ESTONIA
AND THE
ESTONIANS

STUDIES OF NATIONALITIES IN THE USSR

Wayne S. Vucinich, Editor

The Crimean Tatars
  Alan Fisher

The Volga Tatars: A Profile in National Resilience
  Azade-Ayşe Rorlich

The Kazakhs
  Martha Brill Olcott

The Making of the Georgian Nation
  Ronald Grigor Suny

*The Modern Uzbeks: From the Fourteenth Century to the Present;
A Cultural History*
  Edward A. Allworth

Estonia and the Estonians, second edition
  Toivo U. Raun

ESTONIA AND THE ESTONIANS

SECOND EDITION

Toivo U. Raun

HOOVER INSTITUTION PRESS
Stanford University
Stanford, California

Hoover Press Publication 405

Copyright 1991 by the Board of Trustees of the
  Leland Stanford Junior University

Second edition, first printing, 1991
First edition, 1987

Manufactured in the United States of America

96 95 94 93 92 91   9 8 7 6 5 4 3 2 1

Library of Congress Cataloging-in-Publication Data

Raun, Toivo U.
    Estonia and the Estonians / Toivo U. Raun. — 2nd ed.
        p.   cm. — (Studies of nationalities in the USSR)
    Includes bibliographical references and index.
    ISBN 0-8179-9131-X
    ISBN 0-8179-9132-8 (pbk.)
    1. Estonia—History. 2. Estonia—History—Autonomy and
independence movements. I. Title. II. Series.
DK503.54.R38   1991
947'.41—dc20   91-17297
                                                        CIP

Design by P. Kelley Baker

For my parents

Contents

List of Maps   ix

Foreword   xi

Preface to the Second Edition   xv

Preface   xvii

Photographs following page 96

PART ONE:
ESTONIA BEFORE 1710

1   The Prehistoric Era   3

2   Medieval Livonia, 1200–1561   15

3   Polish and Swedish Hegemony, 1561–1710   27

PART TWO:
ESTONIA UNDER IMPERIAL RUSSIA

4   The Zenith and Eclipse of Serfdom, 1710–1860   37

5   National Awakening and Russification, 1860–1900   57

6   Revolution and War, 1900–1917   81

PART THREE:
INDEPENDENT ESTONIA

7   The Emergence of
      Estonian Independence, 1917–1920   99

8   The Republic of Estonia, 1920–1939   112

9   Estonia in Crisis, 1939–1940   139

PART FOUR:
SOVIET ESTONIA

10   The First Year of Soviet Rule, 1940–1941   149

11   The German Occupation, 1941–1944   157

12   The Stalinist Era, 1944–1953   169

13   The Post-Stalin Era, 1953–1985   189

14   Rebirth and De-Sovietization, 1985–1991   222

      Epilogue   240

      Appendixes   243

      Glossary   251

      Notes   253

      Bibliography   297

      Index   325

List of Maps

Area of Ethnic Estonian Settlement, c. 1200   4

Medieval Livonia, c. 1500   14

Estonia under Swedish Rule, c. 1629   26

Estonia under Imperial Russia, c. 1850   58

Independent Estonia, 1939   138

Soviet Estonia, 1985   221

Foreword

The author and the publishers are proud to issue a second edition of Professor Toivo U. Raun's *Estonia and the Estonians*, the first edition of which was highly praised by scholars and other readers and which quickly sold out. Professor Raun, who has continued to follow closely the recent developments in the country, provides us with a masterful analysis of the new situation. This was no easy task; only a scholar with an intimate knowledge of Estonia and an excellent academic background could unravel and assess the complexities of the current picture of this country.

The past few years have constituted some of the most exciting moments in the history of the Estonian people, marking the rebirth of a nation. We are witnessing an emergence of many talented, nationally conscious and politically aware men and women who stand ready to struggle for a free Estonia. The new leaders, though educated in a Communist environment, have found little difficulty in accepting the spirit and principles of parliamentary democracy. To build a new political and socioeconomic order, the leaders have devised democratic ways to direct the nation toward a free political existence. They have given all their citizens, Estonians and non-Estonians alike, the opportunity to voice their opinions, have sought to mobilize domestic and foreign support, and, so far, have done all this without engaging in a bloody confrontation with the Soviet Union.

With the growth of the Estonian liberation movement, many important issues have been placed on the agenda. The Nazi-Soviet Pact of August 1939 and the subsequent Soviet annexation of Estonia in 1940 have been openly and unequivocally repudiated. Soviet military service and citizenship have been widely defied. Distortions in the Soviet historiography on Estonia were expunged, and major steps have been initiated to restore and revive national culture. Within a relatively short period of time, many historical monuments have been restored and preserved.

In the economic arena, progress toward privatization and marketization has been steady, though not without difficulties. The administrative apparatus and judicial and educational systems are being de-Sovietized. A powerful ecological movement has emerged to stop the disastrous consequences of the Soviet industrialization drive and to draw public attention to other environmentally hazardous policies.

Although there has been important progress in the many spheres of national activity, it has become obvious that political questions must be settled before serious reform can be effected in the country's economy. The country must win independence and establish a democratic system of government, for the emerging autochthonous government and the Soviet central government function at cross-purposes.

By 1991 the Soviet system of government had been thoroughly undermined and is now in a state of upheaval. Much still depends on the direction Mikhail Gorbachev will take. Threatened by destabilizing forces, he has, for the moment at least, adopted a conservative position; there is little indication that he will voluntarily allow the dissolution of the Soviet Union, although he will accept its fundamental transformation.

What is important, however, is that Estonia has already won substantial political gains. It has proclaimed sovereignty, elected a democratic national representative body, acquired a responsible government, and has, in effect, established a multiparty system. The minorities have been permitted to organize their own parties and participate in the elections with their own candidates.

Estonians requested permission to participate in the Conference on Security and Cooperation in Europe summit in Paris, in November 1990, a permission that was at first granted and then rescinded after Soviet protests. Estonians also asked to be observers at the meeting of European foreign ministers in June 1991 in Dublin. Estonia has received both economic and political support from the Scandinavian countries but has received only qualified encouragement from Western Europe and the United States, although there is strong popular and congressional support for Estonia in these countries.

Meanwhile, the democratization and de-Sovietization of Estonian society continues. February 24 has been designated as Independence Day, and the blue, black, and white tricolor has replaced the Soviet Estonian flag. Streets and squares have regained their Estonian names, and national seals, emblems, and symbols have replaced Communist ones. In March 1990 the newly elected

Supreme Council dropped the country's official name, Estonian Soviet Socialist Republic, and took the name Republic of Estonia. Even the republican Communist party split into pro-Moscow and locally oriented parties. In March 1991, Estonia became one of the six Soviet republics that refused to vote on Gorbachev's treaty that would transform the existing Soviet system and change the country's name to the Union of Soviet Sovereign Republics. At the same time, Estonia joined the other five republics in an association called the Assembly of Fronts and Movements. The association's purpose is to enable the members to consult one another and to coordinate efforts in the struggle for independence.

Let us hope that Estonia achieves its national objectives. The road ahead is uncertain, but whatever the ultimate outcome — full independence or autonomy within a truly democratized Soviet system — Estonia has emerged from darkness into light and has left a deep mark on history. Professor Raun is to be commended for his masterful coverage and assessment of Estonia's renaissance.

WAYNE S. VUCINICH

Preface to the Second Edition

The second edition of *Estonia and the Estonians* contains the following changes and additions: a new chapter on the developments during the period of *glasnost'* and *perestroika* up to the spring of 1991, minor changes in chapters 12 and 13 on the post–World War II era, a revised epilogue and index, and updated appendixes and bibliography. Although the process of de-Sovietization, as I call it here, is far from over, given the import of recent events, it seems appropriate to offer a provisional assessment. In drafting the new chapter I benefited from discussions with Toomas Karjahärm and Seppo Zetterberg; Rein Taagepera provided useful comments on the manuscript.

Bloomington, Indiana   Toivo U. Raun
April 1991

Preface

This volume is a survey history of Estonia from the first signs of human habitation to the present day. As the title implies, the emphasis is on the ethnic Estonians although other groups—for example, the Baltic Germans—are covered as well. The approach is chronological, but within each period or chapter the major political, economic, social, and cultural developments are treated. Because of space limitations, the cultural sections deal almost exclusively with the ethnic Estonians. Thus, for example, the important achievements of Baltic German culture in the nineteenth century are not included here. Moreover, the stress is on the modern period, beginning in the mid-nineteenth century. Although various aspects and periods of Estonian history have been studied in depth by both Soviet and non-Soviet scholars, no such detailed overview as presented here exists in any language. Furthermore, much of Estonian historiography has remained inaccessible to Western readers because of the language barrier, and it is one of the purposes of the present work to make the results of this body of literature available to a wider public. Evald Uustalu's useful survey, *The History of Estonian People* (1952), does not go beyond World War II, and a great deal of research has been done on earlier topics as well in the past three decades.

In order to keep the development of Estonian history in proper perspective, certain crucial historical factors should be emphasized at the outset. It would be difficult to overestimate the importance of Estonia's geopolitical location in shaping its history. The eastern Baltic region—with important ports such as Riga, Tallinn (Reval), Narva, and Pärnu (Pernau)—has been highly coveted by all northern European powers, especially since the thirteenth century. In economic terms, Estonia has offered a natural and excellent way station for trade across the Baltic Sea. The strategic importance of the eastern Baltic area has grown steadily in modern times (with the possible exception of the most recent period involving the emergence of nuclear arsenals). A balance-of-power principle has operated during the entire historical era (beginning c. 1200); any crisis situation has invited the intervention of the major European powers in the area. This assertion is graphically demonstrated by the periods 1208–1227, 1558–1629, 1700–1721, 1917–1920, and 1939–1944. In all of these cases, two or more European powers vied for control of Estonia with devastating consequences for the native population.

The small number of Estonians has also been a fundamental factor in their history. The periodic onslaughts of war, famine, and disease would not have been so ruinous had it not been for Estonia's small population. It is worth noting that around 1550 the number of Estonians and Finns was roughly comparable, whereas in 1980 there were nearly five times as many Finns as Estonians living in their respective native countries. From the viewpoint of national security, the limited number of Estonians has been a major factor in their inability to ward off foreign invaders. At the same time, the consciousness of being a small people has significantly affected Estonian thinking. Although there is evidence of an aggressive Estonian naval policy in the twelfth century, the historical era witnessed an end to political and military activism. By the time historical conditions fostered the emergence of a modern Estonian nation, it had long since been surrounded by much larger and more powerful neighbors.

Finally, it is important to note Estonia's role as a multinational crossroads, which is a complement of the country's geopolitical position. The favorable location has attracted neighboring as well as more remote peoples. Nevertheless, it is striking that, with the notable exception of the Baltic Germans and small, isolated pockets of Swedes and Russians, the Estonians have succeeded over the centuries in assimilating the immigrant population. The compactness of the Estonian people has clearly been decisive, along with the small size of any given wave of immigrants. Only in the Soviet period has a large non-Estonian minority emerged in the country. The historical survival of the Estonian people has been predicated on the achievement and maintenance of a minimum critical size; the alternative is shown by the fate of other southern Balto-Finnic ethnic groups—for example, the Livonians and the Votes.

A few comments on usage are necessary. For the sake of convenience, the term "Estonia" is used in discussing earlier historical periods although, strictly speaking, no such entity existed before the twentieth century. The bewildering array of place names in a multiethnic society always presents a problem to the historian. In this volume, geographical terms are given in their Estonian form and the German equivalent is included in parentheses at the first occurrence in the text. In addition, Appendix A provides a comprehensive list of parallel Estonian, German, and pre-1917 Russian place names. Up to February 1 (14), 1918, dates are given according to the prevailing Julian Calendar, which was thirteen days behind the Gregorian Calendar in the twentieth century. For transliterations from Russian, the Library of Congress system without diacritical marks is used.

In writing this book I have had the aid of a number of institutions and individuals whose role I gratefully acknowledge. I wish to thank the libraries at California State University, Long Beach; the University of California, Los Angeles; Indiana University, Bloomington; Helsinki University; the Institute of History, Helsinki University; and the Finnish Literary Society for their help in assembling the materials to prepare this volume. California State University, Long Beach also provided funds for research, and the Hoover Institution at Stanford University defrayed the costs of typing the final manuscript. The late Aksel Linkhorst provided valuable source materials, and I profited from several discussions with Seppo Zetterberg on certain aspects of Estonian history. Parts of the manuscript were read by the late Evald Blumfeldt, Aleksander Loit, Andrejs Plakans, and the late Evald Uustalu. The entire manuscript was read by Alo Raun, Rein Taagepera, and Edward C. Thaden. All made valuable comments that have improved this work considerably, although I alone remain responsible for the views presented here. Joan Mortenson typed the final text and notes quickly and accurately. Patricia Warren typed the bibliography, proofread the entire manuscript, and performed various necessary tasks with dispatch and aplomb. I also wish to thank Eileen Johansen for expertly drawing the maps. My greatest debt of gratitude is to my wife, Epp, without whose encouragement and support this book could not have been written.

Long Beach, California   TOIVO U. RAUN

ESTONIA BEFORE 1710

PART ONE

1   The Prehistoric Era

The prehistoric era—from the first signs of human habitation to the emergence of written records—in the region that would become modern Estonia lasted nearly nine millennia. Little is known about this long period; however, a growing number of archaeological finds and evidence from other disciplines provide the basis for cautious generalizations. Before turning to such issues as the origins of the Estonians and the arrival of their ancestors in the Baltic, it will be useful to make some brief geographical comments.

The area populated by the Estonian people and their ancestors has not changed appreciably in the last 1500 years. Twentieth-century Estonia is approximately the size of the states of Vermont and New Hampshire combined. In comparison to other European states, it is larger than Denmark, Switzerland, the Netherlands, or Belgium. To the west and north, Estonia borders on the Baltic Sea and the Gulf of Finland, affording an avenue of contact with Central Europe and Scandinavia. Other nationalities located on the Baltic, especially the Germans, Swedes, and Danes, have used this open waterway to penetrate Estonian territory. To the east, Lake Peipsi has formed a natural dividing line between Slavic and Finnic worlds for centuries. Only in the twentieth century has the Slavic element moved significantly farther west into traditionally Estonian areas. To the south, Estonia has a land border with the Latvians that gradually moved north until it stabilized in early modern times.

Geographically, Estonia is part of the great East European plain and can be divided into two major regions. Lower Estonia consists of the western and northern coastal regions, including the islands as well as the areas around Lakes

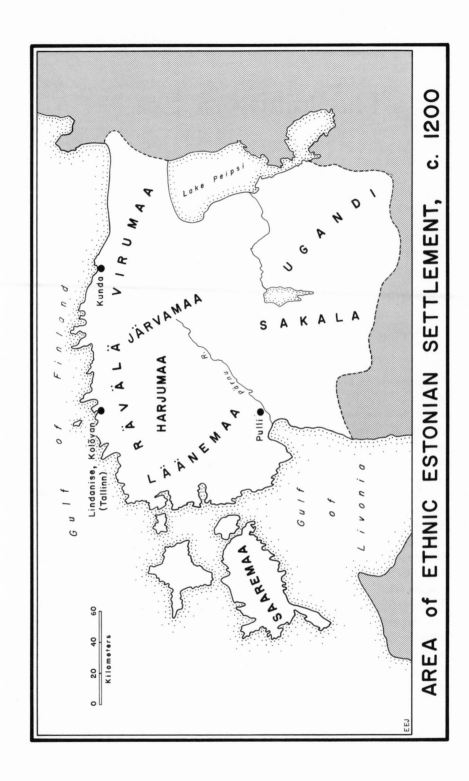

AREA of ETHNIC ESTONIAN SETTLEMENT, c. 1200

Gulf of Finland

Lake Peipsi

VIRUMAA

Kunda

RÄVÄLÄ JÄRVAMAA

UGANDI

SAKALA

Lindanise, Kolõvan (Tallinn)

HARJUMAA

LÄÄNEMAA

Pärnu R.

Pulli

SAAREMAA

Gulf of Livonia

60
40
20
0
Kilometers

EEJ

Peipsi and Võrts (the two largest inland bodies of water). Upper Estonia includes the central and southern regions, excluding the lake districts, and is perhaps best pictured as the areas surrounding the urban centers of Rakvere (Wesenberg), Paide (Weissenstein), Viljandi (Fellin), Tartu (Dorpat), and Võru (Werro). Ninety percent of the country is less than 100 meters above sea level, although the higest point in Estonia at Suur Munamägi in the extreme southeast reaches nearly 318 meters. Whereas Lower Estonia is almost completely flat and often marshy, Upper Estonia is characterized by a more varied landscape and, as a result of glacial deposits, is by far the more agriculturally fertile of the two regions. Estonia possesses no great natural resources. The only mineral wealth of note is oil shale and phosphorite; abundant supplies of limestone and dolomite are available as building materials.

Estonia's climate is characteristic of the continental mixed forest zone, but it is tempered in the winter by the Baltic Sea and the Gulf Stream. The vegetation period (average temperature above 5°C) ranges from 145 to 165 days per year, and the active growing season (average temperature above 10°C) is 110–135 days per year. The warmest areas of the country are the western coastal regions and accompanying islands; there the nights are frost free from four to six months of the year. Average annual precipitation ranges from 21.7 to 25.6 inches.

THE ORIGINS OF THE ESTONIANS

The Estonian language belongs to the Uralic or Finno-Ugric linguistic groups. Uralic, the broader of the two terms, subsumes both Finno-Ugric and the Samoyed languages of western Siberia. The Ugric branch of Finno-Ugric includes Hungarian and the Ob-Ugric subgroup (Vogul [Mansi] and Ostyak [Khanty]), while the Finnic category consists of Perm-Finnic (Votyak [Udmurt] and Zyrian [Komi and Komi-Permiak]), Volga-Finnic (Mordvin and Cheremis [Mari]), Lapp (Sami), and Balto-Finnic. Estonian belongs to the Balto-Finnic subgroup, which can be divided into the two following branches:

Northeastern Balto-Finnic	*Southwestern Balto-Finnic*
Eastern Finnish	Estonian
Ingrian (or Izhorian)	Livonian
Karelian-Olonetsian	Votic
Ludic	Western Finnish
Vepsian	

It should be noted that there is disagreement among linguists with regard to distinguishing among dialects and languages in the Balto-Finnic group. For example, Soviet Estonian linguists recognize Izhorian (Est. *isuri*) as a language spoken in Ingria. Among the Balto-Finns, only the Finns and Estonians have achieved modern cultures. Of the others, only Livonian has a written language, but in the mid-1980s only some 90–100 Livonian speakers (all of them elderly) still remained.[1]

The origins of the Uralic and Finno-Ugric peoples are obscure, but linguistic, archaeological, and anthropological evidence provide important clues upon which credible theoretical constructions can be based. The first major theory on this question was offered by the Finnish scholar M. A. Castrén in the mid-nineteenth century. His so-called Altaic theory postulated a common homeland for the Uralic and Altaic (Turco-Tatar, Mongol, Tungus) peoples in the Altaic mountains of southeastern Siberia. This view is now obsolete, since the alleged connections between Uralic and Altaic have proved problematic. The nineteenth-century mind equated language and race and thus reached the unwarranted conclusion that the Finno-Ugrians were anthropologically Mongoloid. In the 1870s a counterargument to that of Castrén appeared and was later forcefully expounded by the Finnish linguists E. N. Setälä and Heikki Paasonen. Known as the Uralic theory, this view placed the original homeland of the Finno-Ugrians and Samoyeds in the middle Volga region between the Kama and Oka rivers. Gradually the various subgroups broke off: the Samoyeds left first, followed by the Ugrians, Perm-Finns, and Balto-Finns. With certain significant modifications, the Uralic theory has been accepted by most twentieth-century scholars. The archaeologist Richard Indreko has argued that the Finno-Ugrians originated in Western Europe,[2] but his views have not found appreciable acceptance.

There is substantial agreement among Hungarian, Finnish, and Estonian scholars that the original homeland of the Finno-Ugrians is to be found in the forest zone of Eastern Europe west of the Ural mountains. The Hungarian linguist Péter Hajdú places the Uralic homeland on the eastern side of the Urals (6000–4000 B.C.), and he suggests that the Finno-Ugrians crossed over to the European side by 3000 B.C. while the Samoyeds remained in Siberia.[3] The major differences of opinion today concern how and when the Finno-Ugrians split apart and finally reached their later destinations. In particular, archaeologists have tended to push the stages of migration much farther back in time than linguists. However, in recent decades Soviet Estonian scholars from various disciplines have agreed that the ancestors of the Balto-Finns were already in the Baltic area during the third millennium B.C.[4]

It must be remembered that the notion of a compact original homeland with later neat severances by various subgroups is only a theoretical construct based on linguistic data and hardly does justice to the complexity of actual events. The Finnish ethnologist Kustaa Vilkuna has suggested that the concept of an original homeland is itself obsolete and that attempts to locate one are pure speculation. If the idea of a narrow homeland is abandoned, it becomes possible to postulate the Finno-Ugrian region as a long band of thinly populated settlements, perhaps stretching from the Urals to the Baltic area in northeastern Europe.[5] It is also probable that the westward migration of the Finno-Ugrians took place gradually in small waves rather than in any large single movement. Although the Ob-Ugrians show strong Mongoloid characteristics, an anthropological study by the Estonian scholar Karin Mark indicates that the Balto-Finns have overwhelmingly Caucasoid physical features.[6]

PERIODIZATION

The northeastern Baltic area was freed from the last Ice Age in the period 10,000–8000 B.C., and the first signs of human life appear to date from about 7500 B.C. The oldest archaeological find to date is located at Pulli on the Pärnu River. However, the Kunda culture, named for a north Estonian coastal settlement of this period, left few clues about the origins of its founders. It seems reasonable to assume that these early inhabitants, who were hunters and fishermen, came from the south and were probably later assimilated by Finnic elements.[7] The prehistoric era in Estonian history can be divided as follows:

Early Stone Age: 7500–4000 B.C.

Late Stone Age: 4000–1500 B.C.

Bronze Age: 1500–500 B.C.

Pre-Roman Iron Age: 500 B.C.–Birth of Christ

Roman Iron Age: Birth of Christ–400 A.D.

Middle Iron Age: 400–800 A.D.

Late Iron Age: 800–1200 A.D.

Although any such periodization remains artificial to a degree, these approximate dates clearly indicate that the northern Baltic region lagged centuries behind developments in the more favorable climates of Asia, northern Africa, and southern Europe.

The Late Stone Age is the first period for which large numbers of artifacts are available. The greater part of this era was dominated by the so-called comb-ceramic culture, named for the distinctive pottery decorations that suggest the use of a comb-like tool. Today there is substantial agreement that the bearers of this culture were ancestors of the Balto-Finns and that the spread of the comb-ceramic culture all over northeastern Europe to the Urals is likely to be associated with Finno-Ugrian elements. The nomadic nature of the life of the inhabitants, who lived by hunting, fishing, and plant gathering, would also explain the wide geographical spread of the comb-ceramic culture. Around 2000 B.C. a new wave of settlers appears to have entered the Baltic area from the southwest; their most distinctive feature was the use of a previously unknown ax-head in the shape of a boat. Although some linguists have argued that Baltic-Finnic linguistic contact began much later (perhaps 500 B.C.), the Estonian archaeologists Harri Moora and Lembit Jaanits feel that the boat-ax culture was borne by Indo-European or, more specifically, Baltic tribes, who were the ancestors of the Latvians and Lithuanians.[8] Soil cultivation and cattle raising appeared for the first time toward the end of the Late Stone Age and received a major impulse from the boat-ax culture.

The traditional term "Bronze Age" is something of a misnomer when applied to the northern Baltic area. The elements for making bronze—copper and tin—are not native to the region, and few bronze objects have been found from this period. Stone, bone, and wood continued to prevail as the sources for implements and building materials. The period from 1500 B.C. to the birth of Christ was one of a long, gradual transition from nomadic hunting and fishing to agriculture; neither the new nor the old economic system dominated. By the middle of the first millennium B.C., two distinct cultural and ethnic regions had emerged in the area through the process of gradual assimilation. North of the Daugava (Düna, Russ. Dvina) River were the Balto-Finns; to the south were the ancestors of the Latvians and Lithuanians.

Like bronze, iron generally had to be imported to the Baltic region, although a certain amount was produced locally. It was only around the birth of Christ that iron replaced stone as the primary material for implements. The Roman Iron Age witnessed a definite surge in economic activity and was substantially aided by commercial contacts with the south and west. At the same time the process of gradual change to agriculture as the dominant economic system finally reached culmination. This shift can be documented in part by the movement of population centers to the more fertile Upper Estonia and by evidence of more numerous and sophisticated agricultural tools. Before agriculture could dominate in the relatively infertile soil and harsh northern climate, sturdy ploughing implements and some knowledge of fertilizer were necessary. Linguistic evidence indicates that barley was probably the main crop in the first centuries after the birth of Christ. Wheat was also cultivated to a degree, but rye, the later staple crop of Estonia, appears to have played only a minor role.[9]

The Middle Iron Age is generally regarded as a period of economic decline. Previous contacts with the West were then hampered by the unsettling effects of the great European migrations. Whereas earlier contacts had been with Baltic and Germanic peoples to the south and west, toward the middle of the first millennium A.D. Slavs appeared for the first time on Estonia's southeastern border. At the same time, Baltic tribes to the south were pushing the cultural dividing line farther north, perhaps very close to the modern Estonian-Latvian border. An economic upturn began at the start of the last prehistoric period, the Late Iron Age, in the ninth century. The major causal factor was a revival of commercial contacts with the West, especially with Scandinavia. Estonia became an important transit station on the Varangian (or Viking) trade route through Russia to Byzantium in the ninth and tenth centuries. The most important imports were iron, copper, bronze, precious metals, and finished products; the major exported items were bearskins, wax, grain, and cattle. In the twelfth century (and perhaps already in the eleventh), when the Varangian route to the east fell into disuse, the Estonians pursued an active trading and plundering policy to the west on the Baltic Sea. At the same time Estonia retained its importance in the transit trade between Novgorod and the West.[10]

THE ECONOMY AND
SOCIAL ORGANIZATION

Due to the paucity of sources, Estonian social and economic life in the prehistoric era remains relatively obscure. Although agriculture was the dominant economic way of life for some 1,200 years before the German conquest in the thirteenth century, it is not clear what level of technology was achieved by the Estonian farmers and their ancestors. Traditionally, both Baltic German and pre-Soviet Estonian scholars have posited the prevalence of the two-field system and the use of rather primitive implements in this period. However, recent work by Soviet Estonian archaeologists and historians suggests that the more advanced three-field system predated German control in the Baltic. The thirteenth century may well have been a transition period to the new method of cultivation. Furthermore, agricultural implements were not as rudimentary as was once believed; for example, iron ploughshares probably dominated in the Baltic from the eleventh century onward.[11] *The Chronicle of Henry of Livonia*, the unparalleled source for the German conquest of Estonia in the early thirteenth century, suggests the existence of significant expanses of permanent agricultural fields as well as large herds of cattle.[12] Nevertheless, in comparison to the areas populated by the emerging Latvian and Lithuanian nations to the south, where more favorable agricultural conditions prevailed, Estonia was no doubt less developed economically.

Estonian farmsteads in prehistoric times were almost never individual ones, but instead were grouped in two types of villages. On the island of Saaremaa (Ösel) and the western coastal region of Läänemaa (Wiek), a circular or bunched village (*sumbküla*) prevailed. Elsewhere in Estonia row villages were typical—that is, rows of dwellings all located on one side of a road.

Whereas the cultivated land was probably divided into irregular patches by household, the meadow, forest, and pasture lands were held in common. Little is known for certain about rural dwellings in this period, but two noted scholars, Gustav Ränk and Harri Moora, both argue that the distinctive Estonian barn-dwelling (*rehielamu* or *rehetare*) was used even before the thirteenth century. In contrast to the rural housing of neighboring peoples (usually smoke huts), the Estonian rehielamu was a much larger structure (about 20 meters long) that served as both living and working quarters. The building consisted of three main parts: (1) the threshing room, which also served as a granary and, in winter, as a livestock barn; (2) the drying room, located in the middle of the house, which was the only heated room and used for drying grain and for housing the family during the colder months; and (3) the smaller living chambers used during the warmer months. The development of this form of rural housing probably began at least by the twelfth century.[13] With the transition to a more sedentary population, some villages began to be fortified around 750–500 B.C. and others built special fortresses to which the villagers could retreat in times of trouble. Urban life appears to have been in the early stages of development, although it is now known that an Estonian village and trading center existed on the site of the future city of Tallinn at least two centuries before the Danish conquest of 1219.

There is no reason to assume that the nature of Balto-Finnic and Estonian society differed appreciably from that of other cultures at a similar level of development. The Balto-Finns passed through clan and tribal stages while evolving toward distinct ethnic groups; the Estonians probably separated from the other Balto-Finns by about 500 A.D. Estonian family structure in the prehistoric era was probably typical of nomadic and early agricultural societies. In the Stone Age large extended families prevailed, and each family or clan was economically self-sufficient. With the coming of agriculture, families probably declined somewhat in size but did not change their basically extended form. Following Friedrich Engels's theory on the development of family structure, Soviet Estonian scholars posit a matriarchal basis for society in the Baltic area during the nomadic stage of development. According to this view, a patriarchal family structure only developed with the emergence of livestock breeding. Recent studies in folklore and advances in archaeological dating have suggested that the role of women in early prehistoric societies, including Europe, should not be underestimated.[14] Nevertheless, no convincing theory is available on sex roles in early Balto-Finnic society. In any event, it is clear that Estonian society in the early agricultural stage was a fully male-dominated one. The male head of the rural household directed the activity and controlled the property of the family. The position of women was not enviable. Marriage was based entirely on the will of the male (or males). In the early thirteenth century, Henry of Livonia noted the practice of polygamy among some of the Estonians.[15]

The structure of Estonian society in the last centuries before the German conquest was relatively simple. Leaving out the class of slaves (who were primarily non-Estonians), the Estonian population did not show great differences in wealth or social power. There was no concept of a nobility nor of princes or kings in the usual sense of these terms.[16] The elite of Estonian society were what Henry of Livonia called the *seniores* and *meliores* and most likely included the elders at the village, parish, and district levels as well as anyone whose accumulation of wealth (measured mainly in terms of landholdings) placed him above the average level. However, the great majority of the Estonian population probably lived as small landed farmers who were not legally or socially dependent on the will of the elite. These free individuals were men who could own land, bear weapons, and play some role in the societal decisionmaking processes. Virtually nothing is known about the position of women, but it was most likely a strictly subordinate one. At the bottom of the social ladder came a fairly large group of slaves. It appears that the origins of slavery in Estonia go back to the emergence of agriculture as the dominant economic way of life. With the waning of a nomadic lifestyle, the need for inexpensive labor grew. Following what was apparently common practice in northeastern Europe at the time, the Estonians made slaves out of prisoners of war; the male victims of a conquest were usually killed, but the women and children formed a pool for the slave category. Although the existence of a class of slaves is beyond doubt, there is no direct evidence regarding the size of this group. Jüri Uluots has suggested that slaves were the largest social category in prehistoric Estonia, but Soviet scholars have placed their numbers at a much lower level.[17]

POLITICAL ORGANIZATION

The crucial factor in Estonian political history before the German conquest was the lack of a centralized system. On the local level, however, political and administrative subdivisions began to emerge in the first centuries after the birth of Christ. Above the village level, two larger subdivisions appeared: the parish (*kihelkond*) and the district (*maakond*). The parish consisted of several villages, and the term kihelkond is clearly a Scandinavian loan, perhaps originally referring to an area that paid tribute to Viking invaders. It appears that nearly all parishes had at least one fortress, and the defense of the local area was directed by the highest official, the parish elder. The district was composed of several parishes, also headed by an elder. By the thirteenth century the following major districts had developed in Estonia: Saaremaa (Osilia); Läänemaa (Rotalia or Maritima); Harjumaa (Harria); Rävälä (Revalia); Virumaa (Vironia); Järvamaa (Jervia); Sakala (Saccala); and Ugandi (Ugaunia). Military matters were probably decided by a council of elders or occasionally by a more representative group, but the administrative jurisdiction of the parish and district elders was limited and not very institutionalized. The districts themselves remained autonomous, and relations among them were loose.

Although political unity was only nascent, Estonia retained a basic independence before the German conquest. At times tribute was collected by the Vikings from the west and by Kievan Russia to the east, but this was always done on a temporary basis through military force and never became a permanent practice. Parts of Estonia were occasionally dependent on foreigners—for example, the well-known case of the Ugandi district after the campaign of Yaroslav the Wise in 1030. However, this Russian foothold was destroyed by 1061, and the Estonians carried out raids of their own in the Pskov region. Estonia as a whole did not fall under outside rule until the German conquest.[18]

CULTURAL LIFE

Our knowledge of Estonian culture in the prehistoric era is based on linguistic, folkloristic, and archaeological evidence. Toward the middle of the first millennium A.D., Estonian emerged as an independent language when the Balto-Finns separated into discrete groups. Linguistically and culturally, the closest relatives of the Estonians were the Livonians to the southwest and the Votes to the northeast. Estonian itself was already splitting into the two major dialects of later times (North and South Estonian). Some elements of the Estonian oral tradition probably go back at least to the time of the birth of Christ, although it is impossible to date any particular example with exactitude. The old form of popular expression is the *regivärss* folk song, which is characterized by the extensive use of alliteration and assonance and involves the continual repetition or restatement of a theme. The subject matter of the oldest Estonian folk songs includes mythology, weddings and family life, and agricultural work. It is noteworthy that the regivärss folk songs appear to have been created exclusively by women.[19]

The old Estonian folk religion can be reconstructed to a degree on the basis of archaeological evidence. Both the Estonians and their Finno-Ugrian ancestors believed in the principle of animism, that is, the attribution of conscious life or a spirit to material forms of reality. According to this view, spirits (viewed as a psychophysical concept) existed in nature, in humans, and apart from either of these two—such as the *haldjas* or guardian spirit. In all cases, these spirits had to be honored or appeased for such benefits as good fortune, security, and agricultural fertility. By the last centuries of the prehistoric period the Estonians had probably created a world of gods and the rudiments of a mythology, but judging by how little survived into historical times, it could not have been highly developed. Nearly every ancient Estonian village had a sacred grove, with idols of gods as well as sacrificial stones and trees, which served as a place of worship. The most common sacrifices appear to have been grain and animals.

Burial customs among the Estonians and their ancestors show gradual and uninterrupted development and suggest that there had been cultural continuity in the area since the third to second millennium B.C. The first evidence of burials dates from the appearance of the boat-ax culture in the Baltic region around 2000 B.C. Thereafter, and well into the historical era, graves were filled with varying objects (usually tools, weapons, and ornaments), presumably for the use of the deceased's spirit. Toward the end of the Bronze Age, the custom of a stone grave above ground (adapted from Scandinavia or East Prussia) appeared, as well as the practice of cremation. During the Middle Iron Age burial mounds influenced by Slavic practice came into use in southeast Estonia, but the centuries just prior to the German conquest brought only minor modifications in burial customs. It is striking that cremation and simple burial existed as parallel practices for over 2,000 years, which suggests competing religious beliefs.[20]

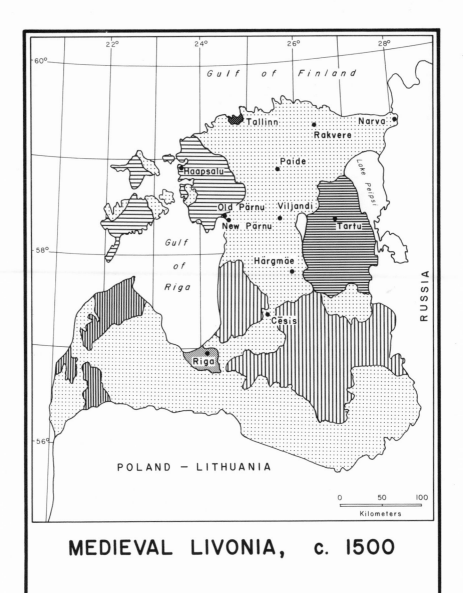

MEDIEVAL LIVONIA, c. 1500

Livonian Order

Bishopric of Kurland

Archbishopric of Riga

City of Riga

Bishopric of Saare-Lääne

Bishopric of Tartu

City of Tallinn

Gulf of Finland

Tallinn

Narva

Rakvere

Paide

Lake Peipsi

Haapsalu

Old Pärnu

Viljandi

New Pärnu

Tartu

Gulf of Riga

Härgmäe

Cēsis

Riga

RUSSIA

POLAND — LITHUANIA

0 50 100
Kilometers

EEJ

2 Medieval Livonia, 1200–1561

Although written records are available for the medieval era of Estonian history, they remain few and far between and tend to be highly partisan accounts. Nevertheless, used with caution, these sources afford a considerably fuller picture of the Estonian past than that revealed by the more indirect evidence from earlier centuries.

THE GERMAN-DANISH CONQUEST

As the German movement eastward reached into the Baltic region at the end of the twelfth century, an abrupt change occurred in the lives of the native peoples of the area. Led by enterprising merchants and crusaders, the Germans became masters of the Baltic littoral, although the process required most of the thirteenth century.[1] The crucial figure in the German conquest proved to be Albert von Buxhoevden of Bremen, Bishop of Livonia in 1199–1229. Although ostensibly a religious leader, Bishop Albert also showed strong political and propagandistic abilities (for example, he made thirteen trips back to Germany to recruit reinforcements), and he became the driving force in the subjugation of the Livonians,[2] Lettgallians,[3] and Estonians. His chief allies as well as rivals for political power were the Order of the Knights of Christ (*fratres militiae Christi*), a crusading order founded in 1202–1203 and confirmed by Pope Innocent III in 1204, and a growing band of German merchants, the first of whom had preceded Albert to the Baltic by some two decades. In 1201

Bishop Albert founded the city of Riga near a Livonian village as a commercial and religious fortress that could be used as a base for German and Christian expansion.

Having subdued the Livonians and the Lettgallians in the early years of the thirteenth century, Bishop Albert and the Sword Brethren, as the German crusading order was popularly known, turned north to the Estonian areas. The struggle against the Estonians lasted nearly two decades (1208–1227) and, if the figures in *The Chronicle of Henry of Livonia* are to be believed, involved considerable bloodshed. Before 1215 the Estonians were able to hold their own, in part benefiting from the frictions between Bishop Albert and the Sword Brethren. The first four years of fighting ended in 1212 with a three-year armistice. However, regionalism remained strong among the Estonians, making it difficult to mobilize sufficient forces against the invaders. At the same time Bishop Albert, an adept practitioner of divide-and-rule tactics, was able to recruit the Livonians and Lettgallians for the war against the Estonians. After the renewal of fighting, Estonian districts began to fall under German domination, beginning with the surrender of Sakala and Ugandi (1215), Järvamaa (1217), and Läänemaa (1218). Guided by Lembitu, the elder of Sakala and an outstanding military leader, the Estonians mobilized a notable *maleva* (military levy) against combined German, Livonian, and Lettgallian forces in August 1217. For the Estonians, however, the battle ended in failure with the death of Lembitu.

As this conflict—the first of several historical struggles for control of the northeastern Baltic region—progressed, other neighboring groups became involved in the battle for hegemony. The Russians, who retained a traditional interest in the area, were at times actively sought by the Estonians as a counterforce to the Germans and their allies. Despite the apparent German successes, Bishop Albert turned to the Danes in 1218 for additional support against the Estonians. With the blessing of Pope Honorious III, Valdemar II of Denmark landed with a large force at the Estonian fortress of Lindanise (or Kolõvan) in the summer of 1219.[4] Overcoming Estonian resistance, the Danes extended their control over much of northern Estonia within the next year. The modern Estonian name Tallinn (*taani linn* or "Danish castle") stems from the rebuilding and expansion of the old Estonian fortress by the Danes. In the summer of 1220 the Swedes established a foothold in Läänemaa, but within a few months the Saaremaa Estonians destroyed the fortress and killed all the inhabitants, thwarting Swedish ambitions in the area for the time being.

By the winter of 1220 nearly all of continental Estonia was under German or Danish domination. However, Saaremaa was relatively populous and naturally protected as an island, and so it remained free of foreign control. Indeed, it was the Saaremaa Estonians who in 1223 led a temporarily successful uprising that overthrew German-Danish power everywhere in the country, except in

Tallinn, and inflicted heavy losses on the Sword Brethren.[5] Nevertheless, the mainland Estonians were again subdued by August 1224, and the more difficult conquest of Saaremaa followed in early 1227 when the Germans and their allies used the frozen sea as an avenue for invasion. The failure of Estonian resistance can be attributed to three major factors: the numerical superiority of the invading forces; the military-technological superiority of the Germans and Danes; and the absence of a centralized Estonian political power, resulting in insufficient native mobilization and failure to secure significant foreign allies. In the end, seven distinct ethnic groups (Germans, Livonians, Latvians, Russians, Danes, Swedes, and Lithuanians) had become involved in the struggle for the northern Baltic area. Estonian forces were severely depleted in the fighting, and they were unable to count on any firm allies among the other combatants. Although the German forces in the Baltic remained relatively small, a crucial factor in their success was the continuous immigration of co-nationals from Central Europe.

The new German ruling class of Livonia considered itself a vanguard for the expansion of Western Christianity and maintained an aggressive foreign policy, but only in proportion to its strength. The first major setback to German expansionism was the disastrous defeat of the Sword Brethren by the Lithuanians and the Semigallians at Saule (in present-day Lithuania) in 1236; this forced the brethren to recoup their losses by uniting with the Teutonic Order of Prussia. Henceforth, the German crusading order in the Baltic was known as the Livonian branch of the Teutonic Knights. Livonia's eastern border became stabilized for some 250 years with the defeat of the Teutonic Knights (along with conscripted Estonian and Latvian units) by Aleksandr Nevskii in the Battle on the Ice on Lake Peipsi in 1242. As Russia fell under the Tatar yoke, the Livonian leaders essentially renounced any dreams of eastward expansion. Much more important for the Teutonic Knights would have been unification by land with the Prussian branch of the Order through Lithuania, but this goal was also shattered in a catastrophic loss to the Lithuanians in 1260. Territorially, medieval (or Old) Livonia remained limited to the approximate area of twentieth-century Estonia and Latvia.

POLITICAL DIVISIONS

The political structure of Old Livonia was motley and fragmented. Estonia—the northern half of medieval Livonia—was divided among Denmark (Tallinn and northeastern Estonia), the Teutonic Knights (southwestern Estonia), and the bishoprics of Saare-Lääne (western Estonia and the islands) and Tartu (southeastern Estonia). The struggle for hegemony in northern Estonia was settled by the Treaty of Stensby in 1238, which resulted in Denmark acquiring Tallinn, Rävälä, Harjumaa, and Virumaa while the Livonian Order received Järvamaa. The Danish presence in Estonia remained nominal; fewer than 20 percent of the vassals in the area were of Danish origin while some 80 percent were German.[6] Although ultimate power theoretically rested with the Danish administrator in Tallinn, in 1259 the local vassals formed a corporation that gradually acquired more power as a political body. This distant colony became too costly for the Danes and, after the great Estonian uprising of 1343–1345, it was sold to the Teutonic Knights of Prussia in 1346 and passed on to the Livonian Order the following year. The transfer significantly enhanced the power of the Teutonic Knights, who, as a body of professional soldiers, remained the strongest military force in medieval Livonia throughout its existence. The Order was an oligarchic organization of a colonial nature; only Germans could join, and by the fifteenth century, only those of knightly estate were accepted. The Livonian branch of the Teutonic Knights was directed by a master (located first in Riga and later Cēsis [Wenden]), who presided over some 30 administrative units.

At a time when the temporal aspirations of the Catholic Church were at their height, it was characteristic that the bishops of Saare-Lääne and Tartu acquired both spiritual and secular power in their dioceses. In the 1220s both were accepted as princes of the German empire. In all of Estonia the sovereigns followed a similar feudal pattern. Land was enfeoffed to vassals—who were overwhelmingly of German origin—in return for military obligations to protect the territory of the sovereign.

The emerging cities were, in theory, subordinate to the sovereigns as well, but they soon developed into virtually autonomous seats of power. This process advanced most rapidly in Tallinn, again aided by the absence of a significant Danish physical presence. In each of the urban centers a city council (*Rat*) emerged in which power was held exclusively by the richest German merchants, who co-opted new members from among their peers. The northern Estonian cities (Tallinn, Rakvere, and Narva) used the Lübeck charter, while all the others (except Old Pärnu, which had a charter granted by the local bishop) followed that of Riga.[7] It would not be an exaggeration to state that Old Livonia was the scene of continual political strife among the Teutonic Knights, the bishops, and the cities; periodically this tension flared into civil war. In the end the political fragmentation proved to be a major factor in Old Livonia's demise. Political decentralization was further heightened by the gradual development of yet another autonomous force in the form of a landed nobility (from the earlier vassaldom). In the 1420s a Livonian diet (*Landtag*) was established that represented the four major political forces, but the deeply rooted vested interests were never able to work together harmoniously.

THE AGRARIAN ECONOMY

The rural economy of Estonia in the Middle Ages (that is, up to the collapse of Old Livonia in 1561) witnessed few innovations. Whatever its origins, the three-field system did become common practice in this period, but no other important changes occurred in agricultural technology or livestock breeding, except for a new breed of horses imported for the Teutonic Knights. The major crop continued to be grain: rye (which had come into use in the eleventh century), followed by barley, oats, and wheat. By the thirteenth century the Estonian farm was calculated in *adramaa* (Ger. *Haken*) or "ploughland" units. The adramaa referred to a unit of land that could be cultivated by one plough with a team of animals along with other complementary agricultural tools. Enn Tarvel has shown that the adramaa is a highly complex and elusive concept that served varying functions (usually involving land measurement and taxation) at different times. Because of insufficient sources, it is impossible to gauge the size of the adramaa or normal peasant farm in medieval times. However, sources for the second half of the sixteenth century suggest an average size of about ten hectares.[8] The nature of the Estonian village and farmhouse appear to have changed very little from earlier times. However, one notable development was the growth of rural artisanry and the emergence of professional craftsmen such as carpenters, tailors, and silver- and goldsmiths.

On the eve of the German invasion the population of Estonia had numbered about 150,000–180,000 and grew gradually, despite periodic setbacks, to around 250,000 toward the middle of the sixteenth century.[9] Old Livonia remained overwhelmingly rural; the maximum urban population reached perhaps 5–6 percent. In the countryside, social and economic developments revolved around the crucial lord-peasant relationship. It is vital to recall that the German expansion eastward failed to settle a German peasantry in the Baltic area. The most expedient policy for the new German overlords was simply to make use of the native peasantry—that is, the Estonians, Livonians, and Latvians—who were collectively referred to as *Undeutsche*. Thus, the social dichotomy of lord and peasant was enhanced by an ethnic one as well.

THE RISE OF SERFDOM

The most fundamental question with regard to agricultural relations in this period is undoubtedly the origins and development of the institution of serfdom. Once again, it should be stressed that the problem is complicated by the scarcity of sources on medieval Livonia. Non-Soviet historians such as Evald Blumfeldt tend to link the origins of serfdom to growing peasant indebtedness and regard the process of enserfment as still incomplete in the mid-sixteenth century. Yet Herbert Ligi, the leading Soviet Estonian historian on this question, argues that restrictions on peasant movement predated indebtedness and also sees a greater decline in the peasantry's condition by 1561.[10] Jerome Blum has suggested that the common feature of European serfdom involved the binding of the peasant "to the will of his lord by ties that were degrading and socially incapacitating and that . . . were institutional rather than contractual."[11] If this view is applied to the Livonian case, it can be argued that serfdom began in the second half of the fourteenth century, grew markedly in the fifteenth, reached near completion in the sixteenth, and received juridical confirmation in the seventeenth century. Closely related to the development of serfdom were the growth of peasant obligations, a decline in legal status, peasant resistance to these changes, and the rise of large seigneurial estates.

Although the burdens on the Estonian rural population were small in medieval times, the obligations grew steadily from the end of the thirteenth century. Demand for peasant labor increased, but taxes in kind remained the most important peasant burden during this period. The major taxes on peasant output, above all on grain, were the tithe or *kümnis* (actually a percentage of the crop, reaching 25 percent in the fifteenth and sixteenth centuries), the *hinnus* (a fixed tax), and the *vakus* (a collective tax usually borne by several peasant villages).[12] Taxes to be paid in money remained extremely small, and labor obligations only grew significantly from the end of the fifteenth century. Yet the Estonian peasant became more and more subject to the will of his lord. Peasant property rights were gradually eroding while the seigneur's judicial powers grew, including the increased use of corporal punishment. In the fifteenth century the peasant became tied to the place of his birth, and the first known instance of the sale of a peasant without land in Estonia was in 1495.[13]

As hopes for improvement in its condition faded in the face of increasing obligations and declining legal status, the Estonian peasantry's resistance changed from an active to a passive phase. In the mid-thirteenth century (1230s to 1260s), the Saaremaa Estonians kept the spirit of revolt alive, and they appear to have succeeded in keeping seigneurial dues at a low level. The great Estonian peasant revolt of the Middle Ages, the *Jüriöö Mäss* or St. George's Night Rebellion of 1343–1345, came at a time when the peasantry's condition was still relatively favorable but beginning to worsen. Centered in Harjumaa, Läänemaa, and Saaremaa, the revolt was a bloody affair that involved the killing of nearly all Germans who remained in the countryside in these districts as well as the slaughter of thousands of Estonian peasants in retribution.[14] Aside from the considerable loss of life, the effect of the uprising's failure on the peasantry was a tremendous loss of confidence and hope for the future. There were no serious peasant revolts between 1345 and 1560. As conditions grew worse, resistance of the peasant became individualized in the form of flight from his lord. Although the seigneurs combated this movement by legal action, it proved impossible to stop, and throughout this period the cities provided a place of refuge since they, too, were anxious to acquire cheap unskilled labor.

The growth of seigneurial estates in Old Livonia contributed to the decline of the peasantry, since the most burdensome dues were those required in the form of labor. This process progressed more rapidly in Harjumaa-Virumaa, where the lords were least dependent on the sovereign. By the end of the fifteenth century 60 percent of the estates in this area had already been established. The emergence of a West European grain market in the second half of the fourteenth and in the fifteenth centuries undoubtedly encouraged this growth. Virgin lands played only a minor role and depopulated peasant farms were only slightly more important as sources of land for new seigneurial estates. The most common basis was the expropriation of peasant land.[15]

SOCIAL STRUCTURE

In terms of numbers, the peasantry was the overwhelming social force in the rural areas. Although the German conquest and the later growth of serfdom undoubtedly had leveling effects on Estonian social groups, important differences remained throughout the existence of medieval Livonia. The following stratification pattern can be distinguished: (1) small vassals, (2) free peasants, (3) adramaa or "ploughland" peasants, (4) *üksjalad* (literally "one-foot men") or peasants with a small amount of land, and (5) landless peasants (the *sulased* and the *vabadikud*). The small vassals were probably members of the old Estonian elite and their descendants who had made their peace with the new overlords. In return for small fiefs, they performed the usual military service. Over time they tended to become Germanized, and their numbers declined toward the end of the period with the growing use of mercenary soldiers. The free peasants were those with sufficient money to buy exemption from other forms of taxation. This group also included some rural artisans and peasant officials on seigneurial estates. By the mid-sixteenth century the small vassals and free peasants tended to come under the same classification.

The adramaa peasants, the largest group, were those who worked normal peasant farms in the Middle Ages; they were the descendants of the former free farmers of the pre-German era but were now subject to seigneurial taxation. The üksjalad peasants appeared in the early fifteenth century and may well have developed from the younger sons of adramaa peasants. Their cultivated land was in all cases smaller than the normal peasant farm. At the bottom of the rural social ladder were the landless peasants. The sulased were agricultural laborers on a yearly contract, and the vabadikud did seasonal work and sometimes had a small piece of land. The previously numerous slaves, while ostensibly emancipated by the Catholic Church in the thirteenth century, lingered on into the early fifteenth century and then gradually melted into the small and landless peasant categories. None of these groups were in any way exclusive, and there appears to have been considerable social mobility.[16]

The two social groups that spanned both rural and urban sectors of Livonian life were the nobility and the clergy. The Baltic German nobility gradually emerged from among the crusaders of higher status who had received fiefs from the Danish king, the bishops, or the Livonian Order. In fact, the composition of the nobility remained motley, but emigration to the Baltic had signified a rise in status for nearly all of them. Presumably for security, the new vassals remained in fortresses in the early decades after the establishment of German control. Only in the second half of the thirteenth century did they move to the open land and begin to create their own estates. By 1259 the Harjumaa-Virumaa vassals had been able to form an autonomous corporation from which a noble estate could develop. Over time the vassals acquired permanent rights to their land, and by the fifteenth century, as noted above, the nobility was already an important political force in the affairs of Old Livonia. It is noteworthy that perhaps as many as 10 percent of the vassals in Harjumaa-Virumaa in the mid-thirteenth century were Estonians.[17] In contrast to the nobility, the clergy (with the exception of the bishops and the highest Church officials) was never able to become a powerful social or political force in medieval Livonia. The rank-and-file clergy lacked the means to acquire great wealth, and an appointment often depended on the local lord. As a formally celibate institution, the Church was constantly required to recruit new members. The priests were virtually all of German nationality, and the majority were recent immigrants to the Baltic area.

URBAN LIFE

The medieval cities of Estonia dated from the thirteenth century, and nearly all were founded at or near the sites of ancient Estonian settlements. In approximate order of importance they included the following: Tallinn, Tartu, Narva, New Pärnu, Viljandi, Old Pärnu, Haapsalu (Hapsal), Rakvere, and Paide. The urban centers were also situated at important water or land junctions. Tallinn and Narva had excellent port locations, and Tartu, Viljandi, and Pärnu were all along the east-west waterway linking southern Estonia with the Russian hinterland. Although the size of the urban population can only be estimated, Tallinn probably had some 4,000 inhabitants in 1372 and perhaps 7,000–8,000 by the mid-sixteenth century. At this latter date Tartu, the second largest city, had a population of about 5,000–6,000.[18]

The economic life of the cities revolved around commerce and artisanry. All the major urban centers were members of the Hanseatic League, and Estonia continued to play an important transit role in east-west trade even after the decline of the Hansa at the end of the fifteenth century. The articles of trade from east to west included bearskins, honey, leather, and (from Estonia itself) rye, barley, and oats; the major imported items from the west were textiles, salt, herring, and precious metals. Craft guilds appeared by the end of the fourteenth century, and in fifteenth-century Tallinn over 70 types of artisanry were practiced.

The immigrant German merchants quickly developed into the new ruling class in the Baltic cities. They dominated both economic and political life through the control of large commerce and the city councils. In Tallinn only the rich merchants could belong to the Great Guild, whereas the guilds of St. Canute and St. Olaf were intended mainly for artisans. In all northern Baltic cities the Estonians were either a large minority or a majority of the population, and in Tallinn as many as a third of the inhabitants were Scandinavians. Gradually, an increasing number of restrictions were placed on Estonians—and other Undeutsche—in an effort to maintain the German nature of the upper echelons of urban society. By the end of the fourteenth century the Tallinn artisans formally prohibited Estonians in the guilds, and Estonian property rights were gradually limited.[19] Although in theory the Estonians were to be restricted to unskilled labor, in practice the only unattainable economic realm for them was large commerce. However, upwardly mobile Estonians were undoubtedly Germanized, and the great mass of their co-nationals did remain at the unskilled level. Ethnic differences continued to be pronounced in the rural areas, whereas the cities were centers of assimilation. It should be noted that both Estonianization and Germanization occurred in the urban areas, although the latter phenomenon was certainly the dominant one. In all cities epidemics and fires periodically devastated the life of the inhabitants; for example, New Pärnu burned down four times between 1488 and 1533.

CULTURAL DEVELOPMENTS

Cultural life in Old Livonia was sharply divided along national and social lines. Although the Baltic Germans were *Kulturträger* in one sense, their culture remained foreign to the Estonian masses. The Catholic Church—the one local institution that might have formed a bridge between the two worlds—was not very successful in this regard. There were almost no Estonian priests, and the church ritual was offered in a foreign tongue. The monastic orders (Dominicans, Cistercians, Franciscans, and the Order of St. Birgitta) were only slightly closer to the common people. Pagan beliefs therefore remained strong among the Estonians, and it would be difficult to assert that they actually accepted Christianity from the Catholic Church. Curious mixtures of pagan and Christian practices appeared, such as the worship of St. Anthony as a house god and the tutelary spirit of the farm.[20] Christian marriage and baptism were slow to take root, and pagan burial customs continued more strongly among the Estonians than among any neighboring people in this period. Although reforms were discussed and even recommended by the Livonian Church (for example, the Riga Synod of 1437), no significant results were achieved before the upheaval occasioned by Martin Luther. Actually, the ideas of the Reformation were slow in coming to the Baltic, and their first application was by the cities as a political weapon against the bishops. The cities went over to the Reformation in the 1520s, but the landed nobility showed little interest in change, and the Catholic Church was able to ward off secularization until the end of medieval Livonia. In the 1530s the first religious services in Estonian were conducted in the urban areas.

Culture in the Estonian language continued to be popular. For example, the oral tradition remained strong, and only the subject matter varied to reflect the changing condition of the Estonian masses. The first few lines of written Estonian, including several names, appeared in *The Chronicle of Henry of Livonia* in the early thirteenth century. However, it was only with the struggle between Catholic and Protestant forces for the hearts and minds of the Estonian people that an extensive Estonian text came into existence. There is some evidence of a Catholic work in 1517 and a Lutheran one in 1525, but no copies of either have been found to date. The first surviving text is a fragment of a Lutheran catechism by Simon Wanradt and Johann Koell, published in 1535 in Wittenberg. Although this work was printed in 1,500 copies, it was removed from sale two years after publication, a victim of the shifting religious views of the early Reformation.[21] The only educational institutions in the Baltic area in medieval times were those associated with the Church or monasteries. Instruction took place in German, and few Estonians were able to attend them.

THE END OF MEDIEVAL LIVONIA

The late Middle Ages witnessed new foreign challenges to Old Livonia as well as continued internecine strife that weakened the entity internally. At the end of the fourteenth century the new political configurations of Poland-Lithuania and the Kalmar Union posed potential threats. In 1410 the Teutonic Knights suffered a catastrophic defeat to Poland-Lithuania at Tannenberg, and in the mid-fifteenth century the Prussian branch of the Order became subordinate to the Polish king. However, the most serious—and eventually fatal—challenge came with the rise of the Muscovite state in the late fifteenth century, although the Livonian Order was able to hold off the Russian threat for another 50 years with the important victory at Smolina (south of Pskov) in 1502. At home, political fragmentation was heightened by the Reformation, and the rising forces of the cities and the nobility continued to struggle against the declining bishops and the Teutonic Knights. It was characteristic of medieval Livonia that on the eve of its demise there was yet another civil war between the Order and the archbishop of Riga.

The Livonian Wars (1558–1583) began with Ivan the Terrible's invasion of Old Livonia in January 1558 with 40,000 men. No serious force could be found to oppose them. In this final crisis the Teutonic Knights were only a pale version of their former strength, and Old Livonia had failed to secure foreign allies. By 1559 the sinking ship began to be deserted as the bishop of Saare-Lääne sold his territories to Frederick II of Denmark, who passed them on to his brother, Duke Magnus. The latter intervened with a Danish military force in northern Estonia in 1560. The Teutonic Knights were finally eclipsed as a fighting force with their total defeat by the Russians at Härgmäe in August 1560. The disintegration of Livonia now became simply a matter of time. In June 1561 the city of Tallinn and the nobility of northern Estonia swore loyalty to Erik XIV, the new Swedish king who began to take an active interest in the Baltic. Medieval Livonia was finally liquidated in November 1561 with the capitulation of the southern regions to the king of Poland, but the struggle for its inheritance was to last over two decades.

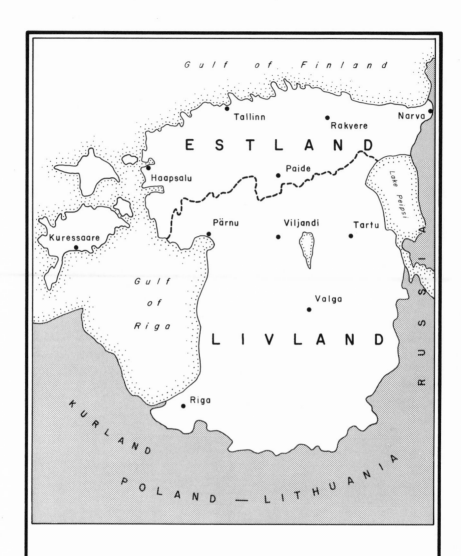

Gulf of Finland

ESTLAND

Tallinn
Rakvere
Narva

Haapsalu
Paide
Lake Peipsi

Pärnu
Viljandi
Tartu

Kuressaare

Gulf
of
Riga

Valga

LIVLAND

R U S S I A

Riga

K U R L A N D

P O L A N D — L I T H U A N I A

ESTONIA UNDER SWEDISH RULE,
c. 1629

EEJ

3 Polish and Swedish Hegemony, 1561–1710

With the collapse of medieval Livonia, four states (Russia, Denmark, Sweden, and Poland) vied for control of the region, and in 1561 Estonia stood partitioned among the first three of these powers. During the next decade the major fighting occurred between Sweden and Poland. In 1570 Duke Magnus concluded a rather bizarre pact with Ivan the Terrible by which he received the title "King of Livonia" and became leader of the Russian forces. In the 1570s the Russians pursued a successful war against Sweden, gaining control of all of northern Estonia except Tallinn by 1576. However, with its naturally protected position, Tallinn was able to withstand two long sieges by Russian forces in 1570–1571 (seven months) and 1577 (seven weeks). The latter failure was crucial for the preservation of Swedish power in the area. Russian fortunes began to decline with the active re-entry of Poland into the struggle in 1579 under Stefan Báthory, and by the early 1580s Ivan the Terrible had tired of the draining and by now unsuccessful war. At Iam Zapolsk (near Novgorod) in 1582 peace was made between Russia and Poland, and the former renounced all rights to Old Livonia. A year later the major fighting between Sweden and Russia ended with a three-year peace. In 1590–1595 these two powers fought a smaller war that finally ended with the more permanent peace of Täyssinä and the recognition of Sweden's right to northern Estonia and Narva. By 1581–1583 an unofficial border had emerged between Swedish and Polish possessions in Estonia, but the struggle for hegemony between these two powers remained unresolved.

The Livonian Wars lasted a quarter of a century and devastated Baltic life.

An early peasant reaction to the wartime dislocations in Harjumaa and Läänemaa in the fall of 1560 was the most serious uprising in over 200 years. At least 4,000 peasants participated in burning down noble estates and murdering several of their owners. The German overlords were forced to expend precious manpower and resources to quell the revolt. In the war itself the Estonian peasantry fought for both major combatants in the area, Sweden and Russia, although probably more for the former. Normal economic life was destroyed by the demands of foreign armies during 25 years of occupation. Plague and famine also became frequent visitors. Urban areas suffered greatly during numerous sieges; Old Pärnu and Rakvere were almost totally destroyed during the Livonian Wars. A Swedish farmstead survey of 1586 reported that the majority of the rural population in northern Estonia had been killed, kidnapped, or had fled in recent years.[1]

The partition of Estonia among Denmark, Sweden, and Poland at the end of the Livonian Wars did not bring a lasting peace. Saaremaa, which had suffered least in the fighting, remained under Danish control until 1645 when it fell to Sweden in the Treaty of Brömsebro. However, the major confrontation occurred between Sweden and Poland in a protracted war with many pauses in the years 1600–1629. The situation had been brought to a head by a dynastic anomaly in which Sigismund III of Poland, a Swede by birth and heir to the Swedish throne, also became king of Sweden in 1592. His obvious Polish sympathies led to his dethronement in Sweden in 1599, but the question remained to be settled by physical force. The first few years of fighting were even more catastrophic for the Estonian population than the Livonian Wars had been. In some parts of Estonia as many as 75 percent of the inhabitants disappeared through the combined effects of war, disease (above all, the plague), and famine.[2] After several armistices and renewed fighting, the Peace of Altmark in 1629 finally established de facto Swedish control of the entire continental Baltic area north of the Daugava River.

POLITICAL INSTITUTIONS

If there was any victor in the Livonian Wars, it was the Baltic German nobility. The field was cleared of two major rivals (the bishops and the Teutonic Knights), and a third threat, the cities, suffered relatively more than the nobility itself. As in medieval times, the nobility was most powerful in northern Estonia. In 1584 the four northern districts of Virumaa, Harjumaa (to which Rävälä had been united in the Middle Ages), Järvamaa, and Läänemaa were combined to form the Swedish Duchy of Estland.[3] In the same year the nobility in these districts formed a single corporation (*Ritterschaft*), which received extensive autonomy and privileges from the Swedish state. In addition to the continuation of nearly full control over their own estates and judicial and police rights over the peasantry, the nobility acquired the exclusive right to be represented at the duchy's Diet (Landtag). The Diet sessions were conducted by the chair of the nobility (*Ritterschaftshauptmann*), and a permanent executive body of twelve councillors (*Landräte*), chosen by their peers, handled everyday affairs. The responsibilities of the Swedish administrator (later governor) in Tallinn were limited, involving only military security and tax collection from state lands. Revenues, however, declined markedly as Sweden followed the practice of enfeoffment and mortgage of these areas to new lords, nearly all of them German, although individual Swedish nobles acquired large tracts of land as well. The Saaremaa nobility also received broad autonomy from the Danish state before 1645, but Denmark kept the majority of the land in its own hands.

In contrast, Poland pursued a much more active—if short-lived—governmental policy in its area of control. The term "Livonia" or Livland now began to refer to the central region of medieval or Old Livonia between the Duchy of Kurland to the south and Swedish Duchy of Estland to the north.[4] These administrative divisions were to continue through the Imperial Russian era to 1917. During the Livonian Wars in 1561, the "Privilegium Sigismundi Augusti," granted by the Polish king, greatly extended the privileges of the Livonian nobility—for example, application of the more favorable Harjumaa-Virumaa inheritance rights. After the wars, however—although Stefan Báthory and Sigismund III did not directly attack the position of the Baltic German nobility—long-term Polish policy was directed toward the complete unification of Livland with the Polish-Lithuanian state. Administrative positions in Livland as well as alienated state lands fell mainly to Poles and Lithuanians, not Germans. It was clear that the pursuit of the Counter-Reformation in Livland also had secular aims, that is, the assurance of political control and closer union with the motherland.

Under Swedish rule in the seventeenth century, however, the Livland nobility made further gains toward decentralization, especially during the reigns of weaker monarchs such as Christina (1632–1654). On the model of their peers in Estland, the Livland nobility received recognition as a corporation in 1634, followed by other privileges over the next two decades. Nevertheless, the Livland Ritterschaft never achieved the degree of autonomy that the Estland body did under Swedish rule. In part because they could conceive of no other social basis for their rule, the centralizing plans of even strong-willed monarchs such as Charles IX and Gustavus Adolphus came to naught in the face of noble opposition. The only successful attack on the political power of part of the Baltic German nobility came in 1694 when Charles XI limited the powers of the Livland Diet and liquidated its permanent executive body. However, these privileges were restored in 1710 by Peter I.

SOCIOECONOMIC DEVELOPMENTS

In spite of repeated dislocations and vast destruction of human resources, rural economic life in Estonia under Swedish, Polish, and Danish rule followed remarkably similar patterns to those of the past. The major crops continued to be rye, barley, and oats, and agricultural technology showed no improvements over the medieval period. Attempts by the Swedish government to standardize the agricultural land unit, the adramaa, failed in the seventeenth century, and it remained a clumsy and irrational basis for the assessment of peasant taxes. The fundamental development in land use in this period was the continued growth of seigneurial estates. This process was significantly advanced by the Swedish and Polish governments, who generously alienated state lands to noble servitors. At the same time the rate of expropriation of peasant land increased, and by the end of the seventeenth century, the ratio between the land worked by the estates and that used by the peasantry had declined to 1:2.8 in Estland and 1:3.4 in Livland.[5] The potentially disastrous effects of Charles XI's state expropriation policy in the 1680s were not felt by the nobility in practice. Although about 83 percent of the seigneurial land in Livland, 53–54 percent in Estland, and 30 percent in Saaremaa were repossessed by the state, the former lords were permitted to remain on the lands as renters, and the whole policy came to naught with the transfer of sovereignty to Russia in the Great Northern War.[6]

In this period of Swedish and Polish rule, the Estonian peasantry experienced the increasing weight of the bonds of serfdom. Although taxes paid in money remained insignificant due to the weakness of the internal market, the growth of noble estates shifted the major burden of peasant obligations from taxes in kind to those in labor by the end of the seventeenth century. At the end of Swedish rule it is estimated that the peasant household was forced to part with 50–80 percent of its output, of which 80 percent went to the lord and 20 percent to the state.[7] Throughout most of this period the burdens on the peasantry were heavier in Estland than in Livland. Some 70 years of war and uncertainty further eroded the peasantry's legal position and property rights, since the buffer of tradition had disappeared. The seigneurs were now more free to work their will; while there was much talk of improving the peasant condition in state circles, neither Sweden nor Poland interfered significantly in the Baltic lord-peasant relationship. Although Charles XI did order some protection for the Livland peasantry on state lands in the 1690s, more characteristic of the period were the Livland rural security regulations of 1671, which can be seen as a milestone in the official sanction of serfdom in the Baltic area.[8] This act formally confirmed the binding of the peasant to his place of birth.

Peasants were sold without land throughout this period. Although there were some localized peasant revolts in the seventeenth century, the major means of resistance continued to be flight. The movement was generally from Estland to Livland or across the border to Russia. Encouraged by the seemingly favorable attitude of Charles XI, the Estonian peasantry flooded Stockholm with petitions to the king at the end of the seventeenth century. In the 1690s the complaints stressed exorbitant taxes, expropriation of peasant land by the lords, unfair treatment, and corporal punishment.[9]

Demographically, Estonia suffered four catastrophic reversals between 1561–1710: the Livonian Wars, the Swedo-Polish War of the early seventeenth century, the famine (called the Great Hunger) of the 1690s, and the Great Northern War. After nearly 70 years of unsettled times, the number of Estonians has been estimated at 60,000–70,000 in 1637–1645 (Juhan Vasar) and the total population of the northern Baltic region at 120,000 in 1640 (Heldur Palli). The next 60–70 years, however, witnessed rapid growth, aided by the influx of numerous immigrants (in particular, Finns, Russians, Latvians, and Lithuanians), who were gradually assimilated by the Estonians. The total population reached 325,000–350,000 (Otto Liiv) or 350,000–400,000 (Palli) by the mid-1690s. The Great Hunger (1695–1697), occasioned by a combination of too much rain and frost, claimed about 20 percent of the population or some 70,000-75,000 people (Liiv).[10] In this weakened condition the inhabitants of Estonia had to face yet another holocaust in the form of the Great Northern War (discussed below).

The years of war and famine also had a leveling effect on the social structure of the Estonian rural population. The small vassals had all but disappeared by the early seventeenth century, and the number of free peasants was also reduced. The peasantry tended to become concentrated at the adramaa-peasant level as the üksjalad peasants and landless laborers moved into the emptied farmsteads. The population upsurge of the second half of the seventeenth century encouraged renewed differentiation, but before the end of Swedish rule the process had not proceeded as far as in medieval times. With incomparably greater resources, the Baltic German nobility withstood the shocks of this period much better than did the peasantry. As in medieval Livonia, the Estland nobility enjoyed the stronger political and economic position—aided by the longer continuity of Swedish rule—whereas in Livland much of the land fell into the hands of Polish, Lithuanian, and, later, Swedish nobles. Nevertheless, only the Baltic Germans formed a coherent force in the region itself. This is not to say that the Baltic German lords were rooted in their rural manors. The life of the nobility, which included numerous military and service obligations, required a great deal of mobility.

Although the liquidation of the Catholic bishoprics and monasteries signified a decline in the fortunes of the clerical estate, Protestantism brought remarkably few changes in the social and economic position of the clergy as a whole. The rural priests continued to be relatively small landholders and overwhelmingly German. However, some Swedes and Finns as well as occasional Estonians (especially in urban congregations) appeared as ministers in the sixteenth and seventeenth centuries.

The Livonian Wars witnessed the beginning of a period of decline in the northern Baltic cities. In proportion to the total population, the urban share decreased for the next 250 years. At the end of the seventeenth century Tartu had fallen to 2,000–3,000 inhabitants, but Tallinn, which managed to escape the downward trend, had grown to about 11,000.[11] The population decline was closely related to a fall in commerce; the economic policies of the new Muscovite state and those of Sweden relegated the Baltic cities to a secondary role in east-west trade as compared to the flourishing medieval era. Instead, the Baltic area became the granary of the Swedish empire and exported increasing quantities of grain. Meanwhile, the urban social structure tended to become even more exclusive as the highly regulated guild system placed further restrictions on economic life. As a result, it became increasingly difficult for non-Germans to enter the higher urban occupations. The movement of peasants to the cities slowed in this period but never completely halted.

CULTURAL LIFE

Under both Polish and Swedish rule Christianity made much greater headway than it had previously in reaching the masses of the Estonian population. The Jesuits, who founded a gymnasium (secondary school) in 1583 and a college in 1595 in Tartu, appear to have been particularly successful in promoting the Counter-Reformation in Livland, if only for a short time.[12] Both the Catholic and Lutheran churches now emphasized the learning of the vernacular by their respective clergy. Yet elements of paganism certainly remained an important part of peasant beliefs, especially in burial customs. The development of written Estonian continued in the hands of non-Estonians but showed marked improvement in the seventeenth century, especially in the orthographical reforms of Bengt Gottfried Forselius in the 1680s. Vital for the spread of works in the Estonian language was the establishment of printing shops in Tartu (1631) and Tallinn (1635); in the seventeenth century about 40 books were published in Estonian. The major demand for works in Estonian came from the clergy, who needed material with which to preach to their parishioners. An Estonian translation of the Bible had been prepared by 1643, but the untimely death of certain individuals, the opposition of the nobility, and later the competition from supporters of the South Estonian dialect postponed publication for nearly a century (1739). The first known example of Estonian literature written by a native Estonian was a poem by Käsu Hans (Hans Kes, a parish clerk from Puhja, in the district of Tartumaa) in 1708, bewailing the destruction of Tartu in the Great Northern War.

The beginning of Estonian elementary education dates from the 1680s and was virtually the work of one man, Bengt Forselius, born in northern Estonia and the son of an immigrant Finnish pastor. From 1684 to 1688 he directed a teacher training school near Tartu that produced 160 schoolmasters. By the time of his death in 1688 there were 38 schools with 800 pupils in the Estonian areas of Livland and eight schools with 200 pupils in Estland. In 1687–1695 the Swedish state ordered a school to be established in each parish. By the end of the seventeenth century the great majority of the teachers were Estonians.[13] Gymnasiums were founded in Tartu (1630) and Tallinn (1631) in order to train future members of the clergy and administration. In 1632 the Tartu gymnasium was raised to the level of a university (Academia Gustaviana) by Gustavus Adolphus. The university operated from 1632 to 1656, from 1690 to 1699, and, having moved to Pärnu, from 1699 to 1710, when it was closed down by the Great Northern War. After 1690 the university was known as Academia Gustavo-Carolina. The overwhelming majority of the students were Swedes, Germans, and Finns; it is not certain that any Estonians were able to attend this university in the seventeenth century.[14]

THE GREAT NORTHERN WAR

The end of Swedish rule came in yet another devastating manner for the population of Estonia. With the accession of the young and inexperienced Charles XII to the Swedish throne in 1697, Peter I of Russia and his Danish, Saxon, and Polish allies recognized an opportunity for an active Baltic policy. Indeed, Sweden was overextended as an empire and ripe for attack. Nevertheless, the first stages of the war were disastrous for Peter; his much larger army was defeated by Charles XII's force at Narva in November 1700. After this, however, the young Swedish king abandoned the Baltic for a campaign in Poland, which wasted his resources with no success and culminated in the catastrophe at Poltava in 1709. With only a small Swedish force left in the Baltic, the Russian armies began to conquer the area, occupying Tartu and Narva in 1704. A three-year lull in the fighting ended in December 1707 when Peter ordered a scorched-earth policy to prevent the Swedes from using the area as a war base. In 1708 in Tartu, for example, every major building was destroyed and the German population was evacuated to Russia. After Poltava, Russian forces returned to the Baltic, forced the surrender of Tallinn in September 1710, and thus ended Swedish power in the area for all practical purposes.

As in the Livonian Wars, the wartime exigencies led to significant peasant unrest. One study has found that 14 percent of the seigneurial estates in Estland and northern Livland experienced some form of mass action by the peasantry.[15] The destructiveness of war (especially the scorched-earth policy) and renewed famine were later accompanied by the plague, which was especially devastating in Estland and in the cities. Perhaps eight-ninths of the population of Tallinn died in the plague epidemic of 1710. The human loss was again catastrophic, although perhaps not as extensive as was once thought. The traditional estimate for the total population of Estonia in 1712 is only 80,000–100,000. However, Palli, who delved more deeply into the available primary sources than anyone previously, has argued that the figure should be revised upward to 150,000–170,000.[16]

ESTONIA UNDER IMPERIAL RUSSIA

PART TWO

4 The Zenith and Eclipse of Serfdom, 1710–1860

During the two centuries of Imperial Russian rule, the Estonian areas of the Baltic littoral enjoyed their longest peaceful era since the Middle Ages, affording a needed opportunity for demographic recovery. In the first 150 years of the tsarist era, Estonian life continued to be dominated by the institution of serfdom, which reached its most extreme form in the eighteenth century and then gradually disappeared both in name and in actual practice by the mid-nineteenth century. The years from 1710 to 1860 can be divided into three major periods. The decades before the reign of Catherine II (1762–1796) were an era of reconstruction from the effects of the Great Northern War as well as one of isolation from the rest of the Russian empire. The 1760s to about 1820 were dominated by an activist state policy, leading to formal emancipation of the Estonian peasantry. The final 40 years were characterized by a deepening agricultural crisis (which had actually begun earlier), culminating in a more meaningful rural reform in Livland (1849–1860) and Estland (1856).

Throughout this entire period the Baltic region of the Russian empire remained a traditional and hierarchical agrarian society, one based on legal and often hereditary social categories (Ger. *Stand*). The Baltic German nobility, clergy, and merchants continued to form the elites in both rural and urban areas. The Estonian population—whether peasants or members of the lower orders in the cities—found little opportunity for upward social mobility, and those who did rise on the social ladder could only do so by adopting the language, customs, and values of the German elites. However, by the latter part of the eighteenth century the traditional order came under increasing attack, both from within Baltic society itself and from a tsarist government seeking to improve its economic and military position as a Great Power. In the first half of the nineteenth century the old order was on the defensive, and it is not coincidental that the first intellectuals who identified themselves as Estonians appeared immediately following liberation from serfdom (1816–1819). Nevertheless, the rise of a national consciousness among the Estonian-speaking population—and, to be sure, only among a small intellectual elite at first—belongs only to the very end of this period.

POLITICAL INSTITUTIONS

Although no fighting occurred in Estonia after 1710, the Great Northern War officially ended only in 1721. By the Peace of Uusikaupunki (Nystad) of that year, Sweden confirmed the loss of the following areas to Russia: Estland, Livland, Ingria, and southeastern Karelia. Although this war marked the effective end of Sweden as a Great Power, in 1710 Peter I still felt it wise to assure himself of the support of the Baltic German elites. In return for the "voluntary" capitulation of the major Baltic city councils and the Estland, Livland, and Saaremaa Ritterschaften, Peter recognized all the previous rights of these bodies and agreed not to interfere with German or Lutheran hegemony in the two provinces. The tsar was generous with the Baltic Germans because he held their local institutions in high regard, and he realized that the Germans of Estland and Livland had important administrative and military skills that could be useful for Russia as an emerging Great Power.[1] For the nobility it was especially important that Peter restored all political and landholding rights that had existed before the reforms of Charles XI of Sweden. Thus, despite the physical devastation caused by the Great Northern War, the Baltic German elites emerged from the rubble politically stronger than ever. It should be noted, however, that the separation and rivalry between the urban merchants and the nobility continued. Whereas the German commercial leaders ruled the cities, the landowning nobility (with the minor exception of a modest role for Riga) had exclusive control of the provincial diets. In fact, the rivalry was no contest, for the nobility was easily able to strengthen its political control in Estland and Livland in the first two-thirds of the eighteenth century, and by the reign of Catherine II the Ritterschaften had a much firmer grip on local affairs than they had ever held under Swedish rule.

In its bid for greater political power, the Baltic nobility was substantially aided by the passivity of the central government with regard to Estland and Livland during the early decades of tsarist rule. It should be recalled that the years between Peter I (d. 1725) and Catherine II were filled by a series of weak and mediocre rulers who followed haphazard policies. The Ritterschaften took advantage of this situation to establish the principle of exclusivity—something never achieved by the Russian nobility. In the 1740s and 1750s matriculation registers were created for the Livland (172 families), Estland (127 families), and Saaremaa (25 families) nobility corporations.[2] Additions could only be made by a 75 percent majority vote of the existing members, thus assuring the self-perpetuating nature of these bodies.[3]

This idyllic situation—from the point of view of the nobility—began to change during the reign of Catherine II. With the growing weakness of Poland and the enhanced status of Russia as a Great Power, the central government was in a much stronger position vis-à-vis the Baltic nobility by the last third of the eighteenth century. Until the end of the tsarist regime, the Baltic area witnessed increasing attempts at encroachment by St. Petersburg. Catherine II's major political sorties into the Baltic were the extension of the 1775 provincial reform to Estland and Livland and creation of the so-called regency (Ger. *Statthalter-schaft*, Russ. *namestnichestvo*) in 1783–1796. Many of the privileges of the nobility and the urban elite were revoked. The permanent executive bodies of the Baltic diets were abolished, and all estate owners, not just the matriculated nobility, received voting rights. In the cities the less wealthy social groups began to participate in the decisionmaking process. For the Ritterschaften this bitter pill was made more palatable by Catherine's recognition of the previously tenuous property rights to their estates. When Paul I acceded to the throne, he essentially restored the pre-1783 administrative system in the Baltic area. Nevertheless, the increased presence of the central government was not dismantled.

In the eighteenth century the highest representative of the central government was called a governor-general or, at times, simply a governor. Estland and Livland were separate administrative units in the period 1719–1775; in the last quarter of the eighteenth century they were administered together. Following the acquisition of Kurland in the Third Partition of Poland, Alexander I established a new office of governor-general for all three Baltic provinces; this office was in effect from 1801 to 1876.[4]

Although most of the officials appointed by St. Petersburg were sympathetic to the Baltic German elites, a turning point can be distinguished in 1845 when the first tsarist official seriously antagonistic to Baltic German hegemony, Evgenii A. Golovin, became governor-general. Although he was removed after three years, Golovin represented the central government's increased desire for greater unification of the Baltic area with the interior of Russia. With regard to administrative regions, there were only minor changes in the eighteenth and early nineteenth centuries. In conjunction with Catherine II's reforms, a fifth district, centered at Paldiski (Baltisch-Port), was created in Estland (later revoked by Paul I); two new districts, Viljandimaa (Kreis Fellin) and Võrumaa (Kreis Werro)—the latter occasioning the foundation of the new city of Võru in 1784—were added to northern Livland.

Despite increased state activism from the time of Catherine II, the control of local affairs remained firmly in the hands of the Baltic German elites. At the top of the local administration stood the diets of Estland, Livland, and Saaremaa, which were limited almost exclusively to members of the nobility corporations. The structure of the leadership of all three diets was essentially the same. The most powerful figures included the permanent executive body of twelve councillors (*Landratskollegium*), elected for life, and the chair of the diet (in Estland called the Ritterschaftshauptmann and in Livland the *Landmarschall*). In Livland a particularly important office was that of residing councillor (*residierende Landrat*) in Riga. The Saaremaa administration was patterned after that of Livland. The jurisdiction of the diets, which gradually adopted the practice of meeting every three years, included virtually any local matter they chose to consider.[5]

The other facets of local administration, all of which continued unchanged from Swedish rule in the eighteenth century, also remained under the hegemony of the nobility or the urban elite. The formal emancipation of the Estonian peasantry in 1816–1819 did not result in any meaningful political independence from the large landowners, since all the decisions of the new peasant administrative organs had to be confirmed by the local estate owner. Furthermore, the nobility retained extensive—in some ways increased—judicial and police powers. Nevertheless, although the postemancipation peasant institutions remained under noble tutelage, they did provide a format for practice in self-government, which would prove useful in later decades.

THE AGRARIAN ECONOMY

The rural economy of the northern Baltic region continued along traditional lines in the eighteenth century. There were no recognizable advances in agricultural technology, and the primitive practices of burning either virgin forest areas or previously cultivated lands were still in use. No improvements had yet evolved in the three-field system, and the concentration on grain cultivation followed established patterns. Major innovations in the second half of the eighteenth century were the increasing turn to alcohol manufacturing on the large estates and the fattening of livestock for slaughter. The emergence of the new market in St. Petersburg encouraged both these processes. The century and a half after the Great Northern War also witnessed the continued growth of noble landholdings. On the one hand, the nobles—who were overwhelmingly Baltic German—acquired much of the land formerly held by Swedish lords in the seventeenth century. In 1758 in Livland, 81.4 percent of the total land (in adramaa units) was held in private estates; the corresponding figure for Estland in 1774 was as high as 95 percent.[6] On the other hand, the nobility increasingly took over the land used by the peasantry. By the early nineteenth century the ratio between land used by the estates and that available to the peasantry in northern Livland had declined to about 1:2, and in Estland it was even lower.[7]

In contrast to the sluggish eighteenth century, the first 60 years of the nineteenth century saw significant changes in the nature of Baltic agriculture. In many ways, this period can be viewed as one of nearly continuous economic difficulty and/or crisis for the noble landowners. The roots of the problem reached back to at least the second half of the eighteenth century, when the nobility, living beyond its means, had fallen increasingly into debt. Although state aid from the time of Alexander I was generous, the magnitude of the problem is indicated by the fact that 97.5 percent of the estates in Estland were mortgaged by 1836 and 71.5 percent of those in Livland by 1839.[8] Moreover, because of growing dependence on the world market, grain and alcohol prices tended to decline, at times disastrously, in the first several decades of the nineteenth century. At the same time, increasing contact with Western ideas, particularly the views of the Physiocrats, led to the establishment of new institutions for the improvement and rationalization of agriculture in the Baltic. The most important were the Livland Public Benefit and Economic Society (*Livländische Gemeinnützige und Ökonomische Sozietät*), which was established in Riga in 1792 and moved to Tartu in 1813, and the chair for agricultural science included among the faculty of the re-established Tartu University in 1802, the first university-level program of its kind in the Russian empire.[9] Thus, agricultural innovation came about as a result of both economic necessity and the influence of new ideas from the West. There was experimentation with new crops (for example, potatoes, clover, and flax) and diversification of the agricultural process (such as raising sheep for wool). Perhaps the major breakthrough in this period was the beginning of the transition from the traditional three-field system to a multifield one on the noble estates.[10] The peasantry, which had only emerged from serfdom in the 1820s, was far less able to practice innovation in agriculture in the early decades after emancipation; however, one important advance by the second quarter of the nineteenth century was the cultivation of flax, especially in the district of Viljandimaa, which proved highly profitable for some segments of the peasantry.

SERFDOM AND MANORIALISM

Serfdom completely dominated agricultural relations in the eighteenth century, and the low point in the status of the Estonian peasantry was no doubt reached in this period. Although the serfs were to a degree shielded by the low population density of Estonia in the first two-thirds of the century, their declining traditional rights had been further undermined by the catastrophic destruction of the Great Northern War. It should be noted that the Russian state, in which serfdom also reigned, was much less concerned with the status of the peasantry than the Swedish state had been. Moreover, the Baltic lords increased their demands on the peasantry in order to support a more expansive style of life. Some authors have suggested that the final and complete enserfment of the Estonian peasantry can be associated with the so-called Rosen Declaration of 1739–1740.[11]Written by the residing councillor in Livland, O. F. von Rosen, and claiming total seigneurial rights over the serfs, the document led to official sanction of the enserfed status of the Baltic peasantry by the central government. However, it is crucial here to stress that enserfment should be viewed as a historical process rather than an event. As suggested earlier, the growth of serfdom was a gradual phenomenon that should be assessed in large blocks of historical time. Although the Rosen Declaration was characteristic of the mid-eighteenth century, its actual significance in the development of the institution of serfdom should not be exaggerated.

As the influence of the Enlightenment penetrated the Baltic region in the second half of the eighteenth century, the condition of the peasantry began to receive more critical attention, especially among the clergy and literati. The gap between lord and peasant had widened to its historically maximum point. The Estonian serf, having been increasingly deprived of legal and property rights, was subject only to the arbitrary will of the lord. For example, the masters now interfered more often in the formation of marriage ties among the peasantry, and the greatest abuses with regard to the sale of peasants without land and the division of families appear to have occurred in this period. Among the most insidious aspects of the lord-peasant relationship under serfdom was the pervasiveness of corporal punishment and physical intimidation. In their abolitionist denunciations of Baltic serfdom at the turn of the nineteenth century, both Garlieb Merkel and Johan Christoph Petri stressed the broken will and ingrained mistrustfulness of the peasantry under unrestricted use of corporal punishment.[12]

In order to understand the nature of the agrarian problem in the Baltic provinces, it is necessary to outline the major features of the farming system under manorialism. Although the number of landed estates was in constant flux through division and consolidation, an approximate figure for the total number of large landholdings in Estland and northern Livland in the second quarter of the nineteenth century is 1,050.[13] On each noble landholding the fields under cultivation were divided into two areas: the "estate" and the "peasant" land. The former consisted of a consolidated whole, whereas the latter was held in scattered strips until at least the 1860s. In return for a farmstead and the right to work the peasant land, the tenant was required to pay dues, which nearly always involved providing laborers for the estate land. Under this system no elements of the actual farming population had any incentive to make economic improvements or to raise productivity. The peasant tenant's right to retain a farmstead remained uncertain, and the irrational strip system made innovation virtually impossible. The peasant laborer, who was maintained by the tenant (and not by the lord), likewise had no motivation to exert himself beyond a minimal effort. The emancipation of 1816–1819 did not significantly change these basic economic relationships, and they continued, in the main, to the 1860s.

PEASANT OBLIGATIONS AND UNREST

The nature and evolution of peasant obligations in the century and a half after the Great Northern War provide an important basis for assessing the condition of the rural farming population. In the eighteenth century there was a noteworthy continuation of the trend from the late medieval era of shifting from taxes in kind to labor dues. With the prevalence of favorable prices in this period, the Baltic landlords concentrated on grain production on their estates for export and use in the manufacture of alcohol. By the early nineteenth century, peasant obligations in Estland and northern Livland were at least 85 percent in the form of labor.[14] Although the peasant population and its economic potential grew markedly in the eighteenth century, the burden of labor dues grew more rapidly. In addition, obligations to the state began to impinge increasingly on the life of the Estonian serf. In 1783 the head (or soul) tax, introduced by Peter I in the interior of Russia, was extended to the Baltic region, and from the start of the reign of Paul I in 1796, the Estonian peasantry became liable for military service in the Russian armed forces. Duty in the pre-reform tsarist army, which required a 25-year term, was akin to penal servitude, and the threat of military service became yet another means by which the Baltic lords could maintain their dominance over the peasantry.

The peasant legislation of the nineteenth century nominally stabilized obligations, although labor dues continued to be overwhelmingly dominant to the 1860s. Following the laws of 1804, peasant rents actually declined 10 percent on the average in Livland while remaining roughly the same in Estland, and the first half of the nineteenth century witnessed no more increases in these norms.[15] However, the dues required were already close to a maximum, and in practice the obligations could be raised through such manipulations as piecework rates. The most burdensome aspect of the dues became the so-called extraordinary labor service (Ger. *Hilfsgehorch*, Est. *abitegu*), which was required of tenants as well as laborers during the most important seasons of the agricultural year. Since the peasant tenants were forced to leave their own fields for substantial periods, this practice sharply reduced the productivity of the peasant land. However, a kind of natural limit to the labor obligations existed, since it was economically disadvantageous to the lord if his tenants went bankrupt. Although the Baltic estate owners were still virtually unanimous with regard to the efficacy of labor rent through the 1830s, money rents began to appear for the first time during the following decade. Yet the great majority of landowners remained unconvinced, and the process did not advance very far before the 1860s. In 1857 only 18.7 percent of the peasant farmsteads in northern Livland paid money rent, and in Estland the shift had hardly even begun.[16]

In the eighteenth century peasant resistance to growing obligations, especially the onerous labor dues, had remained generally passive. Flight from one master to another or across the border to the interior of Russia or to Finland and Sweden had been the major peasant weapon. Sporadic unrest had occurred and had often been connected with new or misunderstood obligations, such as the implementation of the head tax in the 1780s. However, in comparison with the period after 1800, peasant disturbances in the eighteenth century were neither serious nor extensive. With the turn of the nineteenth century and promulgation of new agrarian legislation, the dynamics of peasant resistance in the Estonian areas entered a fundamentally new phase. Motivated by what might be called a "revolution of rising expectations," the Estonian peasantry became much more activist in the pursuit of improved economic conditions. Temporary economic setbacks, such as the crop failures of the 1840s, also led to greater resistance than in the past.

Agrarian reforms in the first half of the nineteenth century did effect some amelioration in rural conditions, and peasant hopes and expectations for more significant and rapid change escalated. In this atmosphere a characteristic form of unrest was to demand more from the new laws than was actually intended. Thus, the disturbances in Estland in 1805, 1817, and 1858, as well as those in northern Livland in 1820–1823, all directly followed the peasant regulations of 1804, 1816–1819, and 1856. The unrest involved peasant refusal to perform the most burdensome types of labor obligations for the lords. Undoubtedly, the most serious disturbance of this kind was the mass action of the Estland peasantry in 1858, which encompassed about 20 percent of the landed estates in the province.[17] Through a singular lack of foresight the authorities had made public the Estland agrarian reform of 1856 at the very beginning of the agricultural year—when the peasantry undertook new rent contracts—in April 1858. When it was further announced that the new law would not go into effect for another ten years, the peasants became incredulous and recalcitrant. The height of the disturbances and the only actual armed clash came in June 1858 at the estate of Mahtra in Harjumaa. Refusing to perform the extraordinary labor dues and seeking safety from reprisals in numbers, 700–800 peasants from the surrounding estates gathered at Mahtra. In a confrontation with half a military company that had been sent on a punitive expedition (popularly known as the "Mahtra War," *Mahtra sōda*), seven peasants were killed and fourteen wounded (of whom three later died) while the military casualties included one officer killed and thirteen soldiers wounded.[18] Although a court-martial in Tallinn sentenced 60 of 65 peasant defendants to death for their part in the Mahtra War, Baltic governor-general Aleksandr Suvorov considerably reduced the severity of the penalties. In the end, 44 received corporal punishment; of these, 35 were also sentenced to forced labor or exile in Siberia. The remaining 21 defendants were released.[19]

An important factor in Estonian peasant unrest in the first half of the nineteenth century was the expectation of aid from the Russian tsar. This involved the revival of the tradition that had arisen in the seventeenth century with regard to the Swedish king. To the peasantry, following the first indications of reform, the tsar began to take on the qualities of a mythical benefactor. The peasantry's growing belief that state aid would be forthcoming was graphically demonstrated during the crop failures of the 1840s, when a new form of peasant resistance to the Baltic lords emerged. In 1845–1848 about 65,000 Estonians in northern Livland (roughly 17 percent of the peasant population) converted from the Lutheranism of the nobility to the "tsar's faith"—that is, Russian Orthodoxy—in the seemingly unshakable belief that this would bring them temporal benefits such as freedom from labor dues, the head tax, and military service.[20]

Fueled by rumors that the tsar was offering free land to colonists in the unpopulated parts of the Russian empire, the Estonian peasantry also turned for the first time to the possibility of legal emigration as a solution to its economic problems. In fact, the basis for the conversion movement was not religious, but social and economic. Although the Orthodox prelates in Livland willingly accepted the new converts, no worldly benefits followed. A similar phenomenon occurred at the end of the 1850s in the religious sectarian movement led by Juhan Leinberg, better known as Maltsvet the Prophet. With a following of 200–300 peasant families who also appeared to have been motivated more by socioeconomic than religious concerns, Maltsvet sought government permission for his flock to emigrate to the Crimea and was at least partially successful.[21] However, he proved to be too unstable a personality to provide any lasting leadership, and the emigration movement remained limited in scope.

THE END OF SERFDOM

Like enserfment, the dismantling of serfdom was a long and gradual process. Although the first tendencies toward restricting this institution appeared in the 1760s, it was nearly a full century before truly fundamental changes were effected in the status of the peasantry. It should also be noted that some vestiges of the customs and regulations associated with the era of serfdom existed until the end of the tsarist regime. The causal factors behind the gradual abandonment of serfdom in the Baltic were undoubtedly complex. Following a Marxist approach, Soviet Estonian historians stress the importance of economic necessity and peasant unrest in the eclipse of serfdom.[22] Unquestionably, the agricultural crisis of the first half of the nineteenth century played a major role in forcing Baltic landowners to try to make their estates more viable economically. Peasant unrest was probably less important, since it hardly reached drastic proportions in the eyes of the nobility. At the same time, estate owners may have feared an emancipated peasantry. Peasant disturbances probably had a greater effect on the policy of the tsarist government.

The decisive role in the initial attack on serfdom in the Baltic was played by the central government, motivated primarily by a desire for increased state revenues. Catherine II's sojourn in the Baltic area in 1764 led to the writing of the first abolitionist tract on serfdom by the German pastor Johann Georg Eisen in the same year and to the first abortive attempts to improve the condition of the peasantry in 1765.[23] As peasant unrest grew in the first half of the nineteenth century, the tsarist government also became concerned with promoting social stability in the Baltic countryside. The Baltic German nobility at first looked askance at suggestions for changes in the traditional agrarian system, but reformist ideas gained increasing acceptance. In addition to economic factors, peasant unrest, and pressure from the central government, the climate of opinion on the agrarian question in the Baltic provinces was also influenced by German writers (for example, Eisen, Heinrich von Jannau, Merkel, and Petri), who expressed Enlightenment and humanitarian notions about the peasantry, and by contemporary developments in the neighboring areas of Europe, especially the abolition of serfdom in the northern German states and Prussia in the early nineteenth century.

The Baltic agrarian reforms in the eighteenth and early nineteenth centuries underwent a long and tortuous evolution. In 1765, Catherine II directed the Livland Diet to assure peasant rights to movable property, stabilize obligations, and limit the use of corporal punishment and the sale of serfs. However, the resulting "protective regulations" were ineffective, since the nobility itself was left to enforce them. A similar fate awaited the paper concessions from both the Estland and Livland nobilities in 1795–1796. With the accession of Alexander I, in contrast, the motivations of both the central government and the Baltic landowners for more serious attempts at reforms increased. Albeit solicitous of the nobility as the major social basis for his rule, Alexander I definitely, if often superficially, turned state policy toward the improvement of the peasantry's condition throughout the Russian empire. At the same time, the Baltic landlords were feeling the increasing pinch of economic difficulties, especially from recent crop failures. As a quid pro quo for a noble credit bank in 1802, the Estland Diet ostensibly promised to establish legal and property rights for the peasantry in the so-called Everyone (*Iggaüks*) Declaration. Similarly, having been granted state credit aid since 1803, the Livland Diet followed with its own peasant regulation in 1804. It is noteworthy that in the reform of the first 60 years of the nineteenth century, the administrative division of Estonia into two separate provinces made for constant comparison and rivalry and served as an impulse to further change.

The 1804 Livland law can be regarded as the first significant step toward agrarian reform in the Baltic area. It established peasant judicial institutions, forbade interference in the choice of marriage partners, prohibited the sale of peasant tenants, and offered them a measure of inheritance rights. As noted earlier, peasant obligations were also codified and reduced somewhat after a land appraisal. Yet the new court system remained under the control of the lords, and inheritance rights proved tenuous in practice. Furthermore, the nontenant majority of laborers among the peasant population received virtually no legal rights and were still subject to the arbitrary will of the lords. In 1804 the Estland Diet also fashioned a new agrarian law, albeit one less favorable to the peasantry than the Livland legislation. In particular, the level of peasant dues continued to be higher in Estland, and norms for corporal punishment were twice as high as those in Livland.[24]

It was clear to the central government that the condition of the peasantry in Estland was markedly poorer than in Livland, and pressure was brought on the Estland Ritterschaft to rectify the situation. In the meantime, the Napoleonic Wars in the first decade of the nineteenth century led to new agrarian legislation in Central and Eastern Europe that offered models for action by the Estland nobility. Furthermore, the effects of Napoleon's Continental Blockade drove down grain prices to the point where the Baltic lords were encouraged to find new ways to raise their income. Reluctantly convinced that renunciation of their rights over the peasant's person did not necessarily mean economic ruin, the noble landowners consented to try emancipation while keeping all economic power in their own hands. In 1811 the Estland Diet accepted the abolition of serfdom in principle, and the emancipation statute, delayed by the war with Napoleon, was finally confirmed by Alexander I in 1816. In Livland emancipation came in 1819 under marked pressure from St. Petersburg, but with more reluctance than in Estland since grain prices had temporarily risen.[25]

The conditions of the emancipation statutes were highly similar in Estland and Livland. Most important, the new laws granted personal freedom to the peasantry while the lords retained ownership of all the land. A major difference between the regulations in the two provinces was the right of the Livland peasantry to keep its agricultural inventory and implements. Although "free competition" was officially espoused and the 1804 obligation norms lost their mandatory character, they continued to be used in practice. The alleged freedom of the peasants was, in fact, severely circumscribed. They remained under the judicial and police control of the landowners, and indeed the norms for corporal punishment in the 1816–1819 laws were higher than had previously been the case. In addition, the lords (and the peasant tenants) could use corporal punishment to discipline anyone working on their lands. The peasant could not leave agriculture as an occupation, and great restrictions continued to exist on his freedom of movement. Before the reforms of the 1860s, only the tiniest fraction of the rural peasant population was able to move to the cities, not to speak of leaving the province. Even moving from one estate to another required the permission of both the old and new lords. It is estimated that less than 1 percent of the male peasantry of Estland changed estates within the province between 1835 and 1849.[26]

For all its shortcomings, the formal emancipation of the Estonian peasantry was yet another step toward independence from the noble landowners. Traffic in human beings and overt interference in peasant family life ended, and the peasantry acquired at least a modicum of economic freedom. Moreover, the psychological impact of emancipation on the self-esteem of the Estonian peasant should not be underestimated. Since the authorities hoped for an orderly transition to the new agrarian system, the laws came into effect gradually, and the process was only completed in 1827 in Livland and 1831 in Estland.

FURTHER AGRARIAN REFORM

The last stage in the development of agrarian legislation before 1860 was the most significant. As noted above, the 1816–1819 agrarian laws had changed rural economic relations very little. The peasantry continued to be overburdened with labor rents to the estates in a system that was organized on a relatively irrational basis. As agricultural prices fluctuated, the nobility discovered that following emancipation they were less able to commandeer peasant labor; at the same time, peasant productivity remained low or even declined. For the 1840s, as for the earlier period, Soviet authors stress the decisive role of a renewed economic crisis for the noble landowners in bringing about agrarian reform. Yet the West German historian Gert von Pistohlkors has argued that political factors were more important. In his view the majority of the Baltic nobility was won over to the side of reform by the fear of centralizing tendencies emanating from St. Petersburg that threatened to sweep away traditional Baltic autonomy and noble hegemony. Most notably, the Orthodox conversion movement in Livland in the mid-1840s, which clearly had some central government support, seemed to portend a full-scale attack on the

Lutheran Church and perhaps on Baltic German institutions in general.[27] Whatever the motivation, some Baltic landowners, led by Hamilkar von Fölkersahm in Livland, began suggesting a full transition to a money economy in the rural areas and the sale of some land to the peasantry. Despite significant opposition by conservative landowners, the Livland Diet accepted a new agrarian law in 1849 on a temporary basis for six years. It served as a model for a similar law in Estland in 1856 and was itself renewed permanently in Livland in 1860.

The 1849 peasant regulation in Livland divided the agrarian land into the following three parts: estate land (*Hofsland*); peasant land (*Bauernland*); and the so-called quota land, which was one-sixth of the land formerly at peasant disposal. Although the noble landowners retained full rights over the estate land as well as the use of the quota land, they were required to rent or sell the rest of the peasant land to the peasantry. Although not made mandatory, money rent was formally recognized as the normal practice. The new Livland law once again regulated labor rents and set them at a somewhat lower level than in 1804. As a solution to the labor problem of the estates, peasant farmsteads were forbidden to allow cottagers (vabadikud) on their land.

The 1856 Estland agrarian law differed from the 1849 Livland legislation only in calling quota land the "one-sixth land" and requiring that the peasant land be consolidated into lots. The Estland and Livland diets remained reluctant to carry out far-reaching reforms in the late 1850s; however, with the accession of Alexander II and the decision to effect major changes in the agrarian system in the interior of the Russian empire, great pressure was brought on the Baltic nobility to follow this trend. In the century following Catherine II's first pressures on the Baltic landowners in the 1760s, the acquiescence of the diets to limited reforms should be seen against the background of their desire to avoid more extensive change.

DEMOGRAPHIC DEVELOPMENTS

The absence of war in the 150 years after the Great Northern War, as well as the disappearance of the plague, had a markedly favorable effect on the demographic situation in Estonia. Aided by immigration on a small scale, the losses of the Great Hunger in the 1690s and the Great Northern War were recouped by the 1760s. Rapid growth continued for the next two decades, and by 1782 the total population of Estland and northern Livland had reached at least 485,000.[28] For the demographic history of the next 80 years the "soul revisions"—that is, periodic censuses of the population subject to the head tax—are an invaluable source. In a study of the evidence for Estland, Sulev Vahtre has offered a much clearer picture of population change than had previously existed. In particular, he has shown that in contrast to the prevailing view (held by Baltic German as well as non-Soviet and early Soviet Estonian historians), population growth, although slowed, never came to a standstill in the years 1782–1816. In Estland the most rapid increases in 1782–1858 came in the two decades following emancipation (1816–1834). Overall, Vahtre suggests a population growth of more than 50 percent in both Estland and northern Livland in 1782–1858, with the total for the end of that period rising to over 750,000. In previous centuries the population had been distributed almost equally between the northern and southern halves of Estonia, but the legacy of the more destructive plague in Estland in 1710–1711 was such that in the mid-nineteenth century 60 percent of the inhabitants were concentrated in northern Livland. Although untouched by the immediate effects of war in these years, the Estonian population witnessed a relative decline in the proportion of males, mainly because of mobilization for the Napoleonic and Crimean wars. There were 89 men for every 100 women in 1858 as compared to roughly an equal number of each in 1782.[29]

RURAL SOCIETY

Like previous wars, the Great Northern War had a leveling effect on the social structure of the Estonian peasantry, and the growth of labor dues in the eighteenth century tended to have the same consequences. However, even though the entire peasantry was subjected to the burden of serfdom, there was social differentiation. For those living on the peasant land, the major division was between the tenants of the peasant farmsteads and the landless laborers (sulased or tüdrukud), who usually worked on the noble estates but were maintained by the tenants. A small, separate group consisted of those peasants who actually lived on the estates and worked there as servants or artisans. Their status depended on their skills and the attitude of the lord. Finally, the cottagers, whose status ranged the entire gamut of the peasant social ladder, formed an extremely motley social category. Some were able to rent small pieces of land to farm while others remained landless laborers. Using soul revisions, Vahtre has suggested the following social composition for the Estland peasantry in 1782 and 1858:[30]

Social group (with families)	1782	1858
tenants	50%	35–40%
laborers	25%	25–30%
cottagers	15%	25%
servants and artisans on estates	up to 10%	up to 10%

The increase in the cottager category, especially after emancipation, reflected a growing desire among the peasantry to avoid laboring on the estates at all cost. The nature of the patriarchal peasant family showed no change in this period, and the division of farm labor followed the patterns laid down by previous centuries.

In the first half of the nineteenth century the quality of peasant life finally began to show definite signs of improvement. At the end of the eighteenth and the beginning of the nineteenth centuries, the first chimneys and glass windows were installed in the dwellings of the rural farming population. Boots also came into general use for the first time, replacing the traditional leather or bark sandals.[31] However, it should be stressed that these innovations spread only gradually, beginning first among the wealthier peasants, especially the tenants. In her limited travels in Estland in 1839–1840, Lady Eastlake, an English traveler, found no evidence of windows or chimneys in the peasant dwellings she encountered.[32] No appreciable changes occurred in the structure of the peasant village or farm buildings.

In many ways, the first century and a half of tsarist rule in Estland and Livland was a golden age for the Baltic nobility. All Russian tsars and tsarinas looked upon the nobility as the first estate of the realm and the major social foundation of their rule. Russian nationalism remained either nascent or muffled in this period, and the central government did not regard the ethnically German character of the Baltic nobility as a shortcoming.

In local Baltic affairs, the political and economic power of the nobility as well as the exclusivity of the Ritterschaften after the mid-eighteenth century brought social dominance and prestige. By its very nature the nobility remained a small fraction of the total population; in Estland from 1782 to 1858, its share of the entire population declined from about 1 percent to 0.6 percent.[33] In social terms the Baltic clergy are best understood as small landowners who were overshadowed by the greater wealth and power of the nobility. Pastorships were relatively fluid and often served as a means for upward social mobility for recent arrivals from outside the Baltic; for example, in the eighteenth century, at least half of the Livland pastors were immigrants from the German states.[34] In terms of status, the clergy occupied a middle position between the nobility and the peasantry, but they remained much closer to the world of the lords.

URBAN LIFE

Economically, the northern Baltic cities continued to stagnate in the eighteenth century. Until 1782 Estland and Livland retained their own tariff system, which created a customs barrier between the Baltic and other parts of the Russian empire. The commercial position of the Baltic ports had received a further blow with the establishment of St. Petersburg in 1703, although Tallinn continued as the most important port in Estonia, specializing in imports, while

Narva and Pärnu concentrated on the export trade. The major imported articles were salt, herring, sugar, coffee, and luxury items; among exports, grain (mainly rye), alcohol, and flax (from Pärnu) dominated. In the eighteenth century the first industrial concerns—paper and glass—began to appear, but their role in the economy remained minimal. The first half of the nineteenth century did not witness any significant economic upswing in the cities, and the sluggishness was particularly apparent between about 1830 and 1860. Nevertheless, an industrial sector of the economy was emerging, particularly with the rise of the textile industry in the second quarter of the century. This development was capped by the founding of the Kreenholm factory, the largest cotton-finishing concern in Europe at the time, in Narva in 1857.[35] New items in the import market such as coal, machinery, and cotton reflected the growing role of industry in the urban economy.

Recovery from the population losses of the Great Northern War required much of the eighteenth century in the urban areas. Until the provincial and urban reforms of Catherine II, the smaller cities in Estonia stagnated because of their dependency on the surrounding noble landowners. Tartu again suffered disaster when two-thirds of the city burned down in 1775, but the re-establishment of the university in 1802—following a 92-year hiatus—began a new period of growth. By 1782 the urban population in Estland and northern Livland had risen to 23,521 (Tallinn: 10,653; Tartu: 3,421), or 5 percent of the total population; urbanization thus remained at a lower level than at the end of the seventeenth century and lower even than the late Middle Ages. In the next 80 years the pace of urbanization increased markedly, and by 1862–1863 the urban proportion of the population had increased to 8.7 percent with 64,031 people. At that time, four cities in Estonia had populations over 5,000: Tallinn: 20,680; Tartu: 13,826; Narva: 8,144; and Pärnu: 6,690.[36]

As urbanization grew, the ethnic composition of the cities underwent distinct changes. In the eighteenth century the Germans held a majority or at least a plurality in all cities, but by the mid-nineteenth century the Estonians, with few exceptions, had become the most numerous urban ethnic group. By 1844 the Estonians had passed the Germans in numbers in Tallinn; in Tartu the same process probably took another fifteen years. Before the reforms of the 1860s, a crucial social division existed between the privileged (untaxed) and unprivileged (taxed) elements of the urban population. The privileged included the nobility, literati (for example, doctors, clergy, teachers, and officials), and honorary citizens; the unprivileged, which included 80–90 percent of the urban inhabitants, consisted mainly of merchants, burghers, artisans, and peasants.[37] However, control of urban affairs remained in the hands of the rich German merchants. The Estonians still formed the lower orders in the cities and lacked any appreciable measure of economic power. Social mobility was considerably limited by the highly regulated economy (with the exception of a short interlude from 1783 to 1796) and the guild system, which continued to the 1860s.

CULTURAL DEVELOPMENTS

Pietism, which came to the Baltic by way of the German states, dominated religious life in Estonia during the eighteenth and early nineteenth centuries. The Moravian Brethren, especially after the visit of Count Nikolaus von Zinzendorf to the Baltic in 1736, provided the major source of influence. Although proscribed from 1743 to 1764, the Moravians continued to work underground and gradually increased their influence after the lifting of the ban. The height of the movement came during the mystical period—the last decade—of Alexander I's reign, but with the increasing secularization of Estonian life by the second half of the nineteenth century, the importance of pietism declined. After their prohibition the Moravians were careful not to allow their movement to be construed as an attack on the established Lutheran Church. As Pietists, the Moravians sought to reach the individual parishioner, and it was probably in large part through their influence that Christianity for the first time became a living element in the lives of much of the Estonian peasantry. Under the leadership of pietistic clergy the New Testament (1715) and the Bible (1739) appeared in the North Estonian dialect, which later became the basis for the standard written language. The Moravian impact on Estonian culture was mixed. Although they clearly promoted literacy, choral music, and temperance, the Moravians also had a destructive effect on traditional Estonian folk culture.[38] For all the importance of pietism, it should not be assumed that paganism disappeared among the peasantry, as is clear from the contemporary complaints of the Lutheran clergy. At no time did the Moravian Brethren ever win the enthusiastic support of the Baltic Lutheran establishment or the parish clergy, both of whom tended to view Christianity on a more rationalistic basis.

A crucial turning point in Baltic religious life came in the 1840s with the massive appearance of Russian Orthodoxy among the Estonian and Latvian peasantry in Livland. According to the official tally of the Orthodox bishop of Riga, 65,683 Estonians and 40,397 Latvians had converted by the spring of 1848. Although the total proportion of the rural Estonian population involved in the movement was about 17 percent, in the districts of Pärnumaa and Saaremaa the share of converts reached 27.7 and 29.8 percent, respectively.[39] As suggested above, the original motivation for the conversions was socioeconomic rather than religious, but the movement did signify the introduction of a new cultural influence and, in many ways, a new world view that broke the monopoly held by the Lutheran Church over the spiritual lives of the peasantry. The competition of Orthodoxy forced Lutheranism to be much more active in minding its flock, but the long-term effect was to encourage religious pluralism and secularism. The conversion movement can also be seen as a precursor of Russification in later decades, since it was only made possible by the guarded blessing of Nicholas I and the central government, who, fearing peasant disturbances, treated the matter in a low-key manner. It is noteworthy that no conversions occurred at the time in Estland or Kurland, despite the similarity of local conditions with those in Livland, because no Orthodox prelates in these provinces accepted proselytes.

As in other aspects of Baltic life, the Great Northern War also had a devastating effect on the emerging school system of late Swedish rule. Although the tsarist government ordered the restoration of the previously established system, elementary education for the Estonian peasantry only began to revive seriously during the reign of Catherine II. In 1765 Catherine, who as an enlightened despot sought to promote education throughout her realm, established the principle that all peasants in the Baltic region be taught to read. At the same time, Baltic German critics of serfdom such as Eisen and Jannau pointed out that education of the peasantry could bring both moral and economic benefits to Baltic society as a whole. By 1786–1787, 275 village schools had been established in northern Livland and 223 in Estland. Nevertheless, this network proved fragile (especially in Estland, where only 29 village schools survived in 1800) in the face of the reaction against Enlightenment ideas occasioned by the French Revolution in the 1790s as well as several bad harvests in that decade.[40]

In the first half of the nineteenth century the rural school system revived and expanded. However, northern Livland remained considerably more advanced than Estland in this regard, aided by a stronger previous base, the presence of Tartu University, and the much more specific educational demands of the peasant emancipation statute in Livland. The more active role of certain Baltic German school officials—for example, the *Oberkirchenvorsteher*—in northern Livland also had an impact. As a result of these differences, in 1856 there were nearly twice as many village schools per capita in northern Livland (one for every 742 peasants) as in Estland (one for every 1,410). The curriculum of the rural elementary schools remained limited in this period; of the three fundamental skills, only reading was taught before the 1840s; writing and arithmetic did not become universal subjects until the 1860s.[41]

In contrast to the slow growth of formal education, literacy made remarkable strides in the eighteenth century, at least on a rudimentary level. Two major factors promoted this development. A growing tradition of teaching children in the peasant home partially compensated for the lack of formal schooling, and the Moravian Brethren concentrated much of their energies on teaching the peasantry to read and even to write, to some extent. Although the ability to write remained limited, parish records from the last decades of the eighteenth century suggest that about two-thirds of the adult peasantry in northern Livland could read. Census data from the late nineteenth century indicate a continual improvement in reading ability among generations born in the early decades of the century. By 1850 probably close to 90 percent of the Estonian population over ten years of age in Estland and Livland could read.[42] It is also noteworthy that by the nineteenth century women had surpassed men as readers among rural Estonians. In any case, literacy was much more advanced in the Protestant Baltic provinces, where a religion that emphasized reading prevailed, than in the Orthodox and Russian areas of the empire.

By the first half of the nineteenth century the influence of modern forms of culture had begun to impinge on the Estonian oral tradition. The alliterative regivärss folk songs, which had prevailed since ancient times, now began to give way to those using the principle of final rhyme. By the mid-nineteenth century the latter form had become dominant, probably through the influence of church hymns, increasing knowledge of poetry, and contact with neighboring peoples.[43] At the same time, traditional Estonian folk dress began to disappear. In the main, however, peasant life and customs continued along established lines. In the peasantry's conception, time was separated into blocks of weeks according to the agricultural year, and traditional saints' days and other holidays provided convenient points of division. Rural weddings were still elaborate and symbolic events that could last as long as a week.

The Estonian printed word developed slowly in the eighteenth century, but the pace of publication increased substantially by the mid-nineteenth century. The total number of books and brochures published in Estonian in the eighteenth century was only 220; that figure quintupled to 1,047 in 1801–1860 and over 60 percent of the output came in the 1840s and 1850s.[44] The majority of publications before 1850 remained religiously oriented, but the availability of secular writings gradually increased, beginning with the appearance of the first Estonian calendar in the 1730s. The first major journalistic undertaking in Estonian was Otto Wilhelm Masing's *Marahwa Näddala-Leht* (Countryfolk weekly) in 1821–1823 and 1825, but the number of subscribers never rose above 200. In the early 1820s, the Estonian peasantry—which was still in the process of emancipation from serfdom—was not ready to support a newspaper, and an Estonian intelligentsia did not yet exist.

During the reign of Nicholas I (1825–1855), the censorship policy of the tsarist regime did not permit the establishment of any new Estonian weeklies. However, calendars and other serials such as Friedrich Reinhold Kreutzwald's *Ma-ilm ja mõnda, mis seal sees leida on* (The world and this and that; 1848–1849), and Johann Voldemar Jannsen's *Sannumetoja* (The messenger; 1848–1851, 1856–1857, 1860), provided didactic information about human relations, agriculture, and the changing outside world. The permanent foundation of Estonian journalism came in the reformist atmosphere of Alexander II's early years with Jannsen's weekly *Perno Postimees* (The Pärnu courier) in 1857, the first Estonian-language publication to use the term "Estonian people" (*eesti rahvas*) rather than "people of the country" (*maarahvas*). This change reflected an emerging national consciousness, and publications like *Perno Postimees* proved instrumental in its spread in the ensuing decades.

The study and development of the Estonian language and culture remained in the hands of German or Germanized intellectuals before the 1840s. By the second half of the eighteenth century, as Enlightenment thinking reached the Baltic area, Estophiles—as these German literati came to be called—had begun to take a much more serious interest in the Estonian language. Johann Gottfried Herder was among the first to give Estonian culture a broader audience through the inclusion of eight Estonian folk songs in his *Stimmen der Völker in Liedern* (1787). The establishment of a lectureship in the Estonian language at Tartu University in 1803 provided an important stimulus for linguistic research, and the first scholarly publication dealing with the Estonian language was Johann Heinrich Rosenplänter's *Beiträge zur genauern Kentniss der ehstnischen Sprache*, which appeared in 22 volumes in 1813–1832. The founding of the Estonian Learned Society (*Gelehrte Estnische Gesellschaft*) in 1838 laid a firm basis for the study of Estonian folklore. It was through this institutional vehicle that Friedrich Robert Faehlmann and Kreutzwald combined forces to create the Estonian national epic. Although the original idea and outline were Faehlmann's, Kreutzwald carried the work to completion in a scholarly Estonian-German edition in 1857–1861. The major impact of *Kalevipoeg* (Son of Kalev), which received strong inspiration from the Finnish epic *Kalevala* (1835), belongs to the period after 1860.

The appearance of the first Estonian intellectuals can be dated from the end of the second decade of the nineteenth century, but it was another twenty years before they began to play a leading role in Estonian culture. The entire question of ethnic identification must be handled with care in this period, since the working language of all educated persons was German, and Estonian remained an underdeveloped instrument for communication. However, the crucial distinction is that some intellectuals of Estonian origin now began publicly to declare themselves to be Estonians. In this change the emancipation of the Estonian peasantry, by raising the status of the Estonians to at least theoretical equality with other European peoples, played a definite role. Although Masing (1763–1832), whose services in the development of the Estonian language were exceptional, never considered himself Estonian, Kristjan Jaak Peterson (1801–1822), a budding poet whose career was cut short by tuberculosis, demonstratively wore Estonian folk dress in educated Baltic circles. Nevertheless, it was characteristic of this period that both Faehlmann (1798–1850) and Kreutzwald (1803–1882), the two outstanding Estonian intellectuals before the 1860s, doubted that the Estonians had a capacity for independent development and felt that they were slated for assimilation.[45]

5 National Awakening and Russification, 1860–1900

The early years of the reign of Alexander II (1855–1881) marked an important watershed in Estonian history. The agrarian reforms of 1849–1860, the spread of education, increasing contacts with the world beyond the Baltic, and the reformist atmosphere of the early part of the new tsar's reign all contributed to the emergence of an Estonian national movement. In its first two decades the movement concentrated on cultural goals—above all, the development of a modern and autonomous Estonian culture. By the late 1870s a political dimension had appeared as well, and the groundwork for a growing Estonian role in Baltic political life after 1900 was laid in the last two decades of the nineteenth century. Industrialization and technological advances were changing the face of the cities and the countryside in this period and afforded the opportunity for increased wealth and upward social mobility. For the first time, significant numbers of upwardly mobile Estonians—through education, marriage, or economic advance—became committed to the goals of the national movement. Nevertheless, many continued to assimilate to the German and, by the late nineteenth century, Russian cultural worlds. The crucial point, however, is that rising Estonians now had a choice, and the Estonian national movement acquired increasing support after 1860.

Although it necessarily remains vague, the term "national awakening" is appropriate to describe the quarter-century from the beginning of the 1860s to the mid-1880s. It was a period of conscious agitation by a growing number of activists who sought to convince others of the merits of a modern Estonian nation and culture. Perhaps the most distinctive feature of these years was the

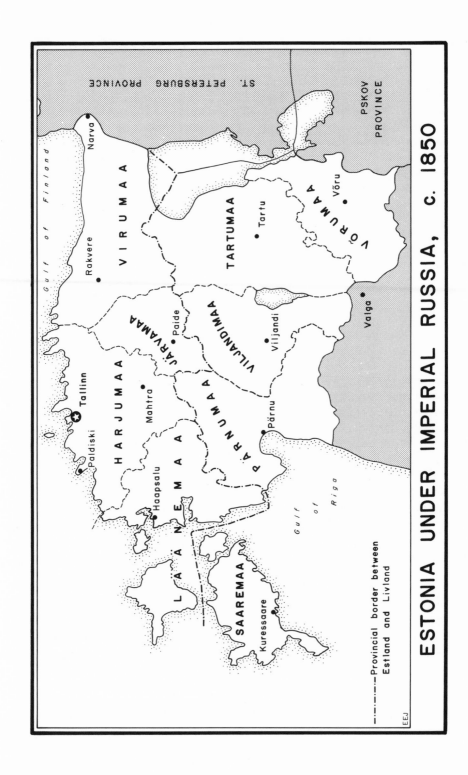

ESTONIA UNDER IMPERIAL RUSSIA, c. 1850

ST. PETERSBURG PROVINCE

PSKOV PROVINCE

Gulf of Finland

Narva

VIRUMAA

Rakvere

TARTUMAA

Tartu

VÕRUMAA

Võru

Valga

JÄRVAMAA

Paide

VILJANDIMAA

Viljandi

Tallinn

HARJUMAA

Mahtra

Paldiski

Haapsalu

PÄRNUMAA

Pärnu

L A A N E M A A

Gulf of Riga

SAAREMAA

Kuressaare

---- Provincial border between
Estland and Livland

EEJ

birth of an Estonian national culture, as seen especially in the emergence of such nationwide efforts as the movement for an Estonian Alexander School (*Eesti Aleksandrikool*), the Society of Estonian Literati (*Eesti Kirjameeste Selts*), and the all-Estonian song festivals. A national romantic tone dominated in the literature, music, and social thought of these years. Although the future remained uncertain, it was generally faced with optimism in the knowledge that apparently the most difficult hurdle—the breakthrough to a national consciousness—had been overcome. However, the pace of the expansion of Estonian nationalism among broad sections of the population should not be exaggerated. It was a process that should probably be measured in decades rather than years.

The last fifteen years of the nineteenth century may be called the era of Russification. This term also lacks precision, and it evokes certain emotional connotations (denationalization, for example) that can be misleading. Nevertheless, like "national awakening," the concept of Russification is firmly fixed in the historical literature of this period, and it does suggest a central feature of the late 1880s and early 1890s: a series of administrative and cultural reforms by the central government in the Baltic provinces that were intended to unite the area much more closely than before with the interior of the Russian empire.[1] Since Russification also involved an attack on certain Baltic German institutions, the Estonians did benefit from some of the changes, especially in the administrative realm. However, disregard for the position of the Estonian language in both administrative and educational reforms occasioned a negative reaction and led to a deep sense of pessimism about the future among some Estonian intellectuals. Coincidentally, an economic downswing added to the mood of despondency, and for nearly a decade Estonian political thought did not rise above humble declarations of loyalty to the tsar. A chastened Estonian national movement thus turned to "small deeds" and eschewed the "senseless dreams" of the national awakening era. With the benefit of hindsight, however, it is clear that contemporaries overestimated the impact of the negative consequences of Russification.

POLITICAL INSTITUTIONS

At the highest level, the three Baltic provinces were administered by a governor-general until 1876, after which separate governors were appointed for Estland, Livland, and Kurland. In general, as agents of St. Petersburg, the governors became stronger advocates of the unification of the Baltic area with the central Russian core of the empire. However, despite threats of more extensive change, the striking fact of Baltic political life in this period—and to the end of the tsarist regime—was the retention of nearly exclusive control of the provincial diets by the Ritterschaften. After 1866 in Estland and Livland (but not Saaremaa), unmatriculated nobles and non-nobles who owned large latifundia (*Rittergüter*) could also participate in the diets, but in practice this proved to be an insignificant concession since these groups remained a small minority of all estate owners. The structure and competence of the diets underwent no basic changes in this period. Beginning in the early 1880s the central government periodically raised the possibility of introducing zemstvo institutions— assemblies in which peasants and urban dwellers would be represented along with the nobility—into the Baltic provinces. Nevertheless, the nobility managed to deflect such thrusts, and the St. Petersburg government never pushed the issue, fearing in part that Baltic zemstvos might actually increase noble influence over the peasantry.[2]

In contrast to provincial administration, significant (if limited) changes took place in the nature of municipal government in the last decades of the nineteenth century. In 1877 the Russian urban reform of 1870 went into effect in the Baltic region. In place of the medieval, estate-based system, the new law enfranchised the entire male taxpaying population 25 years of age and over (roughly 5 percent of the total urban population) and divided it into three unequal parts (curiae) according to the amount paid. Each of the curiae elected a third of the members of the new city council, which varied in number according to the size of the city. Since the Estonian bourgeoisie was only beginning to improve its economic position in the 1870s, the real effect of the reform was to create an Estonian-Russian opposition in the third, or lowest, curia of some cities. The most important opposition bloc emerged in Tallinn in the 1880s.[3] Nevertheless, the Baltic Germans retained control of urban government, although more of them now participated in the political process.

In 1892 the new Russian municipal law was implemented in the Baltic provinces at the same time as elsewhere in the empire. The basis for the franchise shifted to property value, with the result that the number of voters was generally cut in half. Thus, the initial effect was to undercut even further the non-German opposition. However, since the 1892 law abolished voting by curiae and placed all voters on an equal footing, it raised the possibility of an eventual challenge to Baltic German hegemony in the cities by a rising Estonian bourgeoisie, a development that did transpire after the turn of the twentieth century.

Major administrative changes also took place through the Russification of the police and judicial institutions in 1888–1889. In rural areas the Baltic German landowners lost all police power over the peasant township (Est. *vald*), although they retained this power on their estates, which still constituted the majority of the rural land in Estonia. On the district (maakond) and urban levels, the Baltic German role in police affairs was also eclipsed. The central government now appointed all higher police officials, and the entire system was reorganized and placed under the Ministry of the Interior. Although non-Estonians still controlled the police administration, the new Russian officials were more disinterested in local affairs, and the Estonian population generally considered them more even-handed than the German officials had been. The introduction of the Russian judicial system (although Baltic legal codes remained unchanged) signified a rationalization of the entire process and emancipated the Estonians from Baltic German overlordship in this area as well. As in the interior of the empire, purely peasant courts continued on the township level for less serious matters, but for weightier issues in both rural and urban areas the Russian institutions established in 1864 served as a model with minor exceptions. These reforms also brought more impartial justice to the Baltic provinces. However, a serious problem arose through the stipulation that all proceedings in courts above the peasant level be conducted exclusively in Russian. This forced the non-Russian population to hire translators or lawyers, which involved a prohibitive expense for the poorer sections of Estonian society.[4]

At the lower levels of administration other reforms also took place in this period. In 1889 commissars for peasant affairs, appointed by the central government, replaced the abolished district and parish (kihelkond) courts and took on the tasks of supervising peasant government and the application of Baltic agricultural laws in the rural areas. In Livland in 1870 the parish administration was divided into two separate bodies: a parish assembly to deal with overall issues, and a separate council to handle ecclesiastical and educational affairs. Both included peasant representation for the first time, and it is noteworthy that the Livland parish administration remained untouched by Russification.[5]

Most important, the lowest level of local government, the peasant township, underwent significant reform and acquired much greater independence from noble tutelage than had been the case previously. In 1865 the right of the estate owners to administer corporal punishment to peasant landowners and renters was abolished, and the following year a major township reform, probably hastened by a massive petitionary campaign of the northern Livland peasantry in the early 1860s, was decreed by Alexander II. The new law granted voting rights not only to all owners and renters who paid taxes, but also to one representative for every ten landless men. The enfranchised members elected the township officials and—for the first time—a township assembly, which served as the legislative body and had an equal number of seats for the landed and landless. It was required that the township elder, his aides, and the judges be landowners or renters. The jurisdiction of the township government included police functions; administration of taxes, common property, and schools; and care for the sick, aged, and unemployed.[6] Although the townships essentially remained limited to a single social category, the 1866 reform marked a major step forward in peasant self-government.

Overall, the administrative system in Estland and northern Livland in the last four decades of the nineteenth century became a mixture of old and new. Some institutions were Russified; others were not. Although challenged by the central government, the Baltic German elites retained firm control. However, a major change that could not be avoided except in the internal affairs of noble and peasant institutions was the gradual introduction of Russian as the language of administration after 1885. For many educated Estonians who had sought equal rights for Estonian as an administrative language and who had been raised in a German cultural world, this aspect of Russification proved disorienting. The adjustment to Russification was most difficult for the older generations, who had had no exposure to Russian culture and language in their formal education.

POLITICAL IDEOLOGIES
AND PROGRAMS

The clash of political ideologies in the northern Baltic region in the last four decades of the nineteenth century was essentially divided along national lines. The major competing forces included the tsarist Russian government, the Baltic German minority, and the emerging Estonian national movement. In the 1860s the extensive public discussion of the so-called Baltic question forced the central government to reassess its policy in the area. The powerful Russian nationalist reaction to the Polish rebellion in 1863 strengthened the hand of those who favored greater unification of the borderlands with the interior of the Russian empire.

In its perception of Baltic conditions, the St. Petersburg government made a crucial distinction between Germans on the one hand and Estonians and Latvians on the other. Although the Baltic Germans continued to be respected for their administrative abilities, they also came to be feared, especially after the unification of Germany in 1870–1871, as a possible irredentist force. In contrast, the Estonians and Latvians were regarded with more equanimity. Although they constituted the majority of the population in the Baltic provinces, they tended to be viewed as incapable of developing an independent nationality and culture. Nevertheless, much of the urgency behind the policy of cultural Russification in the Baltic provinces stemmed from a fear that the Estonians and Latvians might be Germanized, and thus the area would present an inviting opportunity for territorial expansion by the new Germany of Bismarck or William II. In the 1880s and 1890s tsarist officials were increasingly perceiving "separatist" tendencies among the Baltic natives. From the tsarist standpoint, the Baltic provinces were an exposed flank that constituted a security problem because of their non-Russian character. Russification, both administrative and cultural, was intended to block any potential separatism or foreign intervention by integrating the area more closely with the Russian core of the empire.[7]

In the face of attacks by Russian public opinion and the threat of Russification, the Baltic German minority closed ranks behind the leadership of the nobility corporations. In 1869, in his famous polemic with the Slavophile publicist Iurii Samarin, Tartu University historian Carl Schirren declared that standing fast (*Feststehen*) and perseverance (*Ausharren*) should be the cornerstones of Baltic German policy. Among the majority of Baltic Germans, this attitude did not change in the ensuing decades to the end of the tsarist regime.[8] German rule in the Baltic provinces was based on medieval and corporate principles that simply could not survive in an era of growing nationalism. Attacked by the tsarist government and increasingly threatened by the rising Estonians and Latvians, the Baltic German position was not enviable. An alliance with the tsarist regime and its Russification policy would have meant the destruction of the German identity in the Baltic provinces. The alternative of uniting with the Estonian and Latvian urban and rural bourgeoisie was, in effect, forbidden by the St. Petersburg government. Furthermore, like the Russians, the Baltic Germans on the whole could not overcome a sense of cultural and historical superiority regarding the Baltic natives and were never able to accept them as equal partners. In essence, the historical gap between the Baltic Germans and the Estonians (and Latvians) had been too wide for too long to be bridged successfully in modern times.

In contrast to the relatively stable views of the tsarist government and the Baltic German minority, Estonian political and social thought showed much more diversity and reflected the changes wrought by socioeconomic modernization. For the Estonians, the most politically active years in the last four decades of the nineteenth century came at the end of the 1870s and the start of the 1880s. During the first two decades of the national awakening, political thought developed slowly as the emerging Estonian intelligentsia concentrated on cultural affairs and lacked political self-confidence and maturity. However, two opposing political orientations gradually evolved and became a matter of public dispute by the late 1870s.

The leading spokesmen for the politically moderate or Baltic Estonian position were Jannsen (1819–1890) and Jakob Hurt (1839–1906). Jannsen, who worked as a sexton and elementary schoolteacher before turning to journalism, became the outstanding figure of the first decade of the national movement through his position as editor of the only important Estonian newspapers before 1878: *Perno Postimees* (1857–1864) in Pärnu and *Eesti Postimees* (The Estonian courier; 1864–1880) in Tartu. The essence of Jannsen's political views was gradualism and working within the existing system of Baltic German institutions. He considered Baltic German hegemony inevitable because the established elites were too powerful to be dislodged and the Estonians still too immature politically to assume any real initiative. It is characteristic of Jannsen that in the 1870s he accepted a modest subsidy from the Baltic German establishment, apparently in return for closing *Eesti Postimees* to the more critical voices among the Estonian intelligentsia and maintaining a conciliatory tone in his newspaper.[9] Although Jannsen's motivations have never been fully explained, it is clear that he preferred compromise to confrontation, and in his view the end—that is, continuing to publish at all in the face of Baltic German threats against the Estonian national movement— probably justified the means. Although the existence of this arrangement was widely rumored in his lifetime, it was only conclusively proven in 1940; nevertheless, Jannsen's prestige declined in the 1870s before an incapacitating stroke ended his public career in 1880.

The son of a rural schoolteacher, Hurt took a degree in theology at Tartu University in 1865 and a Ph.D. in philology at Helsinki University in 1886, thus becoming one of the most learned Estonians of his day. He displayed a more theoretical bent than the pragmatic Jannsen and emerged as the primary spokesman for the moderates by the 1870s. Strongly influenced by German romanticism, Hurt viewed each nation as a unique organism with distinctive traits—such as language, character, and customs—and a particular role on earth. Because of the small size of the Estonian population, Hurt concluded that the Estonian mission was in the cultural rather than the political realm.[10] For Hurt in particular and the moderates in general, the Lutheran Church was the foundation of Baltic life, and he regarded the historical separation of the Baltic provinces from the interior of Russia as a positive factor that had helped shape the unique character of the area. Like Jannsen, Hurt called for a conciliatory relationship between Estonians and Baltic Germans that, in effect, accepted the latter's political leadership.

The major proponents of the opposing view, the radical or Russophile position, were Johann Köler (1826–1899) and Carl Robert Jakobson (1841– 1882). Köler rose from a peasant family in northern Livland to become a professor at the Academy of Fine Arts in St. Petersburg. Although not an ideologist, he provided an important link between the tsarist authorities and the Estonian national movement. Jakobson—like Hurt, the son of a rural schoolteacher—had the most checkered career among the leading figures of the national awakening. At various times he was a schoolteacher, tutor to Alexander II's niece, author of both belles lettres and school textbooks, journalist, and farmer. An important influence on the development of Jakobson's worldview was his experience in the 1860s in St. Petersburg, where he met Köler and Krišjānis Valdemārs, the Latvian activist, and acquired a non-Baltic perspective on his homeland. In contrast to the moderates, Jakobson rejected Baltic German dominance, which he saw as historical disaster for the Estonians, and took a strongly anticlerical position on the Lutheran Church, an institution that in his view merely buttressed the status quo in the Baltic provinces. Against the entrenched position of the Baltic Germans, Jakobson sought the aid of the tsar and the central government, dismissing the dangers of Russification and retaining a boundless faith in the good will of the Russian authorities. As opposed to the cultural emphasis of the moderates, Jakobson was the first Estonian leader to demand participatory rights for the Estonians in Baltic provincial politics. In 1878, after finally receiving permission to publish the newspaper *Sakala* (the ancient name for the district around Viljandi) following ten years of fruitless efforts, Jakobson called for equal representation with the nobility for the peasantry and urban dwellers in the Baltic diets. By 1880 he had begun campaigning for the introduction of zemstvo institutions in the Baltic with equal representation for Estonians and Germans.[11]

The major political document of the national awakening era was a memorandum presented by delegates of seventeen Estonian societies (representing some 3,000 members) to Alexander III in June 1881. Although Hurt was a member of the delegation, all of the other representatives, led by Jakobson and Köler, belonged to the radical camp. There is little question that Jakobson had succeeded in winning over the great majority of Estonian public opinion by this time,[12] and the entire memorandum reflected radical and Russophile views. The main points of the document can be summarized as follows:[13]

1. mandatory sale of peasant land by the large landowners at state-regulated prices;
2. inspection of peasant land rental and sale contracts by the central government;
3. equivalent taxation of both estate and peasant land;
4. introduction of zemstvo institutions into the Baltic provinces with equal representation for the Estonians with the Baltic Germans;
5. removal of Estonian elementary education from under the control of Baltic German landowners and clergy and greater emphasis on Russian as a subject in the schools;
6. abolition of the privilege of the large landowners to name the parish clergy;
7. appointment by the central government, rather than election, of justices of the peace in the Baltic provinces;
8. introduction of Russian police and judicial institutions;
9. equal rights for the Estonian language in the judicial process;

10. unification of the Baltic provinces into two administrative units according to the areas populated by the Estonians and Latvians.

As it turned out, four of these points (nos. 2, 5, 7, and 8) were implemented by the tsarist regime at the end of the 1880s.

Shortly after the 1881 audience with Alexander III, the Estonian population of northern Livland had an opportunity to present petitions to Senator Nikolai A. Manasein, who was sent on an inspection tour of conditions in Livland and Kurland in 1882–1883. These requests essentially involved a more detailed repetition of the 1881 memorandum to the tsar.[14] The fact that Estonian representatives had had personal contact with the tsar, as well as Manasein's extensive inspection, raised expectations of significant reform in the Baltic, and Russophile sentiments among Estonian public opinion probably reached their height in the early 1880s.

Despite the differences noted above, there was much that was common to all Estonian political and social thought during the national awakening. All Estonian intellectuals expressed absolute loyalty to the tsar and could conceive of no other form of government for the Russian empire; the first phase of the Russian revolutionary movement in the 1860s and 1870s found no reflection among the Estonians. The ideal world of all Estonian thinkers remained a rural one in which sturdy yeoman farmers practiced scientific agriculture, and private property was regarded as the key to success and happiness.

The beginning of the era of Russification in the Baltic provinces was symbolized by the appointment of Sergei V. Shakhovskoi and Mikhail A. Zinov'ev as governors of Estland and Livland, respectively, in 1885. To some contemporaries it now appeared that the Baltic region would become fully assimilated to central Russian institutions and culture. In addition to the administrative reforms noted above, Russification in education and religion (discussed below) was also implemented in the decade after the mid-1880s. In fact, however, Russification has tended to be overrated by both contemporaries and later observers. No systematic policy of Russifying reforms was ever carried out, and the Estonians benefited from the often sharp differences of opinion between Shakhovskoi and Zinov'ev on local Baltic issues.[15]

The cultural level of the Estonian population had already advanced too far by the mid-1880s for denationalization to be a serious question any longer. Nevertheless, the fact remains that the onset of the Russifying reforms did correspond to the eclipse of the optimism of the national awakening, and in order to understand the prevalent pessimism of the decade between the mid-1880s and mid-1890s, it is necessary to note certain important developments in Estonian public life on the eve of Russification. In part through coincidence, all the major figures of the national awakening had disappeared from the scene by the mid-1880s. Jannsen suffered a stroke in 1880, and the relatively young and vigorous Jakobson died suddenly in 1882. Hurt, who had already accepted a post as a pastor in St. Petersburg in 1880, withdrew from public life when he lost the leadership of the Society of Estonian Literati and the Alexander School movement; Köler, still based in St. Petersburg, could only play an indirect role in Baltic affairs. A crisis of political leadership, to some extent already evident in the internecine struggles between the Hurt and Jakobson forces, emerged full force as no one of sufficient stature came forth to replace them. Thus, even before the onset of Russification, Estonian public opinion was becoming disillusioned with the internal weaknesses of the national movement.

A characteristic Estonian public figure of the Russification era was Ado Grenzstein (1849–1916), editor of *Olevik* (The present) in Tartu from 1882 to 1901. Although he began his journalistic career as a supporter of the Hurt wing of the intelligentsia, Grenzstein began to have doubts about the Estonian national movement in the 1880s and by the early 1890s drew highly pessimistic conclusions about the status of the Estonian people as a minination. Arguing that only those nationalities with at least ten million members were capable of creating an independent culture, he saw no future for the Estonian language. At the same time, Grenzstein asserted that loss of language did not mean the loss of national identity, which—he argued—was determined more by a common heritage and consciousness.[16] It is difficult to assess how representative Grenzstein's views were in this period, but they may have been typical of certain Estonian intellectuals who reached maturity before Russification; in essence, they were disoriented by the new wave and incapable of adapting to it. For all his pro-Russian activity, it is noteworthy that Grenzstein, like Jakobson, never learned Russian well. In the second half of the 1890s, Grenzstein offered a more positive contribution to Estonian political thought through trenchant criticism of German control of Baltic political institutions.[17]

Although it was probably not apparent to contemporaries, the enthusiasm for Russification in the Baltic provinces waned in government circles by the beginning of the reign of Nicholas II in 1894. Coincidentally, the two Russian officials in the Baltic most associated with this policy, Shakhovskoi and Zinov'ev, died in 1894 and 1895, respectively. Among the Estonian intelligentsia in the second half of the 1890s, a new generation that had received its secondary and higher education in the Russian language began to reach maturity. These intellectuals were no more Russified than earlier ones had been Germanized; on the contrary, their sense of Estonian identity appears to have been heightened by the pressure of cultural Russification, and the changed educational system opened up new cultural avenues—for example, Russian literature and radical thought, which had previously been unknown.[18] By the start of the twentieth century a renewed sense of self-confidence was appearing among the Estonian intelligentsia.

MODERNIZATION IN AGRICULTURE

The last four decades of the nineteenth century were a period of major economic change in the rural areas of Estland and northern Livland. Despite the sale of peasant land at high prices and the opportunity to make use of inexpensive peasant labor, the economic condition of the Baltic German estate owners worsened in this period. Mortgage debts remained a plaguing problem, and the number and size of the large estates declined. After 1866 in Livland and 1869 in Estland, the large estates, or Rittergüter, formerly reserved exclusively for members of the nobility corporations, were made available for non-noble ownership; in the following years a number of estates went into the hands of the peasantry, urban bourgeoisie, and foreigners. In 1881, for example, 12 (4.4 percent) of 271 estate owners and 77 (48.1 percent) of 160 estate renters in Estland were Estonians, and the numbers for northern Livland were probably higher (although no figures are available), given the more advanced level of economic development.[19] In an effort to combat this trend, the Estland and Livland Ritterschaften began to entail the large estates by the latter years of the nineteenth century. For all its problems, however, the Baltic German nobility remained by far the most powerful economic force in the countryside. To the end of the tsarist regime, the large estates retained a number of privileges, such as the manufacture of beer and hard liquor, the holding of fairs, and certain hunting and fishing rights.[20]

The most important change in rural economic life in this period was the emergence of a class of peasant landowners. The preconditions for this process were laid by the reforms of the late 1840s and 1850s and the emancipation of the Russian peasantry with land in 1861, reports of which led to rising expectations among the Estonian peasantry. By 1864, following new agrarian laws favorable to the peasantry in the Polish-Lithuanian provinces, the Baltic German estate owners had once again become amenable to some concessions in order to avoid more far-reaching reform. At the same time, an extensive petition campaign by the Estonian peasantry, calling for—among other things—an end to labor rent and the sale of land to the peasants, probably had some influence on tsarist policy.[21] In 1868, under pressure from the central government, the Baltic diets agreed to the abolition of labor rent on peasant land, to be replaced by money rent. In fact, on peasant land the transition to a purely money economy had begun in earnest in the mid-1860s. By 1868, 80.7 percent of the peasant farms in northern Livland were on money rent and 14.3 percent had been sold, while the corresponding figures for Estland were 68.6 and 2.4 percent, and this process continued in the ensuing decades. However, the 1868 regulation said nothing about labor rent on the estate and quota (or one-sixth) lands, and it continued to be used extensively on these lands until 1917.[22]

A thorough study of the transfer of part of the rural land in Estland and northern Livland to the peasantry during the last 60 years of the tsarist regime remains to be done; nevertheless, the broad outlines of the process are clear. In general, the sale of land proceeded much more slowly in Estland where the peasantry was poorer, the estate owners needed less capital (having kept the agricultural inventory for themselves at the time of emancipation), and credit sources were weaker. In Estland, only 11.6 percent of the peasant land had been sold by 1881; thereafter the pace quickened, and the figure reached 50.4 percent in 1897. In northern Livland (with the exception of Saaremaa, where the sale of land was the slowest of all in the Estonian areas), over 50 percent of the peasant land was sold by 1882 and 86.4 percent by 1898. The land was bought by means of long-term mortgages, which proved to be a serious burden for the new owners; at the end of the nineteenth century, less than 10 percent of the peasant farms were free of debt.

It is noteworthy that the Estonian peasants were also able to buy or rent small portions of the estate land, although this remained a distinct minority of the land available to them.[23] Nevertheless, despite the extensive sale of land to the peasantry in this period, the distribution of landholding in general remained highly unequal. On the eve of World War I, the large estates still held about 58 percent of the total rural land and over 42 percent of the agricultural land. Moreover, although the quota land, which proved to be the source of much legal confusion, was ostensibly part of the peasant land, it was often annexed to the estate land. This practice further reduced the land available to the peasants, and up to two-thirds of the Estonian peasantry either remained landless or had a minimal amount of land in this period.[24]

The years from 1860 to 1900 witnessed significant technological innovation in Baltic agriculture. To a large extent, changes took place out of economic necessity, especially with the fall of grain prices on both the world and Russian markets in the last quarter of the nineteenth century, but the growing educational level of the rural population also played a major role. On the peasant land, the basis for innovation was created by the consolidation of the farmsteads into united lots in the 1860s. On both the estate and peasant land, the introduction of agricultural machinery proceeded rapidly. For example, in Estland between 1867 and 1910 the number of agricultural machines in use increased ninefold.[25] By the 1880s, the majority of the estates and newly established farms had replaced the traditional three-field system with much more extensive crop rotation. As a result of these and other innovations, agricultural productivity showed a continuous rise. Rye, oats, and barley—in that order—remained the most important grains. However, the role of grain production in Estonian agriculture declined markedly by the last decades of the nineteenth century as a shift to dairy and cattle farming—at first on the estates and later on the peasant farms as well—began to take place. Among the farms producing for market, those in Estland began to concentrate more on potato cultivation while those in northern Livland continued to specialize in flax.

By the second half of the nineteenth century, agricultural education was reaching many more people than previously; at the university level, the program at Tartu University was joined by one at the Riga Polytechnical Institute in 1862. The expansion of Baltic journalism in the 1860s also contributed markedly to technological progress in agriculture. In 1865 the Livland Public Benefit and Economic Society established the *Baltische Wochenschrift für Landwirtschaft, Gewerbefleiss und Handel*, which served as a model for the first Estonian agricultural periodical, *Eesti Põllumees* (The Estonian farmer), begun in 1869 by Jannsen.[26] For the emerging class of small landowners, an important role was played by the new Estonian agricultural societies, which, for example, held periodic lectures and organized exhibitions. It is characteristic that the first of these societies were founded in the economically more advanced northern Livland (Tartu, 1870; Pärnu, 1870; Viljandi, 1871) with Estland following considerably later (Tallinn, 1888). Although these organizations had a wide influence, their numbers remained limited until the mid-1890s; 45 new groups were established in the last half of that decade. Relations between the Estonian agricultural societies and the Baltic German establishment were ostensibly correct (some of the Estonian societies, for example, were formally connected to the Livland Public Benefit and Economic Society), but political issues, especially during Carl Robert Jakobson's lifetime, often raised tensions.[27]

INDUSTRIALIZATION AND COMMERCE

Another crucial aspect of economic modernization in this period was industrial expansion, which, as in the Russian empire as a whole, was especially noteworthy in the last decade of the nineteenth century. In 1860–1900 the number of industrial workers in Estonia (including Narva) grew from 6,500 to 24,000; however, over half of this increase (9,600) came in the period 1895–1900. Although the textile industry, which was centered at Narva and led by the huge Kreenholm factory, retained its dominance up to 1900 both in terms of value of output and number of workers, the metal and machine industry, based in Tallinn, began narrowing the gap after 1895. In 1900, 41 percent of the industrial workers in Estonia were located in Narva and 33 percent in Tallinn. Pärnu and Tartu continued to be of only secondary importance as industrial centers.[28] Other major industrial branches included pulp and paper, construction materials, and food products. The capital requirements of this industrial expansion were much greater than those that Baltic German or other local sources could supply, and many of the largest concerns were financed by funds from Moscow, Imperial Germany, or France. Given its relatively late start in economic development, the Estonian population played only a minor role in financing industrialization in this period. It was characteristic of these years that an early Estonian economic venture, the Linda Shipping Society (a joint-stock company founded in Tallinn in 1879), went bankrupt in 1893 because of inexperience and mismanagement.

The railroad came to the northern Baltic region in 1870. In that year the Paldiski-Tallinn-Narva-St. Petersburg line was opened; Tartu was connected with it in 1876 and Riga and Pskov (by way of Valga) in 1889. Pärnu became the last major city to receive the railroad (albeit a narrow gauge line) in 1896, and the basic Estonian railway system was completed by the early twentieth century. The density of the railroad network, far above the average for European Russia at the end of the nineteenth century, greatly expanded the range of Estonian markets as well as the mobility of the population. Other revolutionary forms of communication appeared as well. The telegraph came to Estonia during the Crimean War and reached all the larger cities in the 1860s. In the 1880s, Tallinn and Tartu had telephones installed. In Tallinn, the first horse-drawn streetcars began operating in 1888.[29]

Tallinn was the only important Estonian port in this period. It experienced an exponential growth in its foreign commerce in the 1870s following the completion of the Baltic railway and ranked either second, third, or fourth as an import center in the Russian empire during the last three decades of the nineteenth century. Trailing only St. Petersburg in the early 1880s, Tallinn began to slip by the mid-1880s through competition from Odessa and Riga. As in previous centuries, exports remained relatively unimportant and never rose above 20 percent of Tallinn's total foreign trade. The major imports were cotton, coal, coke, machinery, iron, steel, and fertilizers, while the leading exports continued to be grain and alcohol.[30] Internal commerce in Estland and northern Livland expanded rapidly in this period, promoted by industrial and agricultural growth and by the abolition of the guild system in 1866.

DEMOGRAPHIC TRENDS AND SOCIETY

In 1860–1900 the upward demographic trend that had begun after the Great Northern War continued, but the rate of growth slowed by the end of the nineteenth century. As Palli has recently pointed out, a detailed demographic study of this period remains to be done. In an earlier work on Estland, it was noted that in the last two decades of the nineteenth century the average age at marriage increased while fertility declined.[31] The results of two censuses (conducted in 1881 in the Baltic provinces and in 1897 in the Russian empire as a whole) provide more accurate overall data than for previous centuries. In 1881 the total population of Estland and northern Livland was 881,455, of which about 90 percent declared Estonian nationality. Among the ethnic Estonians, slightly over 1 percent indicated that they spoke another language—overwhelmingly German—habitually. This phenomenon occurred much more frequently in the cities than in the rural areas; in 1881, for example, 7.3 percent of the Estonians by nationality in Tallinn said they habitually spoke German.[32] In 1897 the population of Estonia (excluding Narva, which was administratively part of St. Petersburg province in 1802–1917) reached 958,351. The Estonians comprised 90.6 percent of the total while the Russians and Germans—3.9 and 3.5 percent respectively—formed the most important minorities.[33]

A major factor in the demographic balance sheet in these years was emigration. As noted above, freedom of movement had been highly restricted as late as the mid-nineteenth century, but a new passport law in 1863 permitted settlement in any part of the Russian empire. As was generally the case in other parts of Europe in these years, the most important motivation for the emigration movement was economic; the great majority of Estonians who left in these years came from among the landless peasantry. Above all, these colonists sought agricultural land in the Russian empire. The main areas of settlement included St. Petersburg, Pskov, and Vitebsk provinces, while the central Volga region, the Crimea, Siberia, and the Caucasus trailed considerably farther behind. St. Petersburg and Riga, as the two most accessible metropolises, also attracted a significant number of Estonian immigrants. In 1897 about 120,000 Estonians lived outside of Estland and northern Livland (including Narva), and over half of these were located in St. Petersburg province. In the final decades of the nineteenth century, emigration—both to Germany and the interior of the Russian empire—also became a noteworthy phenomenon among the Baltic Germans, which led to a decline in their absolute numbers.[34]

The social structure of the Estonian countryside witnessed important changes in the decades following the reforms of the 1860s. At the top of rural society remained the Baltic German nobility and clergy, although about half of their total numbers resided in the cities. The striking development in this period, fostered by growing wealth and education, was the emergence of increasing social differentiation within the Estonian population. Although the Estonians hardly penetrated the category of estate owners in the nineteenth century and were only beginning to become pastors, a rural intelligentsia that consisted mainly of schoolteachers, administrators on the landed estates, and township officials was growing rapidly. For example, 70 percent of the rural schoolteachers in Estland in 1881 were ethnic Estonians.[35] The Estonian farming population could be divided into three major categories: landowners, renters, and landless. Although many farm owners could not cope with heavy indebtedness, those who managed to keep abreast of the changing agricultural market became relatively wealthy. In general, the farmers of northern Livland continued to be substantially more prosperous than their counterparts in Estland. The majority of the landless peasants worked on the farms, but the least fortunate were clearly those who labored on the large estates and who were still paid only in kind. Nevertheless, the overall quality of rural life, especially housing, showed distinct improvement in this period.[36]

Urbanization, the major social component of modernization, accompanied the process of industrialization. From 1862–1863 to 1897, the population of the Estonian cities nearly tripled, from 64,031 to 189,582, while the overall urban proportion of the total population rose from 8.7 to 19.2 percent. Tallinn (64,572) and Tartu (42,308) retained their positions as the most populous Estonian cities in 1897, while Narva grew to 16,577 (and to 29,882 if the factory suburbs are included). The pace of urbanization in the larger cities was greatest in the 1860s and 1870s.[37] The overwhelming source of urban growth was immigration from the surrounding countryside, a reflection of both the attractiveness of the cities and the economic problems of the rural areas. The national composition of the cities also underwent great changes. Although the Baltic Germans still formed significant minorities (in a few cases, a majority) of the urban population in the 1860s, their share was reduced to 20 percent or less in all twelve Estonian cities except one (Kuressaare: 26 percent) by 1897. As noted above, the German element was declining not only relatively but also absolutely. At the same time, both the Estonian and Russian urban populations were increasing. In 1897 the proportions of the major ethnic groups in the cities of Estland and northern Livland (including Narva) were as follows: Estonians, 67.8 percent; Germans, 16.3 percent; and Russians, 10.9 percent.[38]

In spite of being reduced to small minorities in the cities, the Baltic Germans retained their position at the top of urban society. The great majority of the urban elite—nobility, literati, industrialists, and large merchants—continued to be German. A new element in the middle and upper echelons of urban society was created by the influx of Russian officials beginning in the mid-1880s. At the same time, however, the numerical Estonianization of the cities was accompanied by the emergence of an increasingly stronger Estonian bourgeoisie, including property owners, merchants, minor officials, and a professional middle class of lawyers, teachers, journalists, and physicians. Administrative Russification contributed to a huge increase in the proportion of Estonians employed in the state bureaucracy in the Baltic region. In 1897, Estonians constituted 52 percent of the officials working for the central government in Estland and northern Livland as compared to just 5 percent in Estland in 1881.[39] Nevertheless, it should be borne in mind that German social and cultural influence among the Estonian bourgeoisie remained strong throughout this period.

Among the lower classes in the cities, despite industrial expansion, artisans remained more numerous than industrial workers until the end of the nineteenth century. There was still a significant demand for such skilled artisans as shoemakers, seamstresses, and carpenters. The usual social ills of early industrialization, especially poor working conditions and low wages, accompanied the rise of an urban proletariat. The first major industrial strike occurred in 1872 at the Narva Kreenholm factory, whose work force was about 70 percent Estonian at the time.[40] However, widespread social unrest and political strikes only began in conjunction with the Revolution of 1905.

CULTURAL DEVELOPMENTS

The cultural aims of the national awakening were most clearly expressed in the nationwide efforts of the period: the Estonian Alexander School movement, the Society of Estonian Literati, and the all-Estonian song festivals. Above all, they represented a concerted attempt by the rural intelligentsia, which took the lead in the national movement, to raise the national consciousness of the Estonian people. The fundamental emphasis was on mass culture in an effort to reach as much of the population as possible. The first of these national undertakings, the movement for an Estonian Alexander School (EAS; named in honor of Alexander I as the tsar-liberator), began in the early 1860s among the rural intelligentsia of Viljandimaa. Intended as the first secondary school to use Estonian as the language of instruction, the major purpose of the EAS was to produce a body of well-educated teachers for the growing elementary school network. Nearly a decade passed before the Ministry of the Interior granted permission to begin fund-raising in 1871, but in some fifteen years the required capital (about 100,000 rubles) was gathered through donations. The cultural—and to some extent political—importance of the EAS movement lay in the extent to which it achieved broad participation as the first nationwide Estonian organization through the establishment of local committees in nearly 80 percent of the Estonian parishes, including all but one on the northern Livland mainland. Semiannual plenary meetings of the executive committee and the local representatives in Tartu provided a national forum for the discussion of cultural issues as well as a kind of parliamentary school for the Estonian people.[41]

In the 1870s, Jakob Hurt and the moderate wing of the Estonian intelligentsia led the EAS movement without question. However, in the early 1880s, a power struggle between Hurt and Carl Robert Jakobson and their supporters led to fateful results. Both sides invited the central government to intervene against the other, and by 1884 control of the EAS movement had passed into the hands of tsarist officials. The failure of the Estonian leadership to resolve its differences by itself led to growing pessimism about the future of the national movement among broad sections of the population. Another blow came in

1888 when, in line with the policy of Russification, the EAS opened its doors as a middle school with Russian as the language of instruction. However, until it was closed in 1906 as an alleged hotbed of unrest, the EAS provided a secondary school environment in which all the students were Estonian and the Estonian language was at least a subject of study.[42] In 1914 it was reopened as an agricultural school. Despite its checkered history, the Alexander School movement had a highly educational impact on the Estonian population as a whole.

The idea for the Society of Estonian Literati (SEL) probably originated with F. R. Kreutzwald in the mid-1860s on the model of the Finnish Literary Society, founded 1831. The original intention of the society was to promote eduational literature in Estonian, but the SEL soon took on considerably broader literary aspirations. As with the Alexander School movement, the major rural support for the SEL came from Viljandimaa (and northern Livland in general), but meetings and activities became centered at Tartu as the recognized Estonian cultural center. Officially confirmed in 1871, the SEL was also dominated in the 1870s by Hurt and the moderates. However, the same power struggle—somewhat earlier in the case of the SEL—between the Hurt and Jakobson forces began before the end of the decade. In 1881 the radicals emerged victorious as Hurt and his followers, including the most educated members, resigned from the society. Jakobson became president and managed to overcome this crisis, but after his death in 1882 the SEL went into decline until its closing in 1893 by the tsarist authorities. Because of poor leadership, the disorientation caused by Russification, and internecine quarrels, the SEL provided the tsarist regime with a suitable pretext for ending its activity.[43] Despite its inglorious end, the SEL, although more limited in scope than the EAS movement, afforded another cultural forum for the intelligentsia. In its active years, the SEL made important contributions to the development of the written language and the collection of Estonian folklore.

Certainly no other occasion symbolized the romantic optimism of the national awakening as much as the first all-Estonian song festival held in Tartu in 1869. Despite the fact that Jakobson and Köler saw no reason for celebration, given the crop failures and hunger of the previous year, the song festival—with 845 participants, mainly from northern Livland, and 10,000–15,000 in the audience—was a definite success.[44] Organized by Jannsen and the Vanemuine (mythical god of song, borrowed from Finnish folklore) Society to commemorate the fiftieth anniversary of peasant emancipation in Livland, the event took place amid general harmony. The program included only a modest role for native Estonian music (which, to be sure, was in its infancy), as befitted Jannsen's gradualist views, and a Baltic German pastor presided over the affair. Nevertheless, the first song festival provided a powerful stimulus to the development of Estonian national consciousness and musical culture. The audience, which heard Hurt outline a program for the development of education in

Estonian, carried new ideas and impressions back to the local communities, and Jannsen's *Eesti Postimees* (2,600 subscribers in 1869) provided a full, six-part report on the events.[45]

No less important was the tradition that was established. In the last three decades of the nineteenth century, six all-Estonian song festivals (in 1869, 1879, 1880, 1891, 1894, and 1896) were held, with four of the first five taking place in Tartu. In 1880 Tallinn served as the location for the third song festival, marking its first major participation as a center for Estonian cultural activity. The ostensible occasions for these events were tsarist anniversaries or once again the commemoration of the Livland peasant emancipation in 1894, but the programs became increasingly Estonianized as more native compositions were included; such compositions were a majority in 1880. The number of participants also grew rapidly after 1880, reaching 5,520 in 1896, and estimates for the size of the audience range as high as 50,000 in 1894.[46] The song festivals of the 1890s were particularly important as antidotes to the pessimism occasioned by Russification.

Beginning in the 1860s, another major feature of Estonian life was the emergence of local societies and clubs organized for the advancement of music, theater, adult education, and temperance. The most important of these, the Vanemuine Society in Tartu and the Estonia Society in Tallinn (both founded in 1865), were instrumental in developing musical culture and organizing song festivals. In the 1870s similar organizations were established in other urban centers, and in the following decades they spread into the rural areas as well. The impact of the national song festivals was such that choral and orchestral societies became the most important means of Estonian cultural self-expression on the local level throughout this period. In 1867–1901, for example, the number of Estonian orchestras in Estland and northern Livland (including Narva) jumped from 11 to 224 (160 rural, 64 urban). As in other aspects of Estonian life, northern Livland took the lead in the development of musical culture.[47] In general, the decline of the national movement by the mid-1880s and the Russification era, which included stricter control over local organizations, contributed to a lull in the activity of these groups. However, temperance societies, which began to be founded on the Finnish model in 1889, provided an exception to this trend. Of the 61 such organizations created in the next fifteen years, over half were established in the first part of the 1890s.[48]

The emergence of an Estonian intelligentsia coincided with the beginning of the national awakening. In essence, this meant the appearance of a significant number of educated individuals who believed in the development of a specifically Estonian culture. As suggested by their role in the Alexander School movement and the Society of Estonian Literati, their efforts were not always successful in the second half of the nineteenth century, and more than any other segment of the Estonian population, the older members of the intelligentsia were susceptible to the pessimism of the Russification era. At the same time, Estonian intellectuals remained powerfully under German cultural influence, including the use of German as a means of communication among themselves. In this regard, a major turning point in the evolution of the intelligentsia came at the end of the 1890s. The seemingly contradictory effect of Russification was not to denationalize Estonian intellectuals, but rather to liberate them from the Baltic German cultural world. By the start of the twentieth century, a revolutionary change was occurring among the intelligentsia: the use of Estonian as the habitual means of communication.[49] With a much firmer sense of self-confidence and with growing numbers, the intelligentsia was able to lay a firm basis for a modern Estonian culture after the turn of the twentieth century.

The Estonian language underwent important changes in the latter part of the nineteenth century. In the 1870s two crucial transitions took place in the evolution of written Estonian. First, the so-called new orthography, which is modelled on Finnish and is the basis of modern Estonian, came into general acceptance; second, after centuries of competition, the North Estonian dialect finally emerged as the accepted national language.[50] In the last decades of the nineteenth century, the previously limited vocabulary of Estonian expanded to include new political, social, and cultural terms. Yet many abstract concepts were still lacking in the language, and there was not yet agreement on a single system of grammar.

In many ways, Estonian literature in 1860–1900 reflected the social and psychological conditions of the population as a whole. Whereas romanticism dominated in the belles lettres of the national awakening, critical realism emerged during the era of Russification and at the end of the nineteenth century. It is characteristic that poetry set the tone in the first half of the period and prose seemed more appropriate in the less euphoric later decades. The outstanding literary figure in this era was F. R. Kreutzwald, who became the first Estonian writer to achieve a reputation outside the region, particularly in St. Petersburg, Finland, Germany, and Hungary. Using the traditional regivärss form as well as the themes of Estonian folklore, Kreutzwald's major contribution was the compilation of the national epic, *Kalevipoeg*. In this work he portrays the mythological adventures of Kalevipoeg, which end tragically with the hero— having lost his legs by his own sword—chained to the gates of Hell. However, the final lines of the epic promise that Kalevipoeg will one day return home and create an era of happiness for his people.[51] Among the Estonian population, the importance of *Kalevipoeg* was not so much literary—it took decades to reach a wide audience—as it was symbolic, affirming the historical existence of the Estonian nation. The compilation and study of Estonian folklore, which began on a large scale in the 1880s, received a strong stimulus from the appearance of this work.

In the poetry of the national awakening, the major figure was Lydia

Koidula (1843–1886), Jannsen's daughter, whose most important work was *Emajõe ööbik* (The nightingale of Emajõgi; 1867). In the patriotic evocations of her Estonian homeland, Koidula remained unsurpassed in depth of sentiment and power of expression. Working in the same genre, but of lesser talents, were Mihkel Veske, Ado Reinvald, and Friedrich Kuhlbars. In the late nineteenth century, Juhan Liiv (1864–1913), although troubled by schizophrenia, was by far the most gifted poet. In prose, the typical period piece of the national awakening era was Jakob Pärn's *Oma tuba, oma luba* (A man's home is his castle; 1879), which reflected the ideology of the emerging landowning peasantry. In the 1880s the romanticized historical novel that depicted the Estonian struggle against German invaders came into vogue; the best and most popular of these was Eduard Bornhöhe's *Tasuja* (The avenger; 1880). By the mid-1890s socially critical realism had begun to dominate Estonian prose, especially in the works of Eduard Vilde (1865–1933) and Ernst Peterson-Särgava (1868–1958). Vilde's subjects included both contemporary rural and urban poor in such novels as *Külmale maale* (Banished; 1896) and *Raudsed käed* (Iron hands; 1898). Writing with sharp irony, Peterson-Särgava criticized the conditions of Estonian rural life and satirized the roles of both the Baltic German and Estonian elites. The Estonian theater, founded by Koidula in 1870, remained relatively underdeveloped in this period. August Kitzberg (1855–1927), whose major works came after 1900, was the leading dramatist at the turn of the twentieth century.

The publication of printed matter in Estonian grew rapidly in 1860–1900. During this period the annual output of titles of books and brochures increased nearly sixfold (55 to 312). At the same time, their contents became increasingly secularized; the proportion of religious works declined to 28 percent of the total in 1850–1900 as compared to 53 percent for the first half of the century. In 1861–1900, the number of publishing houses in the northern Baltic region rose from 9 to 44, and Estonians began to own and operate some of them starting in the early 1880s.[52] The most important form of printed matter was the periodical press, which played a decisive role during the national awakening in reaching large numbers of people on a regular basis for the first time. The typical journalistic publication of the awakening era was the weekly newspaper, the number of which quadrupled from two to eight in 1857–1881. With *Sakala* (1878–1882), Jakobson ushered in a new era in the shaping of public opinion and politicized the debate within the Estonian national movement. The Russification period brought a temporary decline in the number of journalistic titles as well as the most stringent censorship practices during the latter part of the nineteenth century. In addition to closing down *Virulane*, the largest Estonian weekly at the time, in 1888, the tsarist authorities rejected numerous requests for new newspapers and journals. Nevertheless, the first Estonian daily—

Postimees (The courier)—emerged in 1891 in Tartu, and the number of titles in the Estonian press surpassed the pre-Russification level by the late 1890s.[53]

Estonian elementary education witnessed significant expansion in numbers and improvement in quality during the national awakening. In Estland, where the educational network had lagged behind, the number of schools doubled in 1860–1872 (from 230 to 461) and finally achieved parity with northern Livland by the early 1880s.[54] The corps of schoolteachers also received better preparation through an expanded number of training institutions, and educational literature was immeasurably improved, especially through Jakobson's readers and the work of the Society of Estonian Literati. However, the rural school system remained under Baltic German control, and beginning in the 1860s there was increasing pressure for the use of German as the language of instruction in the parish (higher elementary) schools.

Russification of the primary educational system in the Baltic provinces brought two fundamental changes: the placement of all rural elementary schools under the jurisdiction of the Ministry of Education in St. Petersburg, and the introduction of Russian as the language of instruction from the third year of school in 1887 and from the first year in 1892 (except for religion in Lutheran schools). The initial effects of Russification in education were chaotic. Many schools were closed when the Baltic German elites withdrew their support in protest against the changes, much of the teaching personnel was either unable or unwilling to learn Russian with sufficient competence to continue in the profession, and the use of a foreign language as the means of instruction led to a marked decline in the quality of education. Nevertheless, the negative effects of Russification should not be overestimated. The tradition of instruction at home in Estonian remained strong, and most teachers appear to have continued to use some Estonian in the classrooms since the tsarist authorities simply lacked the means to enforce Russification. A comparison of the 1881 and 1897 censuses indicates that the Estonian literacy rate (reading only) did not decline, but even increased slightly in the intervening years. In 1897, 96–97 percent of the Estonians ten years of age and older in Estland and northern Livland could read, making the northern Baltic area the most literate region of the Russian empire.[55]

Although secondary and higher education were conducted in German or Russian in this period, they nevertheless offered an important avenue to social and cultural advancement for increasing numbers of Estonians. Above all, it was the growing urban and rural bourgeoisie that was able to send its children to higher schools. A major breakthrough had already occurred in the 1850s when the first secondary schools for girls were established (Lydia Koidula attended one in Pärnu, 1854–1861), and the first girls' gymnasium was founded in Tallinn in 1874. Overall, the total number of secondary school students in Estonia quadrupled between 1857 and 1900 (1,282 to about 5,000), and the proportion of children of burghers and peasants was growing steadily. The number of Estonians at Tartu University also began to grow during the national awakening (5 students in 1860, 41 in 1880). By the early 1890s there were over 100 Estonians enrolled at Tartu, but in the following decade there was a slight decline, probably occasioned by the Russification of the university in the mid-1890s.[56] In addition, by the 1860s increasing numbers of Estonians had begun pursuing higher education at the Riga Polytechnical Institute and, by the 1880s, at institutions in St. Petersburg and Moscow.

In the late nineteenth century, two major issues dominated religious life in Estonia. The more dramatic was the continuing struggle between the Orthodox and Lutheran churches for the allegiance of the Estonian population. Before the mid-1880s, the Orthodox Church did not pursue an active policy in the Baltic provinces, and perhaps as many as one-fourth of the converts of the 1840s (and their offspring) returned to the Lutheran fold in the following decades. However, under Governor Shakhovskoi of Estland (1885–1894), the propagation of Orthodoxy became an important element in the policy of Russification, especially after some 3,400 Estonians in the Läänemaa district of Estland had converted on their own initiative in 1883–1884. Russian officials such as Konstantin Pobedonostsev, procurator of the Holy Synod (1880–1905), and Shakhovskoi saw Orthodoxy as the quickest means to unite non-Russians with the "great Russian family." Despite this active concern, the 1897 census does not indicate any marked success in proselytism. In that year, 17.7 percent of the Estonians in Livland were Orthodox (roughly the same proportion as in the 1840s) while the figure for Estland was 4.6 percent.[57]

The other major religious question in this period was the problem of control of the Baltic Lutheran Church. Although the Baltic German elites retained dominance in Lutheran affairs until the end of the tsarist regime, there was increasing restiveness among the Estonian population. Estonian ire focused on the continued practice of appointment of pastors by the Baltic German landowners with little or no participation by the Estonian congregations, and while the number of Estonian clergymen gradually grew, Germans still constituted the great majority. In his major work, *Herrenkirche oder Volkskirche?* (1899), Ado Grenzstein suggested that the Baltic Lutheran Church be divided into three separate bodies according to nationality—German, Estonian, and Latvian.[58] However, the Baltic German authorities ignored all such proposals.

6 Revolution and War, 1900–1917

The last two decades of the tsarist era were dominated by ferment and revolution throughout the Russian empire, and Estonia was no exception. With the rise of the liberation movement in Russia, all-empire questions began to impinge on Estonian life as never before. At the same time, a new generation emerged at home with a renewed sense of confidence about the Estonian future. The Revolution of 1905 marked a fundamental turning point in Estonian history, particularly a great escalation of cultural and political goals. As the tsarist regime tottered in 1905, the Estonians worked out programs for political autonomy in a federalized Russia and the creation of a modern culture worthy of a European nation. Although the reaction following 1905 dampened hopes for significant political change, the growing socioeconomic power of the Estonian population as well as the cultural flowering of this era could not be halted. The experience of World War I indicated that the Russian empire had not been able to modernize with sufficient speed. It was not a lack of resources, but rather the inability to mobilize them properly that spelled doom for the tsarist regime. The major effect of the war on non-Russian nationalities was a tightening of the tsarist rein, but as the Old Regime disintegrated under external pressure, sweeping changes were in the offing. In February 1917, however, what form those changes would take remained unclear.

BACKGROUND TO 1905

The pessimism occasioned by Russification began to disappear in the final years of the nineteenth century, and Estonian social and political thought now revived in changed circumstances. Leadership of the intelligentsia passed to a new, more educated generation that felt more optimistic about prospects for Estonian development. Jaan Tõnisson (1868–19??), an 1892 graduate in law from Tartu University who became editor of *Postimees* in 1896, was the first major figure to emerge in the post-Russification era. In the second half of the 1890s, Tõnisson worked to restore Estonian self-respect in his editorial debates with Grenzstein's *Olevik*. It was the end of an era in 1901 when Grenzstein, recognizing that he had lost the ideological battle for public support, voluntarily left for permanent exile in Paris.[1] In essence, Tõnisson represented a renewal of the moderate political orientation of the national awakening. Following Hurt and German idealism and romanticism, Tõnisson asserted the moral duty and the right of the Estonian people to exist as a nation. In his view, the attainment of a high level of national and moral consciousness should be the most important goal for the Estonian people. In terms of political aims, Tõnisson envisaged a gradual advance as the Estonians became more educated and, like Hurt and Jannsen, felt that Estonians and Germans could work together for common Baltic development, although he rejected Baltic German tutelage per se. Again sharing Hurt's views, Tõnisson argued that the small size of the Estonian nation meant it could play no role in Russian state politics, and he shunned the all-Russian liberation movement before 1905. As a corollary of this position, he advocated complete loyalty to the tsarist regime.[2]

A crucial shift in Estonian social and political thought came at the start of the twentieth century with the appearance of *Teataja* (The herald; 1901–1905) in Tallinn, edited by Konstantin Päts (1874–1956), and *Uudised* (The news; 1903–1905) in Tartu, edited by Peeter Speek (1873–1968). In contrast to Tõnisson and the *Postimees* group, who tended to represent the wealthier urban bourgeoisie and the landowning farmers, *Teataja* and *Uudised* emerged as the first journalistic voices of the lower classes of the Estonian population. The radicalization of large parts of the Estonian intelligentsia in the years before 1905 reflected the growing differentiation of Estonian society and was also promoted by increasing contacts with the all-empire liberation movement. For the first time, the traditional Estonian loyalty to the tsarist regime began to fade. Within the limits permitted by censorship, *Teataja* and *Uudised* stressed the need for social and economic change. In terms of political reform, both repeated Jakobson's call for zemstvo institutions in the Baltic provinces, and *Uudised* further advocated abolition of all parish-level organs and the creation of a rural township government that would include all social classes, not just the peasantry.[3] In the years before 1905 the first scattered revolutionary circles in Estonia began to appear among intellectuals and secondary school students, especially in Tartu, and among workers in Tallinn and Narva. Their sympathies were generally with the Russian Social Democratic Workers' Party or the non-Russian minority social democratic movements.

THE REVOLUTION OF 1905

Although the tangible changes it effected did not seem far-reaching, the Revolution of 1905 constituted a major watershed in Estonian history. In the Russian empire as a whole, the origins of 1905 reach back to the unresolved political and social problems of the tsarist system. These were in turn compounded by rapid industrialization beginning in the 1890s, which created a discontented working class in the cities; the more immediate crisis was brought on by the failure of governmental leadership in the Russo-Japanese War (1904–1905) and the economic downswing of the early years of the twentieth century. The last straw came with the episode of Bloody Sunday in January 1905, which involved the shooting of hundreds of St. Petersburg workers during a peaceful march. In this volatile situation, the reaction to Bloody Sunday was swift and encompassed the entire empire. Although the immediate origins of the upheaval stemmed from St. Petersburg and the interior of the Russian empire, Estonia participated in the revolution from the beginning.

In January 1905 sympathy strikes by workers broke out in Tallinn, Narva, and Pärnu along with student demonstrations in Tartu, all protesting the killings of Bloody Sunday. Although Tartu University was soon closed, workers' strikes continued periodically throughout the year in Estonia. With the tsarist government thrown off balance, Nicholas II issued a ukase in February that granted his subjects the right to submit proposals for change. In effect, the tsar legalized discussion of reform, and the resultant process of submitting memoranda provided a striking political education for much of the population. By early spring the unrest had spread to the Estonian countryside, and strikes by agricultural workers and cases of arson became increasingly numerous. The most far-reaching reform proposal before the fall of 1905 was offered by *Uudised* at the end of May. Without mentioning the tsar, it called for the creation of a state parliament elected by universal (male and female) suffrage as well as broad autonomy for the non-Russian areas, including Estonia.[4] Beginning in April, periodic arrests of Estonian revolutionaries took place. The major activity of the Russian Social Democratic Workers' Party (RSDWP) in Estland and northern Livland was centered in Tallinn; the Estonian Social Democratic Workers' Party (ESDWP), which had a federalist orientation, was founded in Tartu in August.

As unrest deepened in the summer and early fall and the tsarist regime remained unsure of itself, the revolution reached a crescendo in the two months following mid-October. Within about a week after the start of a railway strike in Moscow in early October, a general strike of unprecedented proportions emerged throughout the Russian empire. In Tallinn, mass meetings called for peaceful reform, and the situation remained calm until October 16. On that day, however, tsarist troops fired three rifle salvos into a peaceful crowd on a market square, killing at least 60 and wounding about 200.[5] The reaction to the Tallinn Bloodbath, as it came to be known, dampened enthusiasm for the October Manifesto, issued by Nicholas II the following day, which promised to grant civil and political rights to the population. Although the tsar had hoped to quell unrest by his action, the October Manifesto satisfied only the most moderate reformists in the empire and actually ushered in the period of greatest upheaval in 1905. During the ensuing "Days of Freedom," which lasted for nearly eight weeks, the population simply appropriated civil rights such as freedom of speech, assembly, and the press. The public meeting became a daily event. In effect, the October Manifesto and the promise of a State Duma—an elected national assembly—permitted the formation of political parties loyal to the reformed regime. In Estland and northern Livland, the only such "legal" parties created were the Baltic Constitutional Party—under Baltic German leadership—and Tõnisson's Estonian Progressive People's Party (*Eesti Rahvameelne Eduerakond*; EPPP), founded in Tartu in November.

The central Estonian political event and the most broadly based expression of public opinion in 1905 was the All-Estonian Congress held in Tartu on November 27–29. Called by Tõnisson and his moderate followers in an attempt to pre-empt the national stage from more radical groups, the congress was presumably permitted by the authorities for that very reason. Although the method of delegate selection was intended to favor moderate forces, the representatives proved to be much more radical than expected.[6] No political parties were formally represented, but the assembly divided into two main groups: the moderate followers of Tõnisson, and a radical opposition. In the balloting for chair, it became clear that the radicals held a majority of the delegates; Jaan Teemant of Tallinn (437 votes) was elected while Tõnisson (101 votes) was even outpolled by one of his own lieutenants. Following a dispute over the election of vice-chairs, the congress split in two as Tõnisson and the moderates (perhaps 300 out of a total of 800 delegates) left the meeting hall. Thereafter the representatives met separately and produced the "Bürgermusse" (moderate) and "Aula" (radical) resolutions.[7]

The two sets of resolutions clearly reflected the major division in Estonian social and political thought that had emerged since the beginning of the twentieth century. Although both called for a constituent assembly elected by universal suffrage, the radicals demanded the overthrow of the tsarist regime by the "revolutionary people," whereas the moderates expected the existing government to call the convention. With regard to means of struggle, the Bürgermusse document sought to remain within the bounds of legality. In contrast, the Aula resolutions advocated use of strikes, boycotts, and the establishment of revolutionary self-government at the local levels. The most striking differences came in the social and economic realm. Whereas the moderates maintained the sanctity of private property, the radicals demanded the expropriation of the large estates and declared the principle of common ownership of all land.

However, there was one common theme in both halves of the congress: the demand for Estonian national autonomy. Yet even here the emphasis differed significantly. Seeking concessions from the existing government, the moderates spelled out their plans for self-government in Estonia. In contrast, the radicals stressed the transformation of the Russian empire as a whole and left the details of Estonian autonomy for later. Nevertheless, both sets of resolutions called for nothing less than the repeal of Russification. The more specific Bürgermusse document demanded the administrative unification of Estland and northern Livland with an autonomous self-government, elected by universal suffrage, operating on three levels: the rural township, the district, and the entire area populated by the Estonians in the Baltic region. The jurisdiction of Estonian local government would include such matters as the police, judicial systems, education, health, and the naming of administrative personnel. Estonian was to become the official language of administration, although German and Russian would have equal rights. In education, Estonian was to become the language of instruction immediately in the elementary schools and in principle on the secondary level (the *Uudised* memorandum in May 1905 had called for the immediate use of Estonian on this level as well). Furthermore, the position of Estonian at Tartu University would be significantly expanded to include professorships in Estonian language and literature, Finno-Ugric languages, and theology as well as lectureships in all faculties. [8]

The three weeks following the All-Estonian Congress proved to be the most agitated period of 1905 in Estonia. Following the Aula resolutions, a number of revolutionary self-governments were established in the rural townships of Estland and northern Livland. At the same time, plans were made to form a workers' soviet in Tallinn. A major congress of rural township representatives was to be held in Tallinn in mid-December, but it never took place, since the tsarist authorities finally began to act with some resolution. On December 10 martial law was declared in Tallinn and Harjumaa, and much of the local committee of the RSDWP as well as a large number of Estonian intellectuals were arrested. Others, such as Päts and Teemant, fled to Finland and later to Western Europe. In reaction to the arrests and in imitation of the Latvian example, bands of workers from Tallinn—joined by some peasants—went to the countryside and partially or totally destroyed up to 120 manorhouses and estates in Estland in the space of a week. Damages to the estates of northern Livland, however, were comparatively slight. [9] Having recovered its balance, the tsarist regime now sent punitive expeditions to the Baltic provinces, which proved to be among the most savage in the entire Russian empire. A Soviet estimate suggests that about 300 people were killed by the punitive expeditions in Estonia and that another 600 received some form of corporal punishment. In addition, 652 additional individuals were court-martialed and sentenced to execution in all three Baltic provinces; another 495 were sent to forced labor.[10]

The political spectrum in Estland and northern Livland in 1905 can be divided into the following major groupings: (1) the Baltic Germans, nearly all of whom supported the Baltic Constitutional Party (allied with the Octobrists in the State Duma); (2) the moderates, led by Tõnisson's EPPP, whose views were comparable to those of the Constitutional Democrats in the empire as a whole; (3) the radicals, never formally organized into a political party and led mainly by Päts and the *Teataja* intellectuals, who held a mediating position between the moderates and the social democrats; and (4) the revolutionaries, divided into the Russian and Estonian Social Democratic Workers' Parties with the RSDWP espousing a centralized, all-Russian movement and the ESDWP following the principles of federalism and local autonomy.

As a movement for immediate and far-reaching political change, the Revolution of 1905 was a failure. Nevertheless, the experience of 1905 signified a turning point in Estonian life. For the first time, broad sections of the population became involved in the discussion of political and social issues, receiving an accelerated education in the process. Above all, political, social, and cultural goals were dramatically escalated in comparison to the pre-1905 era, and the tsarist reaction after 1905 could not turn back the clock.[11]

IDEOLOGICAL DIVISIONS AFTER 1905

For the Baltic German population in Estland and northern Livland, the experience of 1905 also proved to be a watershed. Taken aback by the violence and unrest and feeling abandoned by the tsarist authorities, the Baltic Germans began to look more toward Imperial Germany as a source of potential support. The Baltic German elites also recruited ethnic Germans from elsewhere in the Russian empire for migration to the Baltic provinces and offered them the possibility of land ownership. By 1914 over 20,000 German colonists had arrived in the Baltic area, overwhelmingly in Kurland and Livland.[12] The violence of 1905, coupled with the counterviolence of the punitive expeditions, led to worsened relations between Baltic Germans and Estonians and made a compromise solution to the outstanding political and socioeconomic issues even less likely than before.

For the Estonians, the impact of 1905 set the tone of social and political thought for the remainder of the tsarist era. The right side of the spectrum continued to be dominated by Tõnisson and the EPPP, the only political party tolerated by the tsarist regime after 1905. In general, Tõnisson felt confirmed in his previous views by the experience of 1905. In his opinion, involvement in empirewide political issues was dangerous, and the Estonians should concentrate on their own economic and cultural development instead. Tõnisson also remained committed to rural life as the foundation of Estonian society and emphasized further growth of a class of yeoman farmers.[13]

For the groups to the left of the EPPP, the immediate effect of the repression following 1905 was to eliminate temporarily all political activity. The unorganized radicals and nonconspiratorial ESDWP were scattered by the reaction, but the clandestine and empirewide basis of the RSDWP allowed it to rebound rather rapidly in Estonia. The final ebb of the rebellious mood in the Russian empire came with the dissolution of the Second Duma in June 1907; in the preceding months, the two main RSDWP organizations in Estonia—in Tallinn and Tartu—had suffered devastating arrests. Nevertheless, the more liberal press laws after 1905 permitted the publication of newspapers and periodicals with a veiled social-democratic line, and the RSDWP did have the opportunity to gain a hearing in these years. The differences between Estonian Mensheviks and Bolsheviks only gradually emerged, and they continued to work together as late as 1914.[14]

The most striking phenomenon in Estonian social thought in the post-1905 era was the systematic development of a radical position between the moderates and the social democrats. Gustav Suits (1883–1956), the ideologist of the Young-Estonia (*Noor-Eesti*) movement, offered the first Estonian critique of *both* nationalism and Marxism in 1906. He advocated a synthesis of individualism and undogmatic socialism in which culture would still be national in form but not narrow-minded or chauvinistic. In the period before World War I, the Young-Estonia group concentrated on cultural matters, but in 1914–1916 it published a monthly political and cultural journal entitled *Vaba Sõna* (The free word). The radical intellectuals associated with *Vaba Sõna*—Jüri Vilms and Hans Kruus, for example—were heirs to the federalist tradition established in 1905 by the ESDWP and stressed two major themes of that revolutionary year: democratization and autonomy. In 1917 the major forces in the *Vaba Sõna* group became leading figures in the non-Marxist left in Estonia.[15]

POLITICAL INSTITUTIONS

The only innovation in political institutions as a result of 1905 occurred on the empirewide level: the establishment of the State Duma in 1906. Although the dumas were virtually powerless, participation in the electoral process by much of the male population proved to be an important experience.

In each of the first two dumas, the Estonians had five representatives, but following the limitation of the franchise in 1907, the number was reduced to two in both the Third and Fourth Dumas. The Estonian delegates to the First Duma were all moderates, including Tõnisson and Oscar Rütli from the EPPP, whereas in the Second Duma a radical–social democratic bloc controlled Estland and the EPPP controlled northern Livland. With the change in the electoral laws, the moderates were dominant in the last two dumas. The experience in the dumas also afforded increased empirewide contacts for the Estonian delegates. Following the dissolution of the First Duma in July 1906, Tõnisson was the only Estonian representative to sign the Viipuri (Vyborg) Manifesto, which urged the population of the Russian empire to boycott taxes and military service; as a result of this action, he lost all political rights under the tsarist regime.[16]

Although much discussion of political reform took place in Estland and northern Livland in this period, no change actually occurred. In 1905 the four Baltic diets (Estland, Livland, Kurland and Saaremaa) agreed to a modest reform bill that would have enfranchised propertied Estonians and Latvians, but the tsarist government refused to approve it, and similar proposals in the next two years by both the Ritterschaften and the Estonian moderates foundered on tsarist opposition as well. One striking and unusual example of compromise between the Estonian moderates and the Baltic German elite was the Estland provincial reform project of 1915, sponsored by Päts—who had by now moved to the right—and the Estland Ritterschaft. The plan called for equal representation for large and small property owners and renters in the Estland Diet and would have meant broader representation for the urban and rural Estonian bourgeoisie than they would have had in zemstvo institutions. Once again, the tsarist regime turned down the project. The *Vaba Sõna* group—and probably others to the left of the moderates as well—rejected this proposal as undemocratic.[17]

Despite the lack of political reform, the Estonian bourgeoisie acquired increasing wealth by the early twentieth century and was able to gain control of municipal government in six of the ten major cities in Estland and northern Livland: Valga (in alliance with the Latvians), 1901; Tallinn, 1904; Võru, 1906; Haapsalu, 1909; Pärnu, 1913; and Rakvere, 1914. The city councils of Tartu, Paide, Viljandi, and Kuressaare remained in Baltic German hands until 1917.[18] By far the most important victory came in Tallinn, the capital of Estland and the largest city in the Estonian areas, and subsequent electoral successes there in 1909 and 1913 further contributed to the political maturity and self-confidence of the Estonian bourgeoisie.

ECONOMIC DEVELOPMENT

Although the Revolution of 1905 raised a number of sweeping demands in the agrarian sector, including the expropriation of the landed estates, no major reforms were carried out in the final years of the tsarist era. Nevertheless, despite the lack of any fundamental solution to the agrarian problem, the Estonian peasantry was able to acquire increasing amounts of land in this period. For example, in 1905–1910 the proportion of land in Estland owned by peasants rose from 24 to 34 percent, while in the entire province of Livland the increase was from 35 to 43 percent. By the eve of World War I, the Estonian peasantry had the use of 75 percent of the agricultural land in Estland and northern Livland,[19] including the rental of estate lands. In addition, some aid was forthcoming from the central government through Stolypin's agrarian policy, which included the establishment of branches of the state-sponsored Peasant Land Bank in all three Baltic provinces in 1906 and the sale and rental of state lands to the peasantry.[20] However, these incremental changes in landownership in the Estonian countryside provided no solution to the general problem of peasant land hunger.

In the pre–World War I era, the agricultural sector showed improvement in both output and productivity, particularly in the last five years before 1914. Rye continued to dominate as the main grain for human consumption, and barley and oats were the major crops used for feed. Livestock holdings, especially of hogs, also increased in the prewar years. These improvements in the rural economy were fueled by continuing innovation and mechanization as well as the expansion of agricultural education. By 1910 there were 79 Estonian agricultural societies, one-third of which had been founded in the previous five years, and on the eve of World War I central organizations were established in both Estland and northern Livland to coordinate their activities. In the decade after 1905 the cooperative movement in the Estonian countryside, which had also been encouraged by Stolypin's agrarian policy, expanded rapidly. By 1914 there were 135 milk cooperatives, 138 consumer cooperatives, and 153 machinery cooperatives. In addition, Estonian credit institutions began to emerge after the turn of the twentieth century. In 1902 the first savings and loan association appeared in Tartu, and by World War I there were 129 Estonian credit unions, nearly 60 percent of them in the rural areas.[21]

The industrial expansion that began in the second half of the 1890s in Estonia continued—with a brief pause during the depression of the first few years of the twentieth century—up to World War I. Indeed, the Baltic provinces became one of the most industrialized parts of the Russian empire. In 1908, Estland and Livland ranked fourth and fifth, respectively, both in per capita industrial production and in the number of industrial workers per 100 inhabitants among the 50 provinces of European Russia. From 1900 to 1914 the number of industrial workers in Estonia (including Narva) nearly doubled from 24,000 to 46,000. At the same time, a major shift occurred in the concentration of industrial concerns. By 1914, Tallinn was the center of the rapidly growing metal and machine industry; with 40 percent of all industrial workers, it had passed Narva (with 32 percent) and became the leading Estonian industrial center for the first time. Overall, the textile industry retained its leading position in terms of numbers of workers until World War I, but the gap was narrowing. During the war, with military concerns paramount, the industrial sector underwent sweeping reorientation. With regard to proportion of workers, the metal and machine industry bolted into first place, the textile industry declined slightly, and all other branches fell markedly. The overall number of industrial workers reached a wartime peak in 1916 of about 50,000. In addition, the development of Tallinn as the major Baltic base for the Imperial Russian navy, on which work had begun in 1912, was continued during World War I and grew to include three large shipbuilding concerns.[22]

DEMOGRAPHIC AND SOCIAL CHANGE

No general censuses were conducted in the final years of the tsarist regime; nevertheless, enough statistical information is available to make relatively reliable estimates. An official Ministry of the Interior estimate in 1911 placed the total population of Estland and northern Livland at 1,086,100, about 13 percent higher than in 1897 but far below the rate of increase for the Russian empire as a whole. Population growth in Estonia was affected by a declining rate of natural increase—the lowest in European Russia in the immediate pre–World War I years—and continued emigration.[23] As before, economic factors played the major role in out-migration from the Baltic region, but the political repression following the Revolution of 1905 also contributed to the largest single wave of emigration since 1860. On the eve of the Russian Revolution of 1917, there were nearly 200,000 Estonians living in the empire outside the Baltic provinces and Narva. Over half had settled in St. Petersburg province, and by 1917 their numbers in Petrograd (as St. Petersburg was named in 1914) may have reached 50,000.[24] Emigration outside the Russian empire began to take place in substantial numbers for the first time in this period, but no reliable estimates are available. In the absence of hard data on the ethnic composition of the population, it must be assumed that the Estonians continued to constitute over 90 percent of the total, at least until the distorting effects of World War I. In general, the number of Russians in Estonia increased, especially during wartime industrial expansion, and the number of Germans continued to decline.

The process of urbanization continued during the last two decades of the tsarist regime. In 1913 the population of the Estonian cities reached 253,331, and the overall urban proportion rose to 22 percent in 1914. By 1913 the population of Tallinn (116,132) had nearly doubled compared to the 1897 level, while Tartu (45,088) hardly grew at all. The smaller cities of Pärnu and Narva were both slightly over 20,000. In general, the pace of urbanization tapered off in the years before World War I with the exception of Tallinn and Pärnu. As in the late nineteenth century, the major source of urban growth was immigration; for example, in Tallinn in 1912–1916 the average annual mechanical increase in the population was nearly 11,000. In terms of ethnic composition, the Estonianization of the cities also continued but at a slower rate than in previous decades. In 1913 the three major nationalities in the cities of Estonia (including Narva and Valga) were the following: Estonians, 69.2 percent; Russians, 11.9 percent; and Germans, 11.2 percent. During World War I, the influx of Russian and other non-Estonian workers into the war industries in Tallinn led to a decline in the Estonian share of the population from 72 percent in 1913 to 58 percent in 1917.[25]

Although the upper levels of urban society—which were still dominated by Baltic Germans and some Russians—did not change appreciably in this period, there were major shifts in the middle and lower rungs of the social ladder. The Estonian bourgeoisie continued to grow not only numerically but also in economic strength. This development has been well documented for Tallinn. In 1871 Estonians had constituted only 18.3 percent of the real estate owners in the city, but by 1912 their proportion jumped to 68.8 percent. Increasing wealth accompanied the growth in numbers. In 1871 Estonians had owned only 4.5 percent of the total value of real estate in Tallinn; by 1904–1908, they constituted 75 percent of the property owners under the value of 5,000 rubles and about 33 percent of those above this level.[26]

In the lower social echelons, a multiethnic working class—mainly Estonian and Russian—emerged in Tallinn and Narva in the last two decades of the tsarist regime. The Revolution of 1905 provided a powerful stimulus to worker activism and led to some improvements in wages, hours, and working conditions as well as the establishment of the first trade unions. As elsewhere in the Russian empire, a new wave of strikes began in Estonia in 1910 and became especially noteworthy between 1912 and the beginning of World War I. By 1916, following a lull in the early war years, the strike movement had reached a level comparable to that of 1905. The organization of strikes was aided by the growing concentration of workers in large concerns; by 1916, 75 percent of the labor force in large industry in Estonia was located in factories employing 1,000 or more workers.[27]

CULTURAL LIFE

Although the political goals expressed by Estonians in the early twentieth century were not achieved in tsarist times, the movement for a modern Estonian culture continued apace and received new impetus from the Revolution of 1905. The most conscious efforts in this direction were undertaken by

the Young-Estonia literary and cultural movement, which published five al-
bums (1905–1915) and a journal (1910–1911). The roots of Young-Estonia
reach back to secondary-school circles at the beginning of the twentieth century.
In 1905 its leading figures—Gustav Suits, Friedebert Tuglas (1886–1971), and
Johannes Aavik (1880–1973)—were all 25 years of age or younger. Infected by
the all-empire liberation movement, this new generation sought to emancipate
Estonian culture from its narrow Baltic world. Suits argued that only through
the assimilation of the best of European culture could the Estonians create a
modern culture of their own.[28]

Along with the systematic introduction of West European, Scandinavian,
and Russian belles lettres, Young-Estonia developed a neoromantic literature of
its own. Suits, the first modern Estonian poet, set the tone for the Young-
Estonia movement in 1905 with his volume of verse, *Elu tuli* (The fire of life),
which was powerfully animated by youthful enthusiasm. Although he wrote
highly original prose, Tuglas's most important contribution was the establishment of modern Estonian literary criticism. Aavik's major role came in modern-
izing the Estonian language and greatly expanding its range of expression. As a
movement, Young-Estonia was criticized by the left for its aestheticism and by
the right for its break with tradition and alleged aping of foreign models, but
there is no doubt that it played a fundamental role in the foundation of a
modern Estonian literature.[29]

In all areas of the cultural realm, there was ferment and advance in the early
twentieth century. The written language became more standardized through the
conscious efforts of linguists and other scholars, and in 1910 work began on the
first dictionary of correct usage. Along with Young-Estonia in belles lettres, the
Estonian Literary Society (*Eesti Kirjanduse Selts*)—a conscious revival of the
Society of Estonian Literati, but with much broader and more ambitious
goals—appeared in 1907 and established the first professional Estonian cultural and literary journal, *Eesti Kirjandus* (Estonian literature). At the same
time, such established writers as Eduard Vilde and August Kitzberg were
producing some of their best works. Vilde wrote a historical trilogy on peasant
life in the mid-nineteenth century, including a novel on the uprising of 1858
(*Mahtra sõda* [The war at Mahtra], 1902) and short stories and plays on
contemporary topics (for example, *Pisuhänd* [The hobgoblin], 1913).
Kitzberg's most mature works came after 1905, especially the play *Libahunt*
(The werewolf; 1912).[30] Furthermore, the years after 1905 witnessed the
founding of the first professional theater companies by the Vanemuine and
Estonia societies (both in 1906), the first formal exhibition of Estonian painting
and sculpture (1906), and the establishment of the Estonian National Museum,
which was based on extensive ethnographic collections gathered in the latter
part of the nineteenth century, in Tartu (1909). Finally, the seventh all-Estonian
song festival in Tallinn in 1910 saw a doubling of the number of participants

(12,000) as compared to the previous one in 1896, and it included a program drawn entirely from the works of Estonian composers for the first time.[31]

The turn of the twentieth century also brought a rejuvenation of local cultural organizations. The geographical dispersion of these groups became much broader than in earlier decades. For example, by 1903 some 200 amateur theater groups had been established in the Estonian areas of the Baltic provinces.[32] After 1905, adult education and educational issues in general became a major focus of the local organizations. Some of the local societies, especially the Vanemuine and the Estonia, took on increasing national importance in the transition from amateur to professional forms of culture.

The printed word in Estonian continued to expand in the last years of the tsarist era until World War I. The peak output of titles of books and brochures came in 1913 (702), more than twice the level of 1900 (312), and the total for 1901–1917 exceeded that for the entire nineteenth century. The trend toward secularization also continued: only 17 percent of the titles published in 1901–1917 were religiously oriented. In addition, Estonian journalism experienced substantial growth with a quadrupling of the total number of issues printed in the first decade of the twentieth century. For printed matter in general, the abolition of preliminary censorship in April 1906 proved to be a major boon. Although fines were still meted out and closure of newspapers and periodicals still occurred, the range of expression broadened significantly. Subjects that had been taboo before 1905—for example, Russification—were now treated as a matter of course in the press. However, World War I brought severe limitations on the printed word in Estonian, including a decline in the number of book and brochure titles to less than half of the prewar level. Nevertheless, there was no return to pre-1905 censorship practices.[33]

In the early twentieth century, educational reform became perhaps the most discussed question in Estonian public forums and the press. As noted above, the All-Estonian Congress in 1905 demanded nothing less than autonomous control over the local educational system, including the use of Estonian as the language of instruction in both urban and rural elementary schools and to some degree on higher levels as well. Although the far-reaching aims of 1905 were not realized, it was nevertheless significant that in 1906 Estonian was officially permitted as the language of instruction in the first two years of both urban and rural elementary schools and in nearly the entire curriculum of private schools. By 1910 there were 24 primary educational institutions conducted in Estonian in Estland and northern Livland.[34] Although limited, these concessions did raise expectations for further changes in the future.

On the secondary level, the student body grew rapidly in numbers and became increasingly Estonianized in the years after 1905. In 1913 Estonians constituted over half of the secondary school students in Estland and about 7,000 of the 13,000 secondary school students in the entire northern Baltic region in 1916–1917. Although the tsarist authorities permitted the formation of only four Estonian secondary schools in this period, they too were regarded as a beginning for future development.[35] At Tartu University the Estonian presence increased markedly from less than 100 to a peak of 434—about one-sixth of the total enrollment—in 1914. In fact, the total number of Estonian university students in the Russian empire, including Riga and St. Petersburg, quintupled from about 200 to 1,000 in 1900–1915. Since Russian universities were officially closed to women, the first female Estonian university students at the start of the twentieth century went to Switzerland and Helsinki. Higher education for women at Tartu University finally emerged in the years after 1905, but only as auditors in 1906–1908 and thereafter in private, university-level courses. In 1915 the most popular majors for Estonian students were medicine, law, and engineering, in that order. Theology, a favorite course of study in the second half of the nineteenth century, had dropped far down the list. Although the number of Estonians with a higher education was growing in this period, it was not necessarily easy for them to find suitable positions at home; in 1915, 40 percent of Estonian graduates either sought or had to seek employment outside Estland and northern Livland.[36]

No major changes took place in the structure or administration of the Baltic Lutheran Church in the final years of the tsarist era. Although Estonians made further inroads into the lower clergy, as late as 1909 they still constituted only 13 percent of the pastors in Estland and 29 percent of those in northern Livland. In contrast, that same year fully 61 percent of the Orthodox priests in Estonia were Estonian, a factor that may have contributed to some of the success of the state religion in the northern Baltic region. Nevertheless, Nicholas II's edict of religious toleration in 1906 led to significant defections from Orthodoxy in the ensuing decade, and the balance sheet of religious conversions clearly favored Lutheranism in these years.[37]

WORLD WAR I

The topic of World War I has not been covered in sufficient depth in Estonian historiography. It has been regarded mainly as an epilogue to the tsarist era or a prelude to the ensuing revolutionary one. The outbreak of the war in August 1914 was greeted with mixed emotions in the northern Baltic region. Within the Estonian population, there was some enthusiasm for a struggle against a "historical enemy." For many Baltic Germans, however, war against their co-nationals in Imperial Germany was unthinkable. The tsarist authorities, increasingly suspicious of possible Baltic German collaboration with the enemy, closed down German schools and societies and forbade the public use of German. Inflamed Russian nationalism was directed not only against Germans but against all non-Russian nationalities. Restrictions were also placed on the use of Estonian.[38]

As elsewhere in the Russian empire, the war had a highly disruptive effect on Estonian life. About 100,000 Estonian men—nearly 10 percent of the ethnic Estonian population—were mobilized into the tsarist armed forces. Very little is known of the extent of Estonian losses in the war, and no reliable estimates are available. A reasonable guess might be provided by the proportion of overall tsarist casualties (of the total number mobilized) in World War I: 12 percent killed and 19 percent wounded and sick.[39] Although Latvian national regiments had been established in July 1915, no such Estonian units emerged before the February Revolution of 1917. Some sentiment for creating national units existed among Estonian political leaders in the early period of the war, but there was increasing fear that such forces would simply be used as cannon fodder as the situation worsened. Although Estonia escaped actual wartime destruction, the closeness of the front, which ran along the border of Livland and Kurland in the summer of 1915, led to great distortions in the economy. As noted above, industry was geared to military production while the agricultural sector suffered from the loss of men (about 75 percent of those mobilized came from the rural areas) and livestock as well as the scarcity of machinery and fertilizer. Since the tsarist regime financed the war effort by simply printing new paper money, inflation became an increasingly serious problem. Social unrest, which had declined in the initial patriotic reaction to the declaration of war, gradually increased as the scarcity of consumer goods, especially foodstuffs, grew by 1916.[40]

Friedrich Reinhold Kreutzwald
(1803–1882)—the first major
native Estonian writer and author
of the national epic *Kalevipoeg*
(Son of Kalev), first published
1857–1861.

Main Building of Tartu University—the major center of higher education in
Estonia; completed in 1809, following the reopening of the University in 1802; this
depiction by the artist A. M. Hagen in 1827–1828. Source: Bernard Kangro, ed.,
Universitatis Tartuensis (Lund: Eesti Kirjanike Kooperatiiv, 1970), p. 12.

Jaan Tõnisson (1868–19??)—
Riigivanem (head of state) four
times in the 1920s and 1930s.

Lydia Koidula (1843–1886)—the leading poet of the Estonian national awakening,
shown here with an example of her verse in her own handwriting.

Konstantin Päts (1874–1956)—
Riigivanem five times in the 1920s
and 1930s; president of the Republic
of Estonia, 1938–1940.

The Estonia Theater—financed by private contributions and completed in 1913;
the first Estonian theater and concert hall in Tallinn.

Kristjan Raud, "Kalevipoeg at the Gates of Hell"—illustration
for a new edition of the national epic in 1935 showing
Kalevipoeg at the end of the tale, having lost his legs by his
own sword, now guarding the gates of hell in order to keep
the devil in. Source: Evald Uustalu, *Eesti Vabariik 1918–1940*
(Lund: Eesti Kirjanike Kooperatiiv, 1968), p. 190.

INDEPENDENT ESTONIA

PART THREE

7 The Emergence of Estonian Independence, 1917–1920

The roots of Estonian independence reach back to the national awakening of the 1860s and even farther to the agrarian reforms and educational advances of the first half of the nineteenth century. By the second decade of the twentieth century, political, socioeconomic, and cultural modernization had contributed to the emergence of a modern Estonian nation. The upheavals of World War I, especially the collapse of tsarist Russia and the defeat of Imperial Germany, provided the practical opportunity for the realization of independence.

FEBRUARY–OCTOBER 1917

Given its late start in modernization, the Russian empire proved incapable of withstanding the strains of two and a half years of intensive war in 1914–1917.[1] Surprisingly enough, it was a simple coincidence of strikes, demonstrations, and bread lines in Petrograd in the last days of February 1917 that led to the collapse of the tsarist regime. In Estland and northern Livland the February Revolution was consolidated in the first ten days of March with very limited bloodshed since, as in Petrograd, the existing military forces (roughly 100,000 men in the northern Baltic region) overwhelmingly refused to defend the old order. As elsewhere in the now-defunct Russian empire, the problem of political power became the most immediate fundamental question in Estonia, and the same "dual power" emerged between the forces of the soviets and those owing allegiance to the Provisional Government in the Russian capital.

With the downfall of the tsarist regime, the non-Russian nationalities began to pursue the realization of political autonomy, which had been the widely enunciated goal of the Revolution of 1905 in the borderlands. On March 6, 1917, Finland obtained the restoration of its constitution from the Provisional Government. In the northern Baltic region, the moderate Estonian political forces took the lead in pressing for majority rule and administrative reorganization, pending the final decision of an all-Russian constituent assembly. After extensive lobbying in March by Estonian political figures, including Jaan Tõnisson, as well as a mass demonstration by some 40,000 Estonians (among them 12,000–15,000 soldiers in uniform) in Petrograd, the Provisional Government agreed on March 30 to the reorganization of local self-government in the northern Baltic region.[2] The decree contained two major provisions: (1) the administrative unification of Estland and northern Livland into one consolidated province, marking the fulfillment of a goal first expressed by Carl Robert Jakobson in 1881 and the birth of the political entity known as Estonia in the twentieth century;[3] and (2) the establishment of temporary zemstvo institutions, headed by a provincial (that is, all-Estonian) assembly elected by universal and indirect suffrage, and the appointment of a provincial commissar as the top administrative officer.[4] In addition, the Baltic German–controlled diets and other organs of local administration from the tsarist era were abolished. In April, Jaan Poska (1866–1920), the Estonian mayor of Tallinn at the time of the February Revolution, was appointed commissar of Estonia by the Provisional Government.

In conjunction with the elections to the provincial assembly (Est. *Maapäev*) in May 1917, political parties emerged on a broad basis for the first time in Estonian history. Representatives from the rural areas were chosen in two-tiered elections in May and June; those from the cities joined the Maapäev only at the end of September after municipal elections. Including both the rural and urban results, the 62 members of the Maapäev were divided as follows among the political forces: Bolsheviks, 5; Estonian Social Democrats (SD; formerly Mensheviks), 9; Estonian Socialist Revolutionaries (SR), 8; Labor Party, 11; Democrats (formerly the Estonian Progressive People's Party), 7; Radical Democrats, 4; Agrarian League, 13; German and Swedish minorities, 2; and nonparty representatives, 3.[5]

Given the length of time required to complete elections to the Maapäev, this institution was not able to play an active role in practical matters before the fall of 1917. However, it did become a sounding board for approaches to the implementation of Estonian self-determination. Throughout the summer and early fall of 1917, the consensus was that Estonia should become part of a democratic Russian federation. Nevertheless, as early as August 25, after the German conquest of Riga, Tõnisson noted the weakness of the Provisional Government and urged his colleagues to consider other options for warding off

German occupation. After debate, the Maapäev (with only one member opposed) agreed to create a foreign delegation for the purpose of protecting the interests of Estonian self-determination.[6]

The first test of political strength by direct voting in 1917 came in the municipal elections of late July and early August. The results indicated a significant fractionalization of the political spectrum, complicated by the presence of large numbers of non-Estonian soldiers, especially in Tallinn where over 16 percent of the registered voters were members of the military. Indeed, it is important to bear in mind that the number of troops stationed in Estonia grew from about 100,000 in February–March 1917 to some 200,000 by October.[7] In general, moderate political forces dominated in the smaller urban areas and Tartu while the left proved to be stronger in the industrial cities of Tallinn and Narva. In Tallinn, where the population had been swelled by industrial expansion and wartime refugees, the Bolsheviks (31 percent), SRs (22 percent), and the bloc of Estonian SDs and Russian and Latvian Mensheviks (12 percent) received nearly two-thirds of the vote. About half of the SR representatives and one-fifth of the Bolsheviks were non-Estonians.[8]

Like those in Petrograd and elsewhere in the former tsarist state, the soviets that emerged in Estonia after the February Revolution were at first dominated by the moderate socialists: the SRs and Mensheviks. The major soviets were concentrated in the larger cities and the military garrisons, and they showed a distinctly non-Estonian character. This was especially the case in Tallinn, where the Soviet Executive Committee in May 1917 consisted of at least 75 percent non-Estonians, mainly Russians.[9] At the First Congress of Estonian Soviets in July, the SR-Menshevik candidate for chair defeated the Bolshevik candidate by a 34–24 margin. However, as the Provisional Government and the parties associated with it proved incapable of solving the country's problems, the leftward swing grew apace. On September 5 a Bolshevik resolution passed in the Tallinn Soviet, and at the Second Congress of Estonian Soviets in mid-October, 18 of the 26 delegates present were Bolsheviks.[10] Throughout the eight months from February to October 1917, the relationship between the Estonian soviets and the local administrative organs under the Provisional Government remained uneasy and unsettled. In May, for example, the Tallinn Soviet unsuccessfully sought to have Poska removed as commissar of Estonia for failing to follow its directives.

After the February Revolution and especially following the achievement of limited political autonomy at the end of March, sentiment for the formation of national military units began to grow in Estonian political circles. Although permission in principle for such units was granted in April 1917, the following month Alexander Kerensky (then minister of war), under pressure from the soviets, restricted their establishment to a single regiment.[11] Nevertheless, the first Estonian regiment had grown to about 8,000 men (twice the originally intended size) by the end of July, and the Provisional Government allowed the formation of a second regiment in September. Within Estonian military ranks, political moderation dominated in the first months of the revolutionary period as witnessed in mid-June at the first Estonian military congress, where 150 delegates represented up to 50,000 troops. From the beginning, the Estonian Bolsheviks opposed national military units; they were joined in this view by both the Tallinn and Petrograd soviets as well as by some members of the Russian military leadership. Among the latter, however, especially General Lavr Kornilov and Kerensky himself, the attraction of disciplined troops proved stronger than fears of non-Russian separatism.[12]

THE BOLSHEVIKS IN POWER

On October 27, 1917, following the Bolshevik Revolution in Petrograd, Viktor Kingissepp (1888–1922), in the name of the Estonian Military Revolutionary Committee, took over the reins of power from the Provisional Government's commissar, Poska. However, the actual consolidation of Bolshevik control was a much more difficult task and, indeed, one that remained incomplete when the German invasion in February 1918 drove the Bolsheviks from Estonia. The new masters attempted to rule with the Provisional Government's civil servants, but the latter refused and went on strike until the end of Bolshevik power. Moreover, the Estonian Bolsheviks were simply not strong enough to destroy or replace the existing local administrative organs immediately and were only gradually able to undertake this process. Even in Tallinn, the stronghold of Bolshevism in Estonia, the city council (with a non-Bolshevik majority) was not removed until the end of January 1918.[13] Nevertheless, de facto power was in the hands of the Estonian Military Revolutionary Committee and the Executive Committee of Estonian Soviets, headed by Jaan Anvelt (1884–1937). Throughout its nearly three-month existence to mid-January 1918, the Military Revolutionary Committee appears to have had a substantial majority of Russians in its membership.[14] On November 13, 1917, Anvelt informed the Maapäev that it would be disbanded in two days and elections to an Estonian Constituent Assembly would be held in the latter part of January 1918. In response to this challenge and just before its dissolution on November 15, the Maapäev declared itself the sole sovereign power in Estonia until the convening of a democratically elected constituent assembly.[15] Lacking the physical power, however, to make good its claim at that time, the Maapäev was forced to go underground and transferred power to its Committee of Elders, which was to act in the Maapäev's stead.

Within a few weeks of the Bolshevik Revolution, the major test of political strength in Estonia—excluding the German-occupied Saaremaa and other islands in the west—came in the Russian Constituent Assembly elections on November 12–14, 1917. The results of the voting are summarized below:[16]

Party	Number of votes	Percentage
Left		
Bolsheviks	121,520	40.2
Russian SRs	3,271	1.1
Estonian SRs	17,394	5.8
Estonian SDs	9,202	3.0
Center & Right		
Labor Party	64,998	21.5
Democratic Bloc	68,342	22.6
Radical Democrats	17,600	5.8
Total	302,327	100.0

It should be noted that members of the armed forces in Estonia, which consisted mainly of non-Estonians, voted in special military districts and their votes are not included in the above returns. In examining the results, it is striking that the socialist and nonsocialist vote was almost evenly divided. Of the three major parties in the election, the Bolsheviks and the Labor Party were strongest in Tallinn (Bolsheviks, 47.6 percent) and northern Estonia, while the Democratic Bloc was most successful in Tartu (53.4 percent) and southern Estonia. The results clearly reflected the all-Russian trend toward Bolshevism in the fall of 1917 as well as the relative weakness of the SRs in Estonia, where agrarian conditions and institutions differed markedly from those in the ethnically Russian areas of the former tsarist empire. Furthermore, the failure of the Provisional Government (and thus of the parties associated with it) to carry through on promises of reform and self-determination in Estonia no doubt worked to the benefit of the Bolsheviks.[17]

Bolshevik policies in Estonia in the three and a half months following the October Revolution produced a mixed record. On the one hand, the Bolsheviks were able to effect change in areas in which Commissar Poska and the Maapäev (in part because of the Provisional Government's opposition) had not—for example, the introduction of Estonian as the language of administration in the judicial system, local control over education, and the establishment of workers' control in the factories. On the other hand, they alienated much of the population with the following policies: failure to share power with other parties, except on their own terms; persecution and closure of the non-Bolshevik press; failure to divide the expropriated Baltic German landed estates; and a negative view on the question of Estonian independence. Soviet Estonian historiography emphasizes the latter two positions as the most serious policy mistakes by the Estonian Bolsheviks in this period.[18]

The uncompleted elections to the Estonian Constituent Assembly on January 21–22, 1918, may be taken as an approximation of a referendum on Bolshevik rule. Despite having full freedom to propagate their cause, unlike other political parties, the Bolshevik share of the partial vote showed a decline from the Russian Constituent Assembly elections in November 1917 (37.1 vs. 40.2 percent).[19] In fact, the elections were not carried out in Tartu, Narva, or much of the rural areas, and it is likely that the Bolshevik percentage would have been still lower had the vote been completed. In contrast, the Labor Party emerged as the real winner, raising its share of the total to 29.8 percent (an increase of 8.8 percentage points over the November elections), while the Democratic Bloc held firm at 23.2 percent. Overall, the nonsocialist vote climbed to over 56 percent, including an even larger majority for the parties supporting Estonian independence. Faced with a clear political defeat, the Bolsheviks first postponed and then, on January 27, cancelled the rest of the election process. A convenient but not believable excuse for this action was found in the alleged existence of a conspiracy between the Baltic German nobility and the Estonian bourgeoisie to overthrow Soviet power with the aid of invading German troops.[20]

THE DECLARATION OF ESTONIAN INDEPENDENCE

In the weeks following the October Revolution, the parties represented in the Maapäev became increasingly less sanguine about the possibilities for a democratic Russian federation as Bolshevik policies unfolded, and they began to assess other options for the realization of Estonian self-determination. By the end of December 1917, these options included a non-Bolshevik Russian federation, a Scandinavian alliance, a Finnish-Estonian union, and an independent Estonia. However, Scandinavia and Finland remained cool to the idea of an Estonian or Baltic connection, and Soviet Russia appeared to be consolidating its position. Above all, as peace negotiations between the Soviet Union and Germany at Brest-Litovsk dragged on, it was the threat of German occupation that galvanized Estonian thinking toward independence. As early as December 24, the Maapäev's Committee of Elders agreed, in the event of a German occupation, to declare Estonian independence in order to internationalize the Estonian question. By mid-January 1918, with the exception of the Bolsheviks, all Estonian parties—including the Estonian SRs and SDs, who had hesitated as late as December 1917—supported the idea of independence.[21] Political sentiments in the Estonian military units were also moving in the same direction. After the October Revolution, the Bolsheviks did not—or could not—break up these units, perhaps thinking that they could be made politically reliable.

However, at the Second Congress of Estonian Soldiers in the second week of January 1918, an SR resolution backing Estonian independence passed by a vote of 62–38 with two abstentions.[22]

In order to garner international support for an independent Estonia, the Committee of Elders decided on January 10–11 to expand its foreign delegation and send representatives to the major Western powers, Germany, and Scandinavia with this specific mission for the first time. Of these chargés d'affaires, the most active and successful were Ants Piip (Great Britain), Kaarel R. Pusta (France), and Jaan Tõnisson (Scandinavia). In conjunction with the cancellation of the Estonian Constituent Assembly elections on January 27, the Bolsheviks began a crackdown against their political opponents. The main targets were the Baltic Germans, who were declared guilty of treason and of whom over 500 were arrested and deported to Russia; this action contributed to growing sentiment in influential circles in Imperial Germany for a military move into the northern parts of the Baltic provinces.[23] Estonian political figures were subject to arrest as well, and given this situation, a more conspiratorial organizational form seemed necessary. On February 19 (Gregorian Calendar), the Committee of Elders delegated decisionmaking power to a three-member Rescue Committee: Konstantin Päts, Konstantin Konik, and Jüri Vilms.[24]

In February 1918 the central Soviet leadership agreed to try out Trotsky's "no war, no peace" policy toward Germany, which was predicated on the hope of imminent revolution in Central Europe. As Lenin put it, "We will only risk losing Estonia or Livonia, and for the sake of a good peace with Trotsky, . . . Livonia and Estonia are worth losing."[25] In fact, no revolution transpired in Central Europe at that time, and the Germans began their attack on the Estonian mainland to the apparent surprise of the local Bolsheviks, who rapidly evacuated to Soviet Russia. Since the Estonian military units in Haapsalu made known their neutrality in a German-Soviet war, there was virtually nothing to stop the German advance. With the Bolsheviks retreating and a German occupation nearing, the moment appeared ripe for the declaration of Estonian independence. On February 24, 1918, in Tallinn the Committee of Elders of the Maapäev declared Estonia an "independent and democratic republic" within its "historical and ethnographic borders." Simultaneously, a new Estonian provisional government, headed by Konstantin Päts, was created.[26] In practice, however, these remained only symbolic gestures, since the invading German troops reached Tallinn on February 25.

THE GERMAN OCCUPATION

From late February to mid-November 1918, German rule in Estonia proved to be a much more stringent dictatorship than the previous

Bolshevik one. As might be expected, most of the Baltic German population welcomed the occupation and looked forward to rapid union with the German empire. The Estonians themselves were permitted very little say on this issue; the assemblies called by the German authorities included only the rural township elders from among the Estonian population. At the meeting of Livland representatives, fifteen Estonian elders signed a protest, stating that the Germans had no authority to speak on political issues and that the Maapäev had already declared Estonian independence. Nevertheless, a carefully picked *Landesrat*, including token Estonian and Latvian peasant representatives from Estland and Livland, met in Riga in April 1918 and unanimously requested a personal union with the king of Prussia. Although William II was quite receptive to the idea, his government remained divided, and the center and left of the *Reichstag* were strongly opposed. Soviet Russia renounced sovereignty over Estland and Livland in late August, but no formal ties between the Reich and the two northern Baltic provinces were established prior to the German defeat in November 1918.[27]

The German military occupation in Estonia involved a restoration of the pre-Russification Old Regime under Imperial German tutelage. Such relics of the past as the estate police were resurrected, and in cities where the Baltic Germans had previously lost control of municipal government, the military authorities restored them to power. The Germans went farther than the Old Regime, however, and closed all Estonian societies, forbade virtually all newspapers, and instituted a more severe censorship than in the worst of tsarist times. In March 1918 the Estonian national military units were ordered to disperse, and throughout the occupation all activity by Estonian political parties was strictly banned. Of all social groups, the working class suffered most through massive layoffs and wages lowered to starvation levels. The unabashed aim of the Baltic German elite was rapid Germanization of the entire area. The new educational system was geared to this end, and the Estland and Livland nobles were prepared to offer about one-third of the arable land on their estates to German colonists.[28]

The Maapäev's Rescue Committee suffered major losses during the German occupation. Seeking to join the Estonian foreign delegation abroad in April, Vilms was apprehended near Helsinki by German and Finnish soldiers and executed. For his role as the author of the protest made by the fifteen Livland Estonian township elders, Päts was arrested in June and imprisoned, primarily in German-occupied Belorussia, until November.[29] While Estonian political organizations were proscribed at home during this period, the foreign delegation actively sought support for Estonian independence from the Western Allies. Piip in London and Pusta in Paris were successful in obtaining British and French sympathy for Estonian self-determination, but both powers refused to commit themselves to what they viewed as a hasty division of the former Russian empire. In Washington, President Wilson and the U.S. government thought in terms of a united Russia and wanted nothing to do with the representatives of the Estonian Maapäev. During the period of German rule, representatives of the Estonian provisional government were also present in Petrograd, where they lobbied for the Estonian national cause with the Bolshevik authorities.[30]

In effect, the German occupation temporarily halted the activity of Estonian political forces at home who were working for independence, but more important, it brought about the evacuation of all Soviet military forces and the destruction of the Bolshevik organizational network in Estonia. Thus, when German defeat came in the fall of 1918, there was no possibility of an immediate seizure of power by the Bolsheviks.[31] Instead, a prolonged struggle began between the fledgling independence movement and the Estonian Bolsheviks, who were now forced to press their cause (allied with Soviet armed might) from outside Estonia.

THE WAR OF INDEPENDENCE

On November 11, 1918, when the armistice ending World War I was signed, the struggle for power in Estonia was renewed. Although both the Estonian provisional government and the Tallinn Soviet began functioning almost immediately, the eclipse of German rule left a temporary power vacuum. Into this breach stepped Soviet Russia in the second half of November and began a broad offensive to recover the areas of the former Russian empire that had been under German occupation. The Estonian Bolshevik leadership, in exile in Soviet Russia, enthusiastically supported the Red Army thrust into Estonia along two fronts, beginning at Narva on November 22. Although the initial attack was repulsed by German troops still in Narva, they soon withdrew, leaving the city in the hands of weak Estonian national forces. The Soviets conquered Narva on November 28 and the following day proclaimed the Estonian Workers' Commune, led by Jaan Anvelt.[32]

In this situation, the Estonian provisional government, which was once again headed by Päts following his return from imprisonment on November 20, faced seemingly insurmountable odds. It had to organize its military forces immediately against a potentially much more powerful foe. As Narva fell, the Maapäev accorded the provisional government full and unlimited powers to prosecute the war effort, and the latter declared martial law and a general mobilization. However, the creation of an efficient military organization required time; for example, the commander-in-chief of the Estonian forces, Colonel Johan Laidoner (1884–1953), was not named until December 23, since he had only managed to return from Petrograd a few days earlier; meanwhile, the Soviet offensive pushed forward.[33] In December 1918, at the most critical moment, the Estonian provisional government received crucial aid from two outside sources. On December 12 a British fleet of twelve ships delivered machine guns, rifles, and ammunition to the Estonian national forces. Even more important, this fleet prevented a Soviet naval descent on Tallinn or the northern coast. The Finnish government arranged loans totaling 20 million Finnish marks and provided weapons. In addition, although declining to send regular troops, the Finnish authorities permitted the recruitment of volunteer soldiers to aid the Estonian cause.[34]

By the end of December 1918, the Estonian national cause appeared next to hopeless. Soviet forces controlled roughly half of Estonia, and by the first days of January 1919 they would be within 35 kilometers of Tallinn. On December 26, Päts informed the Finns that if support did not arrive within three days, there would be no need to send it after that. In fact, the first 140-man company of Finnish volunteers arrived on December 30, but the Finns were most significant as a boost to flagging morale rather than on the battlefield since they only reached the front on January 8, after the decisive turn in the fighting.[35] In the first week of January, the Bolshevik advance was halted on all fronts, and the Estonian national forces began a counterattack on January 7. Once the tide had turned, the offensive rapidly gained momentum, and Estonia was virtually cleared of Soviet troops by the start of February. Yet a long period of consolidation of these gains remained, complicated by the continuing Russian Civil War and the attitudes of the Western Allies. A peace treaty with Soviet Russia did not transpire for another year.

Since figures cited in the available sources vary considerably, it is difficult to assess the relative strength of the military forces on either side. However, one generalization stands out: the great majority of men fighting for an independent Estonia were Estonians, while the vast majority of those on the Soviet side were non-Estonians. On January 3, 1919, about 4,800 men on the Estonian national side faced some 6,200–6,500 Soviets. Thereafter, both sides increased rapidly in numbers. The Soviets have never revealed the exact ethnic composition of their armies on the Estonian front, but an estimate by the Estonian national army in mid-February 1919 reported that of 35 Soviet regiments (600–700 men each), only four were partially Estonian and the rest Russian and Latvian. For the Soviets, one of the most bitter moments of the campaign came at the end of May 1919 near Pskov, when an entire Estonian Communist regiment (about 1,000 men) and a divisional commander, L. Ritt, deserted to the national side.[36] By that time, the Estonian national army numbered about 74,500, including 2,750 Russians of the Northwestern (White) Army, 1,500 Latvians, 300 Ingrians, and 300 Finns, Swedes, and Danes. Overall, about 3,700 Finns, 200 Danes, and 178 Swedes fought as volunteers for the Estonian national forces, along with up to 700 Baltic Germans who joined the fight against Bolshevism.[37]

By the early spring of 1919, the provisional government felt sufficiently secure to schedule elections to the Estonian Constituent Assembly on April 5–7, 1919. Realizing that they could not take part as a legal party, the Estonian Bolsheviks called for a boycott of the elections. However, in contrast to the Russian Constituent Assembly elections in November 1917, voter participation—including soldiers at the front—was much heavier (80 vs. 57 percent). The results are summarized below:[38]

Party	Percentage of vote	Number of seats
Left		
Social Democrats (SDs)	33.3	41
Independent Socialists (SRs)	5.8	7
Center		
Labor Party	25.1	30
National Party	20.7	25
Right		
Christian National Party	4.4	5
Agrarian League	6.5	8
Ethnic Minorities	3.8	4
Others	0.4	0
Total	100.0	120

Overall, the vote showed the continuing dominance of the center and left parties. The only striking change was the replacement of the Bolsheviks by the SDs as the major party on the left. Convening on April 23, the Constituent Assembly elected August Rei (1886–1963), a Social Democrat, as chair. The first Estonian cabinet was headed by Prime Minister Otto Strandmann (Labor Party) and Foreign Minister Jaan Poska. On May 19, 1919, the Constituent Assembly voted unanimously (with the Russian and German minority representatives abstaining) to affirm Estonian independence.[39] The search for international recognition became the primary foreign-policy goal of the new government. On the domestic scene, the major piece of legislation enacted by the Constituent Assembly in 1919 was the far-reaching land reform in October (discussed below).

In addition to intermittent fighting on the eastern front in the spring and summer of 1919, the Estonian national forces participated in various actions in northern Latvia and secured their southern border. The most dramatic of these was doubtless the so-called *Landeswehr* War in June. In this brief but bloody conflict the Estonians emerged victorious over the *Landeswehr* (a Baltic German military force) and the Iron Division, composed of Baltic and Reich Germans and led by General Rüdiger von der Goltz, who, under the cover of fighting

Bolshevism, sought to acquire the Baltic area for Germany.[40] For many Estonians there was a symbolic significance in this sound victory over German forces as a kind of revenge for the original German conquest some 700 years earlier. On the Soviet front, relations between the White Army of General Nikolai Iudenich and the Estonian national army remained tense and ill-defined. Since Iudenich repeatedly refused to recognize Estonian independence or even the right to self-determination, the Estonians were less than enthusiastic about his drive against Petrograd in the fall of 1919. However, the Western Allies were seeking a united front against Bolshevism and thus put pressure on the Estonians to aid Iudenich. In the end, the Estonian national forces gave only token support to Iudenich, and when his defeated army retreated to Estonia in November 1919, it was disarmed by unanimous order of the Constituent Assembly.[41]

In July 1919 the Estonian Bolshevik leader, Viktor Kingissepp, announced the liquidation of the Estonian Workers' Commune, which had led only a formal existence since February. Coupled with growing war weariness among the troops, this signal from the Soviet side encouraged the development of a peace policy within the Estonian government. Interrupted by the Iudenich offensive in October, Soviet-Estonian peace negotiations began in September 1919 and were resumed on December 5. Throughout that month the Soviets mounted several offensives along the Narva front in an effort to influence the negotiations. Each time, however, they were thrown back, and an armistice finally came into effect on January 3, 1920. A formal peace treaty between Estonia and Soviet Russia was signed a month later in Tartu on February 2. According to this document, Soviet Russia recognized Estonian independence de jure and renounced all sovereign rights to the territory of Estonia in perpetuity. As partial compensation for evacuated factories, confiscated pension funds, and other problems, the Soviets agreed to pay Estonia 15 million gold rubles from the tsarist reserves. In resolution of the border question, the Estonians received a ten-kilometer-wide strip of land east of Narva in the north as well as the area of Setumaa in the southeast, which coincided with the actual front in that region at the time of the armistice.[42]

Thus, within a three-year period, Estonia, with a population of slightly over one million, was transformed from one and a half tsarist provinces to an independent country. How was such a sweeping change possible for an admitted minination? To begin with, the defeat of both Russia and Germany, the two traditional Great Powers in the area, and their subsequent weakness permitted the emergence of a series of successor states in Eastern Europe. For the independence movements in Estonia and the other Baltic states, the protracted nature of the Russian Civil War was especially important, for it allowed them precious time to mobilize their forces. In addition, the Western Allies offered crucial financial and military support, made possible by the avenue of the Baltic

Sea. However, the emergence of independence was not merely the result of a favorable international situation. Between the 1860s and 1917 a growing sense of Estonian national identity had emerged and resulted in a strong desire for self-determination. Thus, although Estonian independence was certainly not inevitable, as some nationalist historians might claim, it can only be understood by taking into account both the prevailing constellation of international forces and the recent historical development of the Estonian people.

In any final assessment of this period in Estonian history, one must ask whether it was more a war of independence (the prevailing view of non-Soviet Estonian historiography) or a civil war (as Soviet Estonian historians claim). In support of the latter viewpoint, it can be argued that there was a bonafide Estonian Bolshevik movement with a native leadership. However, Bolshevism in Estonia appears to have reached its peak at the time of Russian Constituent Assembly elections in November 1917. By January 1918, the trend was away from Bolshevism. Moreover, despite their control of about half of Estonia at the start of January 1919, the Bolsheviks were unable to mobilize significant grass-roots support in this area. The one major rebellion against the Estonian provisional government in this period took place on the island of Saaremaa in February 1919. However, there was no Bolshevik organization on Saaremaa at that time, and the uprising was mainly a spontaneous resistance to forced military mobilization.[43] Above all, as noted earlier, the military forces fighting for a Bolshevik Estonia were overwhelmingly non-Estonian, in contrast to those on the side of independence where the reverse was true. In the case of Estonia, no unbridgeable class or regional divisions created a typical civil war situation. In April 1919, while armed combat continued, 80 percent of the population voted for parties across the entire political spectrum who favored independence. Thus, although elements of a civil war certainly existed, the war of independence model is a much more appropriate one for Estonia in 1918–1920.

8   The Republic of Estonia, 1920–1939

Following the peace treaty with Soviet Russia in February 1920, the territory of the new Estonian state (47,549 square kilometers) was about 5 percent larger than the combined area of the tsarist provinces of Estland and northern Livland. In addition to the nine existing administrative districts from the tsarist era, two new ones were established. Valgamaa, on the Latvian border, was created out of the southern parts of the surrounding districts and included the city of Valga (Lat. Valka), which was partitioned between the new Estonian and Latvian republics in 1920. Petserimaa or Setumaa, an area of nearly 2,000 square kilometers and formerly part of Pskov province under tsarist Russia, was entirely new territory; it formed the southeastern border with Soviet Russia. In 1922 the population of Petserimaa was about two-thirds Russian and one-third Estonian. Most of the latter were Setus, Orthodox Estonians who had lived in this borderland between the Estonian and Russian worlds for centuries.[1] In the north, the city of Narva and the area to the east of the Narva River was added to the district of Virumaa. On the local level, the historical trend toward consolidation of rural townships continued during the independence period.

THE POLITICAL SYSTEM

The first permanent constitution of the Republic of Estonia was approved on June 15, 1920. Drawing on the models provided by the Weimar, Swiss, French, and U.S. constitutions, this document reflected the democratic idealism of the center-left majority in the Estonian Constituent Assembly. Above all, it established parliamentary superiority in the new political system. The State Assembly (*Riigikogu*), elected by all men and women twenty years of age and over on the basis of proportional representation, consisted of 100 members who sat for a three-year term. The Constitution of 1920 provided for no independently elected executive; instead, the *Riigivanem* (literally, State Elder), selected by the State Assembly, acted as prime minister and presided over the cabinet. Thus, the government served entirely at the pleasure of the State Assembly and could be dismissed at any time, although its members did have to belong to the legislature. It is also noteworthy that Supreme Court judges were elected by parliament. Furthermore, the constitution provided for referendum and popular legislative initiative by demand of 25,000 voters. For approval of constitutional amendments, a referendum was required.[2]

The political history of the Estonian republic may be divided into two major periods: an era of liberal democracy (1920–1934), and an era of moderate authoritarianism (1934–1940). The results of the five State Assembly elections (1920–1932) are summarized below:[3]

	NUMBER OF SEATS IN STATE ASSEMBLY				
Party	*1920*	*1923*	*1926*	*1929*	*1932*
Left					
Communists	5	10	6	6	5
Independent Socialists (SRs)	11	5	—	—	—
Social Democrats (SDs)	18	15	—	—	—
Socialist Workers	—	—	24	25	22
Center					
Labor Party	22	12	13	10	—
National Party	10	8	8	9	—
Homesteaders	—	4	14	14	—
Other Parties	—	6	—	—	—
National Center	—	—	—	—	23
Right					
Christian Nationalist Party	7	8	5	4	—
Farmers' Party	21	23	23	24	—
United Agrarian Party	—	—	—	—	42
Landlords	1	2	2	3	—
National minorities	5	7	5	5	8
Total	100	100	100	100	100

In comparison to the Constituent Assembly elections in 1919, those for the First State Assembly in 1920 showed a powerful swing to the right among the voters. It appears certain that much of the radicalism of the previous years had been defused by the sweeping land reform in the fall of 1919. During the 1920s, the division of the political spectrum as represented in the State Assembly remained remarkably equal and stable, although the fortunes of individual parties showed wide fluctuation. In the four elections between 1920 and 1929, the right, center, and left each received close to one-third of the parliamentary seats; the national minorities won five to seven seats. In 1932 the distinctions between right and center were blurred by a new regrouping of parties, but these entities proved to be highly unstable. On the left, the Communists were never formally proscribed, but their open attacks on the sovereignty of the Estonian republic precluded the possibility of a public existence.[4] Nevertheless, the Communists were able to participate in elections under the guise of front organizations. Their most successful effort—under the rubric United Front of the Working People (*Töörahva ühine väerind*)—came at a time of economic distress in 1923. In 1925 the non-Communist left (the SDs and the Independent Socialists) merged to form the Socialist Workers' Party.

Despite the radical beginning in the Constituent Assembly, the era of liberal democracy in Estonia was completely dominated by the right and center. Of the 21 Estonian cabinets in 1919–1933, ten were headed by members of the Farmers' or United Agrarian parties and another nine went to the National Party, Labor Party, and National Center. As head of state, the most active individual politicians were Konstantin Päts (Farmers' and United Agrarian parties), who was Riigivanem five times, and Jaan Teemant (Farmers' and United Agrarian parties) and Jaan Tõnisson (National Party and National Center), who were head of state four times each. Only once was the office of Riigivanem held by a Socialist (August Rei in 1928–1929) although the Socialist Workers' Party was the largest one in parliament in 1926–1932. The National Center and its main components, Labor and the National Party, were involved in sixteen cabinets while the Farmers, including their role in the United Agrarian Party, participated in fourteen. In contrast, the Socialist Workers and SDs took part in only six cabinets. Like the Weimar Republic, Estonia faced the problem of multiplicity of political parties. Since the Socialists (with few exceptions), Communists, and national minorities—together holding generally one-third of the seats in parliament—remained excluded from the government, the difficulties in forming coalitions were heightened even more. The average tenure of cabinets in 1919–1933 was eight months and twenty days, a duration no shorter, however, than those prevailing at the time in Weimar Germany or in a more established multiparty democracy such as France.[5]

Although the decade of the 1920s was, in general, a politically stable period, the most difficult years for the Republic of Estonia proved to be 1923–1924. In large part as a reaction to economic problems, the May 1923 national elections witnessed the strengthening of both the extreme left and right as well as the greatest fractionalization of the State Assembly (fourteen parties) in the parliamentary era. In Tallinn, Narva, and Pärnu, the Communist front organization received 35–36 percent of the vote in the municipal elections of 1923.[6] The Estonian Communist Party had officially affiliated with the Comintern in 1920, and it subsequently continued underground activities with strong Soviet backing. For example, in May 1922, within two weeks after the execution of Viktor Kingissepp by an Estonian court-martial on charges of high treason, the Soviet Union renamed the border town of Iamburg (near Narva) after that Estonian revolutionary. The culmination of Communist activity in the early 1920s came in the attempted coup of December 1, 1924.

Although some of the details of this attack on the Estonian republic remain obscure, the outlines are clear enough. The Estonian Communist leadership in exile, led by Jaan Anvelt, and its Soviet allies clearly perceived a developing revolutionary potential in Estonia in 1923–1924. Widespread economic distress, including high unemployment, and growing electoral strength of the Communist front (at least in the larger cities where it mattered) presumably lent credence to this view. By late November 1924, as the Estonian economy began to improve, there may well have been a sense that the most favorable moment for action was passing. In addition, intrigues within the Comintern—especially pressure from its head, Grigorii Zinov'ev—appear to have contributed to the launching of the coup. In fact, aside from a few initial successes, the attempted uprising was an utter failure. Instead of several thousands of men, as planned, only 300–400 gathered to participate in the action. Above all, the insurrectionists failed to mobilize expected support from the working class in Tallinn. It is noteworthy that the Soviets ordered a partial mobilization along the Estonian border at the time of the attempted coup, but when the effort had obviously failed, the troops were quickly withdrawn. Following the abortive uprising and the resultant government crackdown, the Communist Party never again attained its pre-coup electoral strength and became a relatively minor factor in the political life of the Estonian republic.[7]

CONSTITUTIONAL CRISIS, 1932–1934

For all its potential shortcomings, the Estonian political system worked well enough during the era of economic stability in the 1920s. Calls for constitutional revision by some of the center and right parties in the second half of the decade did not evoke broad support. However, with the collapse of the world economic order and the onset of the Depression in Estonia in the early 1930s, a political crisis of the first order emerged. The number of workers in middle and large industry declined 17 percent in 1929–1932, and the low point of the economic downswing was reached in the winter of 1932–1933.[8] In a situation demanding decisive action, the weaknesses of the Constitution of

1920 became increasingly apparent. In 1932 alone there were four changes of government, occasioned by both economic and political problems. Attempts to provide political stability through the creation of unified right (United Agrarian Party) and center (National Center) parties proved to be mere palliatives, and by May 1933 the agrarian groups had split apart once again.[9]

The phenomenon that entirely changed the complexion of Estonian political life in this period was the emergence of the movement led by the League of Veterans of the Estonian War of Independence (*Eesti Vabadussõjalaste Liit*).[10] Originally established as a pressure group for veterans' interests, the organization became politicized in the years of economic crisis. Although it was a native Estonian movement, the League of Veterans must be seen in the context of the rise of fascism and the radical right in interwar Europe. Its main foreign models appear to have been the Finnish Lapua movement, the German Nazis, and the Italian Fascists, although there is no hard evidence of any direct collaboration with the latter two. Since the League of Veterans was never able to consolidate political power, its ultimate goals remain somewhat nebulous. Nevertheless, both its style and ideological pronouncements showed the strong influence of European fascism. Led by the youthful lawyer Artur Sirk (1900–1937) and establishing a highly centralized organization, the league pursued its aims through energetic propaganda campaigns supported by a paramilitary force. The members wore berets and armbands (and sometimes uniforms), gave Nazi-style salutes, and engaged in mass marches and parades. In general terms, their ideology professed militant nationalism, anti-Marxism, and anti-Semitism.[11]

The dramatic rise of the league's popularity in Estonia was based mainly on the exploitation of one specific and local issue: the problems of the existing parliamentary system. The Veterans appeared to be especially successful in mounting a kind of populist attack on alleged corruption and nepotism among the political parties in power. As one alternative to the discredited parliament, the league, inspired by the Italian example, called for corporative institutions with representation by occupation.[12] Like the German *Freikorps*, the core of the movement in Estonia consisted of veterans who were unable to adjust to peacetime life after World War I and the War of Independence. Without the Depression, however, the League of Veterans would have remained a fringe phenomenon. It was the threatened pauperization of the Estonian middle class with the concomitant fear of loss of status that provided the mass social basis for the movement. However, it is noteworthy that its support cut across class lines and included at least some elements of both the working and upper classes.

The economic crisis deepened, and demands were thus increasingly aired for a reduction of the State Assembly's overriding powers and the corresponding establishment of a strong executive branch of government. In essence, the initial phase of the political crisis became a competition between, on the one hand, the right and center parliamentary parties and, on the other, the League of Veterans; the question was whose constitutional amendment bill would be approved by the voters.[13] Between August 1932 and October 1933 three national referendums were held on proposed constitutional changes; the first two were offered by the State Assembly and the third by the League of Veterans through the initiative process. It is striking that, despite a wide variance in voting patterns, the three bills differed only on a few points and these were not substantial. All three created a strong executive power with the right to issue laws by decree, although the second State Assembly bill had more restrictions in this regard, including a parliamentary veto power over all decreed legislation. The results of the three referendums were as follows:[14]

	Percentage for	Percentage against	Percentage of eligible voters voting
First State Assembly bill	49.2	50.8	90.5[a]
Second State Assembly bill	32.7	67.3	66.5
League of Veterans' bill	72.7	27.3	77.9

[a] Voting was compulsory for the first referendum.

The dramatic shifts in voter support can only be explained by an increasing loss of confidence by the electorate in the State Assembly, especially after the narrow defeat of the latter's first reform bill. The State Assembly's second bill was no doubt viewed as a step in the wrong direction—that is, toward a weaker executive than called for in its first draft—and there was substantial public resentment over the parliament's attempts to block passage of the league's bill (for example, by raising the quorum to 50 percent of all *eligible* voters). In addition, the State Assembly remained sharply divided on the question of constitutional reform, and its parties proved unable to transcend their traditional and limited constituencies. The Socialists opposed both State Assembly bills, and their lack of support was crucial in the defeat of the first one. In general, the existing parties could not bridge class or urban/rural differences, and this fragmentation lessened their ability to resist the mushrooming League of Veterans movement. In the final analysis, the major reasons for the victory of the latter's constitutional reform bill must be sought more in the divisions and errors of the parliamentary parties than in the ideological appeal, although undeniably strong, of the league itself.[15]

Given the far-reaching nature of the constitutional changes effected by the league's bill, it is appropriate to refer to the result as the Constitution of 1933. Whereas the Constitution of 1920 had made the Riigivanem a servant of parliament, the one in 1933 transformed the head of state into a powerful and independent executive, directly elected by the people for a term of five years. The Riigivanem appointed and dismissed the cabinet and had extensive suspensive veto powers over laws passed by parliament. The State Assembly was also reduced by half in size to only 50 members, and the head of state could dissolve it at any time and call new elections.[16] Above all, it was the right to issue laws by decree "in case of urgent state necessity"[17] that in effect provided the Riigivanem the basis for ruling with or without parliament.

The passage of the Constitution of 1933 served merely to exacerbate the existing political crisis. Before resigning in October 1933, the Tõnisson cabinet ended the state of martial law (which had been in effect since July), and Päts formed a transitional government that was supported mainly by the Farmers' and Socialist Workers' parties to implement the approved constitutional changes. When it seemed that the electorate was behind them, the Veterans decided to enter the political arena directly as an organized party. One of their first political maneuvers in December 1933 reflected the militant anti-Marxism of the League of Veterans movement: an abortive attempt to convince the center and right parties of the State Assembly to outlaw the Socialist Workers' Party. However, in the urban elections of January 1934, the Veterans won a smashing victory by capturing majorities in Tallinn and Tartu as well as strong positions on other city councils. That the Veterans represented primarily an urban movement is shown by their lack of strength in the countryside; in rural elections held at the same time, they received only a little over 10 percent of the vote.[18]

On January 24, 1934, the new constitution came into effect with Päts as acting head of state. Elections for Riigivanem and the new State Assembly were scheduled for the second half of April. Buoyed by their recent successes at the ballot box, the Veterans launched increasingly militant attacks on the established parties, and some of their speakers threatened violence if the party was not voted into power. During the first week of collection of signatures for nominations for head of state (March 5–11), the Veterans demonstrated their organizational abilities. General Andres Larka, the league candidate, far outdistanced the combined total of his three opponents (Laidoner, Päts, and Rei) by 52,346 to 29,975.[19] Larka's strength was overwhelmingly in the urban areas. The rest of the campaign promised to raise political tensions to a new height.

AUTHORITARIANISM TRIUMPHANT: "THE ERA OF SILENCE"

On March 12, 1934, Konstantin Päts, citing "urgent state necessity," began a series of decisive steps. After declaring a state of martial law for six months and appointing General Laidoner as commander-in-chief of the armed forces, Päts shut down all League of Veterans' organizations, arrested some 400 of their leading members, and prohibited all political activity by any group.

Following approval of these steps by the lame-duck parliament, Päts decreed the postponement of elections for Riigivanem and the new State Assembly until the termination of martial law. He also ordered the removal of members of the League of Veterans from local government, the civil service, the armed forces, and the Defense League (*Kaitseliit*)—a voluntary citizen militia. Since the postponement of elections by decree was expressly forbidden by the Constitution of 1933, Päts had, in effect, carried out a coup d'état.[20] How and why was he able to do this?

Although the official justification for the emergency actions of March 1934 was the existence of an alleged plot by the League of Veterans for an armed coup, later investigation found no clear evidence of this. However, at the time the idea seemed plausible, given the vehement agitation by the league and widespread rumors of such a move. Päts and his followers could also claim, quite convincingly, that his actions averted civil war. The latter view was accepted by the Socialist Workers' Party, the stronghold of the democratic left, which regarded Päts as the only suitable politician to deal with the crisis of democracy and the threat posed by the league. Indeed, Socialist support was crucial in the emergence of Päts as acting head of state and in parliamentary acquiescence to his first steps in March 1934. Nevertheless, the differences between Päts and the Veterans before March 1934 should not be exaggerated. It is significant that although he was rejected, it appears that Päts sought the candidacy of the League of Veterans for Riigivanem in the April 1934 elections. Furthermore, although Päts found his main constituency in the rural areas and the Farmers' Party whereas the Veterans were strongest among the urban middle class, both Päts (acting with Laidoner) and the Veterans had significant support among the armed forces, the Defense League, and business circles. Thus, while Päts and Laidoner appeared to act in the interests of the Estonian republic in March 1934, they also moved to insure their own political futures.[21]

The years 1934–1940 have been appropriately termed the "era of silence" (*vaikiv ajastu*) by Kaarel Eenpalu (Einbund until 1935), the prime minister during most of this period. Martial law and restrictions on civil and political rights were continued throughout these years, and the elections for Riigivanem and a new State Assembly were never held as mandated in the Constitution of 1933. Indeed, the constitutional crisis lasted, in effect, until 1938. Päts took the position that political passions had surpassed all permissible bounds from the point of view of *raison d'état*, and his stated purpose in the years after March 1934 was to bring about a gradual healing of the Estonian body politic. When the existing State Assembly convened a special session in the fall of 1934 and displayed opposition to government restrictions, Päts permanently postponed the session and, in March 1935, abolished all political parties. Immediately thereafter the government established the Fatherland League (*Isamaaliit*), an organization designed to promote national unity and insure state stability.

During the "era of silence" this was the only political organization, although it claimed to stand above the politics of the past and represent the true interests of the people.[22] Päts also created a series of corporative institutions in which various elements of the population were represented according to occupation, as had been proposed earlier by the League of Veterans. By the end of 1936, seventeen of these organizations (two predating the Päts era) had come into existence.[23]

In the meantime, the government proceeded with the liquidation of the League of Veterans movement. In the first series of trials in June and September 1935 some of the Veterans were treated quite leniently, receiving sentences ranging from six months to six years. However, following the unmasking of plans for an armed coup led by Sirk himself (who had escaped to Finland in November 1934), the Päts regime finally settled scores with the Veterans, and in May 1936 their leaders were sentenced to fifteen to twenty years at hard labor.[24] Although the democratic opposition approved of the crackdown on the League of Veterans, there was dissatisfaction with the continuing constitutional crisis and the prohibition of political activity even after the danger seemed past. Furthermore, it appeared to many that Päts was using his sweeping powers to neutralize not only the Veterans but also any political opposition. For example, in reaction to criticism of government policy in Tõnisson's *Postimees* in June 1935, Päts sequestered the newspaper and removed Tõnisson as editor, thereby depriving his longtime rival in Estonian public life of any means of expression. Perhaps the most dramatic indication of opposition in the "silent" years came in November 1936 in a memorandum to Päts from four former Estonian heads of state (Jaan Tõnisson, Jaan Teemant, Johan Kukk, and Ants Piip), which was published in the Finnish press because of censorship at home. Citing the fact that Päts himself had pronounced the Estonian people "healthy" again, the four men called for an end to martial law and rule by decree as well as a return to the exercise of civil rights and the democratic traditions of the past.[25]

Having ruled without a parliament for a considerable period, Päts nevertheless declared himself ready to return to a constitutional order. In February 1936 he asked the population by referendum whether a bicameral Constituent Assembly (*Rahvuskogu*) should be convoked in order to amend or replace the Constitution of 1933. Of those voting, 75.4 percent (62.3 percent of the entire electorate) assented to the proposal. The constitutional legality of Päts's actions has been questioned by many observers, and it is noteworthy that no public opposition to Päts's proposal was permitted.[26] Elections to the lower house of the Constituent Assembly were held in December 1936, but despite the advice of the four former heads noted above, the Päts regime refused to permit any organized oppositional or party activity. As a protest against these restrictions, no nongovernmental candidates were nominated in 50 of the 80 electoral districts, and in the remaining 30, voter participation was low. The upper house

(40 members) included representatives of corporative organizations, local administration, and other bodies as well as Päts's own appointees.[27] Given the nature of the selection process, it is not surprising that the Constituent Assembly overwhelmingly followed the government's lead.

The assembly convened in February 1937, accepted Päts's proposals as a basis for discussion, and approved what must be called, given his dominant role in the process, the Päts Constitution in July. (After finishing its work, this assembly disbanded.) Like the Constitution of 1933, that of 1937 provided for a powerful chief executive, now called the president, who had to be at least 45 years of age and was to be elected for a six-year term. Candidates for this office were to be nominated by the two houses of parliament and an assembly of local government representatives. The chief executive would appoint and dismiss the cabinet, have a suspensive veto over legislation, and be able to dissolve both houses of parliament. Nevertheless, in contrast to the Constitution of 1933, the president could only issue decrees when the legislature was not in session.

The lower house of parliament—the Chamber of Deputies (*Riigivolikogu*)—would consist of 80 members elected by universal suffrage in single-member constituencies for a term of five years. Only the Chamber of Deputies, albeit through a unified effort of at least one-fifth of its members, could initiate legislation. The upper house, the State Council (*Riiginõukogu*), would be a close copy of the same body in the Constituent Assembly of 1936. It would comprise 40 members serving five-year terms; of these members, ten were to be appointed by the president, six were included ex officio (the commander-in-chief, the heads of the Lutheran and Orthodox churches, two university rectors, and the president of the state bank), and 24 were elected by corporative organizations, local government, and other public institutions. The State Council, where presidential influence could easily dominate, was clearly intended as a check on the actions of the lower house. It is also noteworthy that the voting age was raised to 23 and, in comparison to earlier constitutions, civil rights were to be relatively circumscribed.[28]

In the elections to the Chamber of Deputies held in February 1938, the Päts regime again refused to allow any activity by the previously existing political parties, and the only organization permitted to campaign was the government's own National Front for Implementation of the Constitution (*Põhiseaduse elluviimise rahvarinne*). In 8 of the 80 electoral districts where only National Front candidates were nominated, no elections were held. In the remaining 72 districts, 71 percent of the eligible voters went to the polls. The National Front collected 54 seats, including the 8 uncontested ones, versus 26 for the opposition. When the Chamber of Deputies convened, ten of the opposition members joined the government bloc. Nevertheless, the popular vote was hardly an overwhelming victory for the Päts forces. A recent Soviet Estonian work, based on archival sources, provides a tally of 46.6 percent of the total vote for the

National Front (not including the votes of the ten deputies who later joined it).[29] No doubt, the National Front benefited from the new, individual constituency system and the large number of candidates (241). The Päts regime's strength continued to be firmly rooted in the countryside, where it captured a majority of the representatives in all but two (Läänemaa and Petserimaa) of the eleven districts. Yet the opposition won half of the seats in Tallinn and all of them in Tartu. Although allegations of irregularities in the 1938 elections have been made, no information that can be substantiated is available on this question.[30]

As stipulated in the Constitution of 1937, the Chamber of Deputies, the State Council, and an assembly of local government representatives met in April 1938 to nominate one candidate each for president. Päts was the only candidate advanced in the latter two bodies, and he easily defeated Tõnisson in the Chamber of Deputies, 65 to 14. Since only one candidate was nominated, a "joint electoral meeting of the three bodies" was convened in which Päts received 219 of 238 votes. As called for in the constitution, Päts was immediately declared president, since a vote of 60 percent or more by the electoral meeting for a single nominee obviated a popular election.[31]

Although Päts returned to constitutionalism in 1938, there proved to be little change from the authoritarianism of the post–March 1934 period. Political parties remained proscribed, the government continued to issue legislation by decree, and the new parliament played a minor role in public life. At the same time, a more definitive "ideology of the 12th of March" began to emerge. Prime Minister Kaarel Eenpalu, the principal spokesman for the Päts regime, termed the new system "guided democracy." The emphasis was on unity, discipline, and leadership from above. For example, new laws issued in 1938 increased the power of mayors and major rural officials who were themselves now either appointed or subject to increased control by the central government. It is also characteristic that the State Propaganda Office, an institution founded in September 1934 for the stated purpose of explaining governmental policies and activities to the nation, received added emphasis in the late 1930s.[32]

Any definitive assessment of the Päts regime in 1934–1940 must await open access to Soviet Estonian archives. Nevertheless, a brief review of the existing historiography and an evaluation based on available sources can be offered here. The Soviet Estonian view has maintained that the League of Veterans and the Päts regime constituted two competing forms of fascism, wherein the latter beat the Veterans at their own game.[33] In contrast, Western observers (for example, Uustalu) have tended to emphasize that Päts justifiably used authoritarian means to deal with a potential totalitarian threat and was gradually returning to democratic practices in the late 1930s. Others (for example, Joseph Rothschild and Tõnu Parming) have noted the relative mildness of Päts's authoritarianism in the Baltic and Central and East European context of the 1930s. At the same time, recent studies by Parming and Imre Lipping have questioned Päts's commitment to a return to democracy in the years before the Soviet takeover in 1940.[34]

Thus, the Päts era remains ambiguous. On the one hand, Päts presided over a rapid recovery from the Depression in Estonia and helped avert civil war and military dictatorship. Karl Ast, a leader of the Socialist Workers' Party in the 1930s, has argued that a Päts dictatorship was far preferable to one by the League of Veterans, and given his broad support in the military and the police, Päts was the most realistic candidate for liquidating the Veterans movement. Under his mild authoritarianism there were no political executions, and it is striking that he granted amnesty to nearly all of his opponents on both the extreme right and left (the Veterans and the Communists) in May 1938.[35] On the other hand, as we have seen, both contemporary and later critics have argued that Päts's authoritarianism went further and lasted longer than necessary if his aims were limited to curbing the threat of the League of Veterans and healing the Estonian body politic.

Regarded as a societal phenomenon, the emergence of authoritarian regimes in Estonia and other East Central European states has been linked to the absence of a tradition of "civic culture," that is, experience in political democracy.[36] In all cases, stunted political participation in the Habsburg, Hohenzollern, and Romanov empires augured poorly for the health of democracy in the successor states. It is crucial, however, to view the Estonian situation in an international context in the 1930s. With the rise of totalitarian powers—an expansionist Nazi Germany and Stalinist Russia—on either side of Estonia, it appears that much of the Estonian population countenanced a departure from democracy in order to insure domestic stability and ward off the threat of foreign intervention. The tranquility of the Päts years probably reflected both a desire for order at home and a fear of the consequences of rising international tensions.

FOREIGN RELATIONS

The single overwhelming theme that dominated Estonian and Latvian foreign policy in the 1920s and 1930s was the problem of security. This was true as well in Lithuania, although there the Vilna question also played a major role. Having once established their sovereignty, these three mininations had to find a formula for survival in a Europe and a world dominated by large powers. Historians have remained divided over the viability of the Baltic states as independent entities. One school of thought maintains that, given the resurgence of both Germany and the Soviet Union in the 1930s, Estonia, Latvia, and Lithuania would inevitably have fallen into the sphere of influence of one of their two large neighbors. An opposing view suggests that as a unified force, the

Baltic states could have played a significant role in determining their own future, and it was largely their own ineptitude and lack of cooperation that sealed their fate.[37] In the 1920s the most promising sources for supporting Estonian independence appeared to be a regional alliance or the League of Nations. By the 1930s both these options had proved illusory, and with the rise of Nazi Germany and a revived Soviet Russia, Estonia faced a choice among an alliance with one of its large neighbors, a limited Baltic union, or strict neutrality.[38]

It will be recalled that with regard to the territories of the former Russian empire, the Western Allies tended to give first priority to the re-establishment of stability in the area. Thus, they were reluctant to commit themselves to the independence movements of the non-Russian nationalities, and it is not surprising that the first nation to give de jure recognition to Estonia was Soviet Russia itself in the Peace of Tartu in February 1920. Great Britain and France recognized Estonian sovereignty in January 1921, and the United States waited until July 1922. In addition to official acceptance by the Great Powers, the admission of Estonia to the League of Nations in November 1922 raised high hopes among the leaders of the fledgling state. However, the weaknesses of the league, especially the absence of the United States as a member and its inability to deter aggression in the 1930s, rendered it a woefully inadequate guardian of the rights of small nations. In the early years of independence, the most propitious basis for insuring Estonia's security appeared to lie in a regional alliance of Scandinavia, Finland, Poland, and the Baltic states. Nevertheless, the idea of a "Greater Baltic Union" foundered on geopolitical realities as well as on problems in the relations of the states involved. The Scandinavian states were not willing to risk their own independence for the sake of their smaller and weaker Baltic neighbors. Although Finland had serious security concerns, it also feared foreign entanglements, and political opinion on possible alliances remained deeply divided. Thus, Finland vetoed two major attempts to establish a "border-state" alliance in 1920–1922. Looking back to its earlier historical role in eastern Europe, Poland regarded itself as the leader of a potential smaller Baltic union (that is, without Scandinavia or perhaps Finland), but such a bloc was sabotaged by the continuing bitter enmity between Lithuania and Poland over the Vilna question. Furthermore, Latvia and Estonia had some fears of Polish domination of such an alliance. Finally, neither Germany nor the Soviet Union had any interest in a large regional bloc on their borders, and both did all they could to discourage movement in that direction.[39]

Although a broad alliance proved impossible, a narrow Baltic entente consisting of Estonia, Latvia, and Lithuania finally emerged in September 1934. For Estonia and Latvia, the choice of Lithuania rather than Poland was occasioned by the latter's overly cordial rapprochement with Germany in their nonaggression treaty of January 1934. With the Soviet Union at its back, Estonia could not afford to steer its foreign policy overtly toward Nazi Germany. The Treaty of Friendship and Cooperation, signed by the three Baltic states for an initial ten-year period, called for periodic conferences of their foreign ministers and consultation on foreign policy matters of mutual interest. However, the most significant point about the Baltic entente is that it did not include a military alliance, and even the earlier Estonian-Latvian pact in July 1921, which theoretically established military cooperation, did not lead to common defense plans. Indeed, despite the obvious similarities in their security situation, the three Baltic mininations struck remarkably cavalier attitudes in dealing with each other.[40] Thus, the small Baltic union lacked teeth as a basis for Estonian security.

With the resurgence of its powerful neighbors in the 1930s, Estonia found it necessary to conclude cautious nonaggression pacts with both the Soviet Union (May–June 1932) and Germany (June 1939). Following the failure of a regional alliance and the League of Nations, Estonia declined to choose between Nazi Germany and Soviet Russia as an ally and attempted to base its foreign policy on strict neutrality. Despite this official position, during the Päts years the Estonian military and civilian leadership privately showed an increasing preference for Germany over the USSR. To some extent this reflected Estonia's geopolitical position on the border of the Soviet Union and her relative distance from Germany, but it now seems clear that the Estonian military leaders and Päts himself entertained false hopes regarding German intentions in the Baltic.[41] In any case, the Nazi-Soviet Pact of August 1939 (discussed below) caught the Estonian authorities totally off guard. Whether a more sober view of German foreign policy would have made any difference with regard to Estonia's fate in 1939–1940 remains a moot point.

ECONOMIC DEVELOPMENT

At the beginning of the independence era, Estonia's industrial sector faced tremendous problems after nearly six years of upheaval and uncertainty in 1914–1920. To the obvious physical destruction was added the flight of capital and the elimination of traditional markets in the Russian hinterlands. Industrial development in the interwar years can be divided into three phases: (1) a period of gradual but steady growth in the 1920s; (2) the Depression, which hit its low point in Estonia in 1932–1933; and (3) recovery and a period of rapid expansion in the mid- and late 1930s. With the virtual closing of the Russian market, certain industries such as metallurgy and machines shrank drastically in the early years, and Estonia was forced to adjust by establishing an expanded domestic market and seeking new foreign ones. In 1929 the top five branches of industry—according to their share in the value of industrial output—were the following: textiles (24.1 percent), foodstuffs (18.2 percent), paper (13.4 percent), metallurgy (9.2 percent), and woodworking (8.1 percent). In 1939 the five major sectors were textiles (24.5 percent), foodstuffs (17.6 percent), metallurgy (10.7 percent), the chemical industry (10.7 percent), and paper (9.2 percent).[42] In the 1930s the rise of the chemical industry was based on the increasing use of oil-shale deposits in northeastern Estonia, and in 1933–1939 Estonia's oil production quintupled. It is also noteworthy that in the industrial expansion of the 1930s, state-owned industrial concerns played a major role.[43] The role of foreign capital in Estonian industry during the independence era was considerable, although exact figures are difficult to obtain. One estimate suggests that three-fourths of the foreign investments in the mid-1920s were British.[44]

Overall, in spite of the Depression (when the net value of large industrial output fell 20 percent in 1929–1933), Estonian industrial production showed a definite upward trend with few exceptions, as the following figures suggest:[45]

	Average 1924–1928	1933	1938
Oil shale (1,000 tons)	359	500	1,473
Pressed peat (1,000 m³)	164	238	477
Phosphorite (1,000 tons)	4	2	13
Cotton cloth (1,000 m)	25,200	13,481	20,026 (1937)
Woolen cloth (1,000 m)	1,200	1,144	1,515 (1937)
Paper (1,000 tons)	35.3	15	19
Cellulose (1,000 tons)	21.9	65	79
Lighting gas (1,000 m³)	1,253	1,555	2,000

As can be seen, the effects of the Depression varied greatly from one branch of industry to another, but in general the economic crisis led to a partial reorientation of Estonian industry and a new period of industrial modernization in the second half of the 1930s.

Fluctuations in industrial employment provide another index of Estonia's economic fortunes in the years of independence. From a pre–World War I peak of about 46,000 in 1913, the number of workers in large and middle industry plummeted to roughly 31,000 in 1922 as a result of disruption of traditional markets and the evacuation of a substantial number of factories in the interior of Russia. With gradual economic recovery, the number climbed to an average of 35,000 in the second half of the 1920s and, following a slight decline during the Depression, rose rapidly to some 49,000 in 1936 and nearly 60,000 in 1939.[46] The varying levels of labor unrest also reflected the state of health of the Estonian economy. Not surprisingly, the period of greatest labor strife came in the early 1920s (for example, 22 percent of the workers in large and middle industry struck in 1921) when adjustments to the changed post-tsarist conditions were still being made. In the late 1920s and during the Depression, strikes played a minor role in Estonian economic life. In 1935, in the early period of the Päts regime, labor unrest grew significantly, but in the last half of the decade the state increasingly intervened in labor matters and placed legal limits on the right to strike. In 1939, for example, no strikes were recorded, only "labor disputes," all of which were settled by negotiation or compulsory arbitration. Of the twenty cases of compulsory arbitration, workers protested against seven decisions, employers against five, and both against two.[47]

Given the relative absence of industrial raw materials and the limited volume of the Estonian economy, foreign trade represented an important element in national economic life. In spite of the industrial growth of the late 1930s, Estonia remained overwhelmingly a farming country; throughout the interwar years it primarily exported agricultural goods and raw materials and imported manufactured products. In 1936, for example, Estonia's major exports included foodstuffs (especially butter, meat, and livestock), timber, flax, papermaking materials, and textiles. The major imports comprised machinery and metals, chemicals, dyes, paints, textiles, raw cotton, and sugar. Throughout this period, Germany and Great Britain constituted Estonia's principal trading partners, as the following figures indicate:[48]

	PERCENTAGE OF IMPORTS		PERCENTAGE OF EXPORTS	
	1923	*1937*	*1923*	*1937*
Germany	51.0	26.1	10.8	30.6
Great Britain	19.7	16.7	34.1	33.9

The balance of Estonia's foreign trade took place with Scandinavia, the Soviet Union, the United States, and Western Europe. It is striking that trade among the three Baltic countries remained minuscule in the 1920s and 1930s, and one important factor in their less than amicable relations must be seen in their competing, rather than complementary, economies. In general, Estonia's balance of payments tended to be favorable in these two decades, and the foreign debt (mainly covering food and war matériel from the United States and Great Britain) was not a great burden. A prudent devaluation of the Estonian crown (*kroon*) in 1933 not only improved trade balance but also helped reduce the size of the foreign debt.[49]

According to the censuses of 1922 and 1934, nearly two-thirds of the working population in Estonia was engaged in agricultural pursuits,[50] and it is probable that the industrial expansion of the late 1930s only began the process of lowering this proportion. Since up to two-thirds of the rural population remained landless or had little land in 1917, it is clear that the agrarian problem was the most important socioeconomic question faced by the new Estonian state. In this situation, of course, Estonia did not differ from Latvia and Lithuania or from the larger successor states of Eastern Europe. In the Baltic states, however, a particular sense of urgency was lent by both the threat of Bolshevism and the fact that the latifundia were overwhelmingly in the hands of a non-native elite.

The Estonian land reform had been passed by the radically oriented Constituent Assembly in October 1919, and it proved to be the most sweeping piece of social legislation in the independence era. On the eve of the reform, the rural land in Estonia (4,189,102 hectares) was divided among 1,149 large estates (2,428,087 hectares or 58 percent) and 51,640 small farms (1,761,015 hectares or 42 percent). The average estate (2,113 hectares) was about 62 times the size of the average farm (34 hectares). The land reform expropriated 1,065 large estates or 96.6 percent of the land in this category, including the private estates of the Baltic German nobility, tsarist state lands, the agricultural land of the churches, and land belonging to the various *Stände*. As a supplement to the October 1919 land reform, an analogous expropriation was carried out in 1922 in the newly acquired areas east of Narva and in Petserimaa. A modest compensation in long-term bonds to the former estate owners was provided on solely agricultural land as well as on farm animals and implements. However, they were able to apply for restitution of up to 50 hectares of agricultural land.[51]

Of the expropriated area (which was over 50 percent of the entire Estonian republic), slightly less than half was agricultural land slated for division into new farms; the rest was forest and wasteland that remained in the hands of the state. As a result of the land reform, the number of farms in Estonia increased by some two and a half times over the number in 1919:[52]

	1925	1929	1939
Total number of farms	126,561	133,357	139,991
1–5 ha	21,883	23,456	21,987
5–10 ha	19,420	21,600	23,823
10–20 ha	32,025	34,977	40,249
20–30 ha	23,497	24,235	25,438
30–50 ha	⎫	22,185	21,720
50–100 ha	⎬ 29,736	6,433	6,322
over 100 ha	⎭	471	452

The new farmsteads could be purchased by means of a long-term loan or leased on the basis of perpetual tenure from the state. After the division of expropriated agricultural land in the first half of the 1920s, the modest growth in farm units was based on the creation of new homesteads from state-owned meadow and forest land. According to the censuses of 1929 and 1939 the average Estonian farm had 23 hectares of agricultural land, although during the 1930s the extremes in size declined and the number of farms in the range of 5–30 hectares increased. In effect, the land reform established a relatively satisfied agrarian sector with the small, individual family farmstead as the ideal. A recent analysis suggests that Estonia in 1939 had achieved a strikingly high degree of equality in land distribution on a comparative world scale.[53]

In the 1920s Estonian agriculture continued along the same lines as in the late tsarist period, with a strong concentration on dairy farming and livestock breeding. Because of the vagaries of the effects of the Depression, it proved advantageous to shift to a greater emphasis on cereals. Nevertheless, in 1937–1938, 54 percent of Estonia's agricultural output still came from livestock (mainly cattle, hogs, poultry, and sheep) while 46 percent accrued from the cultivation of the land (especially grain, potatoes, and flax).[54] Presumably because of adjustments to the establishment of large numbers of new farmsteads, productivity in cereals and potatoes remained roughly comparable to pre–World War I levels throughout the 1920s. In the 1930s, however, wheat, rye, oats, and potatoes all showed considerable gains in yield per hectare. In general, in the early 1930s the productivity of cereal and potato farming in Estonia ranked substantially below that of the Scandinavian countries, but was comparable to the levels achieved in Latvia, Lithuania, and Poland. With regard to the breeding of livestock, the first decade of independence witnessed modest growth, and significant increases were realized in the 1930s, especially in hogs, sheep, and poultry. During the Depression and the Päts years, it is noteworthy that Estonian agriculture received substantial price supports and subsidies from the state, thus helping it to weather the economic crisis rather well.[55]

DEMOGRAPHIC AND SOCIAL CHANGE

As noted earlier, the rate of population growth in Estonia had slackened in the decade and a half before 1914, and World War I and its aftermath contributed to a negative rate of natural increase (– 5.8 per 1,000 population in 1915–1919). A demographic estimate for 1920 for the territory of independent Estonia suggests that the total population had fallen to 1,059,000.[56] Later, the Republic of Estonia registered overall population figures of 1,107,059 (December 28, 1922, census), 1,126,413 (March 1, 1934, census), and 1,134,000 (January 1, 1939, estimate).[57] In the 1920s and 1930s, the birth rate tended to decline more rapidly than the death rate, resulting in generally lower rates of natural increase, as indicated at the top of the next page.[58] On a comparative international level, Estonia's birth rate ranked near the lowest among European countries while its death rate remained relatively high, especially as compared to Western and Northern Europe. A tradition of late marriage (in 1938, for example, the average age for first marriages was 30 for men and 27 for women) strongly contributed to the low birth rate.[59]

	Birth rate[a]	Death rate[a]	Natural increase
1920–1924	19.6	16.5	+ 3.1
1924–1929	17.8	16.5	+ 1.3
1930–1934	16.8	14.9	+ 1.9
1935–1939	16.1	15.0	+ 1.2

[a] Average per year per 1,000 population.

Since the natural population increase was so modest, differences between in- and out-migration played an important role in the demographic balance sheet. Under the terms of the 1920 peace treaty, over 38,000 persons residing in Soviet Russia had emigrated to Estonia by May 1922, and the overwhelming majority of them were Estonian by nationality. This shift provided the basis for the population growth of the early 1920s. However, in the second half of that decade, a net out-migration in effect neutralized a small natural increase in population. During the 1930s a net in-migration prevailed until 1939, when the number of emigrants rose sharply to over 13,000. The great majority of these emigrants were ethnic Germans who feared that Estonia would fall completely into the Soviet orbit following the Nazi-Soviet Pact of August 1939.[60] Notwithstanding a temporary comeback during World War II, this out-migration signified the effective end of the 700-year history of the Baltic German community in Estonia.

The ethnic composition of Estonia during the independence era showed moderate change as compared to tsarist times. For the census years, the percentage breakdown according to nationality was as follows:

	Estonians	Russians	Germans	Swedes	Jews	Others
1922	87.7	8.2	1.7	0.7	0.4	1.3
1934	88.2	8.2	1.5	0.7	0.4	1.0

Compared to 1897, the percentage of Russians in Estonia more than doubled due to the acquisition of the new eastern territories in the peace treaty of 1920. The proportion of Germans, however, showed a continual decline and by 1934 was less than half of what it had been in 1897. In terms of nationality, Estonia was one of the most homogeneous of the successor states of Eastern Europe and was not saddled with any serious minority problems. Indeed, if the area of Estland and northern Livland is taken as the basis of comparison, the ethnic Estonian share rose from 89.8 percent in 1881 to 92.9 percent in 1934.[61] Probably reflecting the new status of Estonian as the state language, denationalization among ethnic Estonians declined. In the decades between the censuses of 1881 and 1922, the proportion of those declaring Estonian nationality but speaking another language habitually remained relatively stable at around 1 percent; by 1934 this figure had reduced by half to less than 0.5 percent.[62]

Estonian cities were more subject to political and socioeconomic vicissitudes than rural areas, and thus they suffered large population losses in the aftermath of the Russian Revolution. In 1917–1919, for example, the population of Tallinn declined by over one-third (159,193 to 102,860); however, in the next two decades, a gradual recovery took place and the city's population reached 144,794 in 1938. In 1939 only three other urban centers numbered over 20,000: Tartu (60,281); Narva (23,384); and Pärnu (21,886). In general, except for the Depression years of the early 1930s, Estonian cities witnessed a moderate rate of growth in the independence era, as suggested by the following figures:

	Percentage Urban	Percentage Rural
1922	25.0	75.0
1934	28.7	71.3
1939	32.8	67.2

As in earlier times, this urbanization was a result of immigration from the countryside rather than a natural increase in the cities themselves. Overall, however, Estonia remained an overwhelmingly rural country, and with the emigration of the Germans, the urban population declined by over 10,000 (nearly 3 percent) between April 1939 and April 1940.[63]

In terms of ethnic composition, Estonian cities in the 1920s and 1930s showed a continuation of the historical trend begun in the nineteenth century. Following the relaxation of restrictions on the peasantry's freedom of movement, the urban areas became increasingly Estonianized. Overall, the ethnic Estonian share in the cities reached 82.3 percent in 1922 and 85.5 percent in 1934. In the larger cities, the percentage breakdown by nationality in 1934 was as follows:

	Estonians	Russians	Germans	Others
Tallinn	85.8	5.8	4.8	3.6
Tartu	88.0	4.5	4.6	2.9
Narva	64.8	29.7	2.1	3.4
Pärnu	90.7	2.3	4.3	2.6

In the rural townships, the Estonians constituted 89.6 percent of the population in 1934. The Russians formed a majority (65 percent) in Petserimaa and a substantial minority in Virumaa and Tartumaa. In the central and western districts (with the exception of Läänemaa, which had a Swedish minority of 8 percent), the Estonian share ranged from 96 to 99 percent.[64]

In the Estonian countryside, the land reform of 1919 brought about sweeping social change. On the one hand, the position of the Baltic German agrarian elite was undermined through the expropriation of its estates. On the other hand, the land hunger of the Estonian peasantry was to a large extent satisfied by the creation of new homesteads. Indeed, the 1934 census shows that two-thirds of the agricultural population lived on family farms that hired no outside labor. The remaining one-third was divided mainly between agricultural workers (17.6 percent) and the farmers who hired them (15.6 percent).[65] Thus, the landless rural population had been reduced by a factor of four since late tsarist times. The continuing mechanization of traditional agricultural activities, especially grain threshing, also contributed to significant changes in farm life. Although the rehielamu continued to be built in the 1920s and 1930s, the construction of farm dwellings separate from the threshing area became increasingly common.[66]

In the urban areas, the German bourgeoisie was able to retain substantial economic strength throughout the independence era. In 1936, for example, Germans owned over one-fourth of the value of all industrial concerns in Estonia. Nevertheless, an expanding Estonian middle class dominated numerically. In 1936, 84 percent of all industrialists were Estonian and 59 percent of the value of urban commercial transactions was in Estonian hands. In the new republic established in their name, Estonians found greatly expanded occupational opportunities in the governmental and military bureaucracies, the educational system, and other professions. By 1928, for example, the German share among lawyers and physicians in Estonian cities had been reduced to just over one-fourth.[67] In the urban areas in 1934, the working class was over two-thirds industrial with the rest distributed among commerce, transportation, communication, and domestic service. In contrast to the rural sector, where family farms prevailed, 62.3 percent of those employed in urban industry were wage workers. In terms of standard of living, Estonia's position was comparable to that of other successor states in Eastern Europe. In 1927–1928, per capita income in Estonia lagged far behind Western Europe and much of Scandinavia, but the level was close to that in Finland and considerably higher than in Poland and Lithuania.[68]

The establishment of the Republic of Estonia contributed to significant advances in the position of women. The Constitution of 1920 granted women the right to vote and declared the principle that all citizens were equal before the law. For the first time in Estonian history, elimination of restrictions on freedom of association permitted women to organize and pursue specific aims. By the early 1930s, for example, the League of Estonian Women (*Eesti Naisliit*) included 38 organizations with about 15,000 individual members.[69] Neverthe-less, the inertia of previous centuries was not reversed overnight. After the Constituent Assembly in 1919, which had seven female members of a total of 120, women never formed more than 3 percent of the representatives in the State Assembly in 1920–1934. In the new Estonian parliament that was elected and appointed in 1938, there was only one woman among the 120 members of both houses. Despite some improvement in practice, there was no official reform of existing family law that (in striking contrast to the principles of the Estonian constitution) relegated women to a subordinate position, especially in terms of property rights and decisionmaking. In the labor market, the share of women among salaried workers rose slightly from 33.0 percent to 35.4 percent in 1922–1934. Female participation in the different sectors of the work force showed considerable variation. In 1934, while the proportion of women em-ployees in agriculture and industry was about equal (30–31 percent), over 90 percent of those engaged in domestic service but only 10 percent of those working in transportation and communication were women.[70]

CULTURAL DEVELOPMENTS

The 1920s and 1930s brought to fruition the goal first enunciated during the national awakening: the creation of a modern and independent Estonian culture. The establishment of an Estonian-language educational sys-tem and of professional cultural institutions directed by Estonians themselves marked the beginning of a new era in Estonian culture. Having finally achieved cultural autonomy for itself, Estonia took steps to guarantee the same for its ethnic minorities. The Constitution of 1920 provided for education in the mother tongue for all citizens, and a specific law on cultural autonomy in 1925 granted minorities of at least 3,000 persons the right to establish state-sup-ported governing councils to deal with their cultural affairs. In spite of the emphasis on nationalism in the Päts years of the 1930s, there was only a minor retreat from this liberal minority policy.[71]

By the beginning of independence, the Estonians were already a highly literate nation. By the end of the nineteenth century, the ability to read among Estonians ten years of age and older had neared 100 percent. In the decades between 1881 and 1922, the ability to write among the Estonian population had jumped from about 40 percent (for those fourteen years of age and older) to over 90 percent (for those ten years of age and older). During the 1920s and 1930s, a further consolidation of these gains took place. A comparison of literacy rates (for those ten years of age and older, including all nationalities) in the two census years reveals the following figures:

	1922	1934
Able to read and write	89.1%	94.0%
Only able to read	5.3%	2.1%
Unable to read or write	5.6%	3.9%

It is noteworthy that a large proportion of the illiterate population was located in the eastern border regions where there were few Estonians. If Petserimaa and the area east of Narva are excluded, the total literacy rate in 1934 would rise to 95.7 percent and the total illiteracy rate would decline to 2.1 percent.[72]

The principle of free, compulsory primary education in the mother tongue (beginning at eight years of age) was established at the start of Estonian independence. Since the tsarist educational network provided a meager foundation, virtually all of the 1920s were required to achieve this goal on a national basis. In the educational reform of 1934, which was enacted by decree of the Päts government and reflected the influence of the agrarian parties, the maximum age for compulsory attendance was reduced from sixteen to fourteen. As a result, the number of pupils leaving elementary school before graduation increased, since many farming families took their children out of school at age fourteen whether or not they had graduated. In 1936–1939, 50 percent of the pupils in rural elementary schools did not complete their education whereas only 14 percent in urban schools failed to do so. Nevertheless, despite differing attitudes toward education in the rural and urban areas, the primary school system was virtually universal in scope. In 1939–1940 only 0.5 percent of the school-age children in the cities and 1.2 percent of those in the countryside had not been exposed to formal education.[73]

Secondary education in the 1920s and 1930s was voluntary and based on the payment of a modest tuition. Between 1922 and 1934 the proportion of those over ten years of age who had received at least some secondary education rose from 7.6 percent to 12 percent. However, a large share (40 percent) of those who entered secondary schools in the 1920s and 1930s did not complete their course of study, and a similar phenomenon existed on the university level. Aiming toward fewer but better-prepared students, the 1934 reform lengthened the period of study in secondary schools by one year and encouraged enrollment in vocational schools as an alternative. Through a substantial increase in state support, vocational education was considerably expanded in the late 1930s. In 1939–1940 there were approximately 16,500 students in Estonian secondary schools and just over 13,000 in vocational schools.[74]

After a brief period under German aegis in 1918, Tartu University was reorganized as an Estonian institution in the fall of 1919. From an opening enrollment of 374, the student body grew rapidly to 4,726 in 1926. Enrollment declined over the next several years to 3,057 in 1932, which probably reflected unfavorable economic conditions and the problem of intellectual unemployment. Throughout the rest of the 1930s, the number of students at Tartu stabilized at slightly over 3,000. In December 1939, however, with the tensions raised by World War II and the emigration of the Baltic Germans, enrollment dropped to 2,689. The nationality breakdown of the students at Tartu tended to correspond to the overall ethnic composition of the country. For example, in 1925 the student body was 81.7 percent Estonian, 6.8 percent German, 5.1 percent Russian, and 3.9 percent Jewish. In 1919–1939, 5,751 students graduated from Tartu University (73 percent men and 27 percent women), but over 50 percent of those entering the university failed to complete their studies. A second institution of higher learning, the Tallinn Technical Institute, was established in 1918. After a temporary move to Tartu in the mid-1930s, it was reestablished in Tallinn in 1936 and the following year took the name Tallinn Technical University. During the independence era, the technical university graduated 320 students, and in December 1939 it had an enrollment of 491.[75]

Following the establishment of independence, the Estonian printed word underwent a new wave of expansion. By 1923 the pre–World War I annual high for books and brochures (702 in 1913) had been surpassed (752), and output doubled by 1933 (1,520). Overall, nearly 25,000 book and brochure titles appeared in 1918–1940, approximately 1.75 times greater than the previous total output. Subject matter became increasingly secular; in 1918–1934 only 5.4 percent of Estonian books and brochures were of a religious nature.[76] In part as a result of the proliferation of political parties and the lively competition for seats in the State Assembly, the number of newspapers in Estonia also grew rapidly. A peak of 121 was reached in 1933; thereafter, the Päts regime quickly reduced the number to 49 by 1936. Yet magazines and journals showed fairly continuous growth (104 in 1926; 217 in 1936). In 1939 there were eleven daily newspapers in Estonia (eight in Estonian, two in German, and one in Russian). The politically independent *Päevaleht* in Tallinn was the largest newspaper in the 1920s and 1930s with a circulation of 40,000–50,000.[77]

The religious persuasions of the population of Estonia did not show appreciable change in the first third of the twentieth century. As noted earlier, the conversion movement to Orthodoxy halted by about 1900, and there was a slight return to Lutheranism from the tsarist state religion after 1905. During the independence era, the relative strengths of the major religions remained virtually unchanged. In 1934, 78 percent of the entire population was Lutheran and 19 percent Orthodox. Among Estonians in 1922 (the 1934 census did not correlate nationality and religious preference), 86 percent had professed allegiance to Lutheranism while 12 percent had chosen Orthodoxy.[78] The Russian Revolution and the establishment of the new Estonian state brought a thorough reordering of organized religious life. The Constitution of 1920 separated church and state, and both the Lutheran and Orthodox churches became independent and purely voluntary organizations. Under the Päts regime, however, the state showed an increasing interest in regulating religious affairs. A new law of December 1934 required all churches and religious organizations to have their bylaws confirmed by the government. In addition, the Päts government reserved the explicit right to intervene in the affairs of any religious organization if its activities were deemed injurious to the state and public order. The new bylaws of the Estonian Lutheran Church, which were confirmed by the government in May 1935, created a much more centralized administrative structure than had previously existed. Among the parish clergymen in the Lutheran Church, Estonians played an increasingly greater role: they constituted 44 percent of the pastors in 1919 and 78 percent in 1939. The independence era also witnessed some decrease in the practice of religious rites. In 1922–1933 the proportion of christenings of newborn children and the share of church weddings declined from 93–94 to 77–78 percent.[79]

The 1920s and 1930s may be called the era of standardization of written Estonian, a culmination of the language reform begun by Johannes Voldemar Veski (1873–1968) and Johannes Aavik at the end of the first decade of the twentieth century. Through borrowing (largely from Finnish) and the creation of neologisms, these two linguists were instrumental in the expansion of the Estonian lexicon. At the same time, Estonian literature experienced a new stage of development. Poetry dominated at both the beginning and the end of the independence era. In 1917–1919 the *Siuru* circle, led by its most gifted member, Marie Under (1883–1980), shocked conventional tastes by its exploration—for the first time in Estonian literature—of sensual and erotic themes. In the second half of the 1930s, the members of the *arbujad* (magicians of the word) group represented a new generation of writers who had received most of their education in independent Estonia, and they turned to neoclassicism and formalism in poetry. Among the arbujad, the leading figures were Heiti Talvik (1904–1947), Betti Alver (b. 1906), and Bernard Kangro (b. 1910). In prose, the work of A. H. Tammsaare (1878–1940) must be singled out; his epic study of Estonian life from the 1870s to the 1920s in the five-volume novel *Tõde ja õigus* (Truth and justice; 1926–1933) remains the outstanding achievement of Estonian fiction. Tammsaare skillfully interweaves realistic detail about both rural and urban life with a more general discussion of philosophical issues and the human condition. Among Estonian playwrights, Hugo Raudsepp (1883–1952) should be mentioned for his popular comedies about rural life, especially *Mikumärdi* (Mikumärdi farm; 1929) and *Vedelvorst* (Lazybones; 1932).[80]

For the Estonian theater, the years of independence were a period of further professionalization. Gradually the dramatic repertoire of the various theaters included more Estonian works; by the late 1930s, the share of original works and translations were about equal. Perhaps the high points for the Estonian theater in these years were the 1929 production of Raudsepp's *Mikumärdi*, which played more than a record 200 times in the original theater alone, and the dramatization of Tammsaare's *Tõde ja õigus* in the 1930s. By the end of the latter decade, the following ten permanent Estonian-language theaters (the first seven professional and the latter three semiprofessional) were in existence: the Estonia, the Workers' Theater, and the Drama Studio Theater (all in Tallinn); Vanemuine (Tartu); Endla (Pärnu); Ugala (Viljandi); the Narva Theater; Kannel (Võru); Säde (Valga); and the Kuressaare Theater. Attendance at Estonian theaters grew from 277,400 in 1920–1921 to 670,254 in 1938–1939. In addition, the Estonian stage expanded its range of activities to include opera and ballet. The first opera using only native vocal talent was performed at the Estonia Theater during the 1918–1919 season, and the first real ballet followed four years later. Rahel Olbrei (1898–1984), the ballet director at the Estonia Theater from 1925 to 1944, played a leading role in raising the standards of the Estonian ballet through such productions as *Giselle* (1929), *The Nutcracker* (1936), and *Swan Lake* (1940).[81]

The emergence of the Estonian republic laid the basis for the establishment of native professional schools in the arts. The Pallas Art School, founded as a private institution in Tartu in 1919, graduated 64 artists in painting, sculpture, and graphic arts during the next twenty years. In Tallinn, the State School of Industrial Arts granted 537 diplomas in the independence era. In 1938 it was divided into two separate institutions: the State School of Industrial and Pictorial Arts, and the Higher State Art School with programs in painting, sculpture, and industrial arts. In 1919 higher schools of music were founded in both Tallinn and Tartu. The Tallinn Conservatory, which became state-supported in 1935, graduated 446 students in 1919–1939 while the smaller and private Tartu music school had 74 graduates. Thus, a new generation of Estonian composers joined those who had received their training at the St. Petersburg Conservatory in the tsarist era. One of the early graduates of the Tallinn Conservatory, Evald Aav (1900–1939), wrote the first Estonian opera, *Vikerlased* (The Vikings), which had its premiere at the Estonia Theater in 1928.[82]

The song festival tradition, which had played such an important role in the national movement in the late tsarist period, continued during independence. National song festivals (the eighth through eleventh, counting from 1869) were held every five years beginning in 1923. The number of participants ranged from about 12,000 in 1923 to some 17,500 in 1938, and at the eleventh all-Estonian song festival in 1938 the size of the audience rose to nearly 100,000 people. The institution of quinquennial national song festivals as well as more frequent local ones provided a strong stimulus for Estonian choral groups and composers. Not only was new choral and orchestral music needed for the festivals themselves, but increasingly the best works from all musical genres were presented during concerts coinciding with the national song festivals.[83]

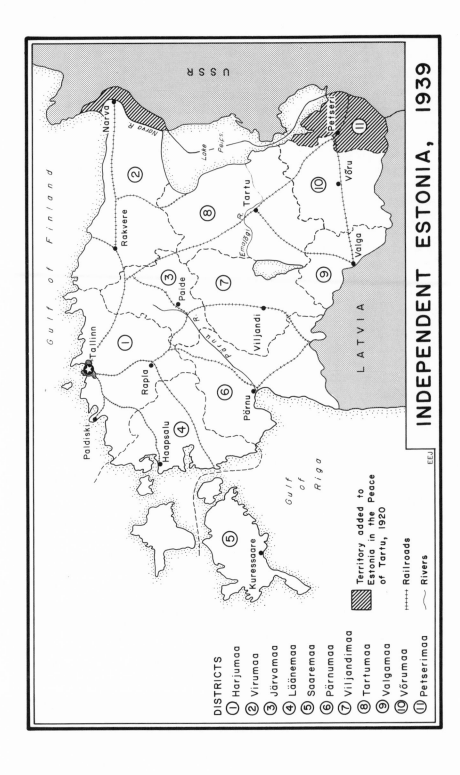

INDEPENDENT ESTONIA, 1939

USSR

Gulf of Finland

Narva

Narva R.

Lake Peips.

Loke

Rakvere

②

⑧

Tartu

Emajõgi R.

⑩

Võru

Petseri

⑪

Võru

Paide

③

⑦

Valga

⑨

Pärnu R.

Viljandi

Tallinn

①

LATVIA

Rapla

⑥

Pärnu

Paldiski

Haapsalu

④

Gulf
of
Riga

Kuressaare

⑤

DISTRICTS
① Harjumaa
② Virumaa
③ Järvamaa
④ Läänemaa
⑤ Saaremaa
⑥ Pärnumaa
⑦ Viljandimaa
⑧ Tartumaa
⑨ Valgamaa
⑩ Võrumaa
⑪ Petserimaa

▨ Territory added to
Estonia in the Peace
of Tartu, 1920

++++ Railroads

⌒ Rivers

EEJ

9 Estonia in Crisis, 1939–1940

THE ESTONIAN-SOVIET MUTUAL ASSISTANCE PACT, SEPTEMBER 1939

As Nazi Germany continued to expand eastward in Europe in the late 1930s, Estonia's security problem became increasingly acute. On the one hand, Hitler had long expressed interest in the Baltic area, and growing Nazi strength did not seem to augur well for the future. On the other hand, the Soviet Union began looking for ways to fortify its western border and increasingly regarded the Baltic states as an important buffer zone against possible German attack. In the spring and summer of 1939, the Baltic states became, in effect, pawns in the diplomatic negotiations of the major European powers. The well-publicized Anglo-French-Soviet talks on a common front against the Nazi threat ostensibly foundered on British unwillingness to agree to Soviet demands for a guarantee of the Baltic states against their will. In fact, however, Great Britain never considered risking war over the fate of Estonia, Latvia, and Lithuania.[1] At the same time, secret Nazi-Soviet negotiations reached fruition on August 23, 1939, in the Molotov-Ribbentrop Pact. With regard to the Baltic region, the now-famous secret protocol to this document assigned Finland, Estonia, and Latvia to the Soviet sphere of influence. On September 28, Lithuania was also transferred to the Soviet sphere in exchange for additional German interests in Poland.[2]

The Estonian political and military leadership appears to have received information on the substance of the Molotov-Ribbentrop Pact's secret clauses within three days of its signing. Reports of Soviet mobilization near the Estonian border also arrived in the last days of August. The previous failure of a Baltic military alliance now came into play. In order to seriously contemplate armed resistance, large-scale mobilization would have had to take place in early

September, but, acting in isolation, neither Estonia nor the other Baltic states were willing to risk the possible repercussions of such a move. By the second half of September, at the same time as the Soviet occupation of eastern Poland, the Red Army had massed some 160,000 troops (a force ten times the size of the Estonian peacetime army) on the Estonian border. Following the escape of the interned Polish submarine *Orzel* from the Tallinn harbor on September 17, the Soviet Union claimed the right to patrol Estonia's territorial waters and its navy began making demonstrative appearances off the Estonian coast. Control of communication by sea was effectively in Soviet hands. In this tense atmosphere, Estonian foreign minister Karl Selter left Tallinn by train on the night of September 22 and arrived in Moscow on September 24 to sign a commercial treaty with the USSR. That same day Soviet bombers began violating Estonian airspace.[3]

On his arrival, however, Selter was greeted with Soviet demands for a military alliance or a mutual assistance pact that would provide for Soviet naval and air bases in Estonia. Soviet commissar for foreign affairs V. M. Molotov, citing the recent escape of the interned Polish submarine, alleged that Estonia alone could not guarantee the security of its section of the Gulf of Finland. More to the point, Molotov declared that the Soviet Union had made great strides in the previous twenty years and was no longer content to "sit in this Finnish 'puddle.'" In a second meeting on September 24, the Soviet side presented a draft of the proposed pact while assuring Selter that the USSR had no intention of infringing on Estonian sovereignty or interfering in its internal affairs. The next day the Estonian foreign minister returned to Tallinn for consultations with his government.[4]

The Estonian government met on September 26 and, with the participation of Selter and the Estonian ambassador to Moscow, August Rei, unanimously decided to enter into negotiations with the Soviet Union on a mutual assistance pact. Päts argued that resistance would not only be futile but that it might also endanger the existence of the Estonian people as a whole. Furthermore, the cabinet found Estonia to be completely isolated. Informal contacts with Germany and attempts to maintain ties with Finland and Latvia had led nowhere, and there was no possibility, considering German and Soviet control of the Baltic Sea, of aid from the Western Allies. As a small and neutral nation, Estonia lacked a war industry, and there was no room for a strategic retreat in the face of overwhelming Soviet quantitative superiority in arms and men. Furthermore, given the meager size of Estonia's air force, the Soviets could quickly claim complete control of the skies.[5]

On September 27 the Estonian delegation, consisting of Selter, Rei, and members of parliament Ants Piip and Jüri Uluots, arrived in Moscow to begin negotiations. In the first session, alleging that an unidentified submarine had sunk the Soviet ship *Metalist* off the Estonian coast, Molotov immediately escalated Soviet demands to include the placement of 35,000 Soviet troops in

Estonia "for the duration of the European war . . . in order to prevent Estonia and the Soviet Union from being drawn into war, and also to protect the internal order of Estonia." After the Estonian side strongly objected to these new conditions, Stalin joined the talks and agreed to reduce the proposed number of Soviet troops to 25,000 and limit the garrisons to the naval and air bases themselves.[6] That evening Selter wired Tallinn for further instructions and learned that Soviet violations of Estonian airspace were increasing, including low sorties over Tallinn and Tartu. In response, the Estonian government ordered the delegation in Moscow to conclude a pact but also to attempt to soften Soviet demands as much as possible. In the final negotiating session, the Estonian side was able to deflect Stalin's demands for a permanent base in Tallinn but not to further reduce the number of Soviet troops to be stationed in Estonia. On the evening of September 28 the mutual assistance pact was concluded, and it was ratified by the USSR on September 29 and by Estonia on October 2.[7]

This treaty and an accompanying confidential protocol provided for Soviet naval and air bases on the islands of Saaremaa and Hiiumaa and at the mainland town of Paldiski, about 50 kilometers from Tallinn. Until the completion of the naval installations at Paldiski, the Soviets were granted the right to use Tallinn harbor for a period of up to two years. The pact itself was to be in effect for ten years, but for the duration of the current war the Soviets could locate up to 25,000 troops at the naval and air bases. In the treaty, the Soviet Union also explicitly renounced any intention of infringing on Estonia's sovereignty.[8] During the first ten days of October, Soviet and Estonian military delegations met in Tallinn to discuss the exact location of the bases. The initial Soviet position, including demands for garrisons in Paide in central Estonia and in Valga on the Latvian border, went far beyond the mutual assistance pact. After a heated debate, which included a meeting between Ambassador Rei and Molotov in Moscow, a compromise solution emerged. The Soviets withdrew their demands for Paide and Valga, but they received (in addition to the already agreed-upon bases in Saaremaa and Hiiumaa and in the Paldiski area) naval and air bases in the Haapsalu region and two air bases near Rapla in northwestern Estonia.[9] At the same time as the military negotiations in Tallinn, the Soviet Union also confronted Latvia and Lithuania with demands for bases and concluded similar mutual assistance pacts with both countries.

With regard to the Estonian-Soviet mutual assistance pact, international public opinion took a pessimistic view of Estonia's future. As the Moscow correspondent for the *New York Times* stated: "Estonia has been reduced to a kind of protectorate." Nevertheless, the immediate reaction in Estonia and the other Baltic states appears to have been one of relief that Soviet demands were not harsher.[10] Since the end of World War II, the prevailing Western interpretation of these events has been that the Baltic states were basically helpless victims of Soviet expansionism and had no alternative but to submit. In more recent years, however, a revisionist position has emerged, which argues that the actions of Estonia's leaders did have a significant impact on the fate of the country and that despite official neutrality, Estonia took an almost overtly pro-German stand in the late 1930s, thus encouraging Soviet suspicions and ignoring Soviet security concerns.[11] Furthermore, it is implied that with better leadership—including possible armed resistance—Estonia could conceivably have limited the Soviet role to a wartime occupation and avoided annexation.[12]

Nevertheless, it is important to view the Estonian case in a broad international context. By the mid-1930s the Western powers were appeasing Hitler, and Estonia could not have counted on Britain for direct aid. Estonia's international isolation was an unfortunate fact of life, and its approaches to Germany in these years can also be interpreted as a means to balance what was seen as growing Soviet pressure on Estonia. Although certain aspects of the September 1939 crisis were not handled as effectively as they might have been, the dilemma facing the Estonian government—how best to provide for the survival of a small nation caught up in a general European war—must be fully appreciated. From Päts's point of view, it was better to face an uncertain future with the Estonian people intact than to resort to armed resistance that would lead to the certain destruction of a significant minority of the nation.[13] In assessing the actions of the Estonian government in the early days of World War II, it is important to bear in mind that the crisis was not of Estonia's own making. When two totalitarian Great Powers decided to divide much of Eastern Europe between them, there was little a minination could do to halt the process. If there was failure of leadership in Estonia and the other Baltic states, it should be seen in the context of the entire independence era and the inability to develop a regional security system.

THE ERA OF SOVIET BASES

In the wake of the mutual assistance pact with the Soviet Union, a reorganization of the Estonian government took place. The two parliamentary members of the delegation that negotiated the treaty, Uluots and Piip (both professors at Tartu University), became prime minister and foreign minister, respectively. The new cabinet, which remained in office throughout the era of Soviet bases (October 1939–June 1940), maintained that Estonia had not yielded any of its sovereign rights through the pact and that rumors of imminent Sovietization were groundless.[14] The basic principle of Estonian foreign policy in this period was to avoid provoking the Soviet Union into making any further demands. Although claiming complete independence, the Estonian government, in practice, felt it had to accommodate Soviet desires in all important matters. For example, during the Winter War (November 1939–March 1940) between Finland and the USSR, Soviet planes flew bombing missions from air bases in Estonia. Although this action was in clear violation of the Estonian-Soviet mutual assistance pact, the Estonian government decided against any protest. In effect, Päts staked his bet for Estonia's future on the trumps of time and aid from some external source. In April 1940 he predicted that war would break out between Germany and the USSR in September and that this would lead to Estonia's deliverance.[15]

The sudden emigration of nearly the entire Baltic German population from Estonia in October 1939 occasioned mixed emotions among Estonians. On the one hand, there was a certain degree of satisfaction at the withdrawal of a historical antagonist. Some Estonian observers also welcomed the final break of the grip of German culture on Estonian life that had remained relatively strong during the independence era. On the other hand, the Estonian population could not but wonder what precipitated the rapid liquidation of a 700-year-old German outpost in the Baltic. With Europe at war and Soviet troops entering Estonia, the future did not appear promising.[16]

On October 18, 1939, Soviet military forces began arriving in Estonia to take up positions at the designated bases. The USSR never publicly revealed the number of troops brought into Estonia in this period. Although the nominal maximum stated in the mutual assistance pact was 25,000, the actual number appears to have risen slightly above that figure by February 1940.[17] During October and November 1939, the Soviets took pains to isolate their troops from the surrounding Estonian population, and except for those people up-rooted by the bases themselves, life appeared almost normal. However, the Winter War between Finland and the USSR also created tensions between Estonia and the garrisoned Soviet troops, and even after the end of this war in March 1940, the number of incidents involving Soviet soldiers and the local Estonian population continued to grow. By the first half of June 1940, Soviet military leaders at the bases were no longer communicating with their Estonian counterparts, and it seemed clear that a new Soviet move was in the offing.[18] Publicly, the only indication of Soviet dissatisfaction with Estonia in the several months before mid-June 1940 came in a May 28 article in *Pravda*, in which the Estonian government was accused of playing down—indeed, concealing from the Estonian people—the role and importance of the USSR for Estonia. *Pravda* also criticized pro-British attitudes within commercial circles and the intelligentsia as well as in the press. Otherwise, as late as May 3, *Pravda* had approvingly quoted General Laidoner's remarks on the correct fulfillment of the Estonian-Soviet mutual assistance pact by both sides.[19]

SOVIETIZATION

With the rapid destruction of France by Nazi invasion in May–June 1940, the Soviet Union decided to take advantage of the secret clauses of the

Molotov-Ribbentrop pact and, at the same time, prepare itself for a possible German move eastward. On June 14, 1940, Lithuania was the first of the Baltic states to be confronted with new Soviet demands. The next day, as the Red Army occupied Lithuania, Soviet armed forces garrisoned at bases in Estonia began marching toward Tallinn and large concentrations of additional troops were massed at the Estonian-Soviet border. On June 16, Molotov presented the Estonian and Latvian ambassadors in Moscow with highly similar ultimatums and, in the Estonian case, demanded an answer in eight and a half hours. In a preposterous charge, the ultimatum accused Estonia of collaborating with Latvia and Lithuania in a military alliance directed against the USSR. In order to deal with this alleged problem, the Soviets demanded that "a government be established in Estonia that would be capable and willing to warrant honest execution of the Soviet-Estonian mutual assistance pact" and that "free passage be promptly ensured to Soviet troops" in order to garrison "the most important centers of Estonia."[20] In this situation, with at least 25,000 Soviet troops already in the country, the Estonian government felt even more compelled to yield than it had nine months earlier, and the terms of the ultimatum were accepted within the allotted time limit.[21]

In Narva on the morning of June 17, General Laidoner, as commander-in-chief of the Estonian armed forces, signed the order permitting the passage of Soviet troops into Estonia. As some 90,000 Soviet troops entered the country in the next two days (bringing the total to at least 115,000), Estonia came under full military occupation. In addition, the civilian population—including the Defense League, which had at that time over 42,000 adult male members—was disarmed.

With military control of the country, the Soviets were in a position to dictate the composition of the new cabinet, and for that purpose A. A. Zhdanov, a Politburo member and one of Stalin's top associates, arrived in Tallinn on June 19. In a meeting with Päts the same day, Zhdanov rejected the Estonian president's candidate, August Rei, and revealed his own—Johannes Vares (1890–1946), a provincial doctor and poet and virtually a political unknown. On June 21, accompanied by Soviet tanks and armed forces, a "spontaneous" demonstration for a new government took place in the central square of Tallinn and at the presidential palace despite an official government ban on public assembly. According to eyewitness observers, among them Ambassador Rei who had returned from Moscow, the overwhelming majority of the demonstrators were Russians, probably including Soviet workers imported to the bases in Estonia, Soviet troops in civilian clothes, and perhaps Russians living in the eastern border regions of Estonia. In any case, on the evening of the same day, Vares revealed the composition of his new cabinet to Päts. By Vares's own admission, the list included only one person of his own choosing—the historian Hans Kruus as deputy prime minister; all the other names had been given to

Vares by Zhdanov.[23] The new cabinet called itself a "people's government" and consisted, to the surprise of many, of left-wing socialists and intellectuals, but it included no known Communists. By raising no substantial objections and confirming the new government in office, Päts apparently clung to the notion that Estonia's best hope for survival remained in avoiding any confrontation with the USSR.[24]

In its first pronouncements, the Vares government promised to maintain Estonian independence and denied any intention of establishing a Soviet regime. However, when Zhdanov temporarily returned to Moscow (June 25–July 2), the new cabinet began closing down existing organizations such as Päts's Fatherland League, the Defense League, and other mass societies. On July 5, following Zhdanov's return and renewed Soviet pressure, Päts ordered new parliamentary elections within ten days, although the existing constitution mandated a period of 35 days for election preparations. The Estonian Communist Party (ECP), which had just been legalized, and other new "democratic" organizations immediately formed an electoral bloc called the Estonian Working People's League (*Eesti Töötava Rahva Liit*; EWPL). Although other candidates were at first permitted, by July 11 only those of the EWPL remained. All opposition candidates had either been coerced and frightened into withdrawing or had been disqualified as "enemies of the people."[25]

Thus, with a single candidate in each electoral district, elections to a new Chamber of Deputies took place on July 14 and 15. The official results indicated that 84.1 percent of the eligible voters participated and 92.8 percent of them approved of the EWPL candidates. However, there is much evidence that the voting took place in a coercive atmosphere and that the results were partially falsified. Soviet soldiers often manned the entrances to polling places, and the official organ of the new regime, *Rahva Hääl* (The people's voice), suggested that it would be imprudent not to vote and only "enemies of the people" would boycott the elections. In some precincts, if the new authorities did not like the results, they simply changed the numbers.[26]

The upper house of parliament, the State Council, was simply dispensed with by the new government. The new Chamber of Deputies, however, met on July 21–23 and unanimously undertook the following far-reaching steps: (1) proclaimed Soviet power in Estonia; (2) declared Estonia's desire to become a member republic of the USSR; (3) declared that all land belonged to the people as a whole; and (4) nationalized banks and large industries. In addition, President Päts was forced to resign on July 22, and his duties were taken over by Prime Minister Vares. In the latter part of July, the political and military leaders of the former Republic of Estonia began to be arrested. Laidoner was deported on July 19 and Päts on July 30. The final step in the first phase of the Sovietization of Estonia took place in Moscow. Having already admitted Latvia and Lithuania, the Supreme Soviet agreed to accept Estonia as the sixteenth republic of the USSR on August 6, 1940.[27]

Following an earlier emphasis on legality in the transfer of power in 1940, Soviet Estonian historiography since 1960 has increasingly stressed the idea of a broadly based, indigenous socialist revolution in Estonia.[28] However, the notion of a "native" revolution is belied by the virtual identity of the process in all three of the Baltic states. For example, the July 1940 elections were all held on the same days, and the published programs of the Working People's League (the organization had the same name in all three states) were identical.[29] Western observers have correctly emphasized the decisive role of Soviet military force in these events.[30]

It is noteworthy that in the spring of 1940 there were only 133 members of the ECP in Estonia, and the ranks of Estonian Communists in the Soviet Union had been decimated by Stalin's purges in the late 1930s.[31] Thus, the role of native Communists in Estonia was perforce a limited one, but it was also in line with Zhdanov's scenario that fellow travelers took the lead in the early stages of the transfer of power. However, it should not be assumed that Vares and the other members of his cabinet were merely Soviet stooges. It appears that the Vares government was not privy to ultimate Soviet goals in Estonia, and when they did become obvious, there is evidence that Vares made a last-ditch effort to obtain a kind of Outer Mongolia status (that is, a people's republic and Soviet hegemony, but no formal annexation to the USSR) for Estonia. There also appears to have been some resistance to the incorporation of Estonia in the USSR at the meeting of the new Chamber of Deputies on July 21, but within 24 hours all opposition was stifled.[32]

Like the events of September 1939, the actions of the Päts government in June–July 1940 have been subjected to critical examination by both contemporary and later observers. Once again, it is the revisionists who argue that Päts deluded himself into thinking that help from Germany was at hand as late as early July. Furthermore, Päts has been taken to task for giving his blessing to the early stages of Sovietization and thus providing the appearance of legal continuity.[33] Päts's executive secretary has also suggested that Päts did not fully grasp the seriousness of the situation facing Estonia in June–July 1940 and remained convinced that the Soviets would soon be forced out of Estonia as a result of a Soviet-German armed conflict.[34] Nevertheless, it must be asked whether anything the Päts government did in the last weeks of independence would have made any difference regarding Estonia's fate. If one argues from the perspective of 1940 (and not from hindsight), it did not seem irrational to postulate that the changing fortunes of war could yet work in favor of the survival of an independent Estonia if the Estonian people could escape physical devastation.

SOVIET ESTONIA

PART FOUR

10 The First Year of Soviet Rule, 1940–1941

Following the incorporation of Estonia into the USSR, the new regime began the process of Sovietization in earnest in all aspects of Estonian life. Nevertheless, the establishment of Soviet norms was by no means complete by June 1941 when Hitler's invasion temporarily ended Soviet control of the Baltic area.

POLITICAL TRANSFORMATION

On August 24, 1940, the Chamber of Deputies reconvened to consider a new constitution and to establish the future form of government for the Estonian SSR. Unanimously adopted the following day, the Soviet Estonian constitution, drawing on the Stalinist model of 1936, proclaimed Estonia "a socialist state of the workers and peasants." While recognizing the leading role of the Communist Party in socialist development, the Constitution of 1940 placed (in theory, at least) ultimate political power in the hands of a new legislative organ, the Supreme Soviet of the Estonian SSR.[1] Civil rights were guaranteed "in conformity with the interests of the working people." Heeding the arguments of its chair, Arnold Veimer (1903–1977), who declared that it would be a "useless waste of time and energy to dissolve ourselves now in order to hold new elections for purely formal reasons," the Chamber of Deputies proclaimed itself the Provisional Supreme Soviet of the ESSR with Johannes Vares as head of its Presidium. Following the USSR model, the executive branch of the government was constituted as the Council of People's Commissars, including the chair (Johannes Lauristin, 1899 –1941), two vice-chairs, the head of the State Planning Commission, and thirteen commissars, or ministers. The commissariats were divided into two groups: those responsible to both the ESSR government in Tallinn and the all-Union one in Moscow (light industry, finance, agriculture, commerce, internal affairs, justice, health, and state control); and those responsible only to the ESSR government (local industry, education, labor, communal economy, and social insurance).[2]

However, the real locus of political power in Estonia after June 1940 was clearly the Communist Party, which was buoyed by the presence of large numbers of Soviet troops. Given its illegal status in Estonia in the 1920s and 1930s, the ECP remained relatively small, and—as noted above—there were no more than 133 known members on June 21, 1940. Moreover, the ECP leadership and rank and file in exile in the Soviet Union had been largely wiped out in Stalin's murderous purges in the late 1930s, and thus the party could count on few reinforcements from outside Estonia. In this situation the ECP was anxious for new blood, and the first recruits included the leading left-wing socialists and intellectuals in the Vares government. The ranks of the party grew to 1,344 members by the start of September 1940 and (following a temporary decline in the latter part of 1940) to 3,732 members by June 1941.[3] Nevertheless, the ECP and the Soviet Estonian government found it necessary to request the presence of over 1,000 Communists (46 in 1940 and 963 in 1941) "from other Union Republics to work at several leading posts in state and economic machinery." It is said that most of these new party members knew Estonian; that is, they were presumably ethnic Estonians who had been living in Soviet Russia.[4]

The top policymaking organ of the ECP was the Buro of the Central Committee, established in September 1940 with Lauristin, Vares, Karl Säre, Nikolai Karotamm (1901–1969), Neeme Ruus, Boris Kumm, and Erich Tarkpea as members. Although all these men had been born in Estonia, they had varying histories. Vares and Ruus only joined the party in July 1940, and Lauristin, Kumm, and Tarkpea had spent extensive time in prison in independent Estonia. By the end of August 1940, Säre, a Comintern operative in Scandinavia in the mid-1930s, and Karotamm, mainly associated with the ECP's foreign bureau in the USSR in the 1930s, became the first and second secretaries, respectively, of the party's Central Committee; they retained these leadership positions at the ECP's Fourth Congress in February 1941. At this meeting, Ruus and Tarkpea were dropped from the Buro while Adolf Pauk, Herman Arbon, Oskar Cher (all three native Estonian Communists who had been in prison in the 1920s and/or 1930s), and Vladimir Tributs (a Soviet Russian naval officer) were added.[5]

In the months between August 1940 and June 1941, the process of political Sovietization proceeded apace. Prominent Estonian political figures from the independence era, including eight former heads of state and 38 former ministers, were arrested and deported to the interior of Soviet Russia. At the same time, Soviet judicial, police, security, and other administrative institutions were established in Estonia. The small Estonian navy and air force were simply absorbed by Soviet forces, while the Estonian army was integrated into the Soviet military structure as the Twenty-second Rifle Corps of the Red Army. During the first months of Soviet rule many Estonian officers were arrested, and in June 1941, simultaneous with the mass deportations throughout the Baltic area, what remained of the older generation of military leaders was sent to Soviet prison camps.[6]

NATIONALIZATION AND AGRICULTURAL REFORM

In the economic sphere in 1940–1941 the new regime focused on the urban sector—industry, banking, transportation, and commerce—while rural economic life was subject to less scrutiny and, therefore, less sweeping change. In the nationalization process, beginning July 26, 1940, top priority was given to large industry and the banks; by the end of August nearly 90 percent of Estonian industry and transport had come under the direct aegis of the state or was run by state-controlled cooperatives. The newly formed People's Commissariats of Light Industry and Local Industry took over the direction of the industrial sector. The nationalization of commerce proved to be a more protracted undertaking, but by June 1941 the state had control of all wholesale trade and 85–90 percent of the retail trade. While large commercial enterprises were simply nationalized outright, the smaller private traders were forced out of business by high rents and taxes.[7] State control over real estate began in August 1940 with the appointment of trustees to regulate the use of large houses and the declaration of a dwelling space norm of nine square meters (or less) per capita. In late October began the nationalization, without compensation, of all buildings with over 220 square meters of "useful floor space" in the larger cities and those with over 170 square meters elsewhere.[8]

As the nationalization of the urban economy proceeded, the Estonian middle and working classes were subjected to a significant decline in standard of living through financial and labor policies and taxation. In November and December 1940 the transition from the Estonian crown to the Soviet ruble as the monetary unit took place at an artificially low exchange rate, roughly eight times lower than would normally have been expected. The resulting drastic decline in purchasing power was further exacerbated in January 1941 by the confiscation of all savings accounts over 1,000 rubles and by rising prices throughout that entire year.[9] In October 1940 the new authorities lengthened the average workday to nine hours and no longer permitted workers to freely change jobs. During the first year of Soviet rule, despite a nominal increase in earnings, the real wages of the average industrial worker (excluding a politically favored minority) fell by perhaps 50 percent. The average worker's tax burden also rose, especially if the purchase of state bonds, which proved to be compulsory in practice, is taken into account.[10]

Perhaps because the agricultural sector employed by far the largest proportion (about two-thirds in the mid-1930s) of the labor force, the new regime moved toward change in this area with greater circumspection. Forced collectivization, for example, was publicly ruled out, and although all land was officially nationalized, "working peasants" were granted "perpetual tenure" on farms up to 30 hectares. In October–December 1940 the Soviet authorities implemented a limited agricultural reform based on the land declaration of the Chamber of Deputies in July. It expropriated, without compensation, all private holdings over 30 hectares, all land belonging to churches and religious groups, and all holdings of cities and other local communities. The lands thus acquired, to which were added the existing state holdings, constituted 742,182 hectares (24.3 percent of all agricultural land) and were declared a state land reserve.[11] The Soviets distributed roughly half of this land to landless peasants and smallholders with an average of about 11 hectares per new farm. In terms of private farming, the result of the land reform was to increase the total number of farms (by about 18 percent compared to 1939) and level their size. Virtually all farms over 30 hectares were eliminated, and farms in the range of 10–30 hectares now constituted over three-fourths of the total. Overall, the average size of all farms in Estonia fell from 22.7 hectares in 1930 to 16.7 in 1941, and the proportion capable of producing for market was sharply reduced.[12]

Given the Stalinist model of collectivization in the USSR in the 1930s, however, it could be presumed that the 1940 land reform in Estonia was only a temporary waystation in Soviet agrarian policy. In addition to the land reform, which ostensibly favored small private farming, the new regime established about 100 sovkhozes (state farms), and the Fourth ECP Congress in February 1941 called for the creation of cooperatives as preparation for the transition to collective production in the agricultural sector. As a prototype for the future, the Soviet authorities organized about ten kolkhozes (collective farms) by the summer of 1941.[13]

Overall, state policy in 1940–1941 favored the collective enterprises and new farmers and discriminated against those proprietors who had established themselves during Estonian independence. By the spring of 1941, the new regime had created 25 Machine Tractor Stations (MTS) and 250 Horse and Machinery Lending Stations (HMLS). Although the MTS—which were founded in 1928 to serve the needs of Soviet kolkhozes—were theoretically available to all, the larger private farmers had to pay more for their use. The HMLS were intended to aid the new small farmers who lacked their own farm animals and implements and to discourage the idea of private property. However, largely because of logistical problems, neither the MTS nor the HMLS were able to fully provide the services they advertised in 1941.[14]

In the spring of 1941 the Soviet authorities also announced a plan for compulsory deliveries of agricultural produce (with a one-year exemption for the new farmers) at fixed and artificially low prices. In fact, the state prices were generally well below cost, and the new delivery policy took no account of the previous production history of Estonian farmers. In addition, in May the regime declared an agricultural profits tax from which, once again, the new farmers were exempt for one year. The average rate of taxation proved to be higher than the average farm income and rose even higher if a farm hired labor. Because of the Nazi invasion in June, these policies were not fully implemented, but their direction was clear. On the one hand, the situation of the older private farms was to be made intolerable; on the other hand, collective farming was to appear as attractive as possible, including exemptions from taxation and compulsory agricultural deliveries.[15]

Although no reliable statistics on agricultural production during 1940–1941 appear to be available, the sudden changes of that year doubtless had an overall negative effect. Such a result is clearly suggested by a comparison of Estonian livestock holdings in July 1939 and September 1941. By the latter date, the number of sheep had declined by 41 percent, cows by 25 percent, horses by 20–25 percent, and hogs by 29 percent. Although the Nazi invasion played some role in this process, the major factor appears to have been voluntary slaughter by farmers for fear of being branded as kulaks (rich peasants) and their desire to avoid possible expropriation of their livestock.[16]

SOCIAL AND CULTURAL DEVELOPMENTS

Political and economic Sovietization in Estonia was accompanied by sweeping social change, especially in the urban areas. The elites of independent Estonia, the economically and politically well-placed, were now dispossessed and many of their members were deported to the interior of the Soviet Union. A new elite, based mainly on political loyalty to the Soviet regime, emerged. At the top of the new hierarchy came the growing number of ECP members and a minority of manual workers who, embracing the new regime, now assumed certain leadership positions. In the middle and lower echelons of society a strong leveling process occurred, although those with some accumulated wealth from the past and with useful mental and manual skills continued to fare the best. Nevertheless, Soviet wage, price, and taxation policies brought pressure on all segments of Estonian society. Less fundamental social change occurred in the countryside, since the larger landowners lost only that portion of their holdings above the new maximum of 30 hectares. In addition, given the small size of their allotments and insufficient state support, the seemingly favored classes in Soviet agrarian policy in 1940–1941—the landless and the smallholders—did not benefit as much as they might have.

Soviet rule in 1940–1941 witnessed extensive losses for the population of Estonia. During the year the Soviet regime executed about 2,000 Estonian citizens and deported approximately 19,000; nearly half of that number was rounded up in a few days in mid-June 1941. The mass deportations of that month, which took place simultaneously with those in Latvia and Lithuania, had been prepared for months and were slated to include the following major categories of people: members of "counterrevolutionary" organizations, former police and prison officials, former higher state officials, former large landowners and industrialists, former officers in the armed forces of independent Estonia, clergymen, and family members of all of the above. The adult deportees appear to have been separated by sex; the men were sent to forced labor camps and the women and children into harsh exile. A recent description by Rutt Eliaser, a surviving deportee, suggests that the death rate among women and children was high, but also that some Estonians were able to return to Estonia after the war.[17]

As the Nazi invasion began, the Soviets quickly mobilized some 33,000 men, mainly in northern Estonia where such action was still possible, and took them along with their retreating forces to the interior of the USSR. Although the exact fate of these men remains unknown, there is enough evidence to indicate that most of them perished in the harsh conditions of Soviet labor camps, and those that actually took part in fighting on the Soviet side were involved in a number of bloody engagements. Thus, it is probable that few of these men survived World War II.

As Soviet forces withdrew from Estonia in the summer of 1941, up to 33,000 additional Estonian citizens, including ECP members and those who in one way or another were tied to the new regime (and their families), joined the eastward evacuation.[18] One final human loss involved emigration in a westward direction: the so-called follow-up resettlement (*Nachumsiedlung*) to Germany in the early months of 1941. In this instance, following new negotiations between the German and Soviet authorities, over 7,000 people, including nearly all the remaining Germans in Estonia as well as a few thousand ethnic Estonians who claimed German ancestry or were married to Baltic Germans, received permission to leave the country. Overall, from mid-1940 to mid-1941, Estonia suffered a total population loss of about 94,000 (40,000 emigrants and 54,000 executed, deported, or mobilized).[19] Of this number, all but those evacuating to the interior of the USSR were permanent losses.

In the cultural realm, the changes wrought in 1940–1941 were far less comprehensive than those in other areas. Two reasons can be given for this: first, the transformation of cultural values and attitudes is a highly complex process, requiring more than a matter of months; second, the Soviet authorities clearly assigned cultural affairs a lower priority than they did to the political and economic spheres. Nevertheless, the new regime did pay considerable attention to the educational sector as the quickest means to reach the younger generations. In the fall of 1940 the state established a new, uniform school system, abolished all private institutions, and reduced the total duration of elementary and secondary education—following the Soviet model—from twelve to ten years. In the curriculum the authorities removed such subjects as religious instruction, ancient languages, and civics, and Russian replaced English as the first foreign language. Furthermore, all subjects were henceforth to be taught in the spirit of Marxism-Leninism. However, the Soviets lacked the personnel to implement this principle immediately. Instead, the existing faculty, except for those with an obviously "counterrevolutionary" past, was slated for retraining, but this process required time and also evoked passive resistance. It appears that, altogether, 10 percent of the schoolteachers in Estonia in 1940–1941 were deported or executed. As a means to circumvent the influence of teachers from the independence era, the new authorities placed great emphasis on the Young Communist League, but its numbers remained small in the first Soviet year.[20]

At Tartu University the Soviet regime moved in the same direction. Before the beginning of the fall semester in 1940, the independence-era administration and several of the more objectionable faculty members, from the Soviet viewpoint, were dismissed, and the theology department was disbanded. Hans Kruus, who had been deputy prime minister in the Vares government, became rector of the university. As at the lower levels of education, Marxism-Leninism was declared the basis for all knowledge and study. However, its guiding role remained limited in 1940–1941, since authoritative texts were not yet available and the new regime lacked educated cadres to enforce its use. By July 1940 the Soviet authorities had liquidated the recently founded Estonian Academy of Sciences, but the scholarly societies associated with Tartu University continued to function. In addition, large numbers of books published before June 1940— including 70,000 volumes dealing with theology that were destroyed outright— were purged from the university library, and similar action was taken in libraries all over Estonia.[21]

In literature and the other arts, 1940–1941 proved to be a year of transition. Soviet Russian models became increasingly visible, but Stalinist norms did not yet prevail to the exclusion of all others. Of the established writers, a small minority embraced the Soviet regime while the others remained publicly noncommittal. In fact, very few literary works that could qualify as socialist realism were produced during the year; even though all publishing houses were nationalized and run by the state, novels such as Hugo Raudsepp's *Viimne eurooplane* (The last European) and Karl Ristikivi's *Võõras majas* (In a strange house), neither of which treated Soviet themes, still appeared. A sign of the times, however, was the growing number of translations from Soviet Russian literature. In theatrical life, the new regime replaced the existing administrators and directors with politically trustworthy substitutes, but the staffs remained relatively unchanged. As in other cultural endeavors, Soviet ideology was declared the norm, but one year could not suffice to effect a real transformation. Although Russian and Soviet plays increasingly entered the theatrical repertoire, the majority of productions were still pre-1940 Estonian or Western.[22]

The Soviet regime regarded religion as a major obstacle to the realization of its aims in Estonia. In the summer of 1940 a frontal attack was launched against both the Lutheran and Orthodox churches, beginning with the expropriation of their property. The abolition of theological studies at Tartu University meant that no new Lutheran pastors could be trained, since no other institution for this purpose existed in Estonia. In January 1941 the Estonian Orthodox Church lost any remaining autonomy through a compulsory merger with the Russian Orthodox Church in Moscow. Given their highly visible ideological position, church officials and clergymen were also ready targets of persecution. In June 1941 the bishops of both the Lutheran and Orthodox churches and a considerable number of their clergy were deported.[23]

11 The German Occupation, 1941–1944

THE NAZI INVASION
AND WORLD WAR II

When Nazi Germany began its attack on the USSR on June 22, 1941, the Soviet Union was still ill-prepared for a total and technologically advanced war. The early German successes are well known and need not be described in detail here.[1] Suffice it to note that the Germans moved rapidly up the Baltic coast and reached Estonia as early as July 5. As elsewhere in the Baltic, they were initially greeted as liberators, especially in the wake of the mass deportations carried out by the Soviets only a few weeks earlier. At the same time, a pro-independence Estonian partisan movement emerged, the beginning of which can be associated with the first wave of men fleeing to the forests to escape the deportations. By the end of June their numbers had grown in reaction to the last-minute Soviet mobilization of draft-age Estonian men. However, as noted above, the Soviets had been successful in conscripting some 33,000 men, largely because many draftees feared reprisals against their families if they evaded mobilization.[2]

On July 3 Stalin made his first public statement since the start of the German invasion; he recognized the necessity of a Soviet retreat but also called for a "scorched earth" policy in the areas to be abandoned. In order to carry out this policy and to cover the withdrawal of its retreating forces, the Soviet regime established so-called destruction battalions (*hävituspataljonid*). As the Nazi forces entered Estonia and in the following weeks, the pro-independence partisans and the destruction battalions fought numerous engagements all over the country. It appears that there were several thousand men on each side, and, although the skirmishes were usually limited in scope, they were at times bloody.[3] Meanwhile, the invading Germans moved quickly into southern Estonia, taking both Pärnu and Viljandi on July 8 and reaching Tartu by July 10. There the Germans temporarily halted their attack, and the battle of Tartu, which lasted two weeks and caused considerable damage to the city, primarily involved Estonian partisans against regular Soviet troops and destruction battalions. Recognizing that complete victory in Estonia was only a matter of time, the Nazi command in the Baltic was apparently content to let the Estonian partisans carry the brunt of the fighting for the time being. However, in the last week of July the Germans began to advance again, and aided by the Estonian partisans, they methodically took Narva on August 17, Tallinn on August 28, and the last of the major Estonian islands on October 21.[4]

In the meantime, most of the Soviet leadership and those connected with the regime had evacuated to the interior of the USSR, although Lauristin perished in the retreat from Tallinn at the end of August. A select group of leading Communists went underground to direct anti-Nazi activities, but most of the leading lights (including Säre, Ruus, Cher, and Arbon) were eventually captured by the Germans. Of the Estonians mobilized into the Red Army, several thousand deserted to the German side, especially after they had left Estonian soil and no longer feared reprisals against their relatives. Most of them were sent to Germany as prisoners of war and were not freed or able to return to Estonia before the spring of 1942. In general in the early months of the war, the German leadership refused to permit the formation of any large Estonian military units, whether based on partisans or Red Army deserters, and the small existing partisan detachments were broken up by the early fall of 1941. Thus, in line with Nazi ideology regarding "inferior" peoples, non-Germans were not yet needed at the front, but Estonians were called on to serve in the Home Guard (*Omakaitse*) to secure the German rear and clean out any remaining troops of the Red Army.[5]

As victory became increasingly elusive on the eastern front and their manpower was stretched thinner, however, the German authorities began to change their attitude. As with other non-German nationalities under Nazi control, an Estonian Waffen-SS unit called the Estonian Legion was established in late August 1942, at first on a voluntary basis. The response among able-bodied Estonian men remained meager for the following reasons: the Germans refused to support Estonian independence, there was little interest in fighting outside Estonia, and the Waffen-SS units were expected to accept Nazi ideology. Indeed, as of October 13, 1942, only 500 volunteers had appeared. Only after additional men were, in effect, drafted from the police did the number rise to 1,280 in the spring of 1943. Called the Narva Battalion, this unit was immediately sent to the south Russian front.[6]

Because of these poor results, the German occupying powers turned to outright mobilization in March 1943, calling up all Estonian men born between 1919 and 1924. Even under these conditions, in March–August 1943 the Germans still only netted 5,300 men for the Estonian Legion and 6,800 for support service (*Hilfswillige*) to the German *Wehrmacht*. After training, these troops were also sent to the front east of Pskov. A later mobilization in October 1943, calling up men born in 1925–1926, also provided limited results. An important consequence of the 1943 mobilizations was the significant wave of Estonian men (perhaps 5,000 in all) crossing the Baltic Sea to Finland, a risky venture in wartime, in order to avoid the German draft. Over half of these men volunteered for service in the Finnish armed forces against the Soviet Union; about 2,300 joined the army and 400 the navy. In addition to avoiding the German army, the volunteers' goal was to acquire military training and experience in order to be of future service to their homeland. Given the emergence of Estonian independence in the rapidly changing fortunes of World War I, the restoration of that same independence did not seem beyond the realm of possibility in the upheavals of World War II.[7]

By January 1944 the German military situation had worsened considerably, and the front began to approach the borders of Estonia once again. At the end of January and the start of February, the city of Narva was almost completely evacuated. On February 1, Hjalmar Mäe, head of the Estonian administration operating under the aegis of the German occupying authorities, called up all men born between 1904 and 1923 for military service. Aided by a radio speech by Jüri Uluots, the last prime minister of the Estonian republic before Soviet intervention in 1940, this mobilization succeeded beyond all expectations and totaled about 38,000 men. The decisive factor seems to have been a desire to stave off Soviet occupation of Estonia until the capitulation of Nazi Germany to the Allies, thus keeping open Estonia's options for the future. Counting the new draftees from February 1944, there were now some 50,000–60,000 Estonian men under arms in Estonia, although they were poorly supplied with weapons, ammunition, and clothes.[8]

With the aid of these reinforcements, the Soviet advance was halted for about six months, and the front was stabilized roughly along the Narva River in the north and near Pskov in the south. In late July, however, as part of a broad offensive on the eastern front, Soviet forces began a relentless attack in the Baltic that led to German evacuation of continental Estonia within two months. The Soviets took Narva on July 26 and reached Võru on the south Estonian front by August 13. Thereafter, with the Germans preparing to retreat (a land connection with Germany had been temporarily cut off by a Soviet breakthrough in Latvia in early August) and aided by their great superiority in numbers, the Soviet forces moved rapidly. Tartu fell on August 27, Tallinn on September 22, Pärnu and Haapsalu on September 24, and the Estonian islands by early October (with the exception of the Sõrve Peninsula on Saaremaa, where the Germans held out until late November). The situation in Estonia was becoming critical by early August 1944, and the Estonian volunteers in the Finnish armed forces voted overwhelmingly to return to aid the defense of their homeland. In late August and early September just over 2,000 of these men made the return trip to Estonia. However, the German authorities, distrustful of their loyalties and uninterested in any movement to restore Estonian independence, quickly dispersed them among other units, thus weakening their potential fighting effectiveness. Even at full strength their efforts could hardly have stemmed the tide, since the decisive factor in Estonia in August–September 1944 was the overwhelming quantitative Soviet superiority in men and matériel.[9]

Finally, an overview of Estonian participation in World War II would be incomplete without a summary of the experience of the Estonian Rifle Corps in the Red Army. Having mobilized some 33,000 Estonians as they were evacuating the Baltic states in the summer of 1941, the Soviets were in no hurry to send these men to the front, especially following the numerous defections to the German side at the time of the Soviet retreat. In fact, it appears that no more than half of these mobilized Estonians were used for military service; the rest perished in Soviet labor camps, mainly in the early months of the war. Estonian national military units within the Red Army began to be formed in January 1942 from among ethnic Estonians living in the interior of the USSR, those who had voluntarily evacuated in 1941, surviving members of the destruction battalions, and the forcibly mobilized Estonians from Estonia itself. A Soviet source suggests that in May 1942 there were nearly 20,000 Estonians in the national units, constituting 89 percent of the total strength of these formations. The Eighth Estonian Rifle Corps, as these units came to be called after September 1942, reached the front at Velikie Luki in December 1942 and suffered heavy losses in battle as well as the defection of about 1,000 men to the German side. After Velikie Luki the Soviets dealt harshly with those suspected of disloyalty, and the corps was replenished with non-Estonians. After a long period of regrouping and retraining, the corps's major activity in the latter part of the war was participation in the Soviet conquest of Estonia, although ethnic Estonians formed only a small portion of the total Soviet forces in that operation.[19]

ESTONIA IN THE GERMAN "OSTLAND"

Although Hitler's general views on *Lebensraum* and German colonization of Eastern Europe and the western Soviet Union are well known, his specific ideas for Estonia are less clear; none of the policies suggested by his lieutenants were ever implemented because of the temporary nature of German hegemony in the Baltic region. Nevertheless, if it can be assumed that Hitler's underlings reflected their leader's own predilections, a reasonably detailed picture emerges.

In April 1941, on the eve of the German invasion, Alfred Rosenberg, Hitler's appointee as Reich minister for the Occupied Eastern Territories, laid out his plans for the East. A Baltic German, born and raised in Tallinn, he regarded his native region as a privileged area of Eastern Europe that, because of the age-old German influence, could even become a constituent part of the new Greater Germany. According to Rosenberg, the entire Baltic area could become truly German through a threefold policy: (1) "Germanization [*Eindeutschung*] of the racially suitable elements"; (2) "colonization by Germanic peoples"; and (3) "exile of undesirable elements." Of the three Baltic peoples, Rosenberg felt the Estonians were the most Germanic, having already reached 50 percent Germanization through Danish, Swedish, and German influence.[11]

In the early months of the war, all things seemed possible to the German conquerors, and Rosenberg and other Nazi planners anticipated the eastward expansion of Estonia's borders to the Leningrad-Novgorod line (a region that Rosenberg called "Peipusland"). Much of the ethnic Estonian population was to be moved into this area to make room for German colonists in the Baltic itself. In fact, such plans were seriously discussed at Hitler's headquarters as late as August 1942, but the Soviet counterattack prevented their realization. Along similar lines, the *Generalplan Ost* of the SS Planning Office in May 1942 called for the population of the eastern *Marken* (frontier regions) to be substantially German or Germanized within 25 years. However, Heinrich Himmler, head of the SS, demanded an amendment of the plan to include, among other things, the complete Germanization of Estonia and Latvia within twenty years. Thus, despite the relatively favorable position of the Estonians in the German ethnic hierarchy in Eastern Europe (as compared to Jews, Gypsies, or Slavs), Nazi ideology, while eschewing physical liquidation, saw no other alternative than rapid denationalization of the Estonian people.[12]

Following the German conquest of the Baltic states in the summer of 1941, the initial administrative system in Estonia was a purely military one. However, in the following months a civilian administration gradually took over in the Baltic region (in Estonia on December 5, 1941). Hinrich Lohse, located in Riga, became the overall head (*Reichskommissar*) of the newly established Ostland, which consisted of the three Baltic states and Belorussia. In Tallinn the highest ranking German official was Commissar General (*Generalkommissar*) Karl Litzmann. In keeping with Hitler's predilection for overlapping jurisdiction, the SS also established a foothold in Estonia, especially in the person of Martin Sandberger, head of the local security forces (*Sicherheitsdienst*).[13]

While retaining all effective power in their own hands, the Germans set up native administrations in the Baltic states in an effort to broaden the appeal of German rule. In Estonia in September 1941, Hjalmar Mäe, a leading figure in the League of Veterans movement of the early 1930s, was placed at the head (*erster Landesdirektor*) of the indigenous administration, which was divided into several directorates: education, internal affairs, economics, agriculture, social matters, and justice. In fact, Mäe had in effect campaigned for this position with a memorandum to the German Foreign Office in June 1941. He flatly claimed that under his and his cohorts' tutelage the Estonian people would accept close ties with the German Reich within six months. Furthermore, seeking to ingratiate himself with the German authorities and assure his own political future, Mäe accepted the idea of partial German colonization in Estonia and called for the territorial expansion of Estonia at the expense of the Soviet Union. All this impressed the Nazi authorities, but Mäe never achieved any significant political base among the Estonian population. Indeed, he alienated the Estonian public through his style, aping Hitler even to the point of wearing the same type of mustache, and his political ineptness—for example, he attacked Konstantin Päts in one of his first speeches and thereby lost any prospect of popular support.[14]

Throughout the occupation period, the official German position on Estonia as a political entity remained immutable. In essence, the Germans argued that since an independent Estonia had ceased to exist in 1940 before their conquest a year later, the question of independence was no longer germane. Yet it is noteworthy that several of Hitler's lieutenants, including Himmler, Rosenberg, and Litzmann, proposed some measure of autonomy or even independence for Estonia for tactical reasons—to encourage the Estonian will to fight—as the military situation worsened. However, Hitler's ideology of Germanic supremacy precluded any concessions, even propagandistic ones, to non-Germanic peoples, and he always vetoed such proposals. In his war of conquest Hitler saw the only alternatives for the Germanic *Herrenvolk* as total victory or total defeat, with no possibility of compromise.[15]

Most of the leading pre-1940 Estonian political figures had been deported to the interior of the USSR by the Soviets in 1940–1941. However, the last prime minister of the Estonian republic before Soviet intervention, Jüri Uluots, was able to avoid deportation, and Article 46 of the Constitution of 1937 states that if the president is unable to discharge his duties, the prime minister acts in his stead. With this constitutional footing and the recognition that Estonia was under military occupation, Uluots tested the waters with the German authorities in a memorandum on July 29, 1941, in which he called for the establishment of an Estonian army under native leadership as well as an Estonian central government. Both of these institutions, said Uluots, would be willing to work closely with the German authorities. As might be expected, given Nazi ideology and aims, the German response was negative, and all later attempts by Uluots and other Estonian political figures to negotiate more power for a genuine Estonian self-government came to naught. For their part, the

Germans made repeated offers to Uluots to replace Mäe as head of the Estonian administration under German aegis, but Uluots refused to accept such a position in a patently occupation regime.[16]

In reaction to the uncompromising policies of the Nazi regime, an underground Estonian resistance movement developed that reflected the pre-1940 political divisions within the Estonian population. On one side, the parties in opposition during the Päts regime (that is, Socialist Workers, National Center, Homesteaders, and Farmers) formed the nucleus of one wing of the resistance; on the other, Uluots and his supporters represented continuity from the Päts era. In March 1944, as the fate of Estonia once again seemed to hang in the balance, the opposition parties, along with like-minded resistance groups in Tallinn and Tartu, established a central organization called the National Committee of the Estonian Republic. Despite their political differences, the National Committee and the Uluots group fully agreed on the necessity of mobilization for defense and seemed to be on the verge of merger in the spring of 1944. However, in April and May the German security forces arrested some 200 Estonian nationalists and political figures. Although the leaders of the Estonian resistance escaped arrest, their activities remained severely curtailed until June. Finally, in August, representatives of the Uluots group joined the National Committee (which was now able to act publicly as the Germans sought all the help they could get) to give it the broadest possible base, and all efforts were concentrated on trying to avoid a new Soviet occupation. When this proved impossible, Uluots, who elected to go into exile but also attempted to maintain continuity from pre-Soviet Estonia, named a provisional government (headed by Otto Tief) on September 18, 1944. However, nearly all its members fell into Soviet hands by the end of the month.[17]

During World War II the international status of Estonia and the other Baltic states remained moot. As noted above, in view of Nazi aims to eventually annex the entire Baltic region, it was expedient for the Germans to regard Estonia as former Soviet territory, thus implicitly recognizing the legitimacy of Sovietization in 1940–1941. However, except for the ECP, all Estonian political forces agreed that the Soviet annexation was not legitimate, and they demanded the restoration of Estonian independence and the pre-1940 state system. To this end, they sought to avoid a new Soviet takeover at all costs; in particular they based their hopes on the Western Allies, since neither the United States nor Britain had recognized the Soviet incorporation of 1940. Furthermore, the declaration of the Atlantic Charter in August 1941, including the principle of restoration of sovereign rights to peoples deprived of them against their will, offered another basis for optimism. Nevertheless, as David Kirby has clearly shown, the commitment of the Western Allies to Baltic independence was only skin-deep, and their major concern was maintaining the Soviet-Western alliance in the fight against Nazi Germany. Although the United States and Britain were never forced to publicly recognize the Soviet annexation of Estonia, Latvia, and Lithuania in World War II (and to this day they do not do so), they never considered risking good relations with Stalin for the sake of the Baltic states.[18]

ECONOMIC CONDITIONS

Given the nature of the Nazi regime in Estonia as a wartime occupation, there is little doubt that the primary short-term concern of the Germans was economic. Above all, they desired food and other support materials for the German armed forces as well as for the civilian population of Germany itself. One estimate, by Harald Nurk, suggests that the value of the goods imported into Estonia during the German occupation was only 10 percent of the value of those exported. In this situation the standard of living in the Estonian population declined more precipitously than in 1940–1941, partly because Soviet rule had effectively eliminated any reserves in goods or money from the independence era. Food was rationed at low norms, and both wages and prices were kept as low as possible. At the same time the German elite lived very well, and even rank-and-file German personnel received higher remuneration than Estonians for comparable work. In terms of labor policy the Nazi regime proved strikingly similar to the Soviet one. Workers could not freely change jobs, and strikes were forbidden.[19]

As with regard to Estonia's political status, the Germans also found it expedient to accept, in practice, the Soviet economic changes carried out there in 1940–1941. Although the Nazi regime in Estonia paid lip service to the idea of private property, only 12 percent of the land confiscated under the Soviets was actually returned to the former owners by June 1944. Other agricultural land was made available to Estonian farmers, but only on a provisional basis, since the occupying authorities retained proprietary rights in the name of the German state (presumably with a view toward future German colonists). In the industrial and commercial spheres as well, reprivatization proved to be a slow and highly bureaucratic process that only reached fruition in a limited number of cases.[20]

In order to maximize their returns from Estonia, the German authorities organized the state sector and other branches of the economy into monopolistic concerns in the form of limited liability companies. The largest of these concerns was in agriculture and included the land nationalized by the Soviets, lands belonging to local governments, and farms of deported persons. In industry and commerce a host of similar institutions were established. In general, the occupation regime retained a firm grip on economic decisionmaking, and freedom of action in the economic sphere for Estonian concerns or individuals remained sharply restricted.[21]

Both the industrial and agricultural sectors of the economy suffered greatly as Estonia became a battleground in the Soviet-German war, especially with the scorched-earth policy of the retreating Soviets. Among the major industrial branches, textiles declined most significantly; several large factories were either partially or entirely destroyed, and they were not rebuilt under Nazi rule. Yet the militarily important oil-shale and metal industries survived the summer of 1941 relatively intact and were immediately mobilized for the German war effort. Soviet deportations and mobilization as well as later mobilizations under the Nazis contributed to an overall decline in the number of industrial workers (from 89,000 in April 1941 to 26,000 in the summer of 1944). In agriculture the same factors (war, mobilizations, and deportations) reduced the labor force by some 50,000 people. The effects of the war and of Soviet and Nazi economic policies are seen in the decline in livestock holdings. Between July 1939 and December 1943 the number of sheep fell by 63 percent, cows by 43 percent, hogs by 38 percent, and horses by 11 percent (the latter figure represents an increase over September 1941). In addition, by the time of the Nazi withdrawal from Estonia, the amount of cultivated land had been reduced by 40 percent as compared to 1941. Estonian farmers had to fulfill substantial norms for the Nazi regime under difficult conditions—for example, they lacked sufficient machinery and fertilizer.[22]

SOCIAL AND DEMOGRAPHIC CONSEQUENCES

The period of the German occupation brought further substantial population losses to Estonia. Any survey of this question is hampered by the lack of hard data, but some reasonable estimates can be made. Population decline in 1941–1944 can be attributed to three major factors: executions, military casualties, and flight. The Nazi regime appears to have executed about 6,000 people in Estonia, most of them Jews, Communists, or alleged Communist sympathizers. Of the 4,434 Jews listed in the 1934 census, some emigrated before World War II, others were deported by the Soviets in 1940–1941, and still others voluntarily evacuated to Soviet Russia at the start of the Nazi invasion. Nearly all the Jews who remained in Estonia in 1941 (perhaps 1,000–2,000) were executed. The execution of non-Jews in this period appears to have been relatively haphazard, and it gave an opportunity for the remains of the League of Veterans movement (some of whom returned from Germany), with Mäe as head of the indigenous Estonian government, to settle old scores.[23]

Estonian military losses through participation, whether compulsory or voluntary, in the German armed forces in World War II are difficult to gauge. It should be recalled that Estonian troops were not only used in Estonia itself but were also scattered over the eastern front. Estimates of Estonian military casualties while in German uniform during the war range from 15,000 to 25,000. By far the largest population loss to Estonia in this period occurred as a result of flight to the West. The movement to Finland in 1942–1944, mainly by men subject to the German draft (discussed above), involved a total of about 6,000 Estonians. At the same time the overwhelming majority of ethnic Swedes living in Estonia emigrated to Sweden. Although the total number of Estonian citizens resettled in Sweden is listed as 7,920, perhaps some 1,500 ethnic Swedes remained in Estonia; since the 1934 census had noted 7,641 Swedes in Estonia and some losses occurred in 1940–1941, there must have been ethnic Estonians (some 1,000–2,000) among those resettled. Finally, the most significant loss took place in the late summer of 1944 as approximately 70,000 Estonians sought to avoid a new Soviet occupation by fleeing to the West, primarily to Sweden and Germany. It is likely that several thousand people perished in the process, but counting other recent emigrants, there may have been up to 100,000 Estonian citizens as refugees in the West by late 1944.[24] Thus, the overall population loss in Estonia in 1941–1944 was probably over 100,000.

The social hierarchy in Estonia during the German occupation—below the Nazi elite at the top—can perhaps best be deduced from the official wage and salary policies established by the occupying authorities. Besides the nature of the work itself, the three major variables were nationality, sex, and age. As seen above, Germans were always paid better than Estonians for comparable work, and the latter earned more than the so-called *Ostarbeiter* (Slavs, literally "Eastern workers"); for example, on the average the wages of an Estonian worker would be 25–35 percent higher than those of an Ostarbeiter. In addition, women and younger workers were always paid less for equal work. Among Estonians, the major socioeconomic division was between those engaged in mental work and management and those performing physical labor, whether in industry or agriculture. At the top, the occupying elite as well as Germans of lesser station took ample advantage of their privileged position.[25]

CULTURAL LIFE

The German occupation regime adopted a relatively laissez-faire attitude toward Estonian culture as compared to the Soviet position in 1940–1941. Although the Nazis ruled longer during World War II than did the Soviets, the primary German concerns were military and economic, and Nazi ideology, in effect, assumed the rapid Germanization of the small Baltic cultures because of their alleged inferiority. Thus, the German viewpoint was much less systematic than the Soviet one, and the Nazi regime allowed considerably more autonomy to Estonian cultural expression.

The German authorities took little interest in Estonian education at the lower levels, and the pre-Soviet curriculum was essentially restored. At Tartu University in July 1941, before the Germans could develop their own policies, the independence era administrative system and faculty were reinstated by former prime minister Uluots, acting as temporary president of Estonia. However, the German authorities only permitted the university to begin functioning in January 1942 and then only those faculties having military importance. By the fall of 1942 all disciplines previously represented at Tartu were again available for study except theology, which began later following formal separation from the university into an institute. Nevertheless, as early as the fall of 1941 the occupying authorities had been discussing the establishment of an Ostland university with German as the language of instruction and the simultaneous liquidation of Tartu University as an Estonian institution. Widespread Estonian opposition, both at the university and in society at large, and presumably lack of time helped abort this project. In 1944, as the front approached Estonia, the Germans offered to evacuate Tartu University to Königsberg, but the administration refused. However, the faculty was left to choose on an individual basis; fully 45 percent of the 1939 teaching staff fled to the West and only 22 percent remained in Estonia (15 percent had died, 5 percent were deported in 1940–1941, and the fate of 13 percent was unknown).[26]

In contrast to the Soviets, the Germans made no attempt to enforce a particular literary or artistic method on the creators of Estonian culture. However, they also did nothing to encourage Estonian cultural expression, since that culture was slated, in their view, for extinction within the coming decades. The results of this policy in literature, for example, led to a meager publication record in 1941–1944, although the ostensible reason offered by the Nazi authorities was always the shortage of paper. Nevertheless, two outstanding literary works were published in 1942: Karl Ristikivi's novel *Rohtaed* (The garden), which dealt with the life of an unworldly Estonian intellectual during the previous 50 years; and Marie Under's poetry collection *Mureliku suuga* (With sorrowful lips). The latter appeared perhaps because it contained references to the dark sides of Soviet rule, including the deportations, in 1940–1941. In the interior of the USSR the minority of Estonian writers who had joined the Soviet evacuation in 1941 produced highly engaged literature intended to spur on the war effort. As Soviet forces closed in on Estonia in 1944, a majority of Estonian writers (and a large number of artists as well) chose flight to the West over the prospect of life under renewed Soviet rule.[27]

As an instrument of public opinion, Estonian journalism remained severely restricted during the German occupation. Only two national newspapers, in limited numbers, were permitted. In Tallinn the largest newspaper of the independence era, *Päevaleht*, was shut down after a brief appearance, and in December 1941, *Eesti Sõna* (The Estonian word)—which was in effect the organ of the Estonian government under Nazi aegis—began publication. In Tartu, *Postimees*, the leading pre-1940 newspaper in southern Estonia, reappeared in July 1941. Although constantly battling with the German censors, *Postimees* managed to survive and still express a guarded nationalist position. However, a special number on the twenty-fifth anniversary of the declaration of Estonian independence in February 1943, despite the censors' approval, led to a major purge of the editorial staff.[28]

The attitude of the Nazi regime in Estonia toward religion and the churches, if not entirely positive, proved to be less hostile than that of the Soviets in 1940–1941. The training of clergy was again permitted at the new Institute of Theology in Tartu, religion could be taught in the schools, and some religious literature was able to be published. In 1944 Estonian clergymen in large numbers joined the flight to the West. Only 77 of 250 Lutheran pastors remained in Estonia while roughly one-third of the Orthodox priests emigrated.[29]

12 The Stalinist Era, 1944–1953

The most significant turning point during post–World War II Soviet rule in Estonia undoubtedly came with the death of Stalin in March 1953. Politically and economically, his absence began to be felt almost immediately. Nevertheless, it took both the Moscow and the Tallinn leadership several years to assess the situation and decide on a new course of action (Khrushchev's secret speech at the Twentieth CPSU Congress in February 1956 is an example of this delayed assessment). Thus, there was a time lag in moving away from Stalinism, and this was particularly the case regarding cultural affairs. The present chapter will deal with the first decade of Soviet rule in Estonia following reannexation in the fall of 1944. Stalin's death marks a convenient terminal date, but in some instances (for example, economic statistics) it may be appropriate to include material up to the mid-1950s.

The Estonian SSR experienced two territorial changes in early 1945, losing about 5 percent of the area that had belonged to the Estonian republic and thus reducing the size of the ESSR to 45,215 square kilometers. First, about three-fourths of the district of Petserimaa was transferred to the Pskov oblast in the Russian SFSR. Second, all of the territory east of the Narva River became part of the Leningrad oblast of the RSFSR.[1] In the first postwar decade the Estonian SSR also underwent numerous administrative reorganizations. In 1945, at the lowest level of rural administration, village soviets (Est. *külanõukogu*) were established in the existing townships (vald); in the late 1940s three new districts (Jõgevamaa, Jõhvimaa, and Hiiumaa) were added to the ten remaining from the independence era. However, the Soviet authorities in the late Stalinist era considered the districts too large as administrative units, and in October 1950 they were replaced by 39 *raion*s (Est. *rajoon*), following the prevailing Soviet model. At the same time the old townships were abolished, leaving only the village soviets, and the five largest cities in Estonia (Tallinn, Tartu, Kohtla-Järve, Narva, and Pärnu) were placed directly under the ESSR Council of Ministers (formerly the Council of People's Commissars). In May 1952, in a further standardization of the ESSR administration with Soviet practice, three oblasts centered in Tallinn, Tartu, and Pärnu were created. All regions and cities in Estonia retained their traditional names with two exceptions: the raion encompassing Saaremaa and the island's administrative center, Kuressaare, were both renamed Kingissepa (for the Estonian Communist Viktor Kingissepp) in 1952.[2]

THE ESTONIAN COMMUNIST PARTY

In the immediate postwar years the ECP witnessed rapid growth. In 1945 membership nearly tripled—from 2,409 at the start of the year to 7,139 at the end—mainly through the influx of returning veterans from the Estonian Rifle Corps. The rate of growth slowed somewhat in the following years, but by the start of 1953 the ECP ranks totaled 22,320 members. Although complete statistics on the ethnic composition of the ECP are not available, enough is known to provide a broad overview. In 1941 the party had been overwhelmingly Estonian (perhaps 90 percent); by 1946, however, the Estonian share had been reduced to 48.1 percent, and the late Stalinist era witnessed a further decline to 41.5 percent in 1952, presumably reflecting the purge of "bourgeois nationalists" in the early 1950s (discussed below).[3] The high percentage of non-Estonians in the ECP in this period suggests not only Moscow's distrust of ethnic Estonians but also a reluctance by Estonians themselves to take part in the Sovietization of their homeland. These figures also disguise the fact that many of the Estonian party members were so-called Russian-Estonians (that is, ethnic Estonians who had spent the bulk of their lives in the USSR), who generally had a different perspective from local Estonians. In the early postwar years the ECP remained a male stronghold (77 percent in 1951) and an overwhelmingly urban institution; in 1951 only 9.7 percent of party members were kolkhozniks while a majority (52.5 percent) were urban, white-collar workers and the rest (37.8 percent) were manual workers both in the urban areas and on the sovkhozes.[4]

The ECP suffered heavy casualties in World War II, especially in leadership positions; it lost about half of its Central Committee and two-thirds of its Buro. To a large extent the slack at all levels was taken up by veterans of the Estonian Rifle Corps, among whom were a high proportion of party members. In 1947, for example, 96 percent of the district party secretaries and executive committee chairs in the ESSR were Rifle Corps veterans. Although there were some local Estonians among the surviving veterans, it should be recalled that Russian-Estonians and Russians held the leading positions in the corps. In the early postwar years established party members from among both Russians and Estonians were sent to Estonia in order to provide the young Soviet republic with additional experienced cadres. In 1945 alone, 376 high-level party functionaries arrived in Estonia.[5]

The Soviets have never published complete lists of the top ECP figures in the late Stalinist era, and biographical information on known leaders is often scarce. Nevertheless, a general portrait of the party leadership and its ethnic composition can be drawn. Nikolai Karotamm, a local Estonian, became the Central Committee's first secretary in September 1944, replacing Karl Säre, who had fallen into German hands in World War II and was later disowned by the Soviets for providing information to the enemy. Two months later, Sergei Sazonov, a Russian sent to the ESSR, was installed as second secretary. Karotamm retained his position until 1950, and he was joined on the ECP Central Committee Buro by some local Estonians, including Boris Kumm, Johannes Vares (until 1946), and Arnold Veimer (after 1948). However, by at least 1948 a majority of the Buro appears to have consisted of Russian-Estonians and Russians.[6]

The most striking shakeup in the ECP leadership occurred in the purge of "bourgeois nationalists" in 1950–1951, and it also had far-reaching effects throughout party and government ranks and in other walks of life. In February 1950 the CPSU Central Committee made public its views on "mistakes and shortcomings in the work of the ECP Central Committee," and in March the purge began at the Eighth ECP Plenum. The major victim of the purge proved to be Karotamm himself. He was accused of ignoring the principle of collegiality in leadership, not fighting "bourgeois nationalism" with sufficient vigor, and providing mistaken guidance in ideological work. By implication, Stalin and the CPSU leadership may have regarded Karotamm as too much of a nationalist, and recently the argument has been made that Karotamm was fired for trying to soften the blow for uprooted Estonian farmers during collectivization in 1949 by allowing them to remain in Estonia rather than be sent to Siberia.[7] The new ECP first secretary was Ivan (Johannes) Käbin, who was born in Estonia in 1905 but left for Russia as a child and only returned in 1941 following Soviet annexation.

By April 1951, at the Sixth ECP Congress, the purge appears to have been completed. In contrast to the Soviet purges in the 1930s and 1940s and to those taking place at the same time in Eastern Europe, the 1950–1951 housecleaning in Estonia was not as murderous. The leading lights only suffered demotions, although lesser party members were often deported and languished or died in labor camps. In 1951 the new Central Committee Buro showed a turnover of at least 75 percent from the last ECP congress in 1948, and the only known local Estonian in the Buro was the writer August Jakobson, who held the relatively ceremonial position of head of the Presidium of the ESSR Supreme Soviet. Käbin, who was reconfirmed as first secretary at the 1951 congress, denounced the remnants of "bourgeois nationalism" in Estonia and all things associated with the independence era, and he praised the unselfish aid of the Russian people. In the early 1950s Vasilii Kosov, a Russian, replaced Sazonov as second secretary. In the Buro and the Secretariat, the two top organs in the party, Russian-Estonians and Russians now completely dominated, reflecting Stalin's distrust of anyone, including Communists, who lacked Soviet training. It is noteworthy that post-Stalin Soviet publications admit that errors were made in carrying out the decisions of the March 1950 plenum, including the exclusion of a number of "honest Communists" from the party.[8]

The 1950–1951 purge in Estonia might be interpreted as Moscow's reaction to too great a show of autonomy by the ECP leadership. However, in the Stalinist era the term "autonomy" would be a misnomer. The ECP second secretary throughout the postwar Stalinist years was always a Russian sent in by the central leadership, and in Moscow an Estonian Bureau, also headed by a Russian, was established at the CPSU Central Committee in November 1944 to provide "practical aid." Even beyond the Moscow-oriented bias of Stalinism, after October 1940 the ECP was not in any sense an independent institution but merely a territorial division of the CPSU. Thus, any party members transferred to Estonia automatically became ECP members as well.[9] Although Lenin may have organized the governmental structure of the Soviet Union on a federal basis and granted formal autonomy to the constituent parts, Leninism also demanded undiluted centralism in the party, and Stalinism was built on this foundation.

THE GOVERNMENTAL SYSTEM

In the fall of 1944, following the collapse of the Nazi position in Estonia, the Council of People's Commissars was reconstituted with the native Estonian Communist Arnold Veimer as its head. Among the four deputy chairs and fifteen people's commissars were a number of members from 1940–1941, and the great majority were native Estonians, including several who had joined the party only in 1940 (for example, Hans Kruus, Nigol Andresen, Aleksander Jõeäär, and Viktor Hion). In March 1946, in accordance with the change at the all-Union level, the people's commissariats were renamed ministries, and the Council of People's Commissars became the Council of Ministers. In the late Stalinist era several new ministries were created for certain industrial sectors.[10]

Among government organs in the Stalinist years, the People's Commissariat for Internal Affairs (NKVD in Russian; MGB since 1946) occupied a special position. As elsewhere in the recently annexed western border areas of the Soviet Union and later in the satellite states of Eastern Europe, the NKVD-MGB in Estonia was charged with establishing the security of the new regime. Although the native Estonian Boris Kumm headed the security forces in 1944–1950, his deputy and much of his staff were Russian. The NKVD was extremely active in Estonia in the first year following the German withdrawal; it screened all residents twelve years of age and older. All those who were considered political opponents were subject to deportation, especially anyone who had served in the German army, in the German-sponsored Home Guard, or any remaining prominent individuals from the independence era. The deportations in the early postwar years (estimates are discussed below) were greater in number than those in 1940–1941, and they set the tone for the fearful atmosphere that pervaded the Stalinist era. If anything, the creation of a separate Ministry for State Security (MGB) in 1946 further strengthened the position of Soviet security forces in Estonia.[11]

In theory, the Supreme Soviet constituted the most important state organ in the ESSR; in practice, it merely executed decisions made by the party or the Council of People's Commissars (Ministers). The ECP Central Committee drew up the list of names for the single-candidate elections, and the Supreme Soviet met only once or twice a year for two or three days at a time. In 1944–1946 the chair of the Presidium of the ESSR Supreme Soviet was Johannes Vares, who had held this post in 1940–1941 after heading the "people's government" of the summer of 1940. In November 1946 Vares died suddenly. It appears that he either committed suicide or was killed by the MGB. He was replaced by Eduard Päll, a Russian-Estonian.[12]

As noted above, the purge of 1950–1951 was not limited to the ranks of the party but also included the leading government figures in the ESSR. In the Council of Ministers the majority of the victims were newcomers to the party, but even long-term, native Estonian Communists such as Veimer and Kumm did not escape dismissal. Indeed, a clean sweep was made of all native Estonians in top government positions. In 1951 Aleksei Müürisepp (1902–1970), a Russian-Estonian, replaced Veimer as chair of the Council of Ministers, and among the 26 members of this body in 1952, seventeen were Russian-Estonians and nine were Russians. Not a single native Estonian Communist remained. One reversal of this pattern took place with the replacement of the Russian-Estonian Päll by the local Estonian August Jakobson as head of the Supreme Soviet Presidium in 1950. However, Päll had publicly defended the Young-Estonia literary movement of the early twentieth century (a patently "bourgeois nationalist" sin), and it should be recalled that his position was a relatively unimportant one in the power structure. The fate of those purged varied greatly.

Some were transferred to lesser positions (for example, Veimer, Päll, and Kumm) while others were sentenced to hard labor (for example, Andresen and Jõeäär).[13]

THE PRO-INDEPENDENCE GUERRILLA MOVEMENT

A striking feature of the postwar Stalinist era in Estonia was the protracted existence of an anti-Soviet guerrilla movement. This phenomenon began to emerge with the rapid Nazi retreat, which stranded thousands of Estonian soldiers who had been drafted into the German army in Estonia. Although some of these men still managed to leave Estonia, many disappeared into the woods and became "forest brethren" (*metsavennad*, the popular Estonian term for the guerrillas).[14] Their numbers were supplemented in the fall of 1944 by other German army veterans and members of the Home Guard seeking to avoid arrest by Soviet security forces. The Soviet authorities carried out two mobilizations in the fall of 1944 and spring of 1945, and this action prompted still others to join the guerrillas or go underground. In addition, those seeking revenge against the Soviet regime for the mass deportations associated with collectivization in March 1949 formed a final source of replenishment for the guerrillas.[15]

Documentation on the guerrilla movement remains sparse, but reports by eyewitnesses permit an overall assessment. The organization of the forest brethren varied, ranging from relatively large military units to individuals operating alone. Arms and ammunition abandoned by the retreating Germans outfitted the Estonian guerrillas in the early postwar years, and subsequent Soviet military supplies became available as the spoils of battle. Food and other basic necessities, along with strategic information, came from the surrounding local population. Regionally, the guerrillas were strongest in Virumaa, Pärnumaa, and Võrumaa, among the most swampy and thickly wooded areas of Estonia. The size of the guerrilla forces is difficult to determine, but one estimate suggests that there were about 5,000 forest brethren in 1944–1946 with 80 percent located in the three above-mentioned districts. In some localities in the early postwar years the guerrillas had effective military control. The high point of guerrilla strength probably came in 1946–1948, when they were capable of fighting substantial military engagements with Soviet forces. Gradually, however, casualties and psychological attrition thinned their ranks. By the early 1950s, despite new blood as a result of the collectivization drive, guerrilla strength had begun to ebb. A post-Stalin amnesty, carried out as promised in 1955, virtually ended the movement.[16]

The goals of the forest brethren must be seen in the context of an expected postwar restoration of Estonian independence through the good offices of the Western Allies. Thus, although the guerrillas realized that they had no hope of bringing down the Soviet regime, they intended to hold out until international pressure (or perhaps a new war) forced the Soviets to withdraw from Estonia. In addition to guarding themselves, the guerrillas sought to protect the local population from acts of violence. By the time of mass collectivization in 1949, the dream of restored independence had vanished, and the major guerrilla motivation became revenge against the Soviet regime. For those slated for deportation, joining the forest brethren was the only other choice.[17]

INDUSTRIAL RECOVERY
AND GROWTH

As a result of once again becoming a battleground in 1944, Estonia suffered extensive destruction to its cities and industry. By the end of the war, for example, 97 percent of the buildings in Narva and nearly half of those in Tallinn and Tartu had been destroyed. The wartime devastation resulted in an overall decline of 45 percent in industrial productive capacity as compared to 1941, and industrial branches such as fuel, textiles, paper, cellulose, and lumber suffered losses of 60–90 percent. As noted above, the Germans only partially rebuilt Estonian industry following the Soviet scorched-earth policy in 1941, and the Nazis carried out their own strategic destruction—especially in the oil-shale industry—during the retreat in 1944. Furthermore, substantial losses occurred during Soviet bombardments in the last several months of German rule in Estonia.[18]

Given this situation, the top priority in the industrial sector in the immediate postwar years was reconstruction, especially in the strategically important oil-shale industry, which was already restored by 1946. The Soviet authorities assigned substantial numbers of German prisoners of war to help in the rebuilding of Estonian industry and restore certain key structures such as the main railroad station and the Estonia Theater in Tallinn. The republic also received a portion of the dismantled German industrial sector brought to the Soviet Union in the postwar years. Estonia became fully integrated into the highly centralized Stalinist economic system, and its major role in the Soviet Union's Fourth Five-Year Plan was to develop its vast oil-shale resources into a major supplier of the energy needs of the northwestern USSR. By 1948, for example, a gas pipeline linking Leningrad to Kohtla-Järve in the Estonian oil-shale region had been put into operation.[19]

Primarily because of the large-scale capital investment in the oil-shale industry, Estonia achieved high industrial growth rates in the first postwar decade: 36 percent per year on the average in 1946–1950 and 14.4 percent annually in 1951–1955, according to Soviet statistics. Indeed, in 1950 Estonia showed the highest industrial growth rate of all Soviet republics in comparison to the 1940 level: 342 percent or nearly twice the overall Soviet average. However, using 1940 as a base year is misleading, since the Soviets at times only include that portion of the year (less than half) when Estonia was under Soviet rule. In 1946–1953 the greatest increases in Estonian industrial output came in the first three years, when recovery was still the major task.[20]

In the postwar era, in part as a continuation of trends begun during wartime, the major divisions of Estonian industry underwent important changes in comparison to the situation in the last years of the Estonian republic. Although the oil-shale and chemical industries expanded rapidly in the late 1930s, the major emphasis remained on light industry, especially textiles and foodstuffs. By 1950, in contrast, a significant shift toward heavy industrial production had taken place. In that year the top branches of Estonian industry, according to their share of investment capital, were the following: fuel and chemical industry (29.7 percent); machines and metallurgy (16.8 percent); light industry, presumably including textiles (15.5 percent); foodstuffs (13.4 percent); and lumber, paper, and pulp (9.6 percent).[21] Once again, these changes reflected the top priority assigned to the development of the oil-shale industry.

Given the considerable population losses Estonia suffered in World War II and the arrests and deportations of the late Stalinist era, it would have been difficult to provide all the human resources for industrial expansion from among local labor. In any case, the pace of industrialization was such that the Soviet authorities recruited workers from the RSFSR for Estonian industry in, for example, the oil-shale region and the large factories in Narva. From the wartime low of 26,000 industrial workers at the end of the German occupation, the number in Estonia more than tripled to 80,800 by 1950.[22] Although no figures are available on the ethnic composition of this labor force, there can be no doubt that non-Estonians constituted a substantial minority.

COLLECTIVIZATION OF AGRICULTURE

The Stalinist era in Estonian agriculture was dominated by first the specter and then the reality of collectivization. As in other spheres of activity, Stalin's rural policies in his later years could offer nothing more than a repetition of the wrenching Soviet experience of the 1930s. However, it is noteworthy that mass collectivization was not begun until some four and a half years after the reestablishment of Soviet rule in Estonia. The new regime moved circumspectly for several reasons. Most important, Estonia and the other newly acquired western regions had not been thoroughly Sovietized before they were lost to the

USSR in 1941. Thus, a certain period of stabilization, especially after three years of Nazi rule, was necessary. Furthermore, the Soviets lacked both cadres and grassroots support in the rural areas, and for all the sociopolitical benefits of collectivization from the regime's point of view, the likely economic conse-quences—such as a disrupted food supply—could not be taken lightly.[23]

In the first three postwar years (September 1944–June 1947), the Soviets implemented a new, more extensive land reform as compared to that of 1940–1941. The regime expropriated all land belonging to persons who had fled Estonia and all otherwise abandoned farms, all land allotted to German colonists under Nazi rule, all land that had been administered by the German occupying authorities, and most of the land belonging to those termed Nazi collaborators. As in 1940–1941, no farm could be larger than 30 hectares, but in addition in 1944–1947, livestock, movable property, and farm buildings belonging to Nazi collaborators or kulaks were subject to expropriation. As a result of these actions the state acquired a new land reserve of 927,047 hectares (25 percent larger than that established in 1940–1941). Two-thirds of this land—and much of the confiscated property—was divided among the landless (with preference for Red Army veterans and their families), those with tiny farms, sovkhozes, Machine Tractor Stations (MTS), Horse and Machinery Lending Stations (HMLS), and other institutions. The remaining third stayed in the state land reserve. Although all farms over 30 hectares were once again eliminated, the share of minifarms (those under 10 hectares) was now 26.5 percent (as compared to 21.4 percent in 1940–1941), and the average farm size was also smaller.[24] In fact, however, the postwar land reform was never intended as anything more than a transition stage on the road to large-scale farming and collectivization.

Compared with what was to follow, 1944–1947 was a relatively benign period in the Estonian countryside. The state quotas for agricultural products did not usually rise above 20 percent of the farm's output, and although farmers had to perform periodic services, such as hauling, road repair, and forest work, the demands did not prove overly burdensome. As in 1940–1941, certain groups received preferential treatment. The new farmers were freed from any agricultural taxes during 1944–1945 and were also eligible for favorable state loans. At the same time the state re-established the various collective enterprises begun in 1940–1941. By June 1947 there were 25 MTS and 232 HMLS, and the number of sovkhozes had risen to 96.[25] In general, the early postwar years witnessed definite improvements in the total amount of land under cultivation and in livestock holdings, but the latter still fell far short of the July 1939 level. In 1947 the number of livestock in Estonia as compared to 1939 was as fol-lows: horses, 84 percent; cattle, 62 percent; hogs, 55 percent; and sheep, 38 percent.[26]

In order to keep the Estonian situation in perspective it should be noted that all the western border regions acquired by the USSR in World War II experienced the process of collectivization more or less simultaneously at the end of the 1940s and the beginning of the 1950s. Furthermore, they all underwent a similar preparatory period. In the case of the Baltic republics the decisive point came in May 1947, when the Moscow Politburo called on the Baltic party organizations to begin the movement toward collectivization.[27] Although the first postwar kolkhoz in Estonia was established in September 1947, collectivization proceeded slowly for the next eighteen months. In October 1948 there were 195 kolkhozes, but they were small concerns and only included 2.2 percent of all Estonian farms. As late as March 20, 1949, only 8.2 percent of the farms had been collectivized. A demand for centralized control, including approval of applications by the ECP Central Committee, and a preference for initiative from among the poor peasantry worked against any rapid development during this eighteen-month period. At the same time Soviet taxation policy prepared the way for mass collectivization. A tax on kulak farms, established at about 40 percent of the expected farm income in the latter part of 1947, rose to 75 percent in 1948. In 1944–1948 taxes on non-kulak farms rose about 50 percent, suggesting to middle and poor peasants that they too could not expect to maintain an independent existence.[28]

As in the USSR collectivization drive in the early 1930s, the kulaks in Estonia were singled out as the root problem in the countryside. By January 1948 kulaks—along with alleged Nazi collaborators and the families of pro-independence guerrillas—were barred from joining kolkhozes.[29] The Soviet Estonian leadership resurrected the Stalinist slogan, "liquidation of the kulaks as a class," and a recent estimate suggests that at least 1,200 families were deported as kulaks in 1947–1948. Furthermore, as was the case in the Soviet Union two decades earlier, the term "kulak" lacked any clear or objective definition; it was thus especially potent as a political weapon.[30]

Nevertheless, anti-kulak propaganda, deportation of individual families, and the promotion of collectivization on a voluntary basis did not bring the desired results. Presumably responding to pressure from Moscow, ECP first secretary Karotamm wrote to Stalin in January 1949 that collectivization would require two to three years and that, by the end of 1949, 25–30 percent of the farms could be collectivized. He also called for the simultaneous deportation of kulak families and those of Nazi collaborators from all three Baltic republics before the spring sowing.[31] Beginning in March 1949, however, it seems that Karotamm received more than he bargained for. The tempo of collectivization in Estonia proved to be much faster than Karotamm had suggested, and the number of deportees appears to have been considerably larger than the 4 percent of farm households he mentioned to Stalin. Within a year Karotamm was removed as first secretary, and although the causal connections remain ambiguous, it seems likely that a major factor in his fall could have been his insufficient realization of Stalinist policies in agriculture.[32]

Beginning on March 20, 1949, the pace of collectivization suddenly became staggering. In the next month fully 56 percent of all Estonian farms were collectivized—20 percent in five days alone (April 5–9). The following figures provide an overview of the speed of collectivization in Estonia:[33]

	Percentage of farms collectivized	Number of kolkhozes	Average number of households per kolkhoz
1949: March 20	8.2	641	17.2
April 5	28	1,534	23.6
April 9	48	2,079	26.7
April 20	63.8	2,753	29.9
May 25	71.1	2,904	31.6
October 1	78	3,003	33.8
1950: January 1	80	—	—
1951: January 1	91.6	2,213	53.6
1952: July 1	97.1	—	—

After the feverish spring of 1949 the pace again slowed, and collectivization gradually reached virtual completion by the end of the Stalinist era.

The sudden upsurge in late March–early April 1949 had one obvious cause: mass deportations during the week following March 23, and the fear of being included among them, began a stampede to join the kolkhozes. No reliable figures are available on the number of deportees. The Soviets have never published comprehensive data on this question, although an occasional Soviet source does suggest that mistakes were made in the deportation and that some persons did not warrant repression.[34] Estimates by Western observers since 1960, based on eyewitness reports and circumstantial evidence, have ranged from 30,000 to 80,000 deportees, and the trend has been upward in recent years. Parming and Järvesoo (1978) suggest a figure of 80,000, and although Taagepera (1980) agrees that this was probably the target number, he argues that perhaps 20,000–30,000 were able to hide or otherwise escape, leaving the total number deported at 50,000–60,000. In any case it appears that 8–12 percent of the rural Estonian population was deported at the end of March 1949.[35] There is little documentation on the fate of the deportees. Death rates for men, who were mainly sent to labor camps in various parts of the USSR, were probably quite high. Women and children usually ended up in Siberia and led a hand-to-mouth existence on desolate kolkhozes.[36]

Although the average number of households per kolkhoz increased with the growing number of collective farms, by early 1950 the Soviet authorities decided that larger units would be more productive and began an all-Union campaign to consolidate the existing small kolkhozes. In Estonia the results were immediately felt. From a peak of over 3,000 at the beginning of 1950, the number of collective farms declined rapidly to 1,137 by the end of 1951 and further to 1,018 by the end of 1952. At the latter date they were divided into 934 agricultural kolkhozes and 84 fishing kolkhozes. With this consolidation the number of households per kolkhoz grew considerably. In the first three months of 1951 the average number doubled (53.6 to 107), and the increase continued in the last years of the Stalinist era.[37]

As in the Soviet Union two decades earlier, the kolkhoz in Estonia became the basic unit of collectivized agriculture. In 1950 the kolkhozes controlled 75 percent of the cultivated land, and by 1955 the figure had risen to 83 percent. Nevertheless, Soviet theory, which is based on the Marxist ideal of the elimination of the differences between town and country, has always noted the superiority of the sovkhoz (run on the analogy of an urban factory) to the kolkhoz (a rural cooperative). Thus, in the Soviet view the kolkhoz is a transition stage between individual farming and the sovkhoz. During the Stalinist era in Estonia the major function of the sovkhozes appears to have been to serve as a model for future development. Although the state farms organized in 1940–1941 were destroyed in World War II, the Soviets created 58 new ones in the fall of 1944, and this figure gradually grew to 130 by the end of 1951, when the consolidation movement began reducing their numbers (115 in 1952). Overall, the sovkhoz share in Estonian agriculture in the first postwar decade remained modest. In 1950 only 4 percent of all cultivated land was in the hands of the sovkhozes, which employed just 12,500 workers as compared to 143,200 on the kolkhozes. The only remaining concession to individual farming was the private garden plots (up to about 0.5 hectare) allotted to kolkhozniks, state farm workers, and some others. In 1950 these individuals still disposed of 18 percent of the cultivated land, but by 1955 their share had declined to 8 percent.[38]

Collectivization in Estonia had serious consequences for agricultural output. For 1946–1950 Soviet statistics indicate an average annual growth rate of 10 percent in agriculture (this may mask higher rates before collectivization and lower ones for 1949–1950); for 1951–1955 output declined by 1.85 percent per year, which meant an overall reduction in farm production of about 10 percent in the first half of the 1950s. In this period crop productivity on all types of agricultural concerns declined as follows, compared to 1946–1950: grain, 32 percent; potatoes, 25 percent; and vegetables, 25 percent. Low state requisition prices for kolkhoz produce no doubt contributed to sluggishness in the agricultural sector. Indeed, for the products in which Estonia specialized— grain, potatoes, vegetables, milk, meat, and eggs—the state prices were considerably lower than production costs. With regard to livestock and poultry holdings, the situation remained fairly stable. For example, in 1951–1955 the number of cattle and hogs declined by 6 and 7 percent, respectively, and the number of poultry grew by 11 percent. There appears to have been no widespread slaughter of livestock in Estonia by farmers entering the kolkhozes, as had been the case in the USSR twenty years earlier.[39]

DEMOGRAPHIC AND SOCIAL CHANGE

The demographic consequences of Stalinism in peacetime proved even more devastating to the population of Estonia than the upheavals of World War II. An assessment of the population changes in 1944–1953 is especially difficult since the Soviets have maintained virtual silence on the period 1944–1950 (and on ethnic composition to 1959). Nevertheless, it is possible to interpolate on the basis of post–1950 Soviet data and on information provided by emigrants and other sources.

An analysis of demographic developments in this period is further complicated by the transfer of about 5 percent of the territory of the Estonian S.S.R. to the RSFSR in January 1945. Parming suggests that about 71,500 people lived in the areas lost by the ESSR. The following data provide an estimate of the overall population changes in Estonia in 1939–1953 (in each case at the beginning of the year):[40]

1939 (pre-1945 borders)	1,134,000
1940 (post-1945 borders)	1,054,000
1945	830,000–854,000
1950	1,096,700
1953	1,141,300

The major unknown demographic factor during World War II is the extent of the military and civilian casualties among residents of Estonia. In any case, between 1940 and 1945 the population appears to have declined by a minimum of 200,000. In the postwar years new deportations took place. A considerable number of Estonian men, including veterans of the German army and members of the Home Guard, were deported in 1945–1946. Purre places their number at 41,000. As noted above, perhaps 50,000–80,000 people were involved in the deportations associated with collectivization in March 1949. Finally, the number of "bourgeois nationalists" banished in 1950–1951 may have reached 3,000.[41]

Given all the population losses during the 1940s, the official Soviet figure cited above for 1950 is strikingly high. The only plausible explanation is that massive immigration occurred in the second half of the 1940s. Although the Soviets have still not published any figures on this period, a recent article does point out that "many people" arrived in Estonia in these years from the Pskov and Leningrad oblasts and from parts of Belorussia.[42] Parming estimates that about 180,000 non-Estonians immigrated in the second half of the 1940s, but the figure may have been higher still if the estimates for losses in the 1940s are close to accurate. A further complicating factor in the early postwar immigration was the influx of significant numbers of Russian-Estonians, certainly involving tens of thousands of people. By the early 1950s, for which data are available, the rate of immigration had dropped markedly; the net number of immigrants in 1950–1953 was 32,600. It is also noteworthy that 1945–1949 witnessed one of the highest birth rates (20.6 per 1,000 inhabitants) in Estonia in the twentieth century. In 1950–1953 the average birth rate was 18.3.[43]

Hard data on the ethnic composition of the population of Estonia in 1944–1953 are simply not available. The task of estimation is made all the more difficult by the fact that as large numbers of Estonians were deported eastward out of Estonia, many Russian-Estonians from the interior of the Soviet Union were moving westward into Estonia. A recent assessment of the native share of the population in Estonia is as follows (in each case at the beginning of the year):[44]

	Number of Estonians (in thousands)	Percentage of total population
1939 (pre-1945 borders)	1,000.1	88.2
1939 (post-1945 borders)	982 ± 5	92
1945	800 ± 25	94 ± 2
1950	845	76 ± 2

Since the population lost in the transfer of the eastern border regions to the RSFSR in early 1945 was heavily Russian (perhaps 75 percent), the ethnic Estonian share increased to over 90 percent despite the wartime losses.[45] However, following the massive influx of non-Estonians in 1945–1950, the native share dropped precipitously, and the decline continued in the early 1950s.

Indeed, the decline was so sharp in the Stalinist years that it has often been asked whether Moscow was following a purposeful long-range Russification policy. Without access to Soviet archives no definitive answer to this question can be given. On the one hand, phenomena such as mass deportations after World War II from all the western border areas newly acquired by the USSR do suggest a centralized policy of denationalization. On the other hand, it could also be that Moscow's primary aim was economic. Rapid industrial expansion in the Baltic demanded a sharp increase in the labor force. In Estonia and Latvia, where native reserves were inadequate to meet the needs, large numbers of non-natives were brought in; in Lithuania local resources were more sufficient, and the native share of the population declined much less under Stalin. Nevertheless, it should be recalled that Stalin cared little about the survival of small nationalities (except perhaps the Georgians), and the immediate postwar era witnessed the height of the "elder brother" concept in Soviet nationality policy.[46]

The postwar industrial expansion in Estonia resulted in highly rapid urbanization. The following figures indicate the Soviet estimates for the urban population in 1940–1953 (in each case on January 1 and applying to the post–1945 borders):[47]

1940	33.6%
1945	31.3%
1950	47.1%
1953	52.5%

Thus, in the second half of the 1940s urbanization grew by an astonishing annual average of 3.2 percentage points, and although the pace slowed in the early 1950s, the rate remained relatively high. On an all-Union basis Estonia ranked first in increase in urbanization between 1939 and 1959.[48] The great influx of non-Estonian immigrants noted above constituted the major basis for this growth. In addition, new cities were established, most notably Kohtla-Järve in 1946 in the oil-shale region, and older ones expanded their territory. The process of migration from rural to urban areas within Estonia itself continued despite the depopulation of the countryside through deportations.[49] It may also have been enhanced by rural Estonians who feared being labeled kulaks.

Few statistics are available on the growth of individual cities in this period, but Soviet estimates on the demographic expansion of Tallinn provide a striking example. In 1944–1955 the population of Estonia's capital city increased as follows:[50]

1944	133,700
1946	167,900
1950	212,400
1955	260,800

In just over a decade the population of Tallinn nearly doubled, and as with the overall urbanization rate, the pace was most rapid in the immediate postwar years. Tartu also grew rapidly in the late 1940s but then showed a slight decline in 1949–1951, which probably reflected the deportations of those years.[51] No published data are available on the ethnic composition of Estonia's cities, but there can be no doubt that the Stalinist era witnessed a drastic drop in the Estonian share from the 86 percent level that prevailed in 1934 and that had probably risen higher by 1944.

Stalinism in Estonia between 1944 and 1953 had far-reaching social consequences. In contrast to 1940–1941, the process of Sovietization was carried to completion in the first postwar decade, and socialism was officially declared to have been reached in January 1953 on the eve of Stalin's death. The growing number of ECP members formed the elite of society, and they were supported by a technical, professional, and artistic intelligentsia that embraced Soviet aims. The party also developed mass social organizations such as the Young Communist League (whose membership jumped from 11,788 in May 1946 to 60,391 in December 1952) in order to mobilize society for Soviet development.[52] The urban and heavy industrial bias of Stalinism meant that manual workers in this economic sector probably fared best of the rank-and-file members of society. The countryside was assigned the lowest position in the Stalinist hierarchy and witnessed the most sweeping social change in this era. Not only were the wealthier farmers physically removed from Estonia but the remaining agricultural population was also subjected to a thorough social leveling. The small minority of sovkhoz workers formed a new rural elite.

Overall, the average Soviet Estonian consumer cannot have fared well under the Stalinist preference for investment over consumption. Although Soviet statistics show an increase in the average monthly wage from 410 to 680 rubles in 1945–1953, it appears that food and other consumer goods, which were rationed until December 1947, were in short supply in the early postwar era, and the collectivization of agriculture further complicated the situation. It is also clear that a serious urban housing shortage ensued because of wartime destruction, rapid urbanization, and the low priority assigned to new construction.[53] A recent Western estimate based on Soviet data suggests that urban per capita living space in Estonia fell from 15.5 square meters in 1940 to 12 in 1945, 9.3 in 1950, and 8.8 in 1955.[54]

CULTURAL LIFE

In the fall of 1944 the Soviet educational system was reintroduced in Estonia. Perhaps the major task was reconstruction, since up to 25 percent of the school buildings had been destroyed or severely damaged during the war. In addition, the number of qualified teachers had been significantly reduced by wartime losses and emigration; in 1944–1945 over one-third of the working teachers in Estonia lacked certification. The rapid population increase in the second half of the 1940s placed added pressure on the schools. The number of students in elementary and secondary schools increased by 36 percent in 1944–1947 (from 108,000 to 147,200), but for the next eight years the level stabilized (149,300 in 1955), which reflected both the wartime decline in birth rates and the mass deportation in 1949. During the Stalinist era the first seven years of school were free and compulsory; for secondary and higher education tuition was charged.[55]

In higher education significant changes transpired in the first postwar decade. As noted above, only a minority of the previous faculty at Tartu University remained in Estonia after the Soviet reconquest in the fall of 1944, and a number of these instructors were considered unreliable by the Soviet regime. In general, the importance of Tartu University in Estonian scholarship declined markedly in this period. The most significant blow came in 1946 when, following the Soviet model, a new Estonian Academy of Sciences was established as the major center for research in the ESSR. Hans Kruus served as the first president until 1950, when he was replaced by the biologist Johan Eichfeld, a Russian-Estonian. In addition, the Estonian Agricultural Academy in Tartu (founded 1951) and the Tallinn Pedagogical Institute (founded 1952) took over the primary training of specialists in these areas from Tartu University. The other institutions of higher learning were the previously established Tallinn Polytechnical Institute (the name for the Tallinn Technical University since 1941) and the Tallinn State Conservatory; in 1950 the ESSR State Art Institute in Tallinn amalgamated the State Art Institute and the State Industrial Art Institute, themselves continuations of analogous institutions from the independence era and World War II.[56] The total number of students in higher education grew rapidly in the latter half of the 1940s (from 3,771 in 1945–1946 to 8,896 in 1950–1951). With the rate of increase slackening markedly in the first half of the 1950s, the total reached 12,085 in 1955–1956.[57]

Publication of books and brochures in Estonian underwent considerable expansion in the early postwar years, but the late Stalinist era witnessed a slight decline. The annual output of titles in Estonian nearly doubled in 1945–1949 (from 469 to 900) but fell to 747 by 1953. By way of comparison, it can be noted that the Stalinist era peak of 900 titles in 1949 had been surpassed in 1924, during the independence period. Overall, the share of Estonian titles in the total ESSR production in the early postwar period varied between 80 and 88 percent. In terms of printed pages there was a high degree of fluctuation. Estonian dominated with 94 percent in 1948, but its share fell to only 55 percent by 1950 (the Russian portion rose thirteen times in these two years) before climbing back to 81 percent in 1952. The circulation of newspapers in Estonia during the Stalinist years remained fairly stable within a range of 372,000 (1945) to 457,000 (1947). In contrast, the number of newspaper titles suddenly jumped from 34 in 1950 to 121 in 1951 as a result of a sharp increase in local administrative organs. In 1950, 76 percent of the newspapers and 86 percent of the magazines published in the ESSR were in Estonian.[58] The largest daily newspapers were *Rahva Hääl* (The people's voice) in Estonian and *Sovetskaia Estoniia* (Soviet Estonia) in Russian.

One of the darkest sides of Stalinism was its impact on cultural output. Although official guidelines were not yet categorical in the early postwar years, the range of cultural expression narrowed dramatically in the late Stalinist era on the heels of the *Zhdanovshchina* (1946–1948) in Russian culture (that is, the extreme enforcement of socialist-realist norms in literature and the arts).[59] Not only did those in the Estonian creative intelligentsia have to eschew "formalism" and strive for ideological purity, but as members of a non-Russian nationality they also had to avoid the sins of "bourgeois nationalism." The bleakest period in Estonian culture under Stalin came in 1948–1953, and the thaw did not begin until the mid-1950s.

Perhaps more starkly than other aspects of Estonian culture, literature in the first postwar decade reflected the distorting influences of Stalinism. Both quantitatively and qualitatively Estonian belles lettres reached a nadir in these years, certainly in comparison to the rest of the twentieth century and perhaps much of the latter part of the nineteenth century as well. It is noteworthy that post-Stalin Soviet works decry the constricting effects of the "cult of personality," and there is even some acknowledgment of a "historical gap" in Estonian culture in the late Stalinist era.[60] Several factors restricted literary output in this period, especially between 1948 and 1955. The stringent ideological guidelines enunciated in 1948 forbade the publication of some works and discouraged the writing of others. In addition to the loss of at least half of the recognized Estonian writers through emigration in 1944, a number of leading authors remaining in Estonia who had established their reputations during the independence era—including Johannes Semper, Friedebert Tuglas, Mait Metsanurk, Nigol Andresen, Betti Alver, Paul Viiding, August Sang, and Kersti Merilaas— were expelled from the Union of Writers and thus lost all opportunity to publish. Two other important writers, Heiti Talvik and Hugo Raudsepp, were arrested and died in prison. One of the major qualifications for publication was simply party membership. For example, in the postwar years up to 1955, the only new poetry collections published were those written by ECP members.[61]

The belles lettres actually published in Estonia during the Stalinist era had an ephemeral quality. In poetry the required didacticism tended to rob the writing of aesthetic quality. It is characteristic that a sharp drop occurred in the number of collections of new verse published in the early 1950s (ten in 1951– 1955 as compared to 29 in 1945–1950). In prose the number of published works was minimal. By far the best proved to be the first volume of Aadu Hint's *Tuuline rand* (The windy coast; 1951), a novel about life on the island of

Saaremaa during the Revolution of 1905. It is also typical of this period that the Russian-Estonian Hans Leberecht's *Valgus Koordis* (The light at Koordi; 1948– 1949), a novel about collectivization written in Russian and then translated into Estonian, received the highest official accolades, and it is striking that it was considered a piece of Estonian literature at all. In drama the work most acclaimed by Soviet critics was August Jakobson's *Elu tsitadellis* (Life in a citadel; 1946), a play about the transformation of a bourgeois professor's consciousness at the time of the Soviet reconquest in the fall of 1944.[62] It is noteworthy that throughout the Stalinist era—and somewhat beyond—Estonian writers in exile in the West, supported by a population of no more than 100,000, produced more and better belletristic literature than their counterparts in Estonia itself. It is also characteristic of this period that in 1950–1954 Russian literature dominated over Estonian in numbers of titles (45 percent vs. 38 percent) and copies (51 percent vs. 32 percent) published in the ESSR.[63]

Estonian theater suffered heavy losses during World War II. All the major theater buildings in Estonia were destroyed, and a substantial portion of the professional staff had emigrated. In the early postwar years, along with the reintroduction of Soviet norms, considerable reorganization took place in theatrical life. By the late 1940s three major institutions had emerged: the Tallinn State Drama Theater; the Estonia Theater in Tallinn, now concentrating solely on musical performances; and the Vanemuine Theater in Tartu, whose activities combined both drama and music. At first, Soviet Russian or Soviet Estonian works dominated the theatrical repertoire; by the early 1950s older Estonian drama had been added. The purge of "bourgeois nationalists" also extended to the theater; the three leading directors in Estonia (Ants Lauter, Priit Põldroos, and Kaarel Ird) all lost their positions at the beginning of the 1950s.[64]

In the figurative arts and music, creative activity was organized under the auspices of the official Union of Artists and Union of Composers. In both cases those artists and composers who had spent World War II in the Soviet interior and then returned to Estonia in 1944 played the leading roles in the first postwar decade. The major themes in art and music included World War II (the "Great Patriotic War"), the building of socialism, and historical motifs, especially those depicting revolutionary struggle. Nevertheless, the Stalinist authorities discovered "formalism" and "bourgeois nationalism" in the artistic and musical fields as well, which resulted in the dismissal of some artists and composers. As in Soviet music in general in the late Stalinist era, Estonian composers were encouraged to develop music that both involved and reached the masses of the people. For example, the operas *Tasuleegid* (The flames of vengeance; 1945) by Eugen Kapp and *Tormide rand* (The stormy coast; 1949) by Gustav Ernesaks depict the historical struggles of the Estonian people.[65]

The Estonian song festival tradition fit neatly into the Soviet concept of mass participation in culture and seemed to offer fruitful ground for the application of the Stalinist principle, "national in form, socialist in content." To this end, Estonian composers were also called upon to expand the existing repertoire of choral music. The twelfth all-Estonian song festival (1947) had over 28,000 participants, and the thirteenth festival (1950) had 30,700; both were by far the largest in Estonian history. In 1947 the audience was estimated at 100,000. On these two occasions a new element appeared in the Estonian song festival tradition when all the various choruses united on the stage to perform a portion of the program. In 1947 Gustav Ernesaks's version of Lydia Koidula's poem, *Mu isamaa on minu arm* (My fatherland is my love), which later developed into an unofficial national anthem, was also performed for the first time at a national song festival.[66] The thirteenth all-Estonian song festival, which took place in July 1950 during the purge of "bourgeois nationalists," lost three of its five main conductors when Alfred Karindi, Riho Päts, and Tuudur Vettik were branded "enemies of the people" and placed under arrest. The heavily Sovietized program included numerous songs in praise of Lenin, Stalin, Moscow, and kolkhozes.[67] Nevertheless, in many ways this powerful musical tradition, reaching back to the national awakening, transcended even the restrictions of the Stalinist era.

The Soviet authorities did not single out religion or the churches as objects of particular concern in the first postwar decade. To be sure, the churches were held in check. The Soviets banned all religious literature, deported the first two postwar Lutheran bishops, and immediately disbanded the theological institute in Tartu that had functioned in 1941–1944. The number of Lutheran clergy in Estonia remained relatively stable (70–80) at less than one-third the prewar level. Nevertheless, there was no frontal attack on religion, and no militant propagation of atheism developed. The Soviet regime, perhaps busy with more pressing matters, opted in this period for a war of attrition with religion.[68]

13 The Post-Stalin Era, 1953–1985

Although the Soviet system did not fundamentally alter in the three decades after 1953, the post-Stalin era witnessed significant changes in Estonian life. For the first time since before Stalinism, the ECP regained some decisionmaking power. After the disastrous first postwar decade, the standard of living improved considerably, especially in the rural areas. The feared security forces were downgraded in importance, and within a few years of Stalin's death many of the surviving deportees returned from the camps and from exile. Gradually the Estonian intelligentsia began to reassert itself, and in the course of the 1960s nothing short of a renaissance was taking place in cultural life. Accompanying these changes was a fundamental shift in Soviet attitudes toward the outside world. Rejecting Stalin's strict isolationism, Khrushchev embraced the notion of peaceful competition with the capitalist world. For Estonia the first contacts were with Finland in 1956. By the late 1950s more and more foreigners visited Estonia, and the number skyrocketed after the opening of the Helsinki-Tallinn boat line in 1965. In the next twelve years the number of tourists from outside the Soviet bloc increased tenfold (from 9,400 in 1965 to 94,100 in 1977). Estonians, albeit in much smaller numbers, were also able to travel abroad for the first time in the post–World War II era.[1]

In the decade following Stalin's death, extensive administrative reorganization continued in Estonia. The oblast system, established in May 1952, was quickly abolished in April 1953. The following year, in coordination with the expansion in the size of kolkhozes and sovkhozes, the number of village soviets was cut in half through consolidation (from 637 to 320). Presumably because of its strategic importance after the discovery of uranium in the area, the small city of Sillamäe near Narva was added to the list of cities directly subordinate to the ESSR Council of Ministers in June 1957. Finally, in the late 1950s and early 1960s the Soviet authorities reduced the number of raions in Estonia from 39 to 15. By 1965 a stable administrative framework had emerged, and no major changes occurred in the next two decades, except for the periodic consolidation of village soviets, which numbered 189 in 1984.[2]

THE ESTONIAN COMMUNIST PARTY

After a brief period of stagnation before the onset of de-Stalinization, the ranks of the ECP swelled markedly in the ensuing years, especially in the first decade after 1956. The following figures provide an overview of ECP growth (in each case at the start of the year):

| | Total ECP membership | ETHNIC ESTONIANS | |
		Number	Percentage
1953	22,320	9,729	43.6
1956	22,524	10,047	44.6
1961	37,848	18,604	49.2
1966	59,094	30,694	51.9
1971	73,168	38,252	52.3
1976	84,250	43,742	51.9
1981	97,923	49,777	50.8

Prior to 1956 Estonia ranked relatively low in proportion of Communist Party membership on an all-Union basis, and as of 1961 the ESSR was only ninth among the fifteen Union republics with regard to party membership per 1,000 population. However, by 1970 Estonia had jumped to third place and retained that position in 1979 as well. A major component of this increase came from ethnic Estonians, whose numbers in ECP ranks tripled in the decade after 1956. In the 1970s, however, non-Estonians outnumbered Estonians among new party members.[3] These trends reflected the initial hopes of the early post-Stalin era that native Estonians could eventually play the leading role in administering Estonia and the disappointment of those hopes by the late 1970s.

In the ECP Central Committee the ethnic Estonian role was more important, ranging between approximately 70 to 80 percent in the 1960s and 1970s.[4] However, a major element among Estonians in the upper ranks of the ECP was still constituted by Russian-Estonians, whose background and outlook differed considerably from those of Communists native to the region. The ECP continued to be a male-dominated institution, although the proportion of female members slowly rose from 28 percent in 1953 to 36 percent in 1981. In terms of social origins, the trend since the mid-1950s was toward a greater role for manual workers in the ECP and a correspondingly lesser one for white-collar workers. In 1955 the party was divided socially as follows: manual workers, 34.5 percent; kolkhozniks, 11.0 percent; and white-collar workers, 54.6 percent. By 1981 the proportions had shifted considerably in the first and third categories: manual workers, 42.6 percent; kolkhozniks, 11.6 percent; and white-collar workers, 45.8 percent.[5]

In the upper echelons of the ECP, continuity from the Stalinist era was more striking than change. To be sure, a substantial turnover of individuals occurred in the ECP Buro in the mid-1950s; however, the patterns of the distribution of power were not significantly altered. During the post-Stalin years a majority of Russian-Estonians and Russians dominated the Buro.[6] It is noteworthy that the Russian-Estonian role grew after 1953 while that of Russians and other non-Estonians declined. After the early 1960s the Buro regularly had only one or two non-Estonians out of nine to eleven members. Yet the relative position of native Estonian Communists on the ECP Buro did not change appreciably between the late 1940s—following the purge of "bourgeois nationalists"—and the early 1980s. In this period native Estonians never constituted more than about one-fourth—and usually less—of that body's membership. In April 1983, however, Johannes Käbin retired from public life and was replaced by Bruno Saul, and in March 1985 Matti Pedak took the place of the Russian-Estonian Vladimir Käo. These changes raised the proportion of native Estonians on the Buro to nearly half (five of eleven members), the highest share in over 35 years.[7] It may finally be that the pool of Russian-Estonians was no longer large enough for this group to continue to play the same role as in the past.

Within the ECP Buro the two top positions, first and second secretaries, remained closed to native Estonians after 1950, and in the post-Stalin era there was little turnover in the chief office, as the following listing shows:[8]

First Secretary	*Second Secretary*
Johannes Käbin (1950–1978)	Leonid Lentsman (1953–1964)
Karl Vaino (1978–1988)	Artur Vader (1964–1970)
	Konstantin Lebedev (1971–1982)
	Aleksandr Kudriavtsev (1982–1985)
	Georgii Aleshin (1985–1989)

The promotion of Lentsman, a Russian-Estonian, to second secretary in August 1953 broke the postwar Stalinist pattern of reserving this post for a

Russian. That pattern was re-established in 1971 when the Russian Lebedev replaced Vader, a Russian-Estonian. It is difficult to gauge the significance of the office of second secretary, but it may not have been coincidental, for example, that the flowering of Soviet Estonian culture occurred in the 1960s when ethnic Russians were absent from this post.

Johannes Käbin was undoubtedly the outstanding figure in the ECP in the post-Stalin era; he presided over the fortunes of the party for nearly three decades, including the uneasy transition from the Stalinist period. Perhaps his most important political talents were the abilities to adapt to changing conditions and to act as a mediator between the ESSR and the central leadership in Moscow. In the late Stalinist era Käbin was certainly far removed from Estonian nationalism, but after 1953 he gradually came to understand and tolerate, if not promote, its aspirations in the Soviet context. Over the years his command of Estonian improved, and in a sense he became re-Estonianized. In the late 1950s the Soviet Estonian press still referred to him as "Ivan"; by the mid-1960s he had become "Johannes."[9] In time, Käbin gained the reputation of a pragmatic and rational leader whose role as a buffer against inordinate demands from Moscow was appreciated.[10]

In the mid-1970s, as Käbin reached his seventieth birthday and his health weakened, the question of succession became opportune. Given that Käbin had legitimized at least a modest form of Estonian nationalism and that Stalin had been dead for over two decades, it did not seem unreasonable to speculate that a native Estonian could once again aspire to the top post in the ECP. The most likely such candidate was Vaino Väljas (b. 1931), who had had a meteoric rise in party ranks, including candidate membership on the Buro at age 24 and appointment as first secretary of the Tallinn City Committee by the time he was 30.[11] In July 1978, however, Käbin moved on to the relatively ceremonial post of chair of the ESSR Supreme Soviet Presidium and was replaced by Karl Vaino (b. 1923), another Russian-Estonian. Born in Siberia, Vaino became a party member in 1947 and was sent to Estonia the same year as an engineer. His career in party work began in 1949, and after holding various lesser positions in the 1950s, he became a party secretary in 1960 and continued in that office until 1978. His highest educational level appears to be graduation from the CPSU Higher Party School in Moscow, a course he completed by correspondence in 1957.[12]

Although the immediate cause for the shakeup in the ECP leadership in 1978 was the death of Artur Vader, who at the time was chair of the Presidium of the ESSR Supreme Soviet, there is no doubt that the move had been in the planning stages for some time. By appointing Vaino, Moscow clearly expressed its continued distrust of Estonian nationalism. Vaino's rise to the top was also something of a surprise in that he had not particularly distinguished himself within the party and had a low profile in 1978. In contrast to Käbin, Vaino was not Estonianized by living in the ESSR and appeared to have no motivation for protecting Estonian national interests. Furthermore, since he lacked Käbin's experience and prestige, Vaino's bargaining power with Moscow was considerably weaker.[13] It can also hardly be coincidental that Vaino's appointment occurred at roughly the same time as Moscow stepped up the all-Union campaign to promote the use of the Russian language. Given Vaino's background and his junior status, the central leadership could probably be sure of his full cooperation in this regard.

The degree to which the ECP enjoyed any autonomy in the post-Stalin era above all depended on the situation in Moscow. Under Khrushchev, decentralizing tendencies were generally in vogue in the Soviet Union and clearly benefited the union republics. For example, the republics' share of the total Soviet budget rose to 55 percent in the early 1960s as compared to only 25 percent in the Stalinist period.[14] The inertia of the Khrushchev years carried over to some extent into the late 1960s, but by the end of the decade recentralization had become the watchword for the Brezhnev leadership. Thus, it should be noted that Vaino became first secretary at a time when autonomist tendencies were increasingly less tolerated by Moscow. Furthermore, Estonians, whether native or brought up in Russia, continue to have virtually no influence within the upper echelons of the Moscow bureaucracy.[15] Among ESSR leaders only the ECP first secretary has traditionally been a full member of the CPSU Central Committee.

THE GOVERNMENTAL SYSTEM

Following the death of Stalin some reorganization of the governmental organs in Estonia took place. As on the all-Union level, the most important permanent change proved to be the substantial decline in the status of the security apparatus. In April 1953 the MGB in Estonia was joined to the Ministry of Interior, and in May 1954 a separate Committee for State Security (KGB) was formally established under the direct jurisdiction of the ESSR Council of Ministers. Although the KGB became a factor to be reckoned with, its role has never compared to that of the security forces under Stalin. In the late 1950s Ivan Karpov, a Russian, headed the Estonian KGB, but in keeping with the gradual Estonianization of leading party and government posts under Khrushchev, he was replaced in 1961 by August Pork, a Russian-Estonian. Pork remained in office until 1982, when he was replaced by Karl Kortelainen, a non-Estonian about whom little is known.[16]

A less permanent change in government structure was Khrushchev's grandiose plan to decentralize economic management in the Soviet Union through a system of regional economic councils (*sovnarkhozes*) in 1957. Arnold Veimer, the native Estonian Communist who was dismissed as chair of the Council of

Ministers under Stalin in 1951, directed the Estonian sovnarkhoz, which corresponded exactly to the territory of the ESSR. The reform involved the elimination of several industrial ministries and the regrouping of their tasks under the new council. In 1964 the Estonian sovnarkhoz managed 160 concerns that produced over 70 percent of the ESSR's industrial output. In 1965 the post-Khrushchev leadership scuttled the regional economic councils on an all-Union basis and returned to the more centralized control of the past.[17]

In the post-Stalin era the size and composition of the Council of Ministers changed considerably. Its membership grew from 26 positions at the end of 1952 to 45 in 1980. In the mid-1950s the major source of expansion was the creation of new ministries, including foreign affairs, defense (later eliminated), various economic posts, and the new office of first deputy minister. In later years, particularly in the 1960s, the heads of newly established committees dealing with cultural and economic matters joined the council. In terms of composition the most striking shift was the declining Russian role on the Council of Ministers. At the end of the Stalinist era in 1952, Russians constituted nearly 40 percent of the membership; in 1980 their share was down to just over 10 percent. In contrast, native Estonians, who were totally unrepresented on the Council of Ministers in 1952, returned to this body in the mid-1950s and by 1980 constituted a substantial minority of its members.[18] However, Russian-Estonians remained the dominant element on the council; after 1953 the post of chair of the Council of Ministers in Estonia was held by two Russian-Estonians, Aleksei Müürisepp (1951–1961) and Valter Klauson (1961–1984). A break in this pattern came only in January 1984 when Bruno Saul, a native Estonian, replaced Klauson on the latter's retirement.[19]

The role of the Supreme Soviet, ostensibly the highest state organ in Estonia, did not change after the Stalinist period. In practice it merely approved the decisions of the ECP leadership and the Council of Ministers, and it met only a few days a year. In contrast to more important political entities, it was characteristic of the Supreme Soviet that the Estonian proportion of its membership was uniformly high in the post-Stalin era. In 1955 approximately 80 percent of the delegates were Estonians, a share that rose to over 85 percent by the end of the 1950s and in the 1960s. In the 1970s a gradual decline began, but in 1980 Estonians still constituted 73 percent of the membership of the Supreme Soviet.[20] Given its relative unimportance, it is not surprising that the office of chair of the Supreme Soviet Presidium changed hands six times in the past 25 years, as the following listing indicates:[21]

August Jakobson (1950–1958)

Johan Eichfeld (1958–1961)

Aleksei Müürisepp (1961–1970)

Artur Vader (1970–1978)

Johannes Käbin (1978–1983)

Arnold Rüütel (1983–)

It is noteworthy that, after a string of four Russian-Estonians, Rüütel was the first native Estonian to hold this post since Jakobson in 1958.

In conjunction with the promulgation of the new all-Union constitution in 1977, a similar one was proclaimed for the ESSR in 1978. In comparison to the 1940 constitution, the new document is much longer and more detailed. For the first time the leading role of the Communist Party was specifically recognized, and the goal of building communism, rather than socialism, set the standard for behavior. Although it updates the 1940 document and eliminates certain obsolete clauses, the practical significance of the new ESSR constitution appears to be limited. Nevertheless, both the all-Union and ESSR constitutions of the late 1970s can be seen as a codification of the centralizing tendencies of the post-Khrushchev era.[22]

DISSENT

Under the Stalinist regime, nonviolent dissent in Estonia had virtually no basis for existence. As noted above, the only visible form of resistance was the violent opposition of the pro-independence guerrilla movement. However, after 1953 the dismantling of most of Stalin's terror apparatus, the rehabilitation of many of his victims, and the return of surviving deportees contributed to a new era of rising political expectations. De-Stalinization implied that the Soviet regime was ready for reforms. Nevertheless, the Khrushchev era passed without fundamental change, and under Brezhnev the Soviet authorities toed an increasingly harder political line. It was disappointment with the unfulfilled promises of reform that first led to the emergence of open dissent in Moscow by the second half of the 1960s.

In Estonia dissent had appeared by 1968, no doubt on the Moscow model, and was fueled by the effects of the invasion of Czechoslovakia in August of that year. It is noteworthy that the first letters of protest from Estonia in the late 1960s were the work of both Estonians and non-Estonians and concerned primarily civil rights issues rather than nationalist ones. By the 1970s, however, nationalism had become the major theme of Estonian dissent. In 1972 the Estonian Democratic Movement and the Estonian National Front, two small dissident groups, demanded the restoration of Estonian independence and called on the United Nations to administer the election of a constituent assembly. In 1975 four members of the two groups were sentenced to five or six years in prison for "anti-Soviet agitation and propaganda."[23]

Despite the crackdown by the authorities, the scope of Estonian dissent broadened in the late 1970s. In 1977 eighteen natural scientists condemned the pollution caused by careless and overly ambitious oil-shale and phosphate mining in Estonia. Estonian dissidents made contact with other Balts, resulting most strikingly in the "Baltic appeal" for self-determination on the fortieth anniversary of the Molotov-Ribbentrop Pact in 1979 and a call for a Nordic nuclear-free zone including Estonia, Latvia, and Lithuania in 1981. One of the Estonian signers of the "Baltic appeal," the long-term dissident and scientist Mart Niklus, was sentenced in 1981 to a ten-year imprisonment. At the same trial, fellow scientist Jüri Kukk, who had declared solidarity with the "Baltic appeal," received a two-year sentence, but he died in mysterious circumstances while on a hunger strike only two months later. The arrest and trial of Estonian dissidents continued in the early 1980s as did various forms of protest against the Soviet regime, including a call for a monthly "silent half-hour" at workplaces and an increase in the number of defections to the West—in some cases by highly placed individuals.[24] Among various Estonian samizdat publications the most important and long-lived was *Lisandusi mõtete ja uudiste vabale levikule Eestis* (Some additions to the free flow of thoughts and news in Estonia). In nineteen issues in 1978–1984 it reported mainly on dissident activity and trials, but it also addressed other matters such as the situation in Poland.[25]

Although a tradition of spontaneous student demonstrations expressing nationalist sentiments dates back to the 1960s, youth unrest increased in the recent past in the major cities. Tartu University was the main center of protests, but the largest demonstration took place in Tallinn in October 1980. About 2,000 secondary-school students marched in the streets and shouted slogans calling for an Estonia free from Russian rule.[26] The use of police force to quell the demonstration as well as clashes with Russian students prompted one of the most remarkable documents of the Soviet era in Estonia. In a signed, open letter, 40 established Estonian intellectuals—some with excellent party credentials—decried the increase in ethnic tensions in the ESSR and spoke out in defense of the Estonian language and culture, which they regarded as increasingly threatened in recent years. A second, unsigned letter from fifteen Estonian intellectuals, dated March 1982, provides a blunter and more graphic description of the growing role of Russians and the Russian language in Estonia. A third, signed letter from thirteen Estonian dissidents in October 1982 appealed to Finnish firms and workers not to participate in the construction of the new Muuga harbor near Tallinn because it would only lead to the further influx of Russians and other non-Estonians into Estonia.[27] In short, during the Vaino years after 1978 the social base of dissent broadened, and its major concern shifted from political demands to the more fundamental issues of national and cultural survival.

STRUCTURE OF THE POST-STALIN ECONOMY

In the decades after Stalin's death the Estonian economy became further integrated into the all-Union one, and Soviet authorities continued to emphasize industrial development. By the late 1950s, for the first time in Estonian history, the number of workers in industry outnumbered those in agriculture. However, in the 1960s and 1970s the proportion of industrial workers remained nearly constant at 34–35 percent, and the share of agricultural workers was cut in half from about 25 percent in 1960 to less than 13 percent in 1980. As might be expected in an increasingly developed economy, employment in trade and in the service sector—material, educational, and cultural—showed the greatest increases.[28] If the structure of the economy is measured by total annual output in rubles, the role of industry remained dominant (60 percent in 1956, 63 percent in 1983). In agriculture growing mechanization partially compensated for the loss of labor, keeping its share at 17 percent of total annual output in 1983 as compared to 24 percent in 1956. The only other economic sector worthy of mention in this regard is construction, whose contribution to total output remained stable at 7–9 percent annually between 1956 and 1983.[29]

Economic ties with the other parts of the Soviet Union played an important role in the Estonian economy in the post-Stalin era. This development reflected the Soviet emphasis on regional specialization as well as Estonia's relative lack of raw materials for its growing industrial sector. In 1977, 82 percent of all imports to the ESSR and 93 percent of exports from it involved other Soviet republics. Of the imports, 40 percent consisted of raw materials and fuel. Among exports from Estonia in the early 1970s, three areas dominated: light industry (30 percent), food products (24 percent), and machinery (19 percent). In 1977, 55–60 percent of Estonia's external trade in both directions was with the RSFSR. The share of the other union republics, from 12 percent for the Ukraine to 0.3 percent for Tadzhikstan in 1972, was generally proportional to their size and inversely proportional to their distance from Estonia. Outside the USSR, Estonia's main trading partners were, in order of importance, Eastern Europe, Finland and Western Europe, and Third World countries in Africa and Asia.[30]

INDUSTRIAL DEVELOPMENT

After 1953, following the principle of regional specialization, the ESSR particularly developed those industrial sectors for which indigenous raw materials are available—for example, oil shale and phosphate. The location of Estonian industry in the post-Stalin era did not change appreciably from earlier twentieth-century patterns. Tallinn retained its leading position, although it suffered a relative decline through competition from the Kohtla-Järve and Narva areas of northeastern Estonia. In the latter part of the 1960s these three cities employed nearly two-thirds of the industrial labor force. Recent decades also witnessed the increasing concentration of Estonian industry. In 1960 only 6.4 percent of industrial concerns employed over 1,000 workers; by 1976 this figure had reached 20 percent.[31]

Under both Khrushchev and Brezhnev a considerable amount of experimentation in industrial management took place in the Soviet Union in general and in Estonia in particular. As noted above, under the sovnarkhoz system (1957–1965), virtually the entire ESSR industrial sector was placed under local control—for example, 98.5 percent in 1959. However, both before and after this temporary reform the share of Estonian industrial output administered directly by all-Union ministries in Moscow was about one-fourth or slightly more (1955, 25 percent; 1975, 31 percent; 1980, 28 percent), and over half the output (60 percent in 1980) was in the hands of Union-republic ministries, thus effectively under central control. Oil-shale mining was entirely managed from Moscow; other industrial branches partially under centralized direction included electricity generation, pulp and paper manufacturing, fisheries, and machinery construction.[32]

The most important permanent economic reform of the post-Stalin era in Estonia began in the mid-1960s. While stressing the crucial role of central planning, the Soviet authorities delegated new powers to local managers, including the right to dispose of their net income (or profits), which now became the ultimate measure of economic efficiency. A new system of incentives was also established to encourage worker productivity.[33] It is noteworthy that in Estonia the tempo of implementation of the reform was more rapid than the all-Union average; in 1969, 96 percent of the industrial output came from enterprises functioning under the new system as compared to 84 percent for the USSR as a whole.[34] In this instance and others in recent decades the Moscow leadership used Estonia as a kind of experimental laboratory for trying out new policies.

After the mid-1950s industrial output in Estonia continued to grow, but at an increasingly slower rate, as seen in the following figures for average annual growth:[35]

1956–1960	11.4%
1961–1965	9.9%
1966–1970	8.6%
1971–1975	7.1%
1976–1980	4.4%

The trend toward slower growth corresponded to the overall Soviet pattern and reflected a number of factors, including the emergence of a more mature economy, a declining labor pool, and concessions to consumers. Among the fifteen union republics Estonia ranked fifth in the 1950s, eighth in the 1960s, and tied for tenth in the 1970s with regard to industrial growth rate. In the 1970s for the first time the ESSR rate fell below the all-Union average.[36]

As a result of industrial expansion the number of workers in this branch of the economy grew substantially, especially in the first post-Stalin decade. In 1955 there were 104,675 industrial workers in Estonia; by 1965 the figure had jumped to 171,400. However, in the following decade the rate of increase slowed markedly, perhaps reflecting increased mechanization as well as a declining rate of industrial growth. In 1975 (the last year for which the Soviets have published such information) the number of industrial workers was 186,500.[37] With regard to the number of employees, the relative positions of the branches of industry did not change appreciably. In the mid-1970s the top five sectors—light industry, machine construction and metalworking, food processing, woodworking and paper and pulp manufacturing, and fuel and energy production—were the same as in the mid-1950s; only the order among the latter three had shifted slightly.[38]

However, if share of investment capital is considered, an entirely different picture emerges. The leading industrial branch by far (36 percent in 1955, 40 percent in 1975) was fuel and energy production, and from an all-Union point of view it was unquestionably the most important one. The basic source for fuel in Estonia is oil shale used to generate electricity. Between 1950 and 1980 the amount of oil shale mined in Estonia increased by a factor of nine (from 3.5 to 31.3 million tons). In 1975 the ESSR's share was 83 percent of the USSR total.[39] During the same three decades the output of electrical energy in Estonia grew by over 43 times (from 0.4 to 18.9 billion kilowatt-hours). By the mid-1970s Estonia was the world's largest producer of oil shale, and it ranked third—after Norway and Canada—in per capita electrical energy production.[40] Two giant oil-shale fired power stations—the Baltic (completed 1966) and the Estonian (completed 1973), both located near Narva and each with a capacity of 1.6 million kilowatts—produce the lion's share of electricity in the ESSR. Although output of oil shale declined slightly and electrical energy leveled off in the early 1980s, a third and even larger power station fueled by oil shale (capacity 2.5

million kilowatts) was slated to be built in northeastern Estonia. When the new plant reaches full capacity, it will result in the doubling of oil-shale consumption as compared to the already high level of 1974.[41]

The pace of oil-shale mining, its wasteful consumption, and the resulting pollution engendered criticism in both official and unofficial publications in Estonia. The rapid tempo would not be necessary to fulfill Estonia's own energy needs; however, the ESSR has long been a major supplier of energy to Leningrad and the northwestern RSFSR. In the mid-1970s nearly two-thirds of the electricity produced in Estonia was exported. Yet technology did not keep up with the pace of oil-shale mining; in the mid-1970s losses approached 50 percent. Moreover, roughly half of the oil shale burned to produce electricity remains on the ground as inorganic ash, and the process contributed to both air and water pollution in the surrounding area.[42] Although there was some official recognition of these problems, it should be recalled that the ESSR government had very little say in policymaking in the fuel and energy production industry.

AGRICULTURE

In the post-Stalin era the agricultural sector of the Estonian economy underwent important changes, which resulted in a major improvement in the lives of the rural population. Indeed, the narrowing of the socioeconomic gap between the city and the countryside must be seen as one of the most significant developments of the three decades following Stalin's death. In the Stalinist system agriculture had been the stepchild of the economy, and it will be recalled that output declined following collectivization in the late Stalinist years. After 1953 a fundamental reordering of priorities in the Soviet Estonian economy took place.

Khrushchev's agricultural reforms, carried out on an all-Union basis, marked the first phase of the rural rebirth. The most important changes dealt with the kolkhozes, which still encompassed the great majority of agricultural land both in Estonia and in the USSR as a whole. In 1953–1956 the Soviet authorities implemented a series of measures designed to raise agricultural productivity and output, including a reduction of rents on private plots and of state norms for private livestock, an increase in state prices for agricultural produce, and provision for more initiative by the kolkhozes themselves. In 1958 the Machine Tractor Stations were transformed into repair centers, and their machinery was sold to the collective farms. Equally important, the agricultural specialists previously based at the MTS now became available for work in residence on the kolkhozes. At the same time, compulsory delivery of agricultural produce to the state at low prices was abolished. The most significant reform of the Khrushchev era also began in 1958: the payment of wages to kolkhozniks in money rather than in kind. In 1959, 14 percent of the ESSR kolkhozes paid their members in money; in 1960 the figure jumped to 68 percent and had reached 100 percent by 1964. It is noteworthy that Estonia completed the transition to money wages before the other Union republics and served as a model in this regard. In addition to these reforms the government began to invest significantly more capital in the agricultural sector than during the Stalinist era. Thus, for example, mechanization proceeded more rapidly than before, and greater quantities of fertilizer became available.[43]

Under Brezhnev the Soviet authorities made changes in the other major institution of collectivized agriculture—the sovkhoz. As in the industrial reforms of the mid-1960s, Moscow sought to increase productivity by tapping local initiative on the state farms. In 1967, 390 sovkhozes in the Soviet Union were placed in an experimental "self-management" (*khozraschet*) program. Among this number were included all 168 sovkhozes in Estonia, which constituted 43 percent of the total. The success of the experiment in the ESSR and elsewhere in the country led to the implementation of the self-management system on all Soviet sovkhozes by 1975. Even more than in industry, Estonia emerged as an important experimental laboratory in Soviet agriculture in the post-Stalin era. The small size of the ESSR, an already developed agricultural base, and the skilled labor force made Estonia an attractive location for such experimentation, which could then provide models for the rest of the Soviet Union.[44]

In terms of organization of collectivized agriculture, Estonia followed the overall Soviet trend in the post-Stalin era toward an increasingly greater role for the sovkhozes and a correspondingly smaller one for the kolkhozes. The proportion of agricultural land allocated to the sovkhozes began to grow markedly in the late 1950s, especially through the establishment of new state farms that took over the lands of weak collective farms. By the mid-1970s the kolkhoz share had fallen below that of the sovkhozes for the first time; in 1983 the kolkhozes held 46 percent of the agricultural land while the sovkhozes held 50 percent.[45] In the case of both collective and state farms the process of consolidation begun in the late Stalinist era continued after 1953. In 1950–1976 the average size of a kolkhoz in Estonia grew sevenfold and that of a sovkhoz nearly ninefold. In this same period the number of agricultural kolkhozes declined from 2,213 to 188 while the figure for sovkhozes remained relatively stable: 127 in 1950 and 148 in 1975. By the latter year the typical Estonian collective or state farm had become a giant undertaking with an average land area of 7,174 hectares. The private sector in agriculture declined from 8 percent of the arable land in 1955 to 4 percent in 1983.[46]

As a result of mechanization and other technological advances—as well as the attraction of urban life—the number of agricultural workers dropped considerably, from 156,000 in 1953 to 108,000 in 1982. On kolkhozes, the number dropped from 140,000 in 1953 to 49,000 in 1976. However, the employment trend on sovkhozes was the reverse: agricultural workers numbered 16,000 in 1953 and rose to 60,000 in 1976.

The decline in the number of kolkhoz workers was sharpest in the 1950s and 1960s. It slowed in the 1970s and appeared to have stabilized at the 1976 level, which held steady for the next six years. Correspondingly, the most dramatic leap in sovkhoz employment occurred in the second half of the 1950s. Here, too, stabilization was reached in the latter part of the 1970s. By 1981 the number of state farm workers had dropped slightly, for the first time in the Soviet era, to 59,000.[47]

Despite the improvement in agricultural conditions in the post-Stalin era, the growth of output in this sector was much less striking than in the industrial one, as seen in the following figures for average annual increase in agricultural production:[48]

1956–1960	13.2%
1961–1965	5.2%
1966–1970	3.2%
1971–1975	4.7%
1976–1980	2.7%

Aside from the late 1950s, growth rates were modest, and the overall trend was clearly downward. Recovery to the 1939 level in agricultural output was only reached in the early 1960s as compared to a decade earlier for the industrial sector. Nevertheless, advances in livestock holdings and crop productivity were significant. Between 1955 and 1980 the number of cattle in Estonia nearly doubled while the number of hogs quadrupled. The pre-Soviet 1939 level for cattle in Estonia was reached in the early 1970s and that for hogs in the late 1950s. The yield per hectare of major crops increased as follows between 1951–1955 and 1976–1980: cereals, 359 percent; potatoes, 61 percent; and vegetables, 50 percent. In general, agricultural labor productivity in Estonia was among the highest in the USSR in the post-Stalin era. Although the share of the private sector in Estonian agriculture declined in recent years, it still played a major role. In 1980, for example, the 4 percent of arable land allotted to private use produced 29 percent of the potatoes, 27 percent of the eggs, 19 percent of the milk, and 14 percent of the dressed meat in the ESSR.[49]

As a result of the improvements noted above, food became more readily available to the consumer in Estonia in the first two post-Stalin decades. Yet by the mid-1970s, reflecting in part the decline in the rate of increase of agricultural output, shortages of food had become evident, including basic items such as potatoes. Other staples such as meat and coffee periodically disappeared from the marketplace.[50]

The structure of the agricultural sector of the Estonian economy did not change appreciably after Stalin. In 1976 approximately two-thirds of the gross output came from cattle and dairy farming while the remaining third consisted of crops, mainly cereals and hay. Furthermore, nearly three-fourths of the crop production served as livestock feed. No changes in this emphasis are to be expected in the foreseeable future. At the Eighteenth ECP Congress in 1981, First Secretary Vaino reaffirmed the commitment to livestock development as the basic task of Estonian agriculture.[51]

DEMOGRAPHIC DEVELOPMENTS

Overall population growth in Estonia after the death of Stalin was moderate but steady, as suggested by the following figures:

1953	1,141,300
1959 (census)	1,196,800
1970 (census)	1,356,100
1979 (census)	1,465,800
1985	1,529,000

The increase in 1959–1982 (25.0 percent) placed Estonia slightly below the Soviet average (28.7 percent). The ESSR ranked barely above the Slavic republics and Latvia, but far below the Central Asian republics and Armenia.[52] In Estonia the greatest growth took place in the 1960s; after that the rate of increase fell off considerably. In 1953–1961 natural increase outstripped mechanical increase; however, after 1962—with the exception of 1974–1976—the situation was reversed. Overall, since 1953, immigration into Estonia outweighed natural increase as a source of demographic growth. The ESSR birth rate was among the lowest in the Soviet Union during this period, and a high death rate prevailed because of the relatively large number of older people.[53]

The low rate of natural increase of the population was not a recent phenomenon. As noted in previous chapters, the birth rate in Estonia had fallen below 20 per 1,000 inhabitants by World War I and since then has only risen above that level once (in 1945–1949) for any five-year period. In the post-Stalin era the trend was once again downward—hastened, no doubt, by the legalization of abortion in 1955—from 18.3 per 1,000 population in 1950–1954 to a low of 14.7 in 1965–1969. After that the birth rate stabilized at about 15 per 1,000 inhabitants. The death rate dropped between 1953 and the mid-1960s

(10.0 per 1,000 in 1964); it then gradually edged upward and was about 12 per 1,000 population after the latter part of the 1970s. Estonia's and Latvia's death rates have been the highest in the USSR since 1953.[54] Average family size in Estonia was also the lowest in the Soviet Union in this period (3.5 members in 1959, 3.1 in 1979); this continues a historical trend, since the figure for the Republic of Estonia in 1922 was only 4.1.[55] Divorce rates in the ESSR mushroomed, increasing sixfold in 1953–1980 (from 8.0 to 47.3 per 100 marriages), which ranked among the highest in the Soviet Union. The two major causes of divorce in the ESSR appeared to be alcoholism and tight housing conditions. Limited space also contributed to a high rate of abortions.[56]

Soviet data on the ethnic composition of the population of Estonia are available for the census years 1959, 1970, and 1979. The following figures provide a breakdown for the major groups for these years (in percentages; see also Appendix B, Table 1).[57]

	Estonian	Russian	Ukrainian	Belorussian	Finnish	Other
1959	74.6	20.1	1.3	0.9	1.4	1.7
1970	68.2	24.6	2.1	1.4	1.4	2.3
1979	64.7	27.9	2.5	1.6	1.2	2.1

In the 1950s the Estonian share of the population remained fairly stable. The ethnic Estonian birth rate was relatively high in that decade, the rate of immigration of non-Estonians was relatively low, and some of the Stalinist-era deportees returned to the ESSR. Arnold Purre estimates that about 9,000 Estonians were granted amnesty in 1956–1958. Furthermore, in the early post-Stalin era some Russian administrators and non-Estonian forced laborers left the ESSR.

In the 1960s and 1970s, however, the Estonian proportion in the ESSR plummeted by 9.9 percentage points—the greatest decline among all union republics in both decades—as the native birth rate fell and Russian and other non-Estonian (mainly Ukrainian and Belorussian) immigration rose to high levels. The rate of decline of the ethnic Estonian proportion dropped markedly in the second half of the 1970s, probably because the pool of potential Slavic migrants in the Soviet Union was shrinking by that time. Net immigration to Estonia rose once again in 1980 (6,800) and 1981 (7,000) but fell in 1982 (5,600) and 1983 (5,100), as compared to an average of 4,800 in 1974–1979.[58] It also appears that Russian-Estonians continued to immigrate to Estonia in the 1960s and 1970s in considerable numbers, although no exact information on this question is available. In any case, the Estonian population of the Soviet Union became increasingly concentrated in the ESSR. In 1979, 92.9 percent of Soviet Estonians lived in Estonia as compared to 90.3 percent in 1959.[59]

Another potential contributing factor to the declining ethnic Estonian proportion in the ESSR was assimilation. The Russian minority grew steadily since the end of World War II and approached one-third of the total population. Moreover, a large fraction of the non-Russians residing in Estonia were themselves Russified (that is, they considered Russian their native tongue)—for example, this was true for 76 percent of the Jews, 65 percent of the Belorussians, and 54 percent of the Ukrainians in 1979. In addition, pressures to learn the Soviet lingua franca grew in the late Brezhnev era, and some aspects of the mass media were dominated by Russian. In 1980, for example, only 17 percent of the Soviet television programming available in Estonia was in the Estonian language.[60]

Nevertheless, the census data for the period between 1959 and 1979 indicated almost no Russification among Estonians in the ESSR. Although the proportion of Estonians in Estonia that habitually spoke another language rose slightly from 0.7 percent in 1959 to 1.0 percent in 1979, the absolute numbers were tiny—3,591 persons—and could be attributed almost entirely to the continuing Russian-Estonian immigration. Indeed, it is noteworthy that in 1979 a larger proportion of Russians were Estonianized (1.56 percent) in the ESSR than Estonians were Russified (0.99 percent).[61] The most probable source of assimilation was ethnically mixed marriages. The rate of such marriages was increasing in Estonia in recent years (13.6 percent in 1970, 15.8 percent in 1979), ranking the ESSR sixth among Soviet republics in 1979 on a scale between Latvia (24.2 percent) and Armenia (4.0 percent). However, the degree of intermarriage by ethnic Estonians was considerably lower. In 1968, only 7.1 percent of Estonian women and 7.6 percent of Estonian men in the ESSR married outside their ethnic group.[62]

Urbanization in Estonia continued to grow after 1953 but at a much slower rate than in the first post–World War II decade. The proportions for urban population for selected years are as follows:[63]

1953	52.5%
1960	57.1%
1970	65.0%
1980	70.1%
1984	71.3%

The average annual increase in urbanization in this thirty-one-year period was 0.6 percentage points, far below the annual increase of 2.7 percentage points for 1945–1952. Furthermore, the rate of growth declined in each successive decade, a trend no doubt related to the drop in the rate of industrial expansion and a reduction in the available pool of immigrants. Nevertheless, in each Soviet census between 1959 and 1979, Estonia ranked first (tied with Latvia in 1959) in the USSR in level of urbanization.[64] Three major factors contributed to continuing urban expansion in Estonia: natural increase (for example, 36 percent of the total growth in the population of Tallinn in 1972–1974 was due to natural increase); migration from rural areas within Estonia (in 1953–1982 the ESSR rural population declined by 20 percent); and immigration from other Soviet republics (for example, in the 1960s, 70 percent of the mechanical increase in Estonian urban areas came from outside the ESSR). It is clear that Russians and other non-Estonian immigrants flocked to the cities in search of employment and urban amenities. In 1970 the non-Estonian population of the ESSR was 88 percent urban.[65]

In terms of individual cities, Tallinn far outstripped any potential rivals, as seen in the following figures on the population of the five major cities in Estonia (in thousands):[66]

	1959	1970	1979	1984
Tallinn	281.7	362.7	429.7	458.3
Tartu	74.3	90.5	104.5	109.9
Narva	27.6	57.9	72.8	78.6
Kohtla-Järve	29.2	68.3	72.7	76.5
Pärnu	36.1	46.3	51.3	52.6

For all major cities the 1960s was the period of greatest growth; Kohtla-Järve and Narva led the way as each more than doubled in size. In the 1970s, however, Kohtla-Järve virtually stagnated, which probably reflected growing mechanization in the oil-shale industry, and the other cities grew only modestly, with Narva achieving the highest rate of increase (26 percent).

Tallinn continued to grow more rapidly than planned or desired. In 1961 it was projected that the city would only reach a population of 350,000 in 1980; in fact, by that year it was already 436,000.[67] In 1959–1984 Tallinn grew by an average of 7,100 new inhabitants per year, and the rate only slightly slackened in the most recent past. Entire new sections of the city were built—Mustamäe and Õismäe to the west and, since 1978, Lasnamäe to the east. The latter region is projected to house 200,000 people when completed. Tallinn's share of the total ESSR population grew from 23.5 percent in 1959 to 30.2 percent in 1984.[68] It should also be noted that the geographic area of the city expanded markedly in the post-Stalin era, although the new sections do not appear to have been heavily populated at the time of their annexation. In 1958–1975 Tallinn grew from 102 to 168 square kilometers, an increase of 65 percent.[69] In 1982 construction began on a new major port at Muuga on the eastern edge of Tallinn. It was to be the largest commercial port in the Soviet Baltic and would have required—by one estimate—about 100,000 new workers if ancillary service concerns were included.[70]

For the post-Stalin era much more information is also available on the ethnic composition of the urban areas in Estonia. For the three census years to 1979 the data on ethnicity are as follows (in percentages):[71]

	1959		1970		1979	
	Tallinn	Other Urban Areas	Tallinn	Other Urban	Tallinn	Other Urban
Estonians	60.2	63.1	55.7	58.7	51.9	56.9
Russians	32.2	29.8	35.0	33.1	38.0	35.5
Others	7.6	7.1	9.3	8.2	10.2	7.6

These figures clearly reflected the continuing immigration of non-Estonians into Estonia. The decline in the native share was particularly striking when compared to the 1934 Estonian proportions in Tallinn (85.5 percent) and the other urban areas (about 86 percent). In 1934 the Russian share of the population of Tallinn was only 5.8 percent.

For the other major cities, data on ethnic composition in 1979 became available through unofficial channels and appear to be quite reliable. For the four cities besides Tallinn with over 50,000 inhabitants in 1979 the figures are as follows (including the 1934 data for comparison):[72]

	PERCENTAGE ESTONIAN		PERCENTAGE RUSSIAN	
	1934	1979	1934	1979
Tartu	88.0	74.4	4.5	20.6
Narva	64.8	4.9	29.7	85.1
Kohtla-Järve	91.8	26.4	6.1	60.4
Pärnu	90.8	74.1(?)	2.3	19.5(?)

With few exceptions (for example, the small city of Paldiski—location of a nuclear naval base—west of Tallinn, which was 94 percent Estonian in 1934 and only 3 percent in 1979), the ESSR urban areas other than Tallinn and those located in the northeastern industrial region remained overwhelmingly Estonian. This was particularly the case in rural areas (91 percent Estonian in 1959, 88 percent in 1979). Even in the raions surrounding Tallinn (78 percent Estonian in 1979) and Narva and Kohtla-Järve (68 percent), a clear Estonian majority was maintained.[73]

SOCIAL CHANGE

In the post-Stalin era, continuing industrialization and urbanization along with the new emphasis on sovkhoz agriculture led to further social
change in Estonia, albeit at a much more gradual pace than in the first postwar
decade. In Soviet parlance the number of workers and employees (white-collar
workers, *sluzhashchie*) grew while the number of kolkhozniks declined. In terms
of employment, one of the major changes in the 1960s and 1970s—in addition
to the decline in agricultural jobs—was the growth of positions in areas not
directly related to material production, such as social services and culture.[74]
Nevertheless, the basic framework of social stratification in Estonia did not
change appreciably from that established by the end of the Stalinist era. The
system continued to favor Communist Party membership, the urban over the
rural areas, and industrial over agricultural labor. Yet the gap between town and
country in terms of living standard narrowed substantially, as noted above.
Wages in kind for kolkhozniks doubled between 1953 and 1956, and their
relative income position appeared to have improved markedly with the full
introduction of money wages by the mid-1960s, although the Soviets did not
publish any systematic data on this question. For sovkhoz workers the improvements were also dramatic; their monthly wages jumped from 68 percent of
those of industrial workers in 1960 to 97 percent in 1975 and seemed to
stabilize at the latter level (95 percent in 1981).[75]

Overall, for the Soviet Estonian labor force (excluding kolkhozniks), wages
rose by 28 percent in the 1950s, 65 percent in the 1960s, and 39 percent in the
1970s; the average monthly wage increased from 63.8 rubles in 1950 and 67.5
rubles in 1953 to 192.8 rubles in 1981. The best-paid workers, who received
consistently above-average remuneration in the 1960s and 1970s, were those in
construction, transportation, and industry. The least-paid were those in cultural work, health services, commerce, and (since 1970) education. In 1981 the
average monthly wage scale ranged from a high of 234.2 rubles for construction
workers (121 percent of the overall average) to 137.8 rubles for those engaged in
cultural work (71 percent of the overall average).[76]

In comparison to the other union republics, there can be little doubt that
Estonia and Latvia maintained the highest standards of living in the USSR in the
post-Stalin era. In the 1960s and 1970s the ESSR consistently ranked first in per
capita trade turnover and first or second in money in savings accounts per
capita.[77] In addition, the availability of consumer products and food was
generally greater in Estonia than elsewhere in the Soviet Union. For example, in
1971 the ESSR ranked first in ownership of radio and television sets per 1,000
inhabitants, and consumption of meat, milk, dairy products, eggs, and fish was
considerably higher in Estonia than the all-Union average throughout the 1960s

and 1970s.[78] Per capita urban living space also grew rapidly from a nadir of 8.7 square meters in 1955 to 17.0 in 1983. In 1979 Estonia ranked first on this index in the USSR. However, despite this progress, it is clear that housing demand substantially outstripped supply, especially in Tallinn.[79]

Despite the relatively high standard of living in Estonia, it is important to distinguish between quantity and quality in the Soviet context. The expansion of urban living space, for example, was not accompanied by a commensurate improvement in the quality of housing. Although Estonia ranked third in the Soviet Union (behind Georgia and Latvia) in the 1960s and 1970s with regard to physicians per 10,000 inhabitants, the population complained to foreign visitors about the quality and availability of local medical care.[80] In a limited series of interviews conducted during a visit to Tallinn in 1970, the Swedish-Estonian journalist Andres Küng found that although people appreciated the benefits of industrial development and rising rural living standards, they also complained about both the shortage and poor quality of consumer goods.[81]

Membership in mass organizations showed a strongly upward trend in the post-Stalin era. Although there were temporary declines in the mid-1950s and late 1960s, the Young Communist League (Komsomol) in Estonia grew from 60,391 members in 1952 (53 per 1,000 inhabitants) to 162,202 members in 1980 (110 per 1,000 inhabitants). As elsewhere in the Soviet Union, the Komsomol in Estonia was not only a training ground for future Communist Party members but also provided workers for major all-Union projects—for example, the development of the Virgin Lands in Kazakhstan in the late 1950s and early 1960s and, more recently, of the Baikal-Amur Mainline in Siberia. Some other mass social organizations with over 100,000 members in 1978 included the state-run trade unions; the Red Cross; the Army, Navy, and Air Force Auxiliary Association (Est. ALMAVÜ, Russ. DOSAAF), which is a paramilitary sports organization mainly for youth; and a union of volunteer firefighters.[82]

Women in Estonia were increasingly integrated into the labor force in the post-Stalin era. Since 1950, when females constituted 47 percent of the workers and employees, Estonia ranked first or second in the USSR in this category. By the early 1970s the figure had reached 54 percent and appeared to stabilize at that level.[83] However, although women constituted three-fourths or more of the work force in health, education, and culture, the leading positions in these areas remained closed to them. Furthermore, the top political posts in Estonia were also off limits to women. For example, no woman has ever been a member of the ECP Buro, and women have constituted only a tiny percentage of the ECP Central Committee. There were also few indications that the burdens of childrearing, household work, and shopping were becoming more equally distributed between husbands and wives.[84] The high rate of female employment in Estonia certainly reflected the large proportion of women in the population as a whole (56.1 percent in 1959 and 53.5 percent in 1983—which is higher than the Soviet average). Moreover, it is likely that the large proportion of working women was related to the low rate of marriage among ethnic Estonian females; this rate was the lowest among the major nationalities in the Soviet Union in both 1959 and 1970.[85]

The most striking social phenomenon in Estonia in this period was the rise of ethnic tensions, especially among the two largest nationalities—the Estonians and Russians. Little documentary evidence is available on ethnic relations in the Stalinist years, but it is not unlikely that tensions were submerged in the overall repressive system. In the immediate post-1953 era, the thaw under Khrushchev and the cultural rebirth of the 1960s (discussed below) permitted a measure of national self-realization by the Estonians in the ESSR. However, by the late 1970s several factors had combined to bring about increasing ethnic tensions: the continuing influx of non-Estonians into Estonia, especially into Tallinn, where the indigenous nationality retained only a bare majority in 1979; the appointment of Karl Vaino, a Russian-Estonian with no interest in ethnic Estonian concerns, as ECP first secretary in 1978; and an all-Union campaign, beginning particularly in the late 1970s, to give the Russian language a greater role in the non-Russian republics. As noted above, the most graphic demonstrations of ethnic unrest in recent years came in the youth protests of October 1980, the subsequent, signed open letter from 40 leading intellectuals, an anonymous letter from fifteen intellectuals dated March 1982, and a signed open letter from thirteen dissidents in October 1982. In the latter three documents the fear was expressed that the Estonian language and culture were in danger of losing their leading role in Estonia as Russian increasingly became the language of administration and was emphasized in education.[86]

Census data for the 1970s suggest a mutual reluctance by Estonians and Russians in the ESSR to learn each other's language, another possible indication of growing ethnic tension. While fluency in Russian (either as a first or second language) grew among all major Soviet nationalities in the 1970s, that among Estonians in Estonia fell from 28.3 percent in 1970 to 24.1 percent in 1979, the lowest among any union republic nationality in the latter year. Such a decline is not credible in any objective terms and should be seen as a form of resistance to the growing role of Russian in Estonian life. At the same time, Russian-Estonian bilingualism among Russians in the ESSR declined slightly, from 14.1 percent in 1970 to 12.9 percent in 1979, which was considerably lower than comparable rates in 1979 for neighboring Lithuania (37.4 percent) and Latvia (20.7 percent) as well as those for the Ukraine, Belorussia, and Armenia.[87]

CULTURAL LIFE

Education in Estonia in the post-Stalin era reflected both all-Union developments and local conditions. As noted above, under Stalin combined elementary and secondary education taught in the native languages of the three Baltic republics lasted a year longer than elsewhere in the Soviet Union (eleven vs. ten years) to facilitate the study of Russian. In 1958 the all-Union school reform lengthened the lower and middle levels of education to eleven years throughout the USSR to include time for vocational training and socially useful work, but no additional year was included in the Baltic schools. In 1964–1965 the central government restored the ten-year school system, eliminating the emphasis on vocational training and practical work, and extended this action to the Baltic schools as well. In Estonia and the other Baltic republics numerous official protests arose against this change. For example, leading members of the ESSR Union of Writers argued that Estonian schools needed a longer educational program than those in the RSFSR because students in the former had to learn three languages (Estonian, Russian, and a foreign language) rather than two. Statements of this kind may have had some impact in central government circles. In any case, in the fall of 1965 an eleven-year program for schools in the local languages was re-established in the Baltic republics.[88]

Other changes also altered the nature of elementary and secondary education in Estonia after 1953. No tuition was charged after 1956 at any level of education, and the period of compulsory attendance rose from seven years to eight (implemented 1959–1962). Moreover, since the mid-1960s specialized elementary and secondary education expanded markedly with the increasing establishment of schools emphasizing a particular subject or approach (for example, a foreign language, music, art, or sports). The pedagogical qualifications of teachers in the ESSR also improved; the proportion of those in general education schools with higher education rose from 31 percent in 1960 to 75 percent in 1983.[89]

Given the continuing influx of non-Estonians into the ESSR in the post-Stalin era, the relative position of the Estonian and Russian languages in the schools became a crucial issue. In 1956–1957, 77 percent of the elementary and secondary schools in Estonia used Estonian as the language of instruction; in 1972 the figure was 73 percent. In both cases this proportion was slightly larger than the ethnic Estonian share of the overall population. No data are available for later years, but it is likely that the proportion of schools conducted in Russian increased along with the growing Russian and other non-Estonian population. Schools with parallel instruction in both Estonian and Russian have not been very popular in Estonia; their share of the total number of schools was 8 percent in both 1956–1957 and 1972.[90]

The relative weight of weekly hours devoted to the study of Estonian in Estonian-language schools did not change substantially after the mid-1950s. In fact, the number of hours per week—in all classes combined—declined for both the study of Estonian (77.5 in 1956–1957, 66 in 1981–1982) and Russian (55.5 in 1956–1957, 41 in 1981–1982). However, by 1981, corresponding to the recent all-Union drive to intensify the learning of Russian by non-Russians, the study of Russian was begun in the first grade of Estonian-language schools for the first time in the Soviet era; Russian was also introduced into Estonian preschools. It is noteworthy that in 1981–1982 the ratio of Russian to Estonian study in Russian-language schools in the ESSR (4.5; that is, 72 hours per week for Russian vs. 16 hours per week for Estonian) was nearly three times the ratio of Estonian to Russian in Estonian-language schools (1.6; that is, 66 hours per week for Estonian vs. 41 hours per week for Russian). The study of Estonian in Russian-language schools in the ESSR began in the third grade.[91] Perhaps in response to the ethnic unrest in Estonia at the beginning of the 1980s the Soviet authorities took some steps to improve the study of Estonian in Russian-language schools, including the establishment of Estonian-language olympiads for Russian students (the first of their kind in the USSR, it appears).[92]

Enrollment trends in higher education in Estonia were similar to those at the lower levels. Overall, the number of students in institutions of higher learning in the ESSR grew steadily from 11,867 in 1955–1956 to 25,554 in 1981–1982. The increase was especially rapid in the first half of the 1960s— from 13,507 in 1960–1961 to 21,363 in 1965–1966—but it was only moderate after that. With regard to individual institutions, the Tallinn Polytechnical Institute (9,872 students in 1981–1982) passed Tartu University (7,701 students in 1981–1982) in the early 1960s and has had the largest student body in Estonia since that time. The number of institutions of higher education remained stable at six after the late 1950s, and enrollments at the other four in 1981–1982 were 4,038 at the Estonian Agricultural Academy, 2,874 at the Tallinn Pedagogical Institute, 544 at the Tallinn State Conservatory, and 525 at the ESSR State Art Institute. Evening and correspondence students constituted about one-third to half of the total enrollment in higher education since the mid-1950s (37 percent in 1981).[93] Less information is available on the ethnic composition of university enrollment, but it is known that the Estonian share of the total ESSR student body declined from 82 percent in 1959–1960 to 72 percent in 1970–1971, which was a more rapid decrease than the overall ethnic Estonian proportion in the republic. At Tartu University the Estonian presence remained high (85 percent in 1974) whereas the Tallinn Polytechnical Institute became increasingly internationalized. In 1981, 40 percent of its graduates were Russian.[94]

As was the general Soviet practice since the time of Stalin, the center for research in Estonia was not the universities but the ESSR Academy of Sciences. The academy received considerably more state funding than the universities, and its scholars were freed from undergraduate teaching responsibilities. Overall, including individuals at all research institutes and universities, the number of scientific workers in Estonia more than quadrupled between 1955 and 1983 (from 1,618 to 6,919). The ethnic composition of the scholarly community in the ESSR remained overwhelmingly Estonian (85 percent in 1973).[95] Neverthe-less, Estonian intellectuals complained about the difficulties in conducting research in their native culture, and it is noteworthy that in the ESSR, as elsewhere in the Soviet Union after 1975, all candidate and doctoral disserta-tions had to be submitted in Russian.[96]

In general, output of printed matter in Estonian showed a strong upward trend between the mid-1950s and early 1970s in terms of numbers of both titles and copies. After the mid-1970s, however, absolute numbers leveled off or even declined. The Estonian-language proportion of printed matter published in the ESSR also fell off considerably since the beginning of the post-Stalin era, as seen in the following percentages.[97]

	BOOKS AND BROCHURES		MAGAZINES		NEWSPAPERS	
	Titles	*Copies*	*Titles*	*Copies*	*Titles*	*Copies*
1955	87	83	78	95	86	—
1965	70	83	75	99	76	86
1975	69	79	69	75	76	83
1985	64	70	68	78	71	85

Nevertheless, the Estonian share of all types of printed matter remained above the native ethnic proportion in the ESSR with the exception of book and brochure titles in 1980, which fell to 61 percent before climbing back to 64 percent in the first half of the 1980s. On an all-Union basis Estonian ranked first in the USSR in copies of books published per capita of ethnic group both in 1970 (9.2) and 1979 (13.0). Indeed, in 1980 Estonian ranked fourth in the Soviet Union (after Russian, Ukrainian, and Georgian) in absolute numbers of published titles of books and brochures.[98] It appears that the central govern-ment in the post-Stalin era was willing to permit relatively high levels of book production in Estonia and the other Baltic republics as a kind of cultural safety valve, recognizing that the influence of printed matter in these languages will not be extensive elsewhere in the USSR. Newspaper circulation in Estonian nearly tripled between 1955 (343,000) and 1975 (990,000), but hardly grew after the latter date (1,043,000 in 1983). The major republican daily news-papers continued to be *Rahva Hääl* in Estonian (circulation of 155,200 in 1977) and *Sovetskaia Estoniia* in Russian (44,900).[99]

The role of electronic media in Estonia continually expanded during the post-Stalin era. Between 1958 and 1980 the average number of daily broadcast-ing hours increased from 17.6 to 34.0 for radio and from 3.9 to 35.3 for television. Whereas radio broadcasting remained overwhelmingly Estonian (89 percent in 1965, 88 percent in 1980), television programming in Estonian declined from 26 percent of the total in 1970–1977 to 17 percent in 1980. The major reason for this striking disparity was that the ESSR radio was entirely local while some two-thirds of the television programs originated in Moscow or Leningrad. Furthermore, it is noteworthy that in 1979 less than half of the local television broadcasting in the ESSR was in Estonian.[100] In the late Brezhnev era, in both public statements and an internal party document that became known in the West, the ECP stressed the role of television in the teaching of Russian.[101] For the Estonian population of the northern third of Estonia, the availability of Finnish television provided a unique avenue to the West. Finland's neutral political stance no doubt contributed to the toleration by Soviet authorities of this bridge to the non-Soviet world. In October 1982, however, the local Estonian newspaper in Tallinn, *Õhtuleht* (Evening newspaper), sharply attacked the influence of Finnish television on Estonian youth and the intelligentsia, suggesting that the purpose was to "dehumanize" Soviet citizens. At about the same time the technical apparatus required to receive the Finnish television signal was removed from some public buildings. Nevertheless, the Soviet authorities probably decided that the effort had been counterproductive in view of the negative international publicity; they quickly called off the campaign and restored the status quo ante.[102]

Developments in the realm of high culture in Estonia in the post-Stalin era can be divided into three major periods: the "thaw" and liberation from the straitjacket of Stalinism in the mid- and late 1950s; a rebirth and flowering in the 1960s; and a period of retrenchment and consolidation in the years 1970–1985. Although official cultural policy in Estonia followed Moscow's lead—for example, in the ebb and flow of the Khrushchev thaw—by the 1960s the cultural output of the Estonian creative intelligentsia had developed a dynamic of its own and considerably expanded the parameters of socialist realism. As in the Stalinist era, belletristic literature in the years after 1953 was the most sensitive barometer of the state of Estonian culture. The thaw in the literary realm in Estonia can be dated from 1955, when most of the authors who had been expelled from the Union of Writers in the late 1940s were reinstated.[103] After that time both quantitative and qualitative improvements were striking.

In contrast to the situation in the late Stalinist era, original native belles lettres once again came to dominate among literary publications in the Estonian language, as the following percentages—referring to belletristic titles—indicate.[104]

	Native Estonian lit.	Russian lit. in Est. trans.	Other Soviet lit. in Est. trans.	Foreign lit. in Est. trans.
1950–1954	38	45	—	—
1955–1965	35	23	6	36
1966–1975	46	15	9	30
1981	48	16	8	28

Compared to 1951–1955, the average annual number of works of Estonian belles lettres published in the ESSR more than doubled by 1971–1974 (from 45 to 96), while the average number of copies per year rose 3.6 times to over 2.5 million.[105] In addition to the declining role of Russian literature, the increased availability of foreign (that is, non-Soviet) belles lettres signified a new opening to the outside world. Beginning in 1957 the weekly *"Loomingu" Raamatukogu* (The library of "Looming") mainly published translations, including many Western classics and works by authors (for example, Beckett, Brecht, and Kafka) whose literary output had not appeared as extensively in Russian translation in the USSR, if at all.[106]

Poetry re-emerged from the doldrums in the mid-1950s, becoming lyric rather than didactic. In 1958 nine new collections of verse were published, as compared to only one in 1954. The outstanding poetic work of the thaw years was by Jaan Kross (b. 1920) entitled *Söerikastaja* (The coal concentrator, 1958); it added a new intellectual dimension to Soviet Estonian poetry and indicated that experimentation with form was now possible. Quantitatively, the height of post-Stalin rebirth in poetry came in 1966 when fully twenty collections of verse appeared. A qualitative leap forward also took place in the 1960s with the appearance of a remarkably large new generation of poets—including Paul-Eerik Rummo (b. 1942), Jaan Kaplinski (b. 1941), Viivi Luik (b. 1945), Mats Traat (b. 1936), Hando Runnel (b. 1938), and Enn Vetemaa (b. 1936)—and the re-emergence of an older generation, especially Betti Alver, August Sang, and Kersti Merilaas. The period after 1970 was characterized by further experimentation and development by already established authors with relatively few newcomers—most notably, Jüri Üdi (b. 1948, later known as Juhan Viiding)—to the poetic scene.[107]

In prose the aesthetic advances in the post-Stalin decades were less impressive, but in 1956 it was clear that a new era had begun with the publication of Rudolf Sirge's *Maa ja rahvas* (The land and the people), a novel about the Estonian countryside in 1940–1941 culminating in the mass deportations of the latter year. Sirge's book was the first Soviet Estonian prose work to avoid stereotyping of ideological adversaries and provide a realistic depiction of everyday life. As such it also suggested that a much broader range of subject matter could now be treated. Nevertheless, the dominant prose genre in the 1960s and 1970s was not the novel, but shorter forms such as the novella and the short story. Three younger authors—Mati Unt (b. 1944), Arvo Valton (b. 1935), and Enn Vetemaa—stood out in the 1960s as innovators who offered fresh perspectives on Estonian life and the human condition. Unt's "Võlg" (The debt; 1964) symbolized the emergence of a post-Stalin generation in prose as well as a kind of youthful rebelliousness. The most significant exception to the leading role of shorter forms of prose was the historical novels of Jaan Kross, which were published in the 1970s and early 1980s.[108] Although he too used the novella, Kross seemed to prefer longer treatments for probing psychological studies of historical figures. His subjects included well-known individuals in Estonian history such as Kristjan Jaak Peterson, Johann Voldemar Jannsen, and Johann Köler, as well as more obscure individuals whose connection with the Estonian world is often tenuous. Firmly grounded in historical fact, Kross's novels seek to penetrate the mental world of past eras that remain only partially accessible today. At the same time the parallels they provide with present-day conditions may not be entirely coincidental.

In drama the peak of achievement in the post-Stalin era came slightly later than in poetry or prose, but still in the same remarkable decade of the 1960s. The years from 1953 to the mid-1960s were dominated by established play-wrights such as Juhan Smuul and Egon Rannet. However, partly as a result of the impact of the East European theater of the absurd, Estonian dramatists turned to allegory and satire by the second half of the 1960s. Artur Alliksaar (1923–1966) provided the breakthrough with *Nimetu saar* (Nameless island) in 1966, a symbolic depiction of the Stalinist system. His successful experiment encouraged others to try their hand at allegory and to move beyond merely realistic portrayals of Soviet life. Perhaps the most powerful application of the techniques of the theater of the absurd was Paul-Eerik Rummo's *Tuhkatriinu-mäng* (Cinderella game) in 1969, which used the old fairy-tale motif to explore the ambiguity and absurdity of the human condition. In the 1970s allegory and elements of absurdism continued to play an important role in Estonian drama but with less boldness and less notable success.[109]

With the cultural thaw of the mid-1950s, the Estonian theater began a period of renewal. Kaarel Ird returned to the Vanemuine Theater in Tartu in 1955, and he and a new generation of directors at various Estonian theaters— especially Volemar Panso, Mikk Mikiver, and Kaarin Raid—created new, more versatile productions, which included some elements of the contemporary Western avant garde. At the same time the repertoire, both dramatic and musical, expanded markedly to include both classical and contemporary West-ern authors and composers. Moreover, beginning in 1965, theatrical contacts beyond the Soviet Union grew steadily, providing a wider range of stimuli for the Estonian stage. Estonians performed in Finland, Sweden, Eastern Europe, and the United States; guest appearances by foreign troups in the ESSR came from Finland, Czechoslovakia, East Germany, and Hungary.[110] The number of professional theaters in Estonia—nine—did not change after the consolidations of the Stalinist era. Five were located in Tallinn (one of which gave performances only in Russian) and one each in Tartu, Pärnu, Viljandi, and Rakvere. Theater attendance grew quite steadily with only occasional reverses from 1955 (1,019,000) to 1979 (1,504,000) before dropping in 1982 (1,387,000).[111]

In the figurative arts, the mid-1950s also formed the major turning point. Here too the range of subject matter and styles expanded far beyond the narrow restrictions of the pre-1953 era. In the next three decades the dominant genre, in terms of both the number of talented artists and the quality of their work, was graphics. Even within this genre the diversity of styles was striking—for example, from the historical motifs of Vive Tolli to the geometric designs of Tõnis Vint to the colorful floral patterns of Malle Leis. Estonian graphic artists also received wide recognition in the USSR as a whole; in 1975, for example, two-thirds of the Soviet graphic artists represented at an exhibition in Yugoslavia were Estonian.[112] As in other forms of culture, growing international contacts served as an inspiration for artistic experimentation—for example, the re-emergence of abstractionism in Estonian painting in the 1960s. Exhibitions of foreign art in Estonia in the Soviet era began in 1957 and included works from Japan, Mexico, Finland, Sweden, and Eastern Europe. Beginning in 1960 Estonian artists had numerous exhibitions abroad, including Scandinavia, Eastern and Western Europe, Canada, the United States, Japan, and India.[113] Since 1958 two noteworthy artistic periodicals, averaging two to three issues annually, have been published in Estonia: *Kunst* (Art) and *Kunst ja Kodu* (Art and home). *Kunst* carries scholarly articles on both Estonian and international art; *Kunst ja Kodu* deals with applied art and design.

In Estonian musical life the immediate post-Stalin era once again constituted a watershed. The cultural thaw and the dismantling of Stalinist orthodoxy encouraged a much greater variety of approaches and techniques in composition. Among the relatively large generation of post-Stalin composers who came on the musical scene, Arvo Pärt (b. 1935, emigrated 1980) and Kuldar Sink (b. 1942) stood out as experimenters in modernistic techniques. In the 1960s, Veljo Tormis (b. 1930) successfully explored the possibilities of using the ancient Estonian folk song in choral composition—for example, his *Eesti kalendrilaulud* (Estonian calendar songs; 1967). In the musical realm as well international contacts provided new sources of enrichment. Among the best Estonian operas of the past three decades was *Barbara von Tisenhusen* (1969) by Eduard Tubin (1905–1982), an Estonian composer who lived in Sweden after 1944; the work was commissioned for performance by the Estonia Theater in Tallinn.

In the post-Stalin era foreign musicians from Eastern and Western Europe, Finland, and Canada performed in Estonia. Fewer Soviet Estonian musicians had the opportunity to perform abroad. The most widely traveled ensemble was Gustav Ernesaks's *Riiklik Akadeemiline Meeskoor* (State Academic Male Chorus), which sang in Finland, Sweden, East and West Germany, Italy, and Switzerland. Neeme Järvi (b. 1937), who was associated with the ESSR State Symphony Orchestra until his emigration in 1980, was among the leading Soviet conductors in the 1970s and had performed in nearly twenty foreign countries.[114]

A special role in Estonian musical life continued to be played by the song festival tradition. Six national song festivals (counting from 1869, numbers fourteen to nineteen) were held at five-year intervals between 1955 and 1980, with the exception of the centennial festival in 1969. Although the number of performers stabilized in the neighborhood of 30,000, the size of the audience continued to grow, reaching roughly 250,000 in 1969 and perhaps 300,000 in 1980. In many ways the seventeenth all-Estonian song festival in 1969, which emphasized the continuity of Estonian musical culture over the past century, proved a fitting climax to a decade of general cultural renewal in the 1960s. The program consisted overwhelmingly of works by native Estonian composers reaching back to the national awakening. Although in 1975 and 1980 the programs were more internationalized and politicized, it is noteworthy that in the latter year Ernesaks's *My Fatherland Is My Love*, which continues to be an unofficial national anthem in Soviet Estonia, became the official finale on the program for the first time.[115] It is safe to say that no other Estonian cultural tradition of the past century and a quarter has proved as powerful or as durable.

After 1953 official policy in Estonia toward religion and the churches showed a great deal of continuity from the Stalinist era. With few exceptions the Soviet authorities adopted a gradualist line, following Marx's dictum that religion will disappear as socialism develops. However, the immediate post-Stalin years witnessed something of a religious revival in Estonia and led to a new antireligious activism by the ECP and the state in 1957. The campaign against religious customs was highly successful over the next decade. In 1957–1968 christenings of newborn children fell from 58.8 to 12.5 percent and religious weddings from 29.8 to 2.6 percent of the total. At the same time, the proportion of eighteen-year-olds undergoing confirmation dropped from 49.0 to 2.2 percent. Only religious burials partially withstood this trend: 64.5 percent in 1957, 46.0 percent in 1968. Nevertheless, although the practice of these outward forms of religion continued to decline, there is also evidence of the substantial strength of religious sentiments in Estonia. Vello Salo has estimated that in the late 1960s nearly 25 percent of ethnic Estonians were church members; after that the number of congregations has remained stable (367 in 1969, 359 in 1978). Despite the difficulty in preparing new clergy and the unavailability of religious literature, the number of congregations relative to the entire population in Estonia ranked substantially above the Soviet average.[116]

POST–STALIN ERA BALANCE SHEET

At the time of Stalin's death in 1953, the Estonian future looked extremely bleak. The elites of the independence era had been physically removed from the scene, primarily through Stalinist repression and wartime emigration. Overall, the ethnic Estonian population declined by a startling one-third in 1939–1955.[117] At the same time, large numbers of non-Estonians, mainly Russians, were immigrating to Estonia. Native Estonians had also been removed from the ECP leadership since, in the postwar era, Stalin apparently trusted only Communists who had spent their entire lives in the Soviet Union. Finally, Estonian culture appeared to be on the verge of extinction in the face of the heavy-handed application of the "elder brother" concept of the superiority of all things Russian.

Nevertheless, in the mid-1950s conditions began to improve markedly, and within the next decade life became almost unrecognizable as compared to the late Stalinist years. Mass repression stopped, and significant numbers of surviving deportees returned. The native Estonian role in the ECP increased considerably, and the hope of an eventual re-Estonianization of the party leadership—along with the autonomy such a change implied—emerged. The economic system became more rational, particularly in the rural sector, and there were major improvements in the standard of living, a development aided by the opening up of contacts with relatives in the West who now sent packages to Estonia. Most striking, Estonian culture had revived and even flowered within the parameters of the Soviet context by the early 1960s. The continued influx of non-Estonians remained cause for concern, but the Estonian share of the ESSR population (75 percent in 1959) was still substantial.

The mid-1960s to the mid-1970s can be characterized as a period of consolidation of the gains made in the earlier post-Stalin years. Living standards continued to rise as did the ethnic Estonian proportion of the ECP, at least until the start of the 1970s. Even Johannes Käbin, the Russian-Estonian who headed the ECP, came to appreciate Estonian national concerns to some extent. There were significant new cultural achievements, and the general mood, despite the impact of the invasion of Czechoslovakia, remained upbeat to the end of the 1960s. The centennial of the first all-Estonian song festival in 1969 proved to be a powerful national demonstration; about one in four Estonians in the ESSR attended the event. Contacts with Western culture also mushroomed through a growing influx of tourists and the availability of Finnish television in the northern third of Estonia.

In the mid-1970s, however, the mood began to shift, and in the next decade there was increasing cause for pessimism. Karl Vaino replaced Käbin as ECP first secretary, thus shattering the hope that native Estonians could once again take charge of local affairs. Living standards no longer improved and may have declined. Non-Estonian immigration fell in the late 1970s but rose again in the early 1980s. The 1979 census revealed that the ethnic Estonian proportion of the total population had dropped to 65 percent and to just over 50 percent in Tallinn; these figures do not include the large numbers of Soviet troops stationed in Estonia. These trends and others—including the growing role of Russian in education, administration, and everyday life; the increasing scarcity of printed matter in Estonian; and restrictions on research in Estonian culture—led to unprecedented social unrest in 1980. Recalling the Russification years of the late nineteenth century under the tsars, the Vaino period was termed the "neo-Shakhovskoi era" by some Estonians.[118] The comparison was not entirely apt, since the position of Estonian in the early 1980s remained more favorable than it was in the 1890s, but it was considerably less favorable than in 1939. The crucial difference between the late tsarist era and the 1980s was that Russians constituted only 4 percent of the population of Estonia in 1897 versus 28 percent in 1979. Thus, the issue of future immigration was vital for the Estonians. Given the decline in Slavic birthrates—those of the most mobile population—in the USSR, it is difficult to know where large numbers of new immigrants might come from. Yet if the industrialization of Estonia continued and all-Union projects such as the Muuga harbor were located there, the necessary labor would have to come from somewhere outside of Estonia itself.

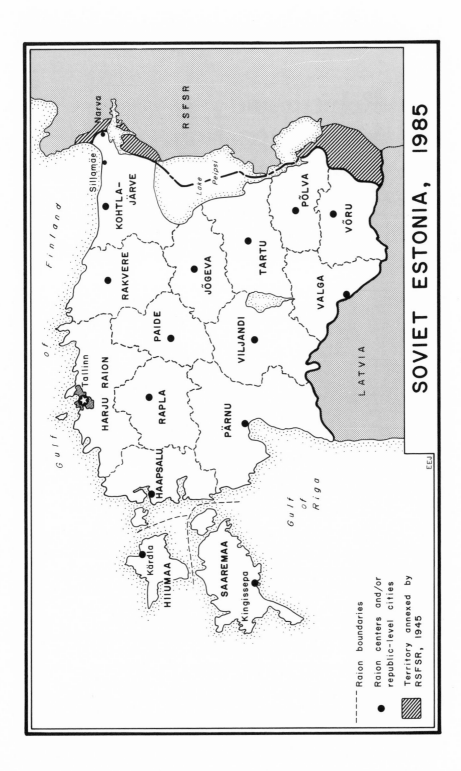

SOVIET ESTONIA, 1985

RSFSR

Finland

Gulf of Finland

Narva

Sillamäe

KOHTLA-
JÄRVE

Lake Peipsi

RSFSR

PÕLVA

VÕRU

RAKVERE

JÕGEVA

TARTU

VALGA

PAIDE

VILJANDI

Tallinn

HARJU RAION

RAPLA

PÄRNU

LATVIA

HAAPSALU

Gulf of Riga

Kärdla

HIIUMAA

SAAREMAA

Kingissepa

- - - - -   Raion boundaries

●   Raion centers and/or
    republic-level cities

▨   Territory annexed by
    RSFSR, 1945

EEJ

14 Rebirth and De-Sovietization, 1985–1991

Life in Estonia changed dramatically in the six years following the succession of Mikhail Gorbachev to power in March 1985. In the manner of the reforming tsars in Russia's past, Gorbachev recognized that the Soviet Union had reached an impasse and announced the need for *perestroika* (restructuring) and *glasnost'* (openness). The reform movement evoked an enthusiastic response in Estonia— as well as in Latvia and Lithuania—and the Baltic states have been in the forefront of the drive for change in the USSR. What has transpired in Estonia since 1985 has involved both a recovery from the alienation and lethargy of the late-Brezhnev era and a simultaneous process of emancipation from Soviet norms.

ORIGINS OF REVIVAL

The movement for change in Estonia can best be characterized as a profound and broadly based desire for the restoration of Estonian political, cultural, and economic self-determination. Its origins must be sought, first of all, at the all-Union level and in Gorbachev's blessing for a frank and open discussion of Soviet shortcomings and the need for far-reaching reform. In Estonia, *glasnost'* opened the way for the rebirth of grass-roots organizations and a revival of the self-help tradition dating back to the independence era and the national awakening of the 1860s and 1870s. One might assume that Stalinism and its legacy during the decades of Soviet rule had destroyed this tradition, but the past few years have shown that the capacity for initiative and activization was not dead but merely dormant. The impact of *glasnost'* was moderate at first, as a wary population gradually and circumspectly tested its limits. By 1987, however, the Estonian population had mobilized; since then the pace of events has moved at a rapid and, at times, breathtaking speed.

The issue that activated the Estonian masses was the environment, specifically the threat of phosphate mining in north-central Estonia, which could result in the possible pollution of some 40 percent of Estonia's water supply (through excavating radioactive materials—chiefly uranium), and increased air pollution through processing at the Maardu phosphate mining site near Tallinn. Furthermore, the project would require another major influx of immigrant labor into Estonia, yet another demographic threat to the native population. The environmental question emerged in late 1986 and came to a head in spring 1987 in an unprecedented public debate. Various institutions that up until then had followed an orthodox line, such as the administrations of Tartu University and the Estonian Soviet Socialist Republic (ESSR) Academy of Sciences, now publicly opposed the mining. Students at universities and high schools also demonstrated against phosphate mining. Indeed, the ESSR authorities could not ignore the public pressure, and there was no attempt at a crackdown.[1] The issue of the environment involved a key concern of the movement for change— who has the right to make decisions regarding Estonia and its natural resources, economy, culture, and other aspects of life—for the phosphate-mining plan was conceived and directed entirely by the central government in Moscow. That question remained in the public eye until late October 1987, when it was announced that the USSR Council of Ministers had shelved the matter for the present.[2]

In 1987 a second activizing episode, which would play a catalyzing role in the next few years and which occurred on the anniversary (August 23) of the Molotov-Ribbentrop Pact, was a demonstration at Hirvepark in Tallinn near the seat of the ESSR government. Estimates of the number of participants range from about two thousand to five thousand. Strikingly, Estonian dissidents who had only recently been released from prison organized the protest; they even obtained official permission for the event.[3] This was the first public protest against the Molotov-Ribbentrop Pact's disastrous consequences for Estonia and the other two Baltic states. Although Tiit Madison, one of the leaders of the Hirvepark demonstration, was forced to emigrate, the event, as with the phosphate debate, emboldened Estonian society and further shook it out of its lethargy. A growing range of issues was held up to public scrutiny, and in this process the so-called creative intelligentsia—writers, critics, artists, journalists, and so on—played a leading role. Another milestone that invigorated public discussion in Estonia occurred at a plenum of the leadership organs of the cultural unions in April 1988. At this meeting, issues taboo during the early years of *glasnost'* were now delineated with a new level of candor, and the plenum called on the nineteenth all-Union Communist party conference to establish genuine federalism and sovereignty for the union republics, organize multicandidate elections, and guarantee cultural rights to all nationalities in the Soviet Union. Speakers at the plenum freely criticized the ruling Communist bureaucracy by name, especially Karl Vaino, the incumbent Estonian Communist Party (ECP) first secretary and the embodiment of the Brezhnev era.[4]

THE HOT SUMMER OF 1988

The six months following the cultural unions' plenum witnessed a whirlwind of activity animated by a romantic optimism not unlike the atmosphere of the nineteenth-century national awakening. On April 13 the economist Edgar Savisaar called for establishing a democratic movement to support restructuring, a *popular front*, as he termed it; an initiative group was founded the same day. A few days later the Estonian Heritage Society (*Eesti Muinsuskaitse Selts*), founded in December 1987, held its Heritage Days in Tartu. This group, which had already taken the lead in the movement to reclaim the Estonian past, increasingly inaccessible in the late years of the Brezhnev era, began filling in the blank spots in the historical record. Its most important act, however, was flying the national colors—blue, black, and white—of independent Estonia at the Tartu days in mid-April. By early June, the traditional Estonian flag was already massively in evidence, such as at the Night Song Festival in conjunction with Tallinn's Old Town Days. This successful breaking of the Soviet taboo, any transgression of which had earlier led to arrest, forced the authorities to react; on June 23 the ESSR Supreme Soviet Presidium officially designated the traditional tricolor as the Estonian national colors.[5] More than anything, restoring the blue, black, and white colors to a place of honor signified the reconnection of Estonians with their past and reestablished a sense of historical continuity.

Grass-roots mobilization was also partially responsible for removing Karl Vaino as ECP first secretary on June 16, 1988, in that Gorbachev and the Moscow leadership were made aware of Vaino's increasing unpopularity. He was replaced—on Moscow's direct recommendation—by Vaino Väljas who had lost out to Karl Vaino ten years earlier and been in "exile" in the 1980s as Soviet ambassador to Venezuela and Nicaragua. Väljas became the first native Estonian to hold the office of ECP first secretary since Nikolai Karotamm was purged in 1950; Väljas quickly gained popularity by speaking out—in perfect Estonian—for republican and Estonian national rights and against the traditional centralized model of the Soviet Union. August 1988 was once again dominated by the specter of the Molotov-Ribbentrop Pact: in midmonth both the Estonian daily *Rahva Hääl* and the Russian-language daily *Sovetskaia*

Estoniia published the text of the secret protocols to the pact. On August 23 demonstrations occurred in several Estonian cities, including one in Tallinn— again organized by former dissidents—that called for an end to Soviet rule in Estonia. The Soviet takeover in 1940 was denounced as a military occupation, not a revolution.[6] In this charged atmosphere an ECP Central Committee plenum took place on September 9–10, 1988. Väljas, who took a strong reformist and anti-Stalinist position, supported, among other things, a new treaty of federation based on equal cooperation by the union republics and raising Estonian to the status of the official language of the ESSR. On the following day, Väljas received a hero's welcome at an all-day rally at the song festival grounds organized by the Estonian Popular Front and attended by about 300,000 people.[7] The gathering mixed political speeches with both traditional and current songs and exemplified what became known in 1988 as the "singing revolution" or *perestroika* Estonian style.

POLITICAL PLURALISM AND DEMOCRATIZATION

Politically, one of the most striking consequences of *glasnost'* and *perestroika* has been the rebirth of pluralism and the emergence of many parties and groupings. A result of spontaneous, grass-roots activism and often looking back to the era of Estonian independence for inspiration, these movements were viewed ambivalently or with outright hostility by the ruling ECP. As noted above, the largest of the new groups, the Estonian Popular Front, began in April 1988 and held its founding congress at the start of October. Led by such reformist Communists as Edgar Savisaar and Marju Lauristin, daughter of Johannes Lauristin, the first head of the Soviet Estonian government, and a journalism professor at Tartu University, the Popular Front sought to prod the ECP and society as a whole toward more rapid and radical change. The front's bylaws barred its leaders from holding top positions in the ECP or in other official organizations. At the congress, Savisaar staked out a middle ground for the Popular Front between unreconstructed Stalinists and what he termed *unrealistic restorationists*, who felt that the pre-1940 republic could be made to reappear despite the passage of fifty years. ECP leader Väljas also greeted the congress but warned the Popular Front not to compete with the party or Soviet institutions. By according the front official status the ECP sought to co-opt and manage the reform movement from below but with a wary eye. By the time of the congress the Popular Front claimed a membership of 100,000, close to that of the ECP itself. A full 91 percent of the front's membership was Estonian, whereas 28 percent of the delegates to the congress also belonged to the ECP.[8]

As a reaction to the growth of the Estonian Popular Front, a self-styled

Internationalist Movement (Intermovement, for short, something of a misnomer because its supporters are almost exclusively Russian speaking) held its
first rally in July 1988 with some two thousand to three thousand participants.
At the first Intermovement congress in March 1989, only 11 [1.5 percent] of
742 delegates were ethnic Estonians; the leaders of Intermovement claimed that
the "nationalist" nature of the Popular Front forced them to take counter-
measures and organize. Above all, Intermovement opposed decentralizing the
Soviet Union and what the March 1989 congress called "creeping counter-
revolution" in Estonia. One should not assume, however, that this movement
represented the great majority of the Russian or non-Estonian population of
Estonia. In an opinion poll taken at the end of 1988, for example, Intermovement received the backing of only 15 percent of the Russian speakers in Estonia.[9] Aside from this hard-line group, however, the Russian population of Estonia remained largely unorganized, although several smaller non-
Estonian and non-Russian minorities (e.g., Jews, Armenians, and Latvians)
quickly established thriving cultural associations as soon as *glasnost'* made this
possible.

Clearly, the major beneficiaries of the greater openness were the Estonians
themselves, who, given their political traditions and their connections via
Finland to the outside world, had perhaps the strongest basis in the Soviet Union
for taking advantage of the situation. With regard to Estonian political parties,
not surprisingly among the first to assume the risk of publicly organizing was
the Estonian National Independence party (ENIP) in August 1988, led by Lagle
Parek, Tunne Kelam, and other former dissidents who had also taken the lead in
raising the issue of the Molotov-Ribbentrop Pact.[10] From its beginning the ENIP
has taken the strongest stand for restoring complete independence to Estonia.

By mid-1990 the Estonian political spectrum had filled out considerably,
with the most noteworthy parties classified according to the following rough
scale (excluding the ECP, which will be discussed below). On the right side of
the spectrum were the ENIP, the Estonian Conservative People's party, the
Estonian Christian Democratic party, the Estonian Christian Union, the Estonian Entrepreneurial party, and the *Res publica* Association. In the center were
the Estonian Liberal Democratic party, the Estonian Democratic party, which
was oriented to the non-Estonian population, and the Estonian Rural-Center
party. On the left wing were the Estonian Green party, the Estonian Social
Democratic Independence party, the Estonian Democratic Labor party, and the
Russian Social Democratic party (in Estonia).[11] The Popular Front, although it
continued to exist as a formal organization, had given birth to a number of the
above-mentioned center and left political parties.

Democratization in Estonia witnessed not only the emergence of a significant number of parties and groupings but also the development of increasingly
freer elections and more sophisticated voters. In March–April 1989 the first

nationwide, multicandidate elections were held in Soviet Estonia to select delegates to the new Congress of People's Deputies in Moscow. There were 119 candidates for thirty-six seats (3.3 candidates on average per electoral district), including 73 Estonians and 46 others. The Soviet Estonian authorities made no attempt to block any candidacies. An impressive 87 percent of the eligible voters took part in the balloting, and Estonians, most associated with the Popular Front, won twenty-nine of the thirty-six seats. The most significant loser in the spring 1989 elections was the hard-line Stalinist wing of the ECP, whose candidates proved highly unpopular with the voters.[12] The population gained further experience in electoral politics in local government elections in December 1989 that achieved a turnout of 72 percent and used an entirely new and relatively sophisticated voting mechanism—the single transferable vote. This same system, with a 78 percent turnout, was applied with similar success to the ESSR Supreme Soviet elections in March 1990. The major dissonant note was four seats being allocated to the Soviet military stationed in Estonia. Between these elections, at the end of February 1990, the Estonian population voted for representatives to the non-Soviet Congress of Estonia, an alternative parliament that denied the legality of Soviet institutions. The turnout there was massive as well, with some 90 percent of the eligible voters participating.[13]

SOVEREIGNTY AND INDEPENDENCE

Ever since Estonian political self-determination emerged as an issue of public debate in 1988, the question was how and in what form this goal could be realized. At first the publicly stated aim remained limited to autonomy and the decentralization of the Soviet Union into a genuine federation or confederation, paralleling the proposal made by four Estonian intellectuals in September 1987 for the establishment of a self-managing economic zone in Estonia.[14] Initially, Mikhail Gorbachev welcomed Estonian and Baltic activism, including the rise of the popular fronts, as a kind of motor for *perestroika*, and he seems to have viewed the Balts as a model for the regeneration of the USSR. As Baltic political aspirations became more radicalized, moving toward full independence, however, Gorbachev and the central authorities reacted with increasing coolness. Although accepting the sweeping changes in East-Central Europe, the Soviet leader apparently insisted that the state borders remain as they had been established in World War II. Nevertheless, by early 1991 the drive for Estonian and Baltic independence could only have been halted by a throwback to the methods of 1956 and 1968, and such repressive force could provide no permanent solution to the Baltic question.

The first notable landmark in the process of political de-Sovietization came with the declaration on sovereignty by the ESSR Supreme Soviet (258 for,

1 against, and 5 abstaining) in November 1988. Despite condemnation from Moscow and pressure to revoke this step, the Supreme Soviet reaffirmed its stand in December by a vote of 150 to 91. This move was all the more remarkable because the Supreme Soviet of late 1988 had been selected by traditional Soviet methods, that is, "elections" with single candidates picked by the ECP authorities. Even this body had become subject to an aroused public opinion, however, especially because 861,000 inhabitants of Estonia (out of a total of about 1.5 million) signed petitions urging that the USSR constitutional revisions proposed by the central government be rejected. *Sovereignty* in this context meant the primacy of local laws over all-Union ones and the right to exercise veto power over all-Union legislation. In promoting this action, the ECP, led by Väljas, placed itself firmly in the forefront of the movement for reform and decentralization in the Soviet Union. In November 1988, Indrek Toome replaced the discredited Bruno Saul, who had defended Moscow's policies regarding phosphate mining, as chair of the ESSR Council of Ministers,[15] which meant that reform Communists now headed both the party and the government in Estonia.

The year 1989 witnessed growing sentiment for complete political independence. A major force moving public opinion in this direction was the Estonian Citizens' Committees, established on the anniversary of the declaration of Estonian independence on February 24, 1989, by the ENIP, the Estonian Heritage Society, and the Estonian Christian Union. Basing its activity on the principle of legal continuity from the independence era, the Citizens' Committees organized the voluntary registration of individuals who were themselves citizens of the pre-1940 republic or descended from such a person. The movement began gradually, registering about 100,000 people by July 1989, but by February 1990 the figure was more than 700,000, well over half the ethnic Estonian population of Estonia. In addition, 34,345 applications for Estonian citizenship were received from post-1940 immigrants.[16] As noted above, the movement held elections in late February 1990 for a non-Soviet Congress of Estonia; this body met three times that year, in March, May, and October. In 1989 the major impact of the Citizens' Committees, through mobilization at the grass-roots level and its uncompromising appeal to legal continuity, was to push other groups and parties toward accepting the goal of complete independence.

In the spirit of *glasnost'* a new phenomenon in Estonia was the appearance of public opinion polls, which provided a unique perspective on the political sympathies of the population. A series of polls conducted by the Mainor public opinion research center over a thirteen-month period in 1989–1990 suggests a substantial increase in proindependence sentiments. The proportion of those favoring complete independence, that is, outside the Soviet Union, was as follows:[17]

	Estonians	*Non-Estonians*
April 1989	56 percent	5 percent
September 1989	64 percent	9 percent
May 1990	96 percent	26 percent

There is every indication that support for independence remained high among Estonians, and proindependence sentiment likely continued to grow among non-Estonians. The proportion of non-Estonians backing the status quo in Estonia declined from 54 percent in April 1989 to 21 percent in May 1990; in the latter poll a plurality (47 percent) of non-Estonians supported the alternative of Estonia as part of a reformed Soviet confederation.

Thus during the course of 1989 the ethnic Estonian population moved from advocating sovereignty in the Soviet context to advocating full independence. In this process the impending fiftieth anniversary of the Molotov-Ribbentrop Pact stimulated further demands that the Soviet authorities come to terms with its consequences for the Baltic states. In June 1989, the Congress of People's Deputies in Moscow established a special commission, eleven of whose twenty-five members hailed from the Baltic republics, to study the Molotov-Ribbentrop Pact and politically and legally assess it. The commission found that the secret protocol did, in fact, exist and recommended that they be declared invalid. The Congress of People's Deputies did this on December 24, 1989, without, however, making a direct link between the pact and the forced annexation of the Baltic states.[18] The fiftieth anniversary of the Molotov-Ribbentrop Pact, on August 23, 1989, witnessed the most dramatic demonstration to date of Baltic determination and solidarity. A human chain, connecting an estimated 1 to 2 million people, stretched for the nearly four hundred miles between Tallinn and Vilnius and evoked condemnation and threats from the CPSU Central Committee, but Moscow's response only solidified the growing consensus on the need for Estonian and Baltic independence.[19] The August rally also highlighted the tendency toward increasing intra-Baltic cooperation. Other examples included the close relations among the three popular fronts, as witness the Baltic Assembly in May 1989; the renewal of the 1934 treaty of cooperation between the Baltic states, including the restoration of the Baltic Council in May 1990; and the joint meeting of all three Baltic parliaments in Vilnius in December 1990.[20]

By fall 1989 a strong consensus emerged among the Estonian population on the goal of independence, especially after the Popular Front joined the bandwagon in October by declaring its final aim for Estonia to be "an independent state in the demilitarized neutral Baltoscandia."[21] The unreformed ESSR Supreme Soviet moved in the same direction on November 12 by declaring legally invalid the incorporation of Estonia into the USSR in 1940 and terming what transpired a "military occupation." The vote was 188 for, 1 against, and 4 abstentions; forty-six deputies (virtually all non-Estonians) walked out before the balloting.[22] The question now became, What would be the most effective means to bring about the restoration of independence? On the one hand, the Popular Front argued that existing institutions, if reformed, could lead the way; a democratically elected Supreme Soviet could become a constituent assembly and then negotiate independence from the USSR. On the other hand, the Citizens' Committees insisted that only a non-Soviet Congress of Estonia could legally resurrect the pre-1940 republic. As it happened, both approaches were tried. Elected in March 1990, the new 105-member Supreme Soviet, now called the Supreme Council, moved on March 30 to declare the start of a transition period to the reestablishment of an independent Estonia. The vote was seventy-three to zero, with twenty-seven non-Estonian deputies present but not voting. Two weeks earlier, on March 11–12, the Congress of Estonia, which regarded itself as an alternative parliament, claimed the moral and legal right to negotiate independence.[23] Nevertheless, the two bodies agreed to cooperate toward their common goal, and the presence of forty-four Congress of Estonia deputies in the Supreme Council seemed to augur well for the future. Soon, however, a falling out took place over strategy and tactics, and because the Congress lacked legislative or administrative authority, it was difficult for it to compete with the Supreme Council in the public eye.

For its part, at the start of April 1990, the Supreme Council designated a new prime minister, Edgar Savisaar, who was to preside over the transition period to independence. Having resigned earlier from the ECP, Savisaar became the first non-Communist head of government in Estonia in fifty years. In the remaining months of 1990 and early 1991, the Savisaar government sought, without apparent success, to carry on serious negotiations with Gorbachev and the Moscow authorities. During this impasse the three Baltic governments worked together for independence, seeking to internationalize the Baltic question because negotiations with Moscow remained stalled. In the latter part of 1990 the Balts approached the Conference on Security and Cooperation in Europe (CSCE), and the three Baltic foreign ministers were invited guests to the CSCE summit in Paris in November. By demand of the Soviet government, however, they were expelled from the Paris meeting.[24] Nevertheless, the Balts were garnering growing support, especially in Scandinavia and Central Europe, although the major Western powers, including the United States, continued to base their policy on Gorbachev and were reluctant to undertake any steps that might weaken his position. In the last few months of 1990, Gorbachev moved to the right, cutting his ties with reformist and democratic elements, and in January 1991 came the bloody crackdown in Lithuania and Latvia. But if anything these chilling events strengthened the resolve of the Estonian population and probably won over more non-Estonians to the goal of independence.

In the process of de-Sovietization the cumulative impact of symbolic changes was not insignificant. In 1989, February 24 was officially designated Independence Day, and the blue, black, and white tricolor replaced the Soviet Estonian flag on Tall Hermann tower in Tallinn. Pre-Soviet names for streets, boulevards, and squares were restored all over Estonia. Victory Square in Tallinn, for example, is now Freedom Square, its name in the 1920s and 1930s, and the main urban center on the island of Saaremaa is again Kuressaare, not Kingissepa. The Soviet era administrative unit, *raion*, was replaced by the traditional *maakond*, "district" (see glossary). In 1989, Estonia also returned to its natural time zone (the same as Finland's), one hour different from Moscow time, which had been imposed during the Soviet period. The most significant symbolic step occurred in May 1990 when the newly elected Supreme Council officially renamed the Estonian SSR the Republic of Estonia. In addition, the Soviet Estonian flag, emblem, and national anthem were dropped, and the blue, black, and white tricolor was restored to the status of state flag of Estonia. Leaders of the Congress of Estonia movement, however, objected to the move as premature because Estonia remained effectively under Moscow's rule.[25]

On the domestic scene in Estonia political life in 1990 remained largely in flux, even after the Supreme Council elections in March. The elected deputies had run as individuals, and because the number of political parties continued to wax and wane, the strengths of the various groupings were not entirely clear. The Popular Front emerged as the strongest faction, although less so than in Latvia or Lithuania. More conservative was the Free Estonia group led by reformist Communists; more radical was a smaller assortment of deputies associated with various new parties. About one-fourth of the Supreme Council members were non-Estonians (nearly all Russians) who opposed Estonian independence and were largely associated with Intermovement.[26] The most dramatic show of opposition by Intermovement and its allies was a pro-Moscow demonstration on May 15, 1990, in front of the Estonian government building. The unruly crowd, although numbering only about two thousand, tried to storm the building; however, it quickly dispersed when Savisaar called out large numbers of Estonian counterdemonstrators on the state radio.[27] The ECP's position became increasingly anomalous, especially after the unreformed Supreme Soviet abolished its leading role in public life in February. Despite its role in generally encouraging reform, events were beginning to overtake the ECP. In 1990 the party lost more than half its members, dropping from 105,600 in January 1990 to 47,000 in January 1991—including a disproportionately large number of Estonians among the dropouts; of those remaining more than half no longer paid party dues. By January 1991 the ECP had formally split into an independent ECP with about five thousand members, which supported Estonian independence, and an ECP led mainly by non-Estonians following the Communist party of the Soviet Union. The size of the latter's active membership remained unclear.[28]

Aside from the primary question of independence and how to achieve it, numerous other difficult issues remained on the public agenda in Estonia in early 1991. Particularly vexing was the question of citizenship. Who among Estonia's present inhabitants had the right to citizenship? Given the demographic distortions created by Stalinist and later Soviet policy, what would be a fair and equitable solution today? What is the appropriate residency requirement for citizenship? These questions have no easy answers, and both the Supreme Soviet and later the Supreme Council have taken their time with these issues, seeking to avoid any precipitate step that might be difficult to reverse. Another matter of serious concern was the Soviet military presence in Estonia and also Estonian participation in the Soviet armed forces. Although the exact number of Soviet troops in Estonia was a well-guarded secret, an Estonian exile estimate for 1984—just over 120,000—is probably not far off the mark.[29] This figure compares with the 115,000 Soviet troops that occupied Estonia in 1940. Given the military's role in the eclipse of Estonian independence and in enforcing Soviet rule, its presence was a particularly sensitive issue. The Balts welcomed the start of the withdrawal of Soviet forces from Central Europe, but some may have been reassigned to the Baltic republics. In any independence negotiations with Moscow, the removal of Soviet troops—probably in a phased withdrawal—is a key issue.

Of more immediate import was the question of military service by Estonian and other young men living in Estonia. Maltreatment of Baltic soldiers became apparent—and perhaps increased—in the age of *glasnost'*, fueling calls for national units and service only in the Baltic region. As a temporary solution, the Estonian Supreme Soviet in March 1990 passed a law permitting alternative civilian service, contravening existing Soviet policy. In 1990 in Estonia less than one-third of those eligible for the military draft responded, suggesting that at least some non-Estonians opposed standard Soviet military service.[30]

THE ECONOMY AND SOCIAL ISSUES

As in the Soviet Union, the Estonian economy declined during the Gorbachev era, a continuation of the downward slide that began in the later Brezhnev years. In the latter part of the 1980s, output of key industrial and agricultural products such as electrical energy, paper, cement, and potatoes either stagnated or fell.[31] Consumers faced numerous shortages and the rationing of many staple items. Nevertheless, Estonia, better off than the neighboring Russian Republic, required—at least in principle—buyers to prove Estonian residence before they could purchase scarce goods. Estonia also benefited from its traditional ties to Finland and Scandinavia; 100,000 Estonians traveled to Finland in 1990, more than did so during the entire previous Soviet era. Many found work there (at minimal wage levels by Finnish standards) and brought home precious foreign goods and hard currency.[32]

Given the critical state of the Soviet economic system and that some 90 percent of Estonia's economy was controlled by decisionmakers in Moscow, the Estonians enthusiastically advocated radical economic reform in the Gorbachev years. In September 1987 four Estonian intellectuals, Siim Kallas, Tiit Made, Edgar Savisaar, and Mikk Titma, put forth a plan for economic autonomy and self-management known as *Isemajandav Eesti* (Estonian acronym IME, which is also the Estonian word for miracle). The plan called for an autonomous, self-managing economic zone in Estonia and decentralizing the Estonian economy. From the start the IME proposal received strong support from the Estonian population, and gradually the ECP came to accept the idea, especially after Väljas became first secretary in June 1988.[33] Despite backing in Moscow, especially in the all-Union Supreme Soviet in 1989, the central government failed to grant any significant self-management powers to Estonia, and the Estonians recognized that the plan would be infeasible in an unreformed Soviet economy. Moscow's vacillations and inability to act decisively on this issue certainly contributed to the growth of proindependence sentiment among the Estonian population.

With the issue of political independence dominating the beginning of the 1990s, any further plans for economic reform in Estonia had to wait until the crucial political questions were resolved. Nevertheless, economists in Estonia looked to the West and to Estonia's experience during the independence era for possible models. The key goals were marketization and privatization. One concrete step was reestablishing private agriculture, although many potential farmers took a wait-and-see attitude given the political uncertainties.[34]

Glasnost' also appeared in the realm of statistics. For example, considerably more information was made available from the 1989 census than from the one in the late Brezhnev era. Overall population growth slowed in Estonia in the 1980s compared with previous decades, following the general trend in the European USSR. The rate of natural population increases grew slightly in the second half of the 1980s, whereas the mechanical increase declined from an average of 8,006 for 1985–1987 to 3,285 in 1988 and 4,611 in 1989. The ethnic Estonian portion of the total natural increase in Estonia jumped from 19 percent in 1986 to 45 percent in 1989; in this same three-year period the annual number of abortions dropped from 36,354 to 25,841.[35]

With regard to the crucial issue of the ethnic composition of the population of Estonia, the census figures for 1989 can be grouped with the earlier postwar data, resulting in the following breakdown for the major groups (in percentages).[36]

	Estonian	*Russian*	*Ukrainian*	*Belorussian*	*Finnish*	*Other*
1959	74.6	20.1	1.3	0.9	1.4	1.7
1970	68.2	24.6	2.1	1.4	1.4	2.3
1979	64.7	27.9	2.5	1.6	1.2	2.1
1989	61.5	30.3	3.1	1.8	1.1	2.2

In the 1980s the Estonian share of the population continued to decline at almost the same rate as in the 1970s. As in the 1960s and 1970s, that decrease was highest among titular union republic nationalities in the USSR. The increase in the Russian share declined somewhat in the 1980s, but the East Slavic total in Estonia in 1989, including the often Russified Ukrainians and Belorussians, reached 35.2 percent.

The absolute increase in the number of ethnic Estonians in Estonia in the years 1979–1989 was only 15,457, resulting in a total of 963,269 in 1989. Part of this growth came from the continued immigration of Russian-Estonians to the ESSR. In 1989, 93.8 percent of all Estonians under Soviet rule lived in Estonia as compared to 92.9 percent in 1979. The low natural increase among ethnic Estonians was due to low birth rates—in part a result of the large number of abortions—and high death rates in an aging population.[37] When the movement for political and cultural self-determination emerged at the end of the 1980s, a probirth attitude was also evidenced in the Estonian press and public opinion.

As in earlier decades assimilation remained a crucial demographic issue in the 1980s. Despite the growing Russian presence in Estonia, almost no cultural Russification occurred among the ethnic Estonian population. In 1989 1.1 percent of Estonians indicated that they spoke another language habitually, only an 0.1 percentage point increase from 1979 and most likely attributed to Russian-Estonian immigrants. Intermarriage by ethnic Estonians in 1988 remained close to the rate that existed twenty years earlier, when 8.6 percent of Estonian men and 8.9 percent of Estonian women married outside their ethnic group.[38]

The rate of urbanization in Estonia stagnated in the latter part of the 1980s, increasing only 0.3 percentage points, to 71.6 percent in the years 1984–1989, suggesting that a saturation level had been reached at least for the time being. In 1989, for the first time in postwar Soviet censuses, Estonia dropped to second place (73.6 percent) in the USSR in level of urbanization after the RSFSR.[39] Tallinn's growth also slowed in the 1980s. Nevertheless, the capital approached half a million (482,300) by 1989, and its share of the total ESSR population increased to 30.8 percent.[40] With regard to ethnic composition in the urban areas, see the following results from the 1989 data (in percentages):[41]

	Tallinn	Total Urban
Estonians	47.4	51.2
Russians	41.2	39.0
Others	11.4	9.8

Thus, for the first time since the midnineteenth century, in the 1980s the Estonian share of Tallinn's population slipped under 50 percent (see Appendix

B, Table 4). For the other four cities numbering more than 50,000 inhabitants in 1989, the Estonian portions were as follows: Tartu, 72 percent; Narva, 4 percent; Kohtla-Järve, 23 percent; and Pärnu, 72 percent.[42]

The above data allude to the most difficult social issue in Estonia: the continuing decline of the Estonian share of the population and the resulting ethnic tensions. During the era of *glasnost'* these tensions came into the open but remained under control. Unlike some parts of the Soviet Union, ethnic relations in Estonia and the Baltics in general did not degenerate into violence. The assertion of their rights by ethnic Estonians led to some non-Estonian (largely Russian and immigrant) backlash by those fearing the loss of their privileged status under Moscow's policies. As noted earlier, Intermovement was established in July 1988 as a reaction to the Estonian Popular Front. Nevertheless, the non-Estonian and Russian communities in Estonia were far from monolithic, as the growing support for Estonian independence among these groups suggests. (A survey by the Estonian Heritage Society in 1989 found no particular correlation between length of residence by non-Estonians in Estonia and their degree of integration with the indigenous population.)[43]

A major factor in the relative lack of communication among nationalities in Estonia was their inability or unwillingness to speak one another's language. The 1989 census showed a moderate increase of Estonians who claimed to speak Russian fluently (33.6 percent versus 23.1 percent in 1979), but a negligible growth of Russians fluent in Estonian (13.7 percent versus 11.3 percent in 1979).[44] Once again, *glasnost'* at the end of the 1980s painstakingly documented the poor quality of language instruction, especially the teaching of Estonian to non-Estonians. In essence, the language issue reflected clashing cultural conceptions. The Estonians argued that Estonian be given a preeminent position because only thus could the Estonian language and culture survive in its traditional homeland, whereas Russians and other non-Estonians spoke of "equal rights" for Russian, as if Estonia were merely a province of the Soviet empire. The argument finally revolved around the legitimacy of Soviet power, which by the end of the 1980s had been rejected by nearly all ethnic Estonians.[45]

ECOLOGY, HISTORY, AND CULTURAL RENEWAL

As noted earlier, the ecological protests of 1987 activated the Estonian population. The powerful environment issue cut across a wide range of economic, social, and political concerns. It also represented a cultural protest in that the environmental demonstrations and the subsequent green movement sought to preserve a traditional Estonia that could be passed on intact to future generations. In addition, the Estonian Greens called for a spiritual rebirth that would change the "collective mindlessness" toward nature that the Soviet system had encouraged.[46]

A striking phenomenon of the *glasnost'* era was an emerging fascination with the past and a need to reclaim it. The Estonian Heritage Society played a major role in this process by restoring historical monuments to the War of Independence that had either been destroyed by the Soviets or hidden by the local population. Twenty-seven such monuments reappeared in 1988 and fifty more in 1989; by August 1990 more than half of the approximately two hundred independence-era memorials were back in place.[47] Particularly important in this respect was the restoration of a 1939 monument to President Konstantin Päts in June 1989 and his reburial in the main Estonian cemetery in Tallinn in October 1990.[48] The Heritage Society also began a massive oral history project that focused on collecting the memoirs of survivors of the Stalin-era repressions.

The initial response among professional historians in Estonia to Gorbachev's call to fill in the "blank spots" in the historical record was unenthusiastic, for most were reluctant to revise the interpretations on which they had built their careers. Writers, artists, and other members of the creative unions, for instance, broke more easily with the official Soviet value system. Nevertheless, by 1988 and especially in 1989, revisionist historians' views increasingly appeared in the monthly or daily press, the characteristic format of debate in the age of *glasnost'*. As might have been expected, it was the younger, less-established historians who took the lead in offering revised approaches or dealing with previously taboo subjects. Revisionism essentially meant a nonideological approach to the past and using previously unavailable or untapped sources.

With regard to blank spots the major concern was—not surprisingly—the twentieth century, especially the period from 1917 to 1953. There was a rush to emphasize the positive contributions of the independence era to Estonian development and to rehabilitate leading political and military figures. Although Konstantin Päts received universal praise for his role in 1917–1920, he was much criticized for his performance in the 1930s, especially in the crisis of 1939–1940.[49] Investigations of World War II and Stalinism shed light on the previously ignored aspects of this period, such as deportations and the postwar guerrilla struggle. Using archival materials, Evald Laasi asserted that 20,702 persons were deported in March 1949, a figure far below standard Western estimates. In addition, he estimated that in the years 1944–1954 at least 30,000 people were arrested and sent to forced labor camps. Beginning in 1989 documentary and archival material, in both Estonian and Russian, especially on the Molotov-Ribbentrop Pact and the events of 1939–1940,[50] became available to a broad reading public.

Glasnost' in Estonia brought a crucial new openness and candor to public life, both in the local press, radio, and television and in relations with the outside world. In the late 1980s the Estonian media became increasingly outspoken, and in February 1990 precensorship was abolished.[51] Even after the central Soviet media began criticizing developments in Estonia following the declaration on sovereignty in November 1988, the Estonian media retained their relative freedom of expression. The new cultural openness also meant the first official recognition of Estonians living abroad and their achievements over the past fifty years. The works of emigré Estonian writers, artists, composers, and scholars were openly discussed and often became available in their home-land. Following his emigration in 1980, the conductor Neeme Järvi became a nonperson in Estonia but in September 1989 made a triumphal return with the Gothenburg Symphony. In June 1989 the Institute of History at the Estonian Academy of Sciences organized a conference to which—for the first time—a number of emigré scholars were invited, and the major archives in Estonia were opened to them. Overall, Estonia was seeking to rejoin Europe after decades of forced isolation. As the writer Lennart Meri, foreign minister in the Savisaar government, argued, Estonia should be seen as the northernmost part of the reemerging region of Central Europe.[52]

To reverse the declining role of the Estonian language in public life, the ESSR Supreme Soviet made it the official state language in December 1988; in January 1989 it passed a language law that, to guarantee the status of Estonian, required all officials and others whose work entailed direct contact with the population to achieve proficiency in the language within one to four years. Six levels of proficiency were established, depending on the degree of education required for a given position. The new law, however, also guaranteed that the Russian language would remain at all administrative levels in the ESSR; a Russian-speaking factory worker, for example, would be under no compulsion to learn Estonian. Despite some delays, in January 1991 the head of the State Language Office said he felt that full implementation was still possible by 1993.[53]

In the *glasnost'* era the traditional Soviet educational system in Estonia came under severe criticism, with demands for a thorough reform of the curriculum and a reshaping of instructional materials. Thus in 1989 a new high school textbook took a decidedly non-Soviet approach to twentieth-century Estonian history, discussing the independence era in positive terms and refer-ring to the military occupation of 1940 and the ensuing deportations.[54] At Tartu University so-called red subjects, that is, Marxism-Leninism, scientific communism, and other courses required by all-Union norms, were dropped from the curriculum. In 1989, numerous fraternities, sororities, and societies were restored. Reformists in higher education stressed the need for decentraliza-tion and faculty autonomy and questioned the validity of Soviet models. Thus by 1991 it looked as though the Estonian Academy of Sciences would not survive in its existing format.[55]

Glasnost's effect on belletristic literature was seen in the appearance of works on previously taboo subjects, such as the Estonian experience in Siberia or in labor camps under Stalin. The text of Heino Kiik's *Maria Siberimaal* (Maria in Siberia) was completed in 1978 but not published until the summer of 1987, when censorship began to loosen in Estonia. Raimond Kaugver, a veteran of the Vorkuta camps, published *Kirjad laagrist* (Letters from the camp) in 1989 in the original text that he had written during the Stalin era. Jaan Kross, a deportee for eight years (1946–54) and Estonia's best-known and most-translated writer, turned to similar topics in "Silmade avamise päev" (Eye-opening day), which was published in 1987, and *Väljakaevamised* (Excavations), published in 1990.[56] Numerous new literary publications of the *glasnost'* years included *Vikerkaar* (Rainbow), which was begun in 1986; its Russian-language version, *Raduga*, was substantially different in content, catering to the Russian-speaking intelligentsia.

The Estonian song festival tradition, which had survived Stalinism and Soviet rule intact, reached new levels during the cultural revival. At the twenty-first all-Estonian song festival in the summer of 1990, gone were all the trappings of Soviet rule, and for the first time in more than fifty years Estonian choruses from abroad participated along with two emigré conductors. Roman Toi from Toronto served as one of three honorary head conductors along with Gustav Ernesaks and Richard Ritsing. The thoroughly non-Soviet program included works by emigré composers, most notably Juhan Aavik's "God Protect Estonia." Some 28,000 singers and musicians participated. The size of the audience was difficult to estimate, but certainly topped the previous high of some 300,000 at the final concert.[57]

Religion in Estonia underwent a striking revival in the latter part of the 1980s. Religious literature once again became available, with large numbers of Bibles donated from abroad, mainly from Finland. In March 1990, the weekly newspaper *Eesti Kirik* (Estonian church), the organ of the Estonian Lutheran church, resumed publication after a fifty-year hiatus. Beginning in 1988 a marked increase in participation in religious rituals took place; in that year there were more than seven times as many baptisms and nearly six times as many confirmations as in 1978. The emergence of several Christian-oriented political parties also testifies to the strength of the revival.[58]

By early 1991 the era of *glasnost'* and *perestroika* had witnessed significant changes in Estonian life, including a broadly based cultural renewal, grass roots environmental and political movements, and an ongoing process of emancipation from Soviet values and control by the central authorities. De-Sovietization was most pronounced in culture because it was least subject to Moscow's control and most closely linked to a reassertive sense of Estonian national identity. In politics the changes were less far-reaching, but among the ethnic Estonian population the consensus moved rapidly from autonomy to full independence. The parallel with the situation in 1917–1920 appeared increasingly germane, with the role of World War I played in the present day by a deepening economic crisis that threatened the legitimacy and very existence of the USSR. A multiparty, democratic political system was developing in Estonia despite Moscow's opposition and threats. In contrast, the economic situation continued to worsen, which added fuel to the movement for decentralization and local control. Social issues seemed intractable as well, as the demographic balance remained precarious and ethnic tensions far from resolved. Overall, the mood in Estonia in the spring of 1991 could be described as wary but determined. No quick solutions appeared in the offing, but too much had changed for Moscow to turn the clock back to the pre-1985 era. In March 1991, Estonia held a nonbinding referendum on the question of independence; 82.86 percent of those eligible to participate did so, and of those 77.83 percent voted yes, meaning that nearly all ethnic Estonians supported independence as well as about 30 percent of the non-Estonians—the highest proportion to date.[59]

Epilogue

The Estonians and their Balto-Finnic ancestors have lived on the Baltic littoral for over four millennia. During the last eight centuries that have comprised the historical era, two major factors have shaped Estonian history: geopolitical location and the small numbers of ethnic Estonians. Appendix B, Table 1 suggests the ruinous role of war and disease in Estonia in the medieval and early modern periods. The two centuries of peace under tsarist Russia contributed to the first uninterrupted period of population growth in historical times. Compared to previous wars and the Second World War, World War I did not constitute a major demographic setback for the Estonians, and it is noteworthy that the near-zero population growth of the independence era was the result of the impact of internal modernization rather than of external pressures. However, such pressures re-emerged in the disastrous decade of the 1940s, when ethnic Estonian numbers fell to the level of the 1880s and from which the Estonians have yet to recover. Throughout the past 800 years, the favorable location of Estonia on the Baltic Sea and the ease of access along the great northern European plain have attracted surrounding powers and peoples.

A modern and conscious Estonian nation, which had its beginnings more than a century and a quarter ago, was a product of both socioeconomic changes and new ideas imported from the outside, chiefly from the West. The Estonian national movement was part of the drive for cultural and political self-determination that was an animating force in Central and Eastern Europe in the latter half of the nineteenth century and the early years of the twentieth. World War I and the Russian Revolution afforded the opportunity for the realization of

Estonian self-determination in the form of independence, although the previous political goal of the national movement had been limited to autonomy. In the 1920s and 1930s, Estonia joined the European family of states and became— along with Latvia and Lithuania—a member of the League of Nations; it shared in the advances and shortcomings of Eastern Europe in this era. An idealistic democratic constitution functioned well enough in the relatively benign decade of the 1920s, but it proved unworkable in the face of economic problems, the lack of a strong tradition of civic culture, and external pressures from Nazi Germany and Soviet Russia. Nevertheless, Estonian authoritarianism in the 1930s was one of the mildest in Eastern Europe—no one was executed for political reasons and virtually all political prisoners were freed in 1938—and the swing was back toward greater political participation in the last years of independence.

The most important achievement of the independence years was the final establishment of a modern Estonian culture. The language became modernized and, for the first time, served a rigorous educational system in the native tongue from the elementary level through postgraduate study. Estonian literature, theater, music, and the other arts had a broader and more sophisticated audience than ever before. It would be unrealistic to expect world-class achievements in such a short period of time as two decades, but figures such as A. H. Tammsaare in prose and Marie Under in poetry suggested a cultural potential on the level of the other smaller nations of Europe.

Estonian political self-determination came to an end with the Nazi-Soviet Pact and the division of Eastern Europe between Hitler and Stalin in World War II. All Soviet attempts to depict the absorption of the Baltic states as voluntary and driven by internal forces in the area remain unconvincing. The three Baltic "revolutions" of 1940 were carbon copies of each other and were clearly orchestrated by Moscow's local emissaries. At each major stage in the establishment of Soviet control the decisive factor was the threat of brutal military force. The Baltic states—the only members of the League of Nations who are not members of the United Nations—may not have physical power on their side; they do, however, command a sense of historical justice and conscience.[1]

The four and a half decades of Soviet rule have been a mixed experience for the Estonians. Under Stalinism there was not only the constant threat to personal security and a significant drop in living standards as compared to the independence era, but the very survival of a native culture was also called into question. However, the thaw years brought a new sense of security and economic improvements, and they promoted a cultural rebirth that in many ways recalled the national awakening of a century earlier. The range of cultural expression expanded markedly and lasting achievements took place. In the post-Stalin era, the foundation built during the independence period stood the Estonians in good stead. At the same time, Moscow came to appreciate the skilled and disciplined labor force in Estonia and often used the ESSR to try out innovations in economic management. After some twenty years of improving conditions, the decade from the mid-1970s to the mid-1980s witnessed retrogression in several areas, including cultural opportunities and the status of the Estonian language, native political representation, and living standards.

In historical perspective the era of rebirth and renewal that began in the late 1980s can be compared with the national awakening of the 1860s and 1870s and the establishment of independence in 1917–1920. In seeking to restore Estonian cultural, political, and economic self-determination, the current movement draws inspiration from these two turning points in modern Estonian history. The serious ecological problems brought on by Soviet rule, the precarious demographic situation, and the threat to the Estonian language and culture from continued immigration add a deep sense of urgency to Estonian demands. To achieve their goals, the Estonians have cooperated much more than in the past with their Baltic neighbors—the Latvians and the Lithuanians—and turned to the countries of Scandinavia and the West for support. In the final analysis a modus vivendi with Moscow must be found. The Estonians, Latvians, and Lithuanians have suggested the relationship between Finland and the Soviet Union as a model for their own future, one that would fit well with their historical role as a crossroads between East and West in Europe.

In 1939 Hans Kruus, the leading Estonian historian of the independence era, wrote an article entitled "The Consciousness of Being a Small People in Estonian Social Thought."[2] Kruus pointed out that Jakob Hurt in the late 1860s and early 1870s was the first to give expression to this viewpoint and to suggest that any Estonian contribution to the world would have to be in the cultural rather than the political or military realm. In the late tsarist period Jaan Tõnisson continued this line of reasoning, arguing that political issues—for example, the exact form of a reformed Russian state—should be secondary for the Estonians; what really mattered was to be able to pursue their cultural aims as they saw fit. During the two decades of Estonian independence such distinctions became blurred, since both cultural and political self-determination seemed assured. However, in struggling back from the nadir of Stalinism, Estonian intellectuals once again turned to Hurt's position. They stressed the uniqueness of Estonian culture: its Finno-Ugric and Uralic base with no more than a total of twenty million speakers, the rich oral tradition painstakingly recorded since the mid-nineteenth century, and the many achievements of modern times—both pre- and post-1940. The small number of ethnic Estonians continues to encourage a heightened commitment to the native tongue, a view expressed by the early nineteenth-century poet Kristjan Jaak Peterson:[3]

> May not the language of this land
> On winds of song and
> Rising to the heavens
> Seek eternity?

APPENDIXES

A: GEOGRAPHIC TERMS

Estonian	German	Pre-1917 Russian*
Eestimaa	Estland	Estliandiia
Haapsalu	Hapsal	Gapsal'
Harjumaa	Harrien	Garrien
Hiiumaa	Dagö	Dago
Jõgevamaa	—	—
Jõhvimaa	—	—
Järvamaa	Jerwen	Erven
Kohtla-Järve	—	—
Kuressaare (1952–1988, Kingissepa)	Arensburg	Arensburg
Liivimaa	Livland	Lifliandiia
Läänemaa	Wiek	Vik
Narva	Narwa	Narva
Paide	Weissenstein	Veisenshtein
Paldiski	Baltisch-Port	Baltiiskii Port
Pärnu	Pernau	Pernov
Pärnumaa	Kreis Pernau	Pernovskii uezd
Petseri	Petschur	Pechory
Petserimaa	—	—
Rakvere	Wesenberg	Vezenberg
Saaremaa	Ösel	Ezel'
Sillamäe	—	—
Tallinn	Reval	Revel'
Tartu	Dorpat	Derpt, Iur'ev
Tartumaa	Kreis Dorpat	Derptskii uezd
Valga	Walk	Valk
Valgamaa	—	—
Viljandi	Fellin	Fellin
Viljandimaa	Kreis Fellin	Fellinskii uezd
Virumaa	Wierland	Virland
Võru	Werro	Verro
Võrumaa	Kreis Werro	Verroskii uezd

* Post-1940 Russian names for geographic terms in Estonia are merely transliterations of the current Estonian forms.

B: POPULATION TABLES

TABLE 1
POPULATION OF ESTONIA, 1200–1989
(in thousands)*

Year	Total Population	Ethnic Estonians
1200	150–180	—
1550	250	—
1640	120	—
1696	350–400	—
1712	150–170	—
1782	485	—
1881	881	792
1897	958	868
1922	1,107	970
1934	1,126	993
1950	1,097	—
1959	1,197	893
1970	1,356	925
1979	1,466	948
1989	1,566	963

* Figures for the pre-1782 years are educated guesses. Censuses took place in 1881 and 1897 (Estland and northern Livland), 1922 and 1934 (independent Estonia), and 1959, 1970, 1979, and 1989 (Soviet Estonia).

SOURCES: Heldur Palli, "O razvitii narodonaseleniia Estonii v sravnitel'no-istoricheskom plane (XIII–XVIII vv.)," *ENSVTA Toimetised* 23 (1974): 357; Heldur Palli, *Estestvennoe dvizhenie sel'skogo naseleniia Estonii 1650–1799*, 3 vols. (Tallinn: Eesti Raamat, 1980), 2: 80; Hugo Reiman, "II rahvaloenduse tulemusi," *Eesti Statistika*, no. 156 (1934): 565; Toivo U. Raun, "The Revolution of 1905 in the Baltic Provinces and Finland," *Slavic Review* 43 (1984): 455; Rein Taagepera, "Baltic Population Changes, 1950–1980," *Journal of Baltic Studies* 12 (1981): 36, 47; *Eesti arvudes 1989. aastal* (Tallinn: Eesti Riiklik Statistikaamet, 1990), p. 10.

TABLE 2

ETHNIC COMPOSITION OF ESTONIA, 1881–1989
(in percentages)*

Year	Estonians	Russians	Germans	Others
1881	89.8	3.3	5.3	1.6
1897	90.6	4.0	3.5	1.9
1922	87.7	8.2	1.7	2.4
1934	88.2	8.2	1.5	2.1
1945	94 ± 2	—	—	—
1959	74.6	20.1	—	5.3
1970	68.2	24.7	0.6	6.5
1979	64.7	27.9	0.3	7.1
1989	61.5	30.3	0.2	8.0

* Based on size of territory at time of census or estimate. Figures for 1881 and 1897 cover only Estland and northern Livland; those for 1922 and 1934 also include Narva and the area east of the Narva River, Petserimaa, and Valga. The figures for 1945 and later are for the territory of Soviet Estonia (independent Estonia minus the area east of the Narva River and three-fourths of Petserimaa).

SOURCES: Hugo Reiman, "Rahvused Eestis," *Eesti Statistika*, no. 164–65 (1935): 354; Rein Taagepera, "Baltic Population Changes, 1950–1980," *Journal of Baltic Studies* 12 (1981): 47 (estimate); Egil Levits, "Die demographische Situation in der UdSSR und in den baltischen Staaten unter besonderer Berücksichtigung von nationalen und sprachsoziologischen Aspekten," *Acta Baltica* 21 (1981): 64; *Statistika Teataja* (1990): 1.

TABLE 3

URBAN POPULATION IN ESTONIA, 1708–1989*

Year	Tallinn	Tartu	Total urban	Percentage of total population
1708	9,801	1,465	—	—
1710	1,962	—	—	—
1782	10,653	3,421	23,521	5.0
1862–63	20,680	13,826	64,032	8.7
1897	64,572	42,308	189,582	19.2
1913	116,132	45,088	253,331	—
1922	122,419	50,342	276,982	25.0
1934	137,792	58,876	323,007	28.7
1959	281,700	74,300	675,500	56.4
1970	362,700	90,500	881,200	65.0
1979	429,700	104,500	1,022,300	69.7
1989	482,300	114,000	1,126,000	71.6

* Including Narva and Valga from 1782.

SOURCES: *Tallinn: Lühientsüklopeedia* (Tallinn: Valgus, 1979), p. 33; Raimo Pullat, ed., *Tartu ajalugu* (Tallinn: Eesti Raamat, 1980), p. 125; Raimo Pullat, *Eesti linnad ja linlased XVIII sajandi lõpust 1917. aastani* (Tallinn: Eesti Raamat, 1972), pp. 37–38; *Eesti NSV ajalugu*, 3 vols. (Tallinn: Eesti Riiklik Kirjastus, 1955–1963; Eesti Raamat, 1971), 2: 114, 116; Hugo Reiman, "II rahvaloenduse tulemusi," *Eesti Statistika*, no. 156 (1934): 557; *Nar. khoz. ESSR 1988*, p. 10.

TABLE 4

ETHNIC COMPOSITION OF THE URBAN POPULATION
OF ESTONIA, 1820–1989
(in percentages)

	TALLINN			TARTU			TOTAL URBAN		
Year	*Est.*	*Ger.*	*Russ.*	*Est.*	*Ger.*	*Russ.*	*Est.*	*Ger.*	*Russ.*
1820	34.8	42.9	17.9	—	—	—	—	—	—
1844	—	—	—	26.8	60.6	9.6	—	—	—
1871	51.8	34.4	11.3	—	—	—	—	—	—
1881	57.4	27.8	11.1	55.1	35.0	6.1	56.1	29.3	11.1
1897	68.7	17.5	10.2	68.6	16.6	8.7	67.8	16.3	10.9
1913	71.6	10.7	11.4	73.3	14.1	6.5	69.2	11.2	11.9
1922	83.9	5.6	6.1	84.4	6.9	4.5	82.3	5.2	8.1
1934	85.8	4.8	5.7	88.0	4.6	4.5	85.5	4.1	7.0
1959	60.2	—	32.2	—	—	—	61.9	—	30.8
1970	55.7	—	35.0	—	—	—	57.5	—	33.9
1979	51.9	0.1	38.0	74.4	—	20.6	54.8	0.3	36.6
1989	47.4	0.1	41.2	—	—	—	51.2	0.2	39.0

SOURCES: Raimo Pullat, *Eesti linnad ja linlased XVIII sajandi lõpust 1917. aastani* (Tallinn: Eesti Raamat, 1972), pp. 58, 60; Raimo Pullat, ed., *Tartu ajalugu* (Tallinn: Eesti Raamat, 1980), p. 128; Hugo Reiman, "Rahvused Eestis," *Eesti Statistika*, nos. 164–65 (1935): 354–55; Friedrich von Jung-Stilling and W. Anders, eds., *Ergebnisse der livländischen Volkszählung*, 3 vols. (Riga: Stahl'sche Buchdruckerei, 1883–1885), 2: 4–5; Raimo Pullat, *Linnad kodanlikus Eestis: Ajaloolis-demograafiline käsitlus* (Tallinn: Eesti Raamat, 1978), p. 135; Rein Taagepera, "Size and Ethnicity of Estonian Towns and Rural Districts, 1922–1979," *Journal of Baltic Studies* 13 (1982): 107, 112; Egil Levits, "Die demographische Situation in der UdSSR und in den baltischen Staaten unter besonderer Berücksichtigung von nationalen und sprachsoziologischen Aspekten," *Acta Baltica* 21 (1981): 64–66; *Statistika Teataja* (1990): 1.

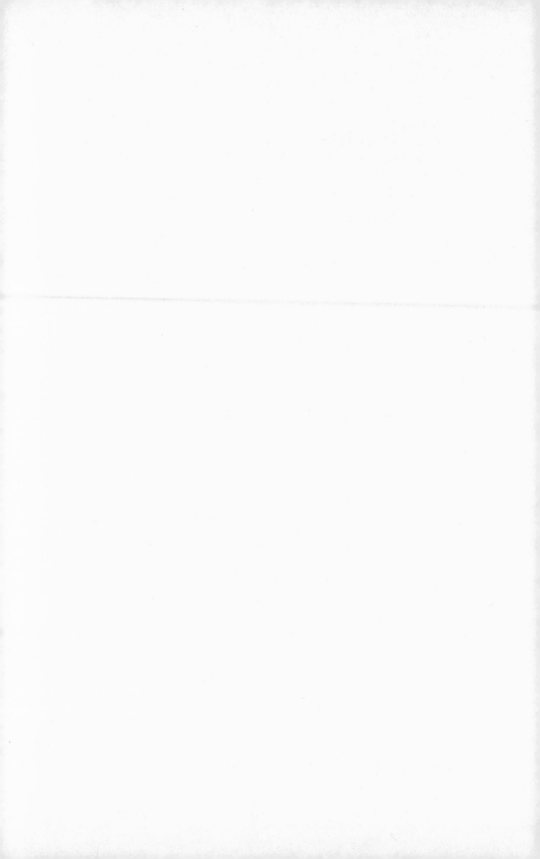

Glossary

Adramaa (Est.)—unit of land (ploughland); Ger. *Haken*

Buro—top decisionmaking body within the communist parties of the Union republics in the USSR; analogous to the Politburo in Moscow

Diet—Ger. *Landtag*; provincial assembly of the nobility in the Baltic region up to 1917

Hinnus (Est.)—fixed tax on the peasantry

Kihelkond (Est.)—parish; Ger. *Kirchspiel*, Russ. *prikhod*; term in use from prehistoric times to the 1940s

Kolkhoz (Russ.)—collective farm

Kolkhoznik (Russ.)—worker on a *kolkhoz*

Kulak (Russ.)—rich peasant; a derogatory, even incriminating term under Soviet rule

Külanõukogu (Est.)—village soviet, the lowest unit of rural administration; established 1945

Kümnis (Est.)—literally "tithe"; in fact, a tax on peasant output as high as 25 percent

Kuningas (Est.)—chieftain or military leader in prehistoric Estonia

Maakond (Est.)—district; Ger. *Kreis*, Russ. *uezd*; term in use from prehistoric era to 1950 and then again beginning in the late 1980s

Maapäev (Est.)—all-Estonian assembly, elected 1917

Meliores (Lat.)—the elite in thirteenth-century Estonia; see also *seniores*

Metsavennad (Est.)—"forest brethren," pro-independence Estonian guerrillas in the Stalinist era

Raion (Russ.)—administrative district established in 1950; Est. *rajoon*

Regivärss (Est.)—traditional Estonian folksong characterized by alliteration, assonance, and repetition or restatement of a theme

Rehielamu (or *rehetare*) (Est.)—barn-dwelling; began to be used before the thirteenth century in Estonia

Riigikogu (Est.)—State Assembly in independent Estonia (1920–1934)

Riiginõukogu (Est.)—State Council (upper house of parliament) in independent Estonia (1938–1940)

Riigivanem (Est.)—state elder, or prime minister, in independent Estonia (1920–1937)

Riigivolikogu (Est.)—Chamber of Deputies (lower house of parliament) in independent Estonia (1938–1940)

Ritterschaft (Ger.)—corporation of Baltic German nobility in Baltic provinces

Seniores (Lat.)—the elite in thirteenth-century Estonia; see also *meliores*

Sluzhashchie (Russ.)—white-collar workers in Soviet Estonia

Sovkhoz (Russ.)—state farm, run on the analogy of an urban factory

Sovnarkhoz (Russ.)—regional economic council in the USSR; functioned in Estonia from 1957 to 1965

Sulased (Est.)—male landless peasants or agricultural laborers on yearly contracts

Sumbküla (Est.)—circular or bunched village in prehistoric Estonia

Tüdrukud (Est.)—as used here, female landless peasants

Üksjalad (Est.)—"one-foot men," or peasants with a small amount of land

Vabadikud (Est.)—agricultural laborers who did seasonal work and sometimes had a small amount of land; cottagers

Vakus (Est.)—collective tax on the peasantry

Vald (Est.)—rural township; Ger. *Gemeinde*, Russ. *volost'*

Vanemuine (Est.)—mythical god of song, borrowed from Finnish folklore (Fin. *Väinämöinen*)

Zemstvo (Russ.)—district or provincial assembly, established in parts of tsarist Russia beginning in 1864

Notes

ABBREVIATIONS

ENSVTA Toimetised	*Eesti NSV Teaduste Akadeemia Toimetised: Ühiskonnateadused.* Tallinn, 1952–.
ERRTM	*Eesti riik ja rahvas Teises maailmasõjas*, 10 vols. Stockholm: EMP, 1954–1962.
Nar. khoz. ESSR	*Narodnoe khoziaistvo Estonskoi SSR. Eesti NSV rahvamajandus*, Tallinn, 1957–. (Statistical annual, usually bilingual)
SPANE	Edgar Tõnurist, ed., *Sotsialistliku põllumajanduse areng Nõukogude Eestis*, Tallinn: Valgus, 1976.

CHAPTER 1

1. "Liivlaste pärandus," *Looming*, no. 6 (1985): 855, citing Eduard Vääri, the leading Soviet Estonian expert on the Livonian language.

2. Richard Indreko, "Soome-ugrilaste päritolust ja asualast," *Virittäjä* 51 (1947): 315.

3. Péter Hajdú, "Linguistic Background of Genetic Relationships," in Péter Hajdú, ed., *Ancient Cultures of the Uralian Peoples* (Budapest: Corvina Press, 1976), pp. 36–38.

4. Karin Mark, *Zur Herkunft der finnisch-ugrischen Völker vom Standpunkt der Anthropologie* (Tallinn: Eesti Raamat, 1970), pp. 101, 105; Paul Ariste, "Über die

früheste Entwicklungsstufe der ostseefinnischen Sprachen," *ENSVTA Toimetised* 10 (1961): 260–61; L. Jaanits, S. Laul, V. Lõugas, and E. Tõnisson, *Eesti esiajalugu* (Tallinn: Eesti Raamat, 1982), p. 125.

5. Vilkuna's argument is cited in Y. H. Toivonen, "Suomalais-ugrilaisten alkukodista," *Virittäjä* 57 (1953): 9. See also Toivo Vuorela, *The Finno-Ugric Peoples*, trans. John Atkinson, Indiana University Publications, Uralic and Altaic Series, no. 39 (The Hague: Mouton, 1964), p. 12, and Ariste, "Entwicklungsstufe," p. 260.

6. Mark, *Herkunft der finnisch-ugrischen Völker*, pp. 42, 48.

7. Jaanits et al., *Eesti esiajalugu*, pp. 27, 53.

8. Harri Moora, "Eesti rahva ja naaberrahvaste kujunemisest arheoloogia andmeil," in *Eesti rahva etnilisest ajaloost* (Tallinn: Eesti Riiklik Kirjastus, 1956), p. 58; Lembit Jaanits, "Soomeugrilaste hargnemisest arheoloogia andmeil," *Keel ja Kirjandus* 16 (1973): 721.

9. *Istoriia Estonskoi SSR*, 3 vols. (Tallinn: Estonskoe Gosudarstvennoe Izdatel'stvo, 1961; Eesti Raamat, 1966–1974), 1: 50. An Estonian version—*Eesti NSV ajalugu*—appeared in the years 1955–1971. In citing this work, vol. 1 of the Russian edition and vols. 2 and 3 of the Estonian edition will be used.

10. *Eesti ajalugu*, 3 vols. (Tartu: Eesti Kirjanduse Selts, 1935–1940), 1: 146–47; Jaanits et al., *Eesti esiajalugu*, pp. 398–99.

11. Paul Johansen, *Siedlung und Agrarwesen der Esten im Mittelalter*, Verhandlungen der Gelehrten Estnischen Gesellschaft, no. 23 (Tartu: Gelehrte Estnische Gesellschaft, 1925), p. 83; Harri Moora and Herbert Ligi, *Wirtschaft und Gesellschaftsordnung der Völker des Baltikums zu Anfang des 13. Jahrhunderts* (Tallinn: Eesti Raamat, 1970), pp. 7, 9.

12. James A. Brundage, ed. and trans., *The Chronicle of Henry of Livonia* (Madison: University of Wisconsin Press, 1961), pp. 103, 178.

13. Gustav Ränk, "The Estonian Dwelling-House," in *Apophoreta Tartuensia* (Stockholm: Eesti Teaduslik Selts Rootsis, 1949), pp. 95, 100–102; Gustav Ränk, *Die Bauernhausformen im baltischen Raum* (Würzburg: Holzner, 1962), pp. 93–95; *Eesti arhitektuuri ajalugu* (Tallinn: Eesti Raamat, 1965), p. 26.

14. *Istoriia Estonskoi SSR*, 1: 23–24, 34–35; Marija Gimbutas, *The Goddesses and Gods of Old Europe, 6500–3500 B.C.: Myths and Cult Images*, rev. ed. (Berkeley: University of California Press, 1982), pp. 9, 237–38.

15. Brundage, *Chronicle of Henry of Livonia*, p. 238.

16. The term *kuningas*, "king," was used by the Estonians at this time, but only in its original Germanic meaning of chieftain or military leader. See Moora and Ligi, *Wirtschaft und Gesellschaftsordnung*, pp. 75–78.

17. Jüri Uluots, *Grundzüge der Agrargeschichte Estlands* (Tartu: Akadeemiline Kooperatiiv, 1935), pp. 16–17; Herbert Ligi, *Talupoegade koormised Eestis 13. sajandist 19. sajandi alguseni* (Tallinn: Eesti Raamat, 1968), p. 26.

18. Ligi, *Talupoegade koormised*, pp. 39, 42–44; Thomas S. Noonan, "The Nature of Medieval Russian-Estonian Relations," in Arvids Ziedonis, Jr., William L. Winter, and Mardi Valgemäe, eds., *Baltic History* (Columbus, Ohio: Association for the

Advancement of Baltic Studies, 1974), pp. 13–19; Raimo Pullat, ed., *Tartu ajalugu* (Tallinn: Eesti Raamat, 1980), pp. 22, 26.

19. *Eesti kirjanduse ajalugu*, 4 vols. (Tallinn: Eesti Raamat, 1965–1984), 1: 37–40, 61; Herbert Tampere, "Eesti regivärsilise rahvalaulu meloodika stiilitüübid," *Etnograafiamuuseumi aastaraamat* 11 (1965): 51.

20. For one interpretation of this phenomenon, see Oskar Loorits, *Grundzüge des estnischen Volksglaubens*, 3 vols. (Lund: Kungl. Gustav Adolfs Akademie, 1949–1957), 3: 111–25.

CHAPTER 2

1. For a recent, nonpartisan account of the Baltic conquest, see Eric Christiansen, *The Northern Crusades: The Baltic and Catholic Frontier, 1100–1525* (Minneapolis: University of Minnesota Press, 1980), pp. 89–99, 105–9.

2. A recent archaeological study estimates the number of Livonians at the start of the thirteenth century at 22,500–28,000. Although the Livonians were already being assimilated by the surrounding Latvians by the eleventh century, the German conquest certainly sped up the process. See Paul Ariste, "Uudset liivlaste minevikust," *Keel ja Kirjandus* 18 (1975): 442.

3. The modern Latvian nation was formed from the following tribal divisions: Lettgallians, Couronians, Semigallians, and Selonians. Like the Estonians, they were all subjugated in the thirteenth century.

4. William Urban, *The Baltic Crusade* (Dekalb: Northern Illinois University Press, 1975), p. 104.

5. Ibid., p. 114. With its location on a natural bluff, the fortress of Tallinn was already showing its relative invulnerability to siege. The Estonians failed in 1221–1223 in three attempts (once with Russian aid) to force the stronghold to surrender.

6. *Eesti ajalugu*, 3 vols. (Tartu: Eesti Kirjanduse Selts, 1935–1940), 2: 58–59.

7. Ibid., p. 103.

8. Enn Tarvel, *Adramaa* (Tallinn: Eesti Raamat, 1972), pp. 66–67.

9. Heldur Palli, "O razvitii narodonaseleniia Estonii v sravnitel'no-istorischeskom plane (XIII–XVIII vv.), *ENSVTA Toimetised* 23 (1974): 357.

10. See the chapter by Evald Blumfeldt in *Eesti majandusajalugu*, vol. 1 (Tartu: Akadeemiline Kooperatiiv, 1937), pp. 84, 86–88; Herbert Ligi, *Eesti talurahva olukord ja klassivõitlus Liivi sõja algul 1558–1561* (Tallinn: Eesti NSV Teaduste Akadeemia, 1961), pp. 210, 238–40.

11. Jerome Blum, "The Rise of Serfdom in Eastern Europe," *American Historical Review* 62 (1957): 809.

12. *Eesti majandusajalugu*, 1: 74–76.

13. Paul Johansen, *Siedlung und Agrarwesen der Esten im Mittelalter*, Verhandlungen

der Gelehrten Estnischen Gesellschaft, no. 23 (Tartu: Gelehrte Estnische Gesellschaft, 1925), p. 35.

14. P. Peter Rebane, "The *Jüriöö Mäss* (St. George's Night Rebellion) of 1343," in Arvids Ziedonis, Jr., William L. Winter, and Mardi Valgemäe, eds., *Baltic History* (Columbus, Ohio: Association for the Advancement of Baltic Studies, 1974), pp. 37, 41, 43; William Urban, *The Livonian Crusade* (Washington, D.C.: University Press of America, 1981), pp. 98, 100, 103.

15. *Eesti majandusajalugu*, 1: 66–69.

16. Ibid., pp. 49–56. See also the lengthy discussion in Ligi, *Eesti talurahva olukord*, pp. 43–117.

17. Harri Moora and Herbert Ligi, *Wirtschaft und Gesellschaftsordnung der Völker des Baltikums zu Anfang des 13. Jahrhunderts* (Tallinn: Eesti Raamat, 1970), p. 91.

18. *Eesti majandusajalugu*, 1: 44; *Istoriia Estonskoi SSR*, 3 vols. (Tallinn: Estonskoe Gosudarstvennoe Izdatel'stvo, 1961; Eesti Raamat, 1966–1974), 1: 300.

19. Vilho Niitemaa, *Die undeutsche Frage in der Politik der livländischen Städte im Mittelalter* (Helsinki: n.p., 1949), p. 64; Paul Johansen and Heinz von zur Mühlen, *Deutsch und Undeutsch im mittelalterlichen und frühneuzeitlichen Reval* (Cologne: Böhlau, 1973), p. 297.

20. Ivar Paulson, *The Old Estonian Folk Religion*, trans. Juta Kõvamees Kitching and H. Kõvamees, Indiana University Publications, Uralic and Altaic Series, no. 108 (The Hague: Mouton, 1971), pp. 157–58.

21. Herbert Salu, *Eesti vanem kirjandus* (Vadstena, Sweden: Tõrvik, 1953), pp. 11–12; *Eesti kirjanduse ajalugu*, 4 vols. (Tallinn: Eesti Raamat, 1965–1984), 1: 112–14.

CHAPTER 3

1. *Eesti rahva ajalugu*, 3 vols. (Tartu: Loodus, 1932–1937), 2: 722.

2. Ibid., 2: 830–31; *Istoriia Estonskoi SSR*, 3 vols. (Tallinn: Estonskoe Gosudarstvennoe Izdatel'stvo, 1961; Eesti Raamat, 1966–1974), 1: 370.

3. To avoid confusion with twentieth-century Estonia, the Swedish and later Russian province (1584–1917) in the northern part of the Baltic littoral will be referred to by its Swedish and German name: Estland.

4. To avoid confusion with medieval Livonia, the Polish-Swedish and later Russian province in the southern part of the Baltic littoral will be referred to by its Swedish and German name: Livland.

5. Herbert Ligi, *Talupoegade koormised Eestis 13. sajandist 19. sajandi alguseni* (Tallinn: Eesti Raamat, 1968), p. 294.

6. Aleksander Loit, *Kampen om feodalräntan: Reduktionen och domänpolitiken i Estland, 1655–1710*, vol. 1, Studia Historica Upsaliensia, no. 71 (Uppsala: n.p., 1975), p. 161; Evald Blumfeldt, "Reduktionen på Ösel," *Svio-Estonica* 14 (1958): 171. The works by Loit and Blumfeldt have, respectively, corrected the traditional

figures for the extent of the repossessions in Estland (33 percent) and Saaremaa (25 percent); see, for example, Evald Uustalu, *The History of Estonian People* (London: Boreas, 1952), pp. 83–84.

7. Juhan Kahk, Herbert Ligi, and Enn Tarvel, *Beiträge zur marxistischen Agrargeschichte Estlands der Feudalzeit* (Tallinn: Eesti Raamat, 1974), p. 44; *Eesti majandusajalugu*, vol. 1 (Tartu: Akadeemiline Kooperatiiv, 1937), p. 202.

8. Arnold Soom, *Der Herrenhof in Estland im 17. Jahrhundert* (Lund: Eesti Teaduslik Selts Rootsis, 1954), pp. 6–7.

9. Otto Liiv, *Suur näljaaeg Eestis 1695–1697* (Tartu: Loodus, 1938), p. 86.

10. See the section by Juhan Vasar in *Eesti rahva ajalugu*, 2: 927–28; Heldur Palli, "O razvitii narodonaseleniia Estonii v sravnitel'no-istoricheskom plane (XIII–XVIII vv.)," *ENSVTA Toimetised* 23 (1974): 357; Liiv, *Suur näljaaeg Eestis*, p. 78.

11. Palli, "O razvitii narodonaseleniia Estonii," p. 359.

12. On Jesuit activity in Tartu, see Vello Helk, "Die Jesuiten in Dorpat," *Zeitschrift für Ostforschung* 12 (1963): 673–87.

13. *Eesti rahva ajalugu*, 2: 1127–32.

14. Helmut Piirimäe, comp., *Tartu ülikooli ajalugu*, vol. 1, *1632–1798* (Tallinn: Eesti Raamat, 1982), pp. 65–66.

15. Elina Öpik, *Talurahva mõisavastane võitlus Eestis Põhjasõja esimesel poolel 1700–1710* (Tallinn: Eesti NSV Teaduste Akadeemia Ajaloo Instituut, 1964), p. 147.

16. Matthias J. Eisen, "Eesti rahva arv," *Eesti Kirjandus* 4 (1909): 258–59; Paul Jordan, *Die Resultate der ehstländischen Volkszählung vom 29. December 1881 in textlicher Beleuchtung* (Tallinn: Lindfors' Erben, 1886), pp. 34–35; Heldur Palli, "Historical Demography of Estonia in the 17th and 18th Centuries and Computers," in *Studia historica in honorem Hans Kruus* (Tallinn: Eesti NSV Teaduste Akadeemia Ajaloo Instituut, 1971), p. 206, 211; Heldur Palli, *Estestvennoe dvizhenie sel'skogo naseleniia Estonii 1650–1799*, 3 vols. (Tallinn: Eesti Raamat, 1980), 2: 80.

CHAPTER 4

1. Edward C. Thaden, "Estland, Livland, and the Ukraine: Reflections on Eighteenth-Century Autonomy," *Journal of Baltic Studies* 12 (1981): 312–13.

2. *Eesti majandusajalugu*, vol. 1 (Tartu: Akadeemiline Kooperatiiv, 1937), p. 269. Under Swedish rule Saaremaa had remained a separate province, but after 1710 it became part of Livland. Nevertheless, the Saaremaa *Ritterschaft* retained an independent existence throughout tsarist times.

3. Additions were made over the years. For example, the Livland *Ritterschaft* had 430 member families by 1875; see Julius Eckardt, *Livland im achtzehnten Jahrhundert*, vol. 1 (Leipzig: F. A. Brockhaus, 1876), p. 539.

4. Erik Amburger, *Geschichte der Behördenorganisation Russlands von Peter dem Grossen bis 1917* (Leiden: E. J. Brill, 1966), pp. 387–89.

5. Reinhard Wittram, *Baltische Geschichte: Die Ostseelande Livland, Estland, Kurland, 1180–1918* (Munich: R. Oldenbourg, 1954), pp. 135–37.

6. *Eesti majandusajalugu*, 1: 277.

7. On the situation in northern Livland, see Juhan Kahk, *Rahutused ja reformid* (Tallinn: Eesti Riiklik Kirjastus, 1961), p. 81; for Estland in the 1840s, *Eesti rahva ajalugu*, 3 vols. (Tartu: Loodus, 1932–1937), 3: 1545, suggests that the estate and peasant lands were approximately the same total area.

8. Calculated from data in *Eesti majandusajalugu*, 1: 310.

9. Hubertus Neuschäffer, "Die Anfänge der livländischen ökonomischen Sozietät (1792–1939)," *Journal of Baltic Studies* 10 (1979): 337–38; Elmar Järvesoo, "Early Agricultural Education at Tartu University," *Journal of Baltic Studies* 11 (1980): 341.

10. V. Fainshtein, "Perekhod ot trekhpol'ia k plodosmenu v Estliandskom pomeshchich'em khoziaistve," in *Eesti NSV ajaloo küsimusi*, vol. 7, Tartu Riikliku Ülikooli Toimetised, no. 290 (Tartu: Tartu Riiklik Ülikool, 1972), pp. 164, 189.

11. *Eesti rahva ajalugu*, 3: 1322; Evald Uustalu, *The History of Estonian People* (London: Boreas, 1952), p. 97.

12. Garlieb Merkel, *Die Letten vorzüglich in Liefland am Ende des philosophischen Jahrhunderts* (Leipzig: Heinrich Gräff, 1797), p. 32; Johan Christoph Petri, *Ehstland und die Ehsten oder historisch-geographisch-statistisches Gemälde von Ehsteland*, 3 vols. (Gotha: n.p., 1802), 1: 310–11, 360, 364.

13. Juhan Kahk, *Die Krise der feudalen Landwirtschaft in Estland (Das zweite Viertel des 19. Jahrhunderts)* (Tallinn: Eesti Raamat, 1969), p. 228.

14. Herbert Ligi, *Talupoegade koormised Eestis 13. sajandist 19. sajandi alguseni* (Tallinn: Eesti Raamat, 1968), p. 295; *Eesti majandusajalugu*, 1: 334.

15. Ligi, *Talupoegade koormised Eestis*, p. 296; Herbert Ligi, "Eestimaa 1804. aasta talurahvaseadus ja feodaalsed koormised," in *Ajaloo järskudel radadel* (Tallinn: Eesti Raamat, 1966), pp. 102–3, 113.

16. *Eesti rahva ajalugu*, 3: 1544.

17. Kahk, *Rahutused ja reformid*, p. 572.

18. Juhan Kahk, *1858. aasta talurahvarahutused Eestis: Mahtra sõda* (Tallinn: Eesti Riiklik Kirjastus, 1958), pp. 149, 153.

19. Hans Kruus, *Grundriss der Geschichte des estnischen Volkes* (Tartu: Akadeemiline Kooperatiiv, 1932), p. 96.

20. Hans Kruus, *Talurahva käärimine Lõuna-Eestis XIX sajandi 40-ndail aastail* (Tartu: Eesti Kirjanduse Selts, 1930), pp. 340, 400.

21. A. Kuusberg, ed., *Materjale Maltsveti-liikumise kohta* (Tartu: Loodus, 1931), pp. 23, 234.

22. Juhan Kahk, Herbert Ligi, and Enn Tarvel, *Beiträge zur marxistischen Agrargeschichte Estlands der Feudalzeit* (Tallinn: Eesti Raamat, 1974), pp. 54–56, 60–61.

23. Hubertus Neuschäffer, "Katharina II. und die Agrarfrage in den baltischen Provinzen," *Journal of Baltic Studies* 14 (1983): 110–11.

24. *Istoriia Estonskoi SSR*, 3 vols. (Tallinn: Estonskoe Gosudarstvennoe Izdatel'stvo, 1961; Eesti Raamat, 1966–1974), 1: 695–96.

25. *Eesti majandusajalugu*, 1: 369–72.

26. Kahk, *Krise der feudalen Landwirtschaft*, pp. 137–38.

27. Gert von Pistohlkors, *Ritterschaftliche Reformpolitik zwischen Russifizierung und Revolution*, Göttinger Bausteine zur Geschichtswissenschaft, no. 48 (Göttingen: Musterschmidt, 1978), pp. 85–86, 110–11; Gert von Pistohlkors, "Juhan Kahk's Interpretation of Feudal Agrarian Economy in Estonia and Northern Livonia, 1825–1850: A Review Article," *Journal of Baltic Studies* 9 (1978): 368–70.

28. Sulev Vahtre, *Eestimaa talurahvas hingeloenduste andmeil (1782–1858)* (Tallinn: Eesti Raamat, 1973), p. 236.

29. Ibid., pp. 236, 240, 242–43, 246. For an example of the "demographic crisis" view of the years 1780–1820, see *Eesti majandusajalugu*, 1: 330–31.

30. Ibid., pp. 162, 167.

31. Mihkel Weske, "Über den Culturfortschritt im Leben der Esten," *Sitzungsberichte der gelehrten estnischen Gesellschaft zu Dorpat* (1876): 40, 43.

32. [Elisabeth Rigby], *Letters from the Shores of the Baltic* (London: John Murray, 1849), p. 51.

33. Vahtre, *Eestimaa talurahvas*, pp. 229, 234.

34. Wilhelm Lenz, "Zur Verfassungs- und Sozialgeschichte der baltischen evangelisch-luterischen Kirche 1710–1914," in Reinhard Wittram, ed., *Baltische Kirchengeschichte* (Göttingen: Vandenhoeck & Ruprecht, 1956), p. 115.

35. Otto Karma, *Tööstuslikult revolutsioonilt sotsialistlikule revolutsionile Eestis: Tööstuse arenemine 1917. aastani* (Tallinn: Eesti NSV Teaduste Akadeemia Ajaloo Instituut, 1963), p. 119.

36. Raimo Pullat, *Eesti linnad ja linlased XVIII sajandi lõpust 1917. aastani* (Tallinn: Eesti Raamat, 1972), pp. 36–38.

37. Ibid., pp. 57–58, 63.

38. Rudolf Põldmäe, "Eesti ainestik Vennaste-uniteedi arhiivis Herrnhutis Saksamaal," *Ajalooline Ajakiri* 19 (1940): 79.

39. Kruus, *Talurahva käärimine*, pp. 344, 400.

40. Lembit Andresen, ed., *Eesti rahvakoolide seadused 18. ja 19. sajandil* (Tallinn: Eesti NSV Kõrgema ja Kesk-Erihariduse Ministeerium, 1973), pp. 21–24; Lembit Andresen, *Eesti rahvakoolid 19. sajandil kuni 1880-ndate aastate koolireformini* (Tallinn: Valgus, 1974), pp. 33–35, 37, 52.

41. Andresen, *Eesti rahvakooli seadused*, pp. 32–43; Andresen, *Eesti rahvakoolid 19. sajandil*, pp. 40, 62–63, 75, 91, 113.

42. Andresen, *Eesti rahvakoolid 19. sajandil*, p. 36; Toivo U. Raun, "The Development of Estonian Literacy in the 18th and 19th Centuries," *Journal of Baltic Studies* 10 (1979): 117–19.

43. *Eesti kirjanduse ajalugu*, 4 vols. (Tallinn: Eesti Raamat, 1965–1984), 1: 314–15.

44. Daniel Palgi, ed., *Raamatu osa Eesti arengus* (Tartu: Eesti Kirjanduse Selts, 1935), pp. 294–95.

45. *Eesti biograafiline leksikon* (Tartu: Loodus, 1926–1929), p. 97; Friedrich R. Faehlmann, "Mein Streit mit Nolcken und Liphart," in *Talurahvaliikumine Eestis 1841.–1842. aastal: Dokumentide kogumik* (Tallinn: Eesti Raamat, 1982), p. 241. For Kreutzwald's views, see the preface to the first edition of *Kalevipoeg*, translated in Fr. R. Kreutzwald, comp., *Kalevipoeg: An Ancient Estonian Tale*, trans. Jüri Kurman (Moorestown, N.J.: Symposia Press, 1982), pp. 293, 295.

CHAPTER 5

1. For a recent reassessment of Russification in the Baltic region, see Edward C. Thaden et al., *Russification in the Baltic Provinces and Finland, 1855–1914* (Princeton, N.J.: Princeton University Press, 1981).

2. Michael H. Haltzel, "The Baltic Germans," in Thaden et al., *Russification*, p. 152; Alexander von Tobien, *Die livländische Ritterschaft in ihrem Verhältnis zum Zarismus und russischen Nationalismus*, 2 vols. (Riga: G. Löffler, 1925; Berlin: Walter de Gruyter, 1930), 1: 157–58.

3. Hans Kruus, "Opositsioon Tallinna linnaomavalitsuses 1877–1904," *Ajalooline Ajakiri* 17 (1938): 105–6, 110–13.

4. Toivo U. Raun, "The Estonians," in Thaden et al., *Russification*, pp. 308–9.

5. Ibid., pp. 309–11.

6. August Traat, "Vallareform Eestis 1866. aastal," *ENSVTA Toimetised* 27 (1968): 13, 15–17, 20–21.

7. Sergei G. Isakov, *Ostzeiskii vopros v russkoi pechati 1860-kh godov*, Tartu Riikliku Ülikooli Toimetised, no. 107 (Tartu: Tartu Riiklik Ülikool, 1961), pp. 178–80; Tobien, *Livländische Ritterschaft*, 1: 158–59; Sergei V. Shakhovskoi, *Iz arkhiva kniazia S. V. Shakhovskogo: Materialy dlia istorii nedavnego proshlogo Pribaltiiskoi okrainy*, 3 vols. (St. Petersburg: V. Eriks, 1909–1910), 3: 209.

8. Ernst Seraphim, "Die baltischen Provinzen in der zweiten Hälfte des 19. Jahrhunderts," *Deutsche Monatsschrift für Russland* 1 (1912): 595; Haltzel, "The Baltic Germans," pp. 126–27.

9. Voldemar Miller, "Eestikeelne ajakirjandus baltisakslaste teenistuses," in *Minevikust tulevikku* (Tallinn: Eesti Raamat, 1972), pp. 12–19.

10. Jakob Hurt, "Meie koolitatud ja haritud meestest," in Hans Kruus, ed., *Jakob Hurda kõned ja avalikud kirjad* (Tartu: Eesti Kirjanduse Selts, 1939), pp. 68, 71, 75–76; Hans Kruus, "Väikerahvalik tunnetus eesti ühiskondlikus mõttes," *Ajalooline Ajakiri* 18 (1939): 137–40.

11. Ea Jansen, *Carl Robert Jakobsoni "Sakala"* (Tallinn: Eesti Raamat, 1971), p. 208; Carl Robert Jakobson, "Kuidas eesti rahvas vaimuharimise teel oma õigusele jõuab," in *Valitud teosed*, 2 vols. (Tallinn: Eesti Riiklik Kirjastus, 1959), 1: 409.

12. With a circulation of over 4,500 in 1880–1882, *Sakala* had quickly overtaken its

main rival, *Eesti Postimees*, which declined from about 4,600 subscribers in 1878 to about 1,500 in 1881; see Meelik Kahu, "C. R. Jakobsoni 'Sakala' levikust," *Keel ja Kirjandus* 7 (1964): 141, and Jansen, *"Sakala,"* pp. 275, 279.

13. "Eesti saadikute märgukiri Vene keiser Aleksander III-le 19. juunist 1881," *Eesti Kirjandus* 15 (1921): 346–49.

14. "Senaator Manasseini revisjonist," in Hans Kruus, ed., *Eesti ajaloo lugemik*, 3 vols. (Tartu: Eesti Kirjanduse Selts, 1924–1929), 3: 292–95.

15. Raun, "The Estonians," pp. 305, 341.

16. Ado Grenzstein, *Herrenkirche oder Volkskirche?* (Tartu: A. Grenzstein, 1899), pp. 129–31; Friedebert Tuglas, *Ado Grenzsteini lahkumine* (Tartu: Noor-Eesti, 1926), p. 19.

17. Peeter Ruubel, *Poliitilised ja ühiskondlikud voolud Eestis* (Tallinn: Varrak, 1920), p. 58.

18. Märt Raud, *Sulg ja raamat* (Lund: Eesti Kirjanike Kooperatiiv, 1962), p. 75.

19. Jüri Uluots, *Grundzüge der Agrargeschichte Estlands* (Tartu: Akadeemiline Kooperatiiv, 1935), p. 161; Ea Jansen, "'Sakala' kaastööliste sotsiaalsest ja kutselisest jagunemisest," *ENSVTA Toimetised* 14 (1965): 447; Paul Jordan, ed., *Ergebnisse der ehstländischen Volkszählung*, 3 vols. (Tallinn: Lindfors' Erben, 1883–1885), 3: 31.

20. Alexander von Tobien, *Die Agrargesetzgebung Livlands im 19. Jahrhundert*, 2 vols. (Berlin: Puttkammer & Mühlbrecht, 1899; Riga: G. Löffler, 1911), 2: 311–12; Uluots, *Grundzüge*, p. 172; "Tartu Ülemaalise Rahvaasemikkude Kongressi Bürgermusse koosolekute otsused," in Hans Kruus, ed., *Punased aastad: Mälestusi ja dokumente 1905. aasta liikumisest Eestis* (Tartu: Eesti Kirjanduse Selts, 1932), p. 225.

21. Artur Vassar, "Eesti talurahva vaated maavaldusele XIX sajandi teisel poolel," in *Eesti talurahva sotsiaalseid vaateid XIX sajandil* (Tallinn: Eesti NSV Teaduste Akadeemia Ajaloo Instituut, 1977), p. 131. For the text of the main Estonian peasant petition to the tsar in the 1860s, see "Polozhenie estov v 1860-kh godakh," *Russkaia starina* 100 (1899): 655–65.

22. *Eesti rahva ajalugu*, 3 vols. (Tartu: Loodus, 1932–1937), 3: 1553; *Eesti NSV ajalugu*, 3 vols. (Tallinn: Eesti Riiklik Kirjastus, 1955–1963; Eesti Raamat, 1971), 2: 62–65.

23. *Eesti NSV ajalugu*, 2: 71; Arno Köörna, *Suure Sotsialistliku Oktoobrirevolutsiooni majanduslikud eeldused Eestis* (Tallinn: Eesti Riiklik Kirjastus, 1961), pp. 37–39; Hendrik Sepp, "Põhja-Eesti majanduslik olustik XIX sajandi teisel poolel," *Ajalooline Ajakiri* 17 (1938): 10–11.

24. Köörna, *Majanduslikud eeldused*, p. 37; Vassar, "Eesti talurahva vaated," pp. 155–56.

25. Jaan Konks, "Maavaldusest Eestimaal aastail 1900–1917," in *Sotsiaalmajandusliku arengu probleeme XVII–XX sajandil*, Tartu Riikliku Ülikooli Toimetised, no. 454 (Tartu: Tartu Riiklik Ülikool, 1979), p. 91.

26. Hubertus Neuschäffer, "Die Anfänge der livländischen ökonomischen Sozietät (1792–1939)," *Journal of Baltic Studies* 10 (1979): 342.

27. Otu Ibius, "Balti mõisnike katsed eesti põllumeesteseltside sõltuvuses hoid-

miseks XIX sajandi teisel poolel," *ENSVTA Toimetised* 15 (1966): 404–5, 409, 413, 415; *Isamaa kalender 1905 aasta jaoks* (Tartu: Schnakenburg, 1904), pp. 154–55.

28. Otto Karma, *Tööstuslikult revolutsioonilt sotsialistlikule revolutsioonile Eestis: Tööstuse arenemine 1917. aastani* (Tallinn: Eesti NSV Teaduste Akadeemia Ajaloo Instituut, 1963), pp. 192–93, 234, 257.

29. Köörna, *Majanduslikud eeldused*, pp. 16–17; *Eesti NSV ajalugu*, 2: 83–85.

30. *Eesti NSV ajalugu*, 2: 110.

31. Heldur Palli, "19. sajandi maarahvastiku loomuliku liikumise uurimisest: Probleeme ja allikaid," *ENSVTA Toimetised* 32 (1983): 128–31; Nikolai Köstner, "Rahva arvu kasvamine Eestimaal," in *Noor-Eesti*, 5 vols. (Tartu: Noor-Eesti, 1905–1915), 5: 67, 88.

32. Jordan, *Ergebnisse der ehstländischen Volkszählung*, 1: 4–5, 68–69; 2: 6; 3: 25; Friedrich von Jung-Stilling and W. Anders, eds., *Ergebnisse der livländischen Volkszählung*, 3 vols. (Riga: Stahl'sche Buchdruckerei, 1883–1885), 3: 148–49; *Eesti arvudes 1920–1935* (Tallinn: Riigi Statistika Keskbüroo, 1937), p. 26.

33. Toivo U. Raun, "The Revolution of 1905 in the Baltic Provinces and Finland," *Slavic Review* 43 (1984): 455.

34. Viktor Maamiagi [Maamägi], *Estonskie poselentsy v SSSR (1917–1940 gg.)* (Tallinn: Eesti Raamat, 1976), pp. 21–22; Kurt Baron Maydell, "Die Baltendeutschen vor ihrer Umsiedlung: Ein statistischer Rückblick," *Jomsburg* 4 (1940): 67–68; Reinhard Wittram, *Geschichte der baltischen Deutschen: Grundzüge und Durchblicke* (Stuttgart: W. Kohlhammer, 1939), p. 176.

35. Toomas Karjahärm, "Eesti rahvusliku haritlaskonna kujunemisest möödunud sajandi lõpul ja praeguse algul," *Keel ja Kirjandus* 16 (1973): 627; Jordan, *Ergebnisse der ehstländischen Volkszählung*, 3: 28.

36. *Eesti NSV ajalugu*, 2: 75–76; Aleksei Peterson, "Taluelamu käsitlus eestikeelses perioodikas aastail 1850–1917," *Etnograafiamuuseumi aastaraamat* 23 (1968): 33–34.

37. Raimo Pullat, *Eesti linnad ja linlased XVIII sajandi lõpust 1917. aastani* (Tallinn: Eesti Raamat, 1972), pp. 37–38; *Eesti NSV ajalugu*, 2: 114, 116; *Entsiklopedicheskii slovar'*, 41 vols. (Leipzig: F. A. Brokgauz; St. Petersburg: I. A. Efron, 1890–1904), 28: 278.

38. Pullat, *Eesti linnad ja linlased*, p. 60.

39. Karjahärm, "Eesti rahvusliku haritlaskonna kujunemisest," pp. 627–28.

40. *Eesti NSV ajalugu*, 2: 166.

41. Hans Kruus, *Eesti Aleksandrikool* (Tartu: Noor-Eesti), pp. 212, 233–34.

42. Ibid., pp. 202, 208, 293.

43. Friedebert Tuglas, *Eesti Kirjameeste Selts* (Tallinn: Eesti Riiklik Kirjastus, 1958; first published, 1932), pp. 191, 217; Sergei G. Issakov [Isakov], "Uusi andmeid Eesti Kirjameeste Seltsi sulgemise kohta," *Keel ja Kirjandus* 13 (1970): 290–91.

44. *1869–1969: Juubelilaulupeo juht* (Tallinn: Eesti Raamat, 1969), p. 36; Rudolf Põldmäe, *Esimene Eesti üldlaulupidu 1869* (Tallinn: Eesti Raamat, 1969), p. 105.

45. Jakob Hurt, "Kõne esimesel Eesti üldlaulupeol 1869," in Kruus, *Jakob Hurda kõned*, pp. 44–47; *Eesti Postimees*, December 25, 1868, p. 415.

46. *1869–1969: Juubelilaulupeo juht*, p. 36; A. Tamman, *Eesti üldised laulupeod XIX aastasajal* (Tallinn: Albert Org, 1923), pp. 89, 105, 125, 137; *Postimees*, June 27, 1894, pp. 1–2.

47. Rudolf Põldmäe, *Kaks laulupidu: 1879–1880* (Tallinn: Eesti Raamat, 1976), p. 242; Ellen Karu, "Muusikaseltside asutamisest Eestis 19. sajandi teisel poolel," in *Eesti talurahva majanduse ja olme arengujooni 19. ja 20. sajandil* (Tallinn: Eesti NSV Teaduste Akadeemia Ajaloo Instituut, 1979), pp. 50, 52–53, 64; Olavi Kasemaa, "Orkestrimänguharrastuse ulatus ja levik Eestis aastail 1818–1917," *ENSVTA Toimetised* 32 (1983): 49, 59–60, 62.

48. *Eesti karskuse seltside aastaraamat*, vol. 8 (Tartu: H. Laas, 1905), pp. 168–71.

49. Otto A. Webermann, "Probleme des baltischen Raumes als Forschungsaufgabe," *Ural-Altaische Jahrbücher* 35 (1964): 294; Juhan Luiga, "Noor-Suomi-Eesti," *Eesti Kirjandus* 12 (1917): 226.

50. Eeva Ahven, *Eesti kirjakeele arenemine aastail 1900–1917* (Tallinn: Eesti Riiklik Kirjastus, 1958), p. 7; George Kurman, *The Development of Written Estonian*, Indiana University Publications, Uralic and Altaic Series, no. 90 (The Hague: Mouton, 1968), p. 33.

51. A full translation of *Kalevipoeg* in English is now available: Fr. R. Kreutzwald, comp., *Kalevipoeg: An Ancient Estonian Tale*, trans. Jüri Kurman (Moorestown, N.J.: Symposia Press, 1982).

52. Daniel Palgi, ed., *Raamatu osa Eesti arengus* (Tartu: Eesti Kirjanduse Selts, 1935), pp. 295–96; Richard Antik, *Eesti raamat 1535–1935* (Tartu: n.p., 1936), pp. 55, 58.

53. Friedrich Puksov, *Eesti raamatu arengulugu seoses kirja ja raamatu üldise arenemisega* (Tallinn: Eesti Raamatukoguhoidjate Ühing, 1933), pp. 73, 91; Toivo U. Raun, "The Role of Journalism in the Estonian Awakening," in Aleksander Loit, ed., *National Movements in the Baltic Countries during the 19th Century*, Studia Baltica Stockholmiensia, no. 2 (Stockholm: Almqvist & Wiksell International, 1985), p. 391; Antik, *Eesti raamat*, p. 90; Raun, "The Estonians," p. 333.

54. Lembit Andresen, *Eesti rahvakoolid 19. sajandil kuni 1880-ndate aastate koolireformini* (Tallinn: Valgus, 1974), pp. 59, 76.

55. Raun, "The Estonians," pp. 316–17; Toivo U. Raun, "The Development of Estonian Literacy in the 18th and 19th Centuries," *Journal of Baltic Studies* 10 (1979): 122–23.

56. Allan Liim, "Keskkoolivõrgu kujunemine ja areng Eestis 19. sajandi teisel poolel," *Nõukogude Kool* 31 (1973): 703; Voldemar Juhanson, "Esimesed eesti üliõpilased Tartu Ülikoolis ja Eesti Üliõpilaste Selts," in Juhan Vasar, ed., *Tartu üliõpilaskonna ajalugu seoses eesti üliõpilaskonna ajalooga* (Tartu: Tartu Üliõpilaskond, 1932), pp. 98–99.

57. Raun, "The Estonians," pp. 324–25.

58. Grenzstein, *Herrenkirche oder Volkskirche?*, p. 144.

CHAPTER 6

1. Friedebert Tuglas, *Ado Grenzsteini lahkumine* (Tartu: Noor-Eesti, 1926), pp. 138–39, 145.

2. Peeter Tarvel, "J. Tõnissoni rahvuspoliitilisi vaateid," in *Jaan Tõnisson töös ja võitluses* (Tartu: Koguteose "Jaan Tõnissoni" komitee, 1938), pp. 439–41, 458.

3. *Teataja*, September 10, 1902, p. 1; *Uudised*, June 8, 1904, p. 1.

4. *Uudised*, May 25, 1905, p. 1; Toivo U. Raun, "1905 as a Turning Point in Estonian History," *East European Quarterly* 14 (1980): 329–30.

5. *Revoliutsiia 1905–1907 gg. v Estonii: Sbornik dokumentov i materialov* (Tallinn: Estonskoe Gosudarstvennoe Izdatel'stvo, 1955), pp. 254–55.

6. The delegates were selected as follows: four from every city, two each from the propertied and working classes; two from each rural township, one landed and one landless; and one from each Estonian local organization or society. Toivo U. Raun, "The Estonians," in Edward C. Thaden et al., *Russification in the Baltic Provinces and Finland, 1855–1914* (Princeton, N.J.: Princeton University Press, 1981), p. 312.

7. *Postimees*, November 29, 1905, pp. 1, 3; Toivo U. Raun, "The Revolution of 1905 and the Movement for Estonian National Autonomy, 1896–1907" (Ph.D. diss., Princeton University, 1969), pp. 170–73.

8. The Bügermusse and Aula resolutions are reproduced in Hans Kruus, ed., *Punased aastad: Mälestusi ja dokumente 1905. aasta liikumisest Eestis* (Tartu: Eesti Kirjanduse Selts, 1932), pp. 220–30, and summarized in Toivo U. Raun, "Estonian Social and Political Thought, 1905–February 1917," in Andrew Ezergailis and Gert von Pistohlkors, eds., *Die baltischen Provinzen Russlands zwischen den Revolutionen von 1905 und 1917*, Quellen und Studien zur baltischen Geschichte, no. 4 (Cologne: Böhlau, 1982), pp. 63–65.

9. Toivo U. Raun, "The Revolution of 1905 in the Baltic Provinces and Finland," *Slavic Review* 43 (1984): 461.

10. Sidney Harcave, *First Blood: The Russian Revolution of 1905* (New York: Macmillan, 1964), p. 241; Toomas Karjahärm and Raimo Pullat, *Eesti revolutsiooni tules 1905–1907* (Tallinn: Eesti Raamat, 1975), pp. 151–52.

11. Raun, "1905 as a Turning Point," p. 332.

12. C. Leonard Lundin, "The Road from Tsar to Kaiser: Changing Loyalties of the Baltic Germans, 1905–1914," *Journal of Central European Affairs* 10 (1950): 225–26; Reinhard Wittram, *Baltische Geschichte: Die Ostseelande Livland, Estland, Kurland, 1180–1918* (Munich: R. Oldenbourg, 1954), pp. 235–36.

13. Raun, "Estonian Social and Political Thought," pp. 65–68.

14. Alma Ostra-Oinas, "Jooni revolutsioonilisest tegevusest," in Kruus, *Punased aastad*, p. 65; *Revoliutsiia 1905–1907 gg.*, pp. 553, 577; August Rei, *Mälestusi tormiselt teelt* (Stockholm: Vaba Eesti, 1961), p. 120.

15. Gustav Suits, "Kaks ilmavaadet," in *Sihid ja vaated* (Helsinki: Yrjö Weilin, 1906), pp. 49, 54–57, 60; Raun, "Estonian Social and Political Thought," pp. 68–71.

16. Anton Jürgenstein, "Jaan Tōnissoni elulugu," in *Jaan Tōnisson: Tagasivaateid ja mälestusi tema 60. a. sünnipäevaks* (Tartu: Postimees, 1928), pp. 19–22.

17. Eduard von Dellingshausen, *Im Dienste der Heimat!* (Stuttgart: Ausland und Heimat Verlag, 1930), pp. 109–10; Gert von Pistohlkors, *Ritterschaftliche Reformpolitik zwischen Russifizierung und Revolution*, Göttinger Bausteine zur Geschichtswissenschaft, no. 48 (Göttingen: Musterschmidt, 1978), pp. 173–81; Toomas Karjahärm and Sirje Kivimäe, "Maaomavalitsusküsimus Eesti ühiskondlikus liikumises kodanlik-demokraatlike revolutsioonide ajajärgul," *ENSVTA Toimetised* 29 (1980): 332–33, 335–37; J. Vilms, "Maaomavalitsuse uuenduskatsed Eestis," *Vaba Sōna*, no. 12 (1915): 320–22.

18. Toomas Karjahärm, "Eesti linnakodanluse poliitilisest formeerumisest 1870-ndate aastate lõpust kuni 1914. aastani (linna- ja duumavalimiste materjalide põhjal)," *ENSVTA Toimetised* 23 (1973): 255–56, 260–62.

19. *Ezhegodnik Rossii* (1907): 210–11; *Eesti NSV ajalugu*, 3 vols. (Tallinn: Eesti Riiklik Kirjastus, 1955–1963; Eesti Raamat, 1971), 2: 457–58; Arno Köörna, *Suure Sotsialistliku Oktoobrirevolutsiooni majanduslikud eeldused Eestis* (Tallinn: Eesti Riiklik Kirjastus, 1961), p. 41.

20. Sirje Kivimäe, "Die Agrarreform Stolypins in den baltischen Gouvernements," in Ezergailis and Pistohlkors, *Die baltischen Provinzen Russlands*, p. 107.

21. Köörna, *Majanduslikud eeldused*, pp. 35, 46–49; *Eesti NSV ajalugu*, 2: 461, 490; Hans Kruus, *Grundriss der Geschichte des estnischen Volkes* (Tartu: Akadeemiline Kooperatiiv, 1932), pp. 194–95.

22. Köörna, *Majanduslikud eeldused*, p. 15; Otto Karma, *Tööstuslikult revolutsioonilt sotsialistlikule revolutsioonile Eestis: Tööstuse arenemine 1917. aastani* (Tallinn: Eesti NSV Teaduste Akadeemia Ajaloo Instituut, 1963), pp. 234, 287, 345, 377; *Eesti NSV ajalugu*, 2: 533–35; Timo Herranen and Timo Myllyntaus, "Effects of the First World War on the Engineering Industries of Estonia and Finland," *Scandinavian Economic History Review* 32 (1984): 124–26.

23. *Ezhegodnik Rossii* (1911): 38–39, 47; H. Reiman, "Demographic Survey of Estonia," *Baltic Countries* 1, no. 1 (August 1935): 53; A. G. Rashin, *Naselenie Rossii za sto let, 1811–1913 gg.* (Moscow: Gosstatizdat, 1956), pp. 227–29.

24. August Nigol, *Eesti asundused ja asupaigad Venemaal* (Tartu: Postimees, 1918), pp. 9–11; Viktor Maamiagi [Maamägi], *Estonskie poselentsy v SSSR (1917–1940 gg.)* (Tallinn: Eesti Raamat, 1976), p. 47; Raimo Pullat, *Peterburi eestlased: Ajaloolis-demograafiline käsitlus XVIII sajandi algusest kuni 1917. aastani* (Tallinn: Eesti Raamat, 1981), p. 22.

25. Raimo Pullat, *Eesti linnad ja linlased XVIII sajandi lõpust 1917. aastani* (Tallinn: Eesti Raamat, 1972), pp. 37–39, 42, 53, 58, 60.

26. Raimo Pullat, "Eesti kodanluse kujunemisest Tallinnas aastail 1871–1912," *ENSVTA Toimetised* 13 (1964): 51–52, 54.

27. *Eesti NSV ajalugu*, 2: 495, 507; Köörna, *Majanduslikud eeldused*, pp. 83, 143.

28. *Noor-Eesti*, 5 vols. (Tartu: Noor-Eesti, 1905–1915), 1: 16–17.

29. Anton Jürgenstein, "Noor-Eesti: Peatükk uuemast Eesti kulturalisest edenemisloost," in W. Reiman, ed., *Eesti Kultura*, 4 vols. (Tartu: Postimees, 1911–1915), 1: 96.

30. Eeva Ahven, *Eesti kirjakeele arenemine aastail 1900–1917* (Tallinn: Eesti Riiklik Kirjastus, 1958), p. 169; August Palm, *Eesti Kirjanduse Selts 1907–1932* (Tartu: Eesti Kirjanduse Selts, 1932), pp. 5, 12–13; Arvo Mägi, *Estonian Literature* (Stockholm: Baltic Humanitarian Association, 1968), pp. 26–29.

31. *Eesti muusika*, 2 vols. (Tallinn: Eesti Raamat, 1968–1975), 1: 135; *1869–1969: Juubelilaulupeo juht* (Tallinn: Eesti Raamat, 1969), p. 36.

32. *Teataja*, March 4, 1903, p. 1.

33. Daniel Palgi, ed., *Raamatu osa Eesti arengus* (Tartu: Eesti Kirjanduse Selts, 1935), p. 296; Richard Antik, *Eesti raamat 1535–1935* (Tartu: n.p., 1936), pp. 63, 90; Benjamin Rigberg, "The Efficacy of Tsarist Censorship Operations, 1894–1917," *Jahrbücher für Geschichte Osteuropas*, NF 14 (1966): 331n.

34. Allan Liim, "Eesti algkoolide õppekeel kahe kodanlik-demokraatliku revolutsiooni vahelisel perioodil," *Nõukogude Kool* 29 (1971): 474; Peeter Põld, *Eesti kooli ajalugu* (Tartu: Akadeemiline Kooperatiiv, 1933), pp. 158–59.

35. Allan Liim, "Keskkoolivõrgu areng Eestis 20. sajandi algul (kuni 1917. a.)," *Nõukogude Kool* 31 (1973): 856–60; *Obzor Estliandskoi gubernii za 1913 god* (Tallinn: Estliandskaia Gubernskaia Tipografiia, 1914), Prilozhenie no. 23.

36. Voldemar Juhanson, "Esimesed eesti üliõpilased Tartu Ülikoolis ja Eesti Üliõpilaste Selts," in Juhan Vasar, ed., *Tartu üliõpilaskonna ajalugu seoses eesti üliõpilaskonna ajalooga* (Tartu: Tartu Üliõpilaskond, 1932), p. 99; Toomas Karjahärm, "Eesti rahvusliku haritlaskonna kujunemisest möödunud sajandi lõpul ja praeguse algul," *Keel ja Kirjandus* 16 (1973): 627–29; *Alma mater Tartuensis* (Tallinn: Valgus, 1977), pp. 27–28.

37. Karjahärm, "Eesti rahvusliku haritlaskonna kujunemisest," p. 630; *Pravoslavie i liuteranstvo v Pribaltiiskom krae po noveishim dannym russkoi pechati* (St. Petersburg: Gosudarstvennaia Tipografiia, 1911), p. 54.

38. Arnold Takkin, *Eesti Esimese maailmasõja aastail* (Tallinn: Eesti Riiklik Kirjastus, 1961), p. 11.

39. *Eesti NSV ajalugu*, 2: 530; *Estonian War of Independence, 1918–1920* (New York: Eesti Vabadusvõitlejate Liit, n.d.), p. 11; Hans Rogger, *Russia in the Age of Modernisation and Revolution, 1881–1917* (London: Longman, 1983), p. 257.

40. Takkin, *Eesti Esimese maailmasõja aastail*, p. 53; Karma, *Tööstuslikult revolutsioonilt*, pp. 385–86; Köörna, *Majanduslikud eeldused*, pp. 93–95.

CHAPTER 7

1. The reader is reminded that all dates before February 1 (14), 1918 (when the Gregorian Calendar was adopted in Russia) are given according to the Julian Calendar (thirteen days behind the Gregorian or Western Calendar in the twentieth century).

2. Eduard Laaman, *Eesti iseseisvuse sünd* (Stockholm: Vaba Eesti, 1964; first published, 1936), pp. 79–80, 82.

3. This new administrative entity included nearly all the Estonians in the northern

Baltic region and, with relatively minor changes in the eastern border, corresponded to the areas of both independent and Soviet Estonia. Thus, beginning with this date, the term Estonia takes on its twentieth-century sense.

4. The Provisional Government's decree is reproduced in English in Robert P. Browder and Alexander Kerensky, eds., *The Russian Provisional Government*, 3 vols. (Stanford: Stanford University Press, 1961), 1: 300–1.

5. Artur Mägi, *Das Staatsleben Estlands während seiner Selbständigkeit*, vol. 1, *Das Regierungssystem* (Stockholm: Almqvist & Wiksell, 1967), pp. 22, 22n.

6. Laaman, *Eesti iseseisvuse sünd*, pp. 131–33; Olavi Arens, "The Estonian *Maapäev* During 1917," in V. Stanley Vardys and Romuald J. Misiunas, eds., *The Baltic States in Peace and War, 1917–1945* (University Park: The Pennsylvania State University Press, 1978), pp. 24–25.

7. Karl Siilivask, *Veebruarist oktoobrini 1917* (Tallinn: Eesti Raamat, 1972), pp. 48, 350, 432.

8. Ibid., pp. 344–45; *Päevaleht*, August 8 and 9, 1917.

9. Siilivask, *Veebruarist oktoobrini*, p. 202. See also Olavi Arens, "Soviets in Estonia, 1917/1918," in Andrew Ezergailis and Gert von Pistohlkors, eds., *Die baltischen Provinzen Russlands zwischen den Revolutionen von 1905 und 1917*, Quellen und Studien zur baltischen Geschichte, no. 4 (Cologne: Böhlau, 1982), pp. 296–97, and Aleksander Hellat, "Revolutsiooni miilitsas," in *Mälestused iseseisvuse võitluspäivilt*, 2 vols. (Tallinn: Rahvaülikool, 1927–1930), 1: 112.

10. *Suur Sotsialistlik Oktoobrirevolutsioon Eestis* (Tallinn: Eesti Riiklik Kirjastus, 1957), p. 227; Siilivask, *Veebruarist oktoobrini*, pp. 421–23.

11. Stanley Page, *The Formation of the Baltic States* (New York: Howard Fertig, 1970; first published, 1959), p. 72; Arens, "Soviets in Estonia," p. 299.

12. Aleksander Tõnisson, "Esimesest Eesti polgust," in *Mälestused iseseisvuse võitluspäivilt*, 1: 159; Evald Uustalu, *Eesti Vabariik 1918–1940* (Lund: Eesti Kirjanike Kooperatiiv, 1968), p. 11; Siilivask, *Veebruarist oktoobrini*, pp. 256–61.

13. Laaman, *Eesti iseseisvuse sünd*, p. 164; Arens, "Soviets in Estonia," p. 312; *Suur Sotsialistlik Oktoobrirevolutsioon Eestis*, p. 673.

14. See the committee's minutes in *Eestimaa Sõja-Revolutsioonikomitee* (Tallinn: Eesti Raamat, 1977).

15. The vote in the Maapäev on the issue of sovereign power was 39–0 in favor with 9 abstentions (some Estonian Social Democrats and SRs); the Bolshevik members had already withdrawn by this time. Laaman, *Eesti iseseisvuse sünd*, p. 162; Ants Piip, *Tormine aasta* (Stockholm: Vaba Eesti, 1966; first published, 1934), pp. 24, 26.

16. Siilivask, *Veebruarist oktoobrini*, pp. 470–71; Olavi Arens, "Revolutionary Developments in Estonia in 1917–18 and Their Ideological and Political Background" (Ph.D. diss., Columbia University, 1976), pp. 243–44. I have corrected some minor internal errors in Siilivask's data (he gives incorrect totals for the Estonian and Russian SRs and the total valid vote), and—as Arens does—I have omitted the totals for Narva since some of the parties there were not comparable to those in the rest of Estonia.

17. Siilivask, *Veebruarist oktoobrini*, pp. 470–74; Page, *Formation*, pp. 74–75.

18. Olavi Arens, "Bolshevik Policies in Estonia During 1917–18" (Paper delivered at the Sixth Conference on Baltic Studies, Toronto, Ontario, Canada, May 11–14, 1978), pp. 11–14; Joosep Saat, *Nõukogude võim Eestis: Oktoober 1917-märts 1918* (Tallinn: Eesti Raamat, 1975), pp. 403–4; *Revolutsioon, kodusõda ja välisriikide interventsioon Eestis (1917–1920)*, 2 vols. (Tallinn: Eesti Raamat, 1977–1982); 1: 297, 306–12, 324.

19. A. Helbe, "Esseeride tegevusest Eestis Oktoobrirevolutsiooni võidu ja Nõukogude võimu kindlustamise perioodil," in *Eesti NSV ajaloo küsimusi*, vol. 6, Tartu Riikliku Ülikooli Toimetised, no. 258 (Tartu: Tartu Riiklik Ülikool, 1970), pp. 371, 375–76. Laaman gives a figure of 35.3 percent for the Bolsheviks and indicates that the election was about two-thirds complete when broken off; see Laaman, *Eesti iseseisvuse sünd*, p. 207.

20. Helbe, "Esseeride tegevusest," p. 376; Saat, *Nõukogude võim*, p. 432; *Revolutsioon, kodusõda ja välisriikide interventsioon*, 1: 302.

21. Piip, *Tormine aasta*, pp. 77, 85; Seppo Zetterberg, *Suomi ja Viro 1917–1919*, Historiallisia Tutkimuksia, no. 102 (Helsinki: Suomen Historiallinen Seura, 1977), pp. 49–58; Laaman, *Eesti iseseisvuse sünd*, pp. 185–86, 189–90, 199, 201–4; Hans Kruus, "Murdekuudel 1917–1918," *Looming*, no. 9 (1933): 1033, 1035.

22. Kruus, "Murdekuudel," pp. 1037–38.

23. Evald Uustalu, "Die Staatsgründung Estlands," in Jürgen von Hehn, Hans von Rimscha, and Hellmuth Weiss, eds., *Von den baltischen Provinzen zu den baltischen Staaten: Beiträge zur Entstehungsgeschichte der Republiken Estland und Lettland, 1917–1918* (Marburg/Lahn: J. G. Herder-Institut, 1971), p. 281.

24. Laaman, *Eesti iseseisvuse sünd*, pp. 234–35.

25. John Wheeler-Bennett, *Brest-Litovsk: The Forgotten Peace, March 1918* (London: Macmillan, 1956; first published, 1938), p. 193.

26. Laaman, *Eesti iseseisvuse sünd*, pp. 235–44. An English translation of the declaration is available in Elmar Järvesoo, "Estonia's Declaration of Independence in 1918: An Episode of Collision Between National-Revolutionary and Bolshevist Ideologies," in Arvids Ziedonis, Jr., William L. Winter, and Mardi Valgemäe, eds., *Baltic History* (Columbus, Ohio: Association for the Advancement of Baltic Studies, 1974), pp. 170–72.

27. Laaman, *Eesti iseseisvuse sünd*, pp. 267–68, 271, 275–76; Wheeler-Bennett, *Brest-Litovsk*, p. 429; Arved Freiherr von Taube, "Von Brest-Litovsk bis Libau: Die baltisch-deutsche Führungsschicht und die Mächte in den Jahren 1918/1919," in Jürgen von Hehn, Hans von Rimscha, and Hellmuth Weiss, eds., *Von den baltischen Provinzen zu den baltischen Staaten: Beiträge zur Entstehungsgeschichte der Republiken Estland und Lettland, 1918–1920* (Marburg/Lahn: J. G. Herder-Institut, 1977), p. 83.

28. Hans Kruus, *Saksa okkupatsioon Eestis* (Tartu: Odamees, 1920), pp. 33–34, 45, 59, 81–82; Eduard von Dellingshausen, *Im Dienste der Heimat!* (Stuttgart: Ausland und Heimat Verlag, 1930), p. 273.

29. A. Saar, "Saksa vangilaagrites," in *K. Päts: Tema elu ja töö* (Tallinn: n.p., 1934), 224, 226, 232.

30. Laaman, *Eesti iseseisvuse sünd*, pp. 286, 289–90, 319–20; Piip, *Tormine aasta*, pp. 250, 271.

31. H. Veem, "Võitlus põrandaalustega," in *Mälestused iseseisvuse võitluspäivilt*, 2: 286.

32. Uustalu, "Staatsgründung," pp. 290–91.

33. Mägi, *Staatsleben Estlands*, p. 29; Laaman, *Eesti iseseisvuse sünd*, p. 368; Uustalu, *Eesti Vabariik*, pp. 27–28.

34. Piip, *Tormine aasta*, pp. 354–55; Johan Laidoner, "Inglaste tulek," in *Mälestused iseseisvuse võitluspäivilt*, 2: 20; Zetterberg, *Suomi ja Viro*, pp. 148–59.

35. Zetterberg, *Suomi ja Viro*, pp. 162, 166.

36. *Estonian War of Independence, 1918–1920* (New York: Eesti Vabadusvõitlejate Liit, n.d.), p. 21; Mihkel Martna, *Estland, die Esten und die estnische Frage* (Olten: W. Trösch, 1919), pp. 181–82; Uustalu, *Eesti Vabariik*, pp. 40–41.

37. *Estonian War of Independence*, p. 31; Zetterberg, *Suomi ja Viro*, p. 161; Uustalu, *Eesti Vabariik*, p. 37.

38. Page, *Formation*, p. 142; Siilivask, *Veebruarist oktoobrini*, p. 470; Mägi, *Staatsleben Estlands*, pp. 321, 324.

39. Laaman, *Eesti iseseisvuse sünd*, p. 486.

40. Robert G. L. Waite, *Vanguard of Nazism: The Free Corps Movement in Post-War Germany, 1918–1933* (Cambridge, Mass.: Harvard University Press, 1952), pp. 98–99, 105.

41. Laaman, *Eesti iseseisvuse sünd*, pp. 583, 645, 663.

42. Ibid., pp. 596–97, 620, 684, 693, 701–3; Uustalu, *Eesti Vabariik*, p. 65.

43. For a Soviet view of the events on Saaremaa in February 1919, see *Eesti NSV ajalugu*, 3 vols. (Tallinn: Eesti Riiklik Kirjastus, 1955–1963; Eesti Raamat, 1971), 3: 142–47.

CHAPTER 8

1. *1922. a. üldrahvalugemise andmed*, 11 vols. (Tallinn: Riigi Statistika Keskbüroo, 1923–1927), 11: 12–13, 21. On the Setus, see Jakob Hurt, "Über die pleskauer esten oder die sogenannten setukesen [sic]," *Anzeiger der Finnisch-ugrischen Forschungen* 3 (1903): 185–205.

2. Malbone W. Graham, *New Governments of Eastern Europe* (New York: Henry Holt, 1927), pp. 291–92, 675–86; Henn-Jüri Uibopuu, "The Constitutional Development of the Estonian Republic," *Journal of Baltic Studies* 4 (1973): 12–15. An English translation of the Constitution of 1920 is available in Graham, *New Governments*, pp. 675–86.

3. Artur Mägi, *Das Staatsleben Estlands während seiner Selbständigkeit*, vol. 1, *Das Regierungssystem* (Stockholm: Almqvist & Wiksell, 1967), pp. 178–79, 321; *Eesti entsüklopeedia*, 8 vols. & supplement (Tartu: Loodus, 1932–1940), 2: 665–66.

4. On the legal status of the Estonian Communist Party, see Tönu Parming, "The Pattern of Participation of the Estonian Communist Party in National Politics, 1918–1940," *Slavonic and East European Review* 59 (1981): 397–99.

5. Mägi, *Staatsleben Estlands*, pp. 187, 200–2, 323.

6. *Eesti NSV ajalugu*, 3 vols. (Tallinn: Eesti Riiklik Kirjastus, 1955–1963; Eesti Raamat, 1971), 3: 250–51.

7. Ibid., 3: 250–59; Imre Lipping, "December 1, 1924—The Communist Coup in Estonia," *Yearbook of the Estonian Learned Society in America* 5 (1968–1975): 43–46; J. Saar, *Enamlaste riigipöörde katse Tallinnas 1. detsember 1924* (Tallinn: Valvur, 1925), pp. 27, 42–43; Tönu Parming, "The Electoral Achievements of the Communist Party in Estonia, 1920–1940," *Slavic Review* 42 (1983): 447.

8. Eduard Laaman, "Põhiseaduse kriisi arenemine 1928–1933," in *Põhiseadus ja rahvuskogu* (Tallinn: Rahvuskogu Üldkoosoleku Juhatus, 1937), p. 32.

9. Mägi, *Staatsleben Estlands*, pp. 321, 323; *Eesti kroonika 1932* (Tartu: Eesti Kirjanduse Selts, 1933), pp. 11, 16.

10. Until August 1933, the official name of the league was *Eesti Vabadussõjalaste Keskliit* (Central League of the Veterans of the Estonian War of Independence).

11. William Tomingas, *Vaikiv ajastu Eestis* (New York: Eesti Ajaloo Instituut, 1961), pp. 26–28; Werner Haas, *Europa will leben: Die nationalen Erneuerungsbewegungen in Wort und Bild* (Berlin: Batschari, 1936), p. 129; Tönu Parming, *The Collapse of Liberal Democracy and the Rise of Authoritarianism in Estonia* (London: Sage, 1975), pp. 39–40; Emanuel Nodel, "Life and Death of Estonian Jewry," in Arvids Ziedonis, Jr., William L. Winter, and Mardi Valgemäe, eds., *Baltic History* (Columbus, Ohio: Association for the Advancement of Baltic Studies, 1974), p. 230; *Päevaleht*, May 27, 1933, p. 5; December 20, 1933, p. 2; Olaf Kuuli, *Vapsidest Isamaaliiduni: Fašismi ja fašismivastase võitluse ajaloost kodanlikus Eestis* (Tallinn: Eesti Raamat, 1976), pp. 76–84. To date there is no thorough study of the Veterans movement in any language. Kuuli's book provides the most detailed (although still elliptical) analysis of the League of Veterans' newspaper, *Võitlus* [The struggle].

12. Kuuli, *Vapsidest Isamaaliiduni*, pp. 78–79.

13. Laaman, "Põhiseaduse kriisi arenemine," p. 35; Heinrich Laretei, *Saatuse mängukanniks* (Lund: Eesti Kirjanike Kooperatiiv, 1970), p. 206. According to the Constitution of 1920, all constitutional amendments required the direct approval of the people.

14. Anatol Tooms, "Rahvahääletused põhiseaduse muutmiseks," *Eesti Statistika*, no. 145 (1933): 608. The first State Assembly bill is summarized by Artur Mägi, *Kuidas valitseti Eestis* (Stockholm: Tõrvik, 1951), pp. 82–84; the second State Assembly bill appears in *Riigi Teataja Lisa*, no. 16 (March 3, 1933): 393–96, and the League of Veterans' bill in *Riigi Teataja*, no. 86 (October 28, 1933): 990–94.

15. Mägi, *Kuidas valitseti Eestis*, pp. 82–87; Parming, *Collapse of Liberal Democracy*, pp. 23, 41–44, 47; Uibopuu, "Constitutional Development," pp. 16–17; August Ots, *Mehed sündmuste kurvidel* (Stockholm: Andromeda, 1976), p. 86; Ilmar Raamot, *Mälestused*, vol. 1 (Turku: Vaba Eesti, 1975), p. 307.

16. *Riigi Teataja*, no. 86 (October 28, 1933): 990–94; Uibopuu, "Constitutional Development," pp. 18, 31n.

17. Section 60, Part 12 of the constitution; the phrase in Estonian is *"edasilükkamatu riikliku vajaduse korral."* However, a decree could not be used for changing the laws regarding referendum, initiative, or election of the State Assembly or the Riigivanem. The decrees were in effect "until changed by the Riigivanem or the State Assembly."

18. *Päevaleht*, December 9, 1933, p. 1; Kuuli, *Vapsidest Isamaaliiduni*, pp. 117, 120–21; *Eesti NSV ajalugu*, 3: 340.

19. *Päevaleht*, March 3, 1934, p. 2; March 13, 1934, p. 3; Haas, *Europa will leben*, p. 130. Sirk (born 1900) could not be a candidate since the constitution required the Riigivanem to be at least 40 years old. On Sirk, see *Eesti biograafilise leksikoni täiendusköide* (Tartu: Loodus, 1940), pp. 306–9.

20. Parming, *Collapse of Liberal Democracy*, pp. 44–45; Uibopuu, "Constitutional Development," p. 19; Kuuli, *Vapsidest Isamaaliiduni*, pp. 137–38.

21. Tomingas, *Vaikiv ajastu Eestis*, pp. 83, 86; Kuuli, *Vapsidest Isamaaliiduni*, p. 139; Karl Ast, "Demokraatliku Eesti loojakul," *Vaba Eesti*, no. 1 (1955): 1–2; Imre Lipping, "The Emergence of Estonian Authoritarianism," in Ziedonis et al., *Baltic History*, pp. 209, 213–14; Raamot, *Mälestused*, p. 309.

22. Tomingas, *Vaikiv ajastu Eestis*, p. I; Parming, *Collapse of Liberal Democracy*, pp. 56–57; Kuuli, *Vapsidest Isamaaliiduni*, pp. 169–70.

23. Kuuli, *Vapsidest Isamaaliiduni*, p. 167; *Eesti kroonika 1936* (Tartu: Eesti Kirjanduse Selts, 1937), pp. 29–30; *Eesti nõukogude entsüklopeedia*, 8 vols. & supplement (Tallinn: Valgus, 1968–1978), 4: 258. The following occupations and groups were represented in the corporative organizations: commerce-industry, agriculture, engineering, physicians, homeowners, veterinarians, agronomists, pharmacists, cooperatives, dairies, fishing, rural workers and small landowners, workers, teachers, artisans, and "officials of private enterprise." In general, workers and employers belonged to different organizations.

24. Parming, *Collapse of Liberal Democracy*, p. 57; *Eesti kroonika 1936*, p. 31.

25. Tomingas, *Vaikiv ajastu Eestis*, pp. 279–80; Ots, *Mehed sündmuste kurvidel*, p. 105; *Vaba Eesti*, no. 6 (1953): 3.

26. Uibopuu, "Constitutional Development," pp. 20–21; Parming, *Collapse of Liberal Democracy*, pp. 58–59.

27. Kuuli, *Vapsidest Isamaaliiduni*, p. 179; *Eesti kroonika 1936*, pp. 36–37.

28. The text of the Constitution of 1937 is available in English in *Estonian Official Guide* (Baltimore: Baltimore Estonian Society, 1972), pp. 121–42. See also Uibopuu, "Constitutional Development," pp. 22–24.

29. Kuuli, *Vapsidest Isamaaliiduni*, pp. 217–19; Parming, *Collapse of Liberal Democracy*, pp. 59–60. *Uus Eesti* (New Estonia), the organ of the Fatherland League, claimed on April 21, 1938, that 57.4 percent of the vote went to the National Front, but this apparently included the totals for 95 individuals — that is, fifteen more than the front's original 80 candidates. Maria Kleitsman, an emigré Estonian author writing in 1960 (cited in Parming, p. 60), offers figures that agree with Kuuli's.

30. Kuuli, *Vapsidest Isamaaliiduni*, pp. 218–20; *Uus Eesti*, February 26, 1938; Parming, *Collapse of Liberal Democracy*, p. 60; Uibopuu, "Constitutional Development," p. 25; Tomingas, *Vaikiv ajastu Eestis*, p. 457.

31. *Estonian Official Guide*, pp. 124–25; *Uus Eesti*, April 23–24, 1938.

32. Mägi, *Staatsleben Estlands*, p. 307; *Eesti kroonika 1938* (Tartu: Eesti Kirjanduse Selts, 1939), pp. 37–38; Friido Toomus, *Konstantin Päts ja riigireformi aastad* (Tartu: Loodus, 1938), pp. 239–40, 249, 276.

33. V. A. Maamägi and H. T. Arumäe, "Fasismi Baltiassa," *Historiallinen Arkisto 72* (1977): 100–4; *Eesti NSV ajalugu*, 3: 339–46.

34. Evald Uustalu, *Eesti Vabariik 1918–1940* (Lund: Eesti Kirjanike Kooperatiiv, 1968), pp. 143–44; Joseph Rothschild, *East Central Europe Between the Two World Wars*, A History of East Central Europe, vol. 9 (Seattle: University of Washington Press, 1974), pp. 376–77, 379; Parming, *Collapse of Liberal Democracy*, p. 61; *Uus Eesti*, May 5, 1938; Lipping, "Emergence of Estonian Authoritarianism," p. 213.

35. Rothschild, *East Central Europe*, p. 374; Ast, "Demokraatliku Eesti loojakul," p. 7; Parming, *Collapse of Liberal Democracy*, p. 61; *Uus Eesti*, May 5, 1938.

36. Rein Taagepera, "Civic Culture and Authoritarianism in the Baltic States, 1930–1940," *East European Quarterly* 7 (1973): 408; Lipping, "Emergence of Estonian Authoritarianism," p. 214n. For balanced surveys of authoritarianism in the Baltic states in the 1930s, see V. Stanley Vardys, "The Rise of Authoritarianism in the Baltic States," in V. Stanley Vardys and Romuald J. Misiunas, eds., *The Baltic States in Peace and War, 1917–1945* (University Park: The Pennsylvania State University Press, 1978), pp. 65–80, and Lauri Hyvämäki, "Fasistiset ilmiöt Baltian maissa ja Suomessa 1920-luvun lopussa ja 1930-luvulla," *Historiallinen Arkisto* 72 (1977): 113–37.

37. For a statement from the "pessimistic" school, see Alexander Dallin, "The Baltic States Between Nazi Germany and Soviet Russia," in Vardys and Misiunas, *Baltic States in Peace and War*, p. 107; for an "optimistic" view, see Edgar Anderson, "The Baltic Entente: Phantom or Reality?" in Vardys and Misiunas, *Baltic States in Peace and War*, pp. 134–35.

38. There is no monographic treatment of Estonian foreign policy in the independence period. For a review of the principal outlines, see Royal Institute of International Affairs, *The Baltic States* (Westport, Conn.: Greenwood Press, 1970; first published, 1938), pp. 62–88, and Uustalu, *Eesti Vabariik*, pp. 196–221.

39. Royal Institute, *Baltic States*, pp. 63–64; Heinrich Laretei, "Iseseisvuse-aegsest välispoliitikast," in *ERRTM*, 1: 202–3; Rothschild, *East Central Europe*, pp. 369–70; Kalervo Hovi, "Polish-Finnish Cooperation in Border-State Policy, 1919–1922," *Journal of Baltic Studies* 14 (1983): 121–26.

40. Royal Institute, *Baltic States*, pp. 82–84; Uustalu, *Eesti Vabariik*, p. 199; Anderson, "Baltic Entente," pp. 128–29; Edgar Anderson, "The Pacts of Mutual Assistance Between the USSR and the Baltic States," in Ziedonis et al., *Baltic History*, p. 240.

41. Seppo Myllyniemi, *Baltian kriisi 1938–1941* (Helsinki: Otava, 1977), pp. 32, 34; Anderson, "Baltic Entente," p. 131; Georg von Rauch, *The Baltic States: The Years of Independence, 1917–1940* (Berkeley: University of California Press, 1974), pp.

200–2, 205, 221; Heinrich Laretei, "Baaside ajastu välispoliitika," in *Minevikust tulevikku* (Stockholm: EÜS Põhjala, 1954), p. 23.

42. J. Janusson, "The Economic Structure of Estonia," *Baltic Countries* 1, no. 2 (December 1935): 191–92, 195; *Eesti entsüklopeedia*, suppl.: 251–54.

43. *Eesti entsüklopeedia*, suppl.: 257–58.

44. Merja-Liisa Hinkkanen-Lievonen, *British Trade and Enterprise in the Baltic States, 1919–1925*, Studia Historica, no. 14 (Helsinki: Suomen Historiallinen Seura, 1984), p. 264.

45. *Eesti entsüklopeedia*, 2: 589–90; suppl.: 251–52.

46. Otto Karma, *Tööstuslikult revolutsioonilt sotsialistlikule revolutsioonile Eestis: Tööstuse arenemine 1917. aastani* (Tallinn: Eesti NSV Teaduste Akadeemia Ajaloo Instituut, 1963), p. 377; "Tööliste arv Eesti tööstuses 1923–1924. a.," *Eesti Statistika*, no. 39 (1925): Appendix I, p. 5; *Eesti NSV ajalugu*, 3: 264; *Eesti entsüklopeedia*, suppl.: 251–54.

47. R. Sõrmus, "Streigid tööstuses," *Eesti Statistika*, no. 98 (1930): 37; Parming, *Collapse of Liberal Democracy*, p. 12; R. Sõrmus, "Töötülid 1939. a.," *Eesti Statistika* (1940): 205–7.

48. Royal Institute, *Baltic States*, pp. 126, 160–63, 165.

49. Ibid., pp. 128, 169, 172–73, 183.

50. Janusson, "Economic Structure of Estonia," p. 192.

51. *Eesti entsüklopeedia*, 5: 806–8; J. Õisman, "Maareformi teostamine Eestis," *Eesti Statistika*, nos. 6–8 (1922): 49–50, 53; Royal Institute, *Baltic States*, pp. 29–30; von Rauch, *Baltic States*, pp. 88–89.

52. *Eesti entsüklopeedia*, suppl.: 241–42.

53. Ibid.; Rein Taagepera, "Inequality Indices for Baltic Farm Size Distribution, 1929–1940," *Journal of Baltic Studies* 3 (1972): 28–29, 31.

54. Janusson, "Economic Structure of Estonia," p. 194; *Eesti entsüklopeedia*, suppl.: 245–46.

55. Royal Institute, *Baltic States*, pp. 110–12, 146–47; "Baltic Yearbook," Appendix to *Baltic Countries* 1, no. 1 (August 1935): 7–8; *Eesti entsüklopeedia*, suppl.: 239–40, 249–50.

56. *II rahvaloendus Eestis*, 4 vols. (Tallinn: Riigi Statistika Keskbüroo, 1934–1937), 4: 152.

57. Hugo Reiman, "II rahvaloenduse tulemusi," *Eesti Statistika*, no. 156 (1934): 557; "Sündimus, suremus, abiellumus ja rahvastikuarv 1938. a. (eelkokkuvõte)," *Eesti Statistika*, no. 208 (1939): 162.

58. "Sündimus, suremus, abiellumus ja rahvastikuarv 1939. a. (eelkokkuvõte)," *Eesti Statistika* (1940): 147.

59. "Sündivus, surevus, abielluvus ja rahvastikuarv 1932. a. (eelkokkuvõte)," *Eesti Statistika*, no. 136 (1933): 164; "Baltic Yearbook," p. 6; A. Tomberg, "Abiellumus, sündimus, suremus ja rahvastiku iive 1938. a.," *Eesti Statistika*, no. 218 (1940): 10.

60. Anatol Tooms, "Opteermisliikumine ja Eesti jõudnud optandid," *Eesti Statis-*

tika, no. 5 (1922): 9; *Eesti arvudes 1920–1935* (Tallinn: Riigi Statistika Keskbüroo, 1937), p. 27; "Sündimus, suremus, abiellumus ja rahvastikuarv 1939. a.," p. 147; Jürgen von Hehn, *Die Umsiedlung der baltischen Deutschen — das letzte Kapitel baltisch-deutscher Geschichte*, Marburger Ostforschungen, no. 40 (Marburg/Lahn: J. G. Herder-Institut, 1982), pp. 94–95.

61. *Eesti arvudes*, p. 26.

62. "Baltic Yearbook," p. 5; Rothschild, *East Central Europe*, pp. 36, 89, 203, 328, 359; *1922. a. üldrahvalugemise andmed*, 1: 34; *II rahvaloendus Eestis*, 2: 47.

63. Raimo Pullat, *Linnad kodanlikus Eestis: Ajaloolis-demograafiline käsitlus* (Tallinn: Eesti Raamat, 1978), pp. 83, 88, 101–2, 115; Reiman, "II rahvaloenduse tulemusi," p. 557; *Eesti NSV ajalugu*, 3: 369; *Eesti Statistika* (1940): 259.

64. Hugo Reiman, "Rahvused Eestis," *Eesti Statistika*, nos. 164–65 (1935): 354–55.

65. *II rahvaloendus Eestis*, 4: 65.

66. *Eesti NSV ajalugu*, 3: 381.

67. Pullat, *Linnad kodanlikus Eestis*, pp. 169, 173, 191; Parming, *Collapse of Liberal Democracy*, p. 25.

68. *II rahvaloendus Eestis*, 4: 65; Eduard Laaman, *Eesti ühiskond* (Tartu: Eesti Kirjanduse Selts, 1936), p. 14.

69 Vera Poska-Grünthal, *Naine ja naisliikumine: Peajooni naisliikumise ajaloost ja probleemistikust* (Tartu: Eesti Kirjanduse Selts, 1936), p. 83; *Eesti entsüklopeedia*, 2: 779.

70. Helmi Mäelo, *Eesti naine läbi aegade* (Lund: Eesti Kirjanike Kooperatiiv, 1957), pp. 177–80, 216–17; *Estonian Official Guide*, pp. 13–15; Vera Poska-Grünthal, *See oli Eestis 1919–1944* (Stockholm: Välis-Eesti & EMP, 1975), pp. 68, 79; *1922. a. üldrahvalugemise andmed*, 3: 19; *II rahvaloendus Eestis*, 3: 152–53.

71. Royal Institute, *Baltic States*, pp. 37–38; Karl Aun, "The Cultural Autonomy of National Minorities in Estonia," *Yearbook of the Estonian Learned Society in America* 1 (1951–1953): 30; Michael Garleff, *Deutschbaltische Politik zwischen den Weltkriegen*, Quellen und Studien zur baltischen Geschichte, no. 2 (Bonn-Bad Godesberg: Wissenschaftliches Archiv, 1976), pp. 111–12, 184–85.

72. Toivo U. Raun, "The Development of Estonian Literacy in the 18th and 19th Centuries," *Journal of Baltic Studies* 10 (1979): 122; Reiman, "II rahvaloenduse tulemusi," p. 565; *Eesti arvudes*, p. 26.

73. *Eesti entsüklopeedia*, 2: 607–10; suppl.: 276–79; Uustalu, *Eesti Vabariik*, p. 159; A. Lepp, "Lõpetanute arv õppeasutisis 1919–1939. a.," *Eesti Statistika* (1940): 217–19.

74. Laaman, *Eesti ühiskond*, p. 27; Lepp, "Lõpetanute arv õppeasutisis," pp. 220–21; *Eesti entsüklopeedia*, suppl.: 277–78.

75. Peeter Põld, "Tartu Ülikool," in *Eesti: Maa, rahvas, kultuur* (Tartu: Haridus-ministeeriumi Kirjastus, 1926), pp. 993, 1001; Uustalu, *Eesti Vabariik*, p. 108; *Eesti entsüklopeedia*, suppl.: 278–79; Lepp, "Lõpetanute arv õppeasutisis," pp. 229, 231, 234.

76. Richard Antik, *Eesti raamat 1535–1935* (Tartu: n.p., 1936), pp. 29, 51; M. Lott, "Raamat kodanlikus Eestis (1918–1940)," in Voldemar Miller, ed., *Eesti raamat 1525–1975* (Tallinn: Valgus, 1978), p. 169.

77. Lott, "Raamat kodanlikus Eestis," p. 185; *Eestis NSV ajalugu*, 3: 424; Uustalu, *Eesti Vabariik*, pp. 170–71.

78. *1922. a. üldrahvalugemise andmed*, 1: 50–52; *II rahvaloendus Eestis*, 2: 118–19.

79. *Eesti entsüklopeedia*, 2: 618–19; suppl.: 280–82; Uustalu, *Eesti Vabariik*, p. 99; Vello Salo, "The Struggle Between the State and the Churches," in Tõnu Parming and Elmar Järvesoo, eds., *A Case Study of a Soviet Republic: The Estonian SSR* (Boulder, Colo.: Westview Press, 1978), p. 204.

80. *Eesti NSV ajalugu*, 3: 417–18; George Kurman, *The Development of Written Estonian*, Indiana University Publications, Uralic and Altaic Series, no. 90 (The Hague: Mouton, 1968), pp. 51–70; Endel Nirk, *Estonian Literature* (Tallinn: Eesti Raamat, 1970), pp. 182–84, 268–71; Arvo Mägi, *Lühike eesti kirjanduslugu*, 2 vols. (Lund: Eesti Kirjanike Kooperatiiv, 1965), 2: 34–41.

81. Lea Tormis, *Eesti teater 1920–1940: Sõnalavastus* (Tallinn: Eesti Raamat, 1978), pp. 141–42, 283, 359, 373–74; Lea Tormis, *Eesti balletist* (Tallinn: Eesti Raamat, 1967), pp. 32, 36, 46, 50; *Eesti nõukogude entsüklopeedia*, 5: 496.

82. *Eesti kunsti ajalugu*, 2 vols. (Tallinn: Kunst, 1970–1977), 1, part 2: 126–27; Lepp, "Lõpetanute arv õppeasutisis," pp. 224–25, 228–29; *Eesti muusika*, 2 vols. (Tallinn: Eesti Raamat, 1968–1975), 2: 24.

83. *Eesti muusika*, 2: 33, 39, 44, 48–49, 51–52; *Eesti: 20 aastat iseseisvust sõnas ja pildis* (Tallinn: Konjunktuurinstituut, 1939), p. 168.

CHAPTER 9

1. Edgar Anderson, "The Baltic Entente: Phantom or Reality?" in V. Stanley Vardys and Romuald J. Misiunas, eds., *The Baltic States in Peace and War, 1917–1945* (University Park: The Pennsylvania State University Press, 1978), p. 127; David M. Crowe, Jr., "Great Britain and the Baltic States, 1938–1939," in Vardys and Misiunas, *Baltic States in Peace and War*, p. 118.

2. Raymond J. Sontag and James S. Beddie, eds., *Nazi-Soviet Relations, 1939–1941: Documents from the Archives of the German Foreign Office* (Washington, D.C.: Department of State, 1948), p. 78; Bronius J. Kaslas, *The USSR-German Aggression Against Lithuania* (New York: Robert Speller & Sons, 1973), pp. 129–30.

3. Richard Maasing, "Eesti ja N. Liidu sõjaväeliste delegatsioonide läbirääkimisi 1939. a. oktoobris," in *ERRTM*, 2: 46; August Torma, "Eesti saatkonnas Londonis," in *ERRTM*, 2: 94; "Testimony of Estonia's Foreign Minister Karl Selter," *Lituanus* 14, no. 2 (1968): 54–56; *Uus Eesti*, September 28, 1939.

4. "Minutes of the Soviet-Estonian Negotiations for the Mutual Assistance Pact of 1939," *Lituanus* 14, no. 2 (1968): 62–71.

5. August Varma, "Läbirääkimised Moskvas ja Tallinnas," in *ERRTM*, 2: 63–64;

Maasing, "Eesti ja N. Liidu sõjaväeliste delegatsioonide läbirääkimisi," p. 49; August Warma, *Diplomaadi kroonika* (Lund: Eesti Kirjanike Kooperatiiv, 1971), pp. 20, 42–43; Alfred Luts, *Heitluste keerises*, 2 vols. (Stockholm: Välis-Eesti & EMP, 1975–1976), 1: 89, 91.

6. "Minutes of the Soviet-Estonian Negotiations," pp. 71–77. After the Soviet annexation of Estonia in 1940, it became obvious that the *Metalist* had never been sunk since the ship appeared in good health in Estonian ports; see Luts, *Heitluste keerises*, 1: 88.

7. "Minutes of the Soviet-Estonian Negotiations," pp. 78–92; "Sündmuste kroonikat 1939–1945," in *ERRTM*, 10: 150.

8. "Pact of Mutual Assistance Between the USSR and Estonia," *Lituanus* 14, no. 2 (1968): 94–96.

9. Varma, "Läbirääkimised Moskvas ja Tallinnas," pp. 69–76; "Pakti elluviimise protokoll," in *ERRTM*, 2: 197–98; August Rei, *The Drama of the Baltic Peoples*, 2d ed. (Stockholm: Vaba Eesti, 1970), pp. 269–72.

10. *New York Times*, September 29, 1939, pp. 1, 8; September 30, 1939, p. 5.

11. Tõnu Parming, "From the Republic of Estonia to the Estonian Soviet Socialist Republic: The Transfer of Rule and Sovereignty, 1939–1940" (unpublished manuscript), pp. 29–30, 45–46, 50–52; Seppo Myllyniemi, *Baltian kriisi 1938–1941* (Helsinki: Otava, 1977), pp. 32, 34, 50, 183.

12. Parming, "From the Republic of Estonia," pp. 47–48, 66–68, 89.

13. Esmo Ridala, "Peajooni Eesti välispoliitikast 1934–1940," *Eesti Teadusliku Seltsi Rootsis Aastaraamat* 8 (1977–1979): 47–48, 55; Evald Uustalu, *Tagurpidi sõudes: Mälestusi ajavahemikult 1914–1943* (Stockholm: Teataja, 1982), pp. 138–43.

14. "Välisminister A. Piibu raadiokõne 28. okt. 1939," in *ERRTM*, 2: 202–4.

15. Heinrich Laretei, *Saatuse mängukanniks* (Lund: Eesti Kirjanike Kooperatiiv, 1970), pp. 240–41.

16. *Päevaleht*, November 12, 1939; Erhard Kroeger, *Der Auszug aus der alten Heimat* (Tübingen: Verlag der deutschen Hochschullehrer-Zeitung, 1967), pp. 106–7.

17. Alo Raun, "Nõukogude Liidu relvastatud jõudude liikumised Eestis seoses niinimetatud vastastikuse abistamise paktiga" (unpublished manuscript), p. 12.

18. Luts, *Heitluste keerises*, 1: 105, 138–43.

19. *Pravda*, May 28, 1940, p. 5; May 3, 1940, p. 6.

20. Hans Kauri, "Punane laine ujutab üle," in *ERRTM*, 3: 7; August Rei, ed., *Nazi-Soviet Conspiracy and the Baltic States: Diplomatic Documents and Other Evidence* (London: Boreas, 1948), pp. 46–48.

21. August Rei, "Traagiliste sündmuste tunnistajana," in *ERRTM*, 3: 17.

22. Luts, *Heitluste keerises*, 1: 150–51; Uustalu, *Eesti Vabariik*, p. 232.

23. According to Rei, the total number of people — including bystanders — on Freedom Square was 2,000–3,000; Rei also suggests that he recognized the Soviet Russians among the demonstrators by the recent Soviet songs they sang. Rei, "Traagiliste

sündmuste tunnistajana," pp. 18–24; Luts, *Heitluste keerises*, 1: 158; *Uus Eesti*, June 19, 1940.

24. Parming, "From the Republic of Estonia," p. 78.

25. "Sündmuste kroonikat 1939–1945," pp. 153–54; A. Soom, "Seadusevastased valimised," in *ERRTM*, 3: 38–41; *Eesti NSV ajalugu*, 3 vols. (Tallinn: Eesti Riiklik Kirjastus, 1955–1963; Eesti Raamat, 1971), 3: 494.

26. *New York Times*, July 15, 1940, p. 1; Soom, "Seadusevastased valimised," pp. 40–43; E. Kuik, "Valimisvõltsimine Viljandimaal," in *ERRTM*, 3: 48; Edgar Tomson, "The Annexation of the Baltic States," in Thomas T. Hammond, ed., *The Anatomy of Communist Takeovers* (New Haven, Conn.: Yale University Press, 1975), p. 227. English translations of twenty documents on the elections appear in Rein Taagepera, "De-Choicing of Elections: July 1940 in Estonia," *Journal of Baltic Studies* 14 (1983): 223–46.

27. "Sündmuste kroonikat 1939–1945," pp. 153–54; *Eesti NSV ajalugu*, 3: 497–98, 500–2.

28. Myllyniemi, *Baltian kriisi*, pp. 156–57. For recent statements of the Soviet Estonian view of this period, see Villem Raud, *Developments in Estonia, 1939–1941* (Tallinn: Perioodika, 1979), and Olaf Kuuli, *Revolutsioon Eestis 1940* (Tallinn: Eesti Raamat, 1980).

29. Ants Oras, *Baltic Eclipse* (London: Victor Gollancz, 1948), p. 65.

30. See, for example, J. Hampden Jackson, *Estonia*, 2d ed. (London: George Allen & Unwin, 1948), pp. 30–36, and Georg von Rauch, *The Baltic States: The Years of Independence, 1917–1940* (Berkeley: University of California Press, 1974), pp. 219–27.

31. Kuuli, *Revolutsioon Eestis 1940*, p. 49; Myllyniemi, *Baltian kriisi*, p. 91.

32. Oras, *Baltic Eclipse*, pp. 77–78; Jaan Siiras, *Viro neuvostokurimuksessa: Piirteitä Viron tapahtumista ja kehityksestä bolševikkivallan aikana vv. 1939–1941* (Porvoo: Werner Söderström, 1942), pp. 98–99.

33. Parming, "From the Republic of Estonia," pp. 71, 78; Myllyniemi, *Baltian kriisi*, p. 151.

34. Elmar Tambek, *Tõus ja mõõn*, 2 vols. (Toronto: Orto, 1964), 1: 380–81.

CHAPTER 10

1. Olaf Kuuli, *Revolutsioon Eestis 1940* (Tallinn: Eesti Raamat, 1980), pp. 156–58.

2. Artur Mägi, "Eesti õiguskorra hävitamine," in *ERRTM*, 3: 60–61; "Riigivolikogu koosseis: Stenograafilised aruanded," in *ERRTM*, 3: 239; Kuuli, *Revolutsioon Eestis 1940*, p. 158.

3. Kuuli, *Revolutsioon Eestis 1940*, pp. 47, 173; *Ülevaade Eestimaa Kommunistliku Partei ajaloost*, 3 vols. (Tallinn: Eesti Riiklik Kirjastus, 1961–1963; Eesti Raamat, 1972), 2: 300–1; 3: 13, 19.

4. Villem Raud, *Developments in Estonia, 1939–1941* (Tallinn: Perioodika, 1979), p. 92.

5. Kuuli, *Revolutsioon Eestis 1940*, pp. 42, 161; *Ülevaade Eestimaa Kommunistliku Partei ajaloost*, 3: 33–34. For brief biographies of the Buro's members (except Säre), see the appropriate volumes of *Eesti nõukogude entsüklopeedia*, 8 vols. & supplement (Tallinn: Valgus, 1968–1978).

6. Evald Uustalu, *The History of Estonian People* (London: Boreas, 1952), p. 248; *Eesti NSV ajalugu*, 3 vols. (Tallinn: Eesti Riiklik Kirjastus, 1955–1963; Eesti Raamat, 1971), 3: 503–4; R. Maasing, "Riigikaitse hävitamine," in *ERRTM*, 3: 211, 214; Meinhard Leetmaa, *Sõjas ja ikestatud Eestis* (Stockholm: Välis-Eesti & EMP, 1979), p. 30.

7. *Eesti NSV ajalugu*, 3: 505–6; H. Nurk, "Eesti majandus punasel aastal," in *ERRTM*, 3: 117, 122–23.

8. Endel Kareda, *Technique of Economic Sovietisation*, East and West, no. 3 (London: Boreas, 1947), pp. 102–3; *Eesti NSV ajalugu*, 3: 506.

9. *Eesti NSV ajalugu*, 3: 507; Nurk, "Eesti majandus punasel aastal," pp. 115, 124–25, 127; Aleksander Kaelas, *The Worker in the Soviet Paradise*, East and West, no. 2 (London: Boreas, 1947), p. 26.

10. Nurk, "Eesti majandus punasel aastal," pp. 119, 124, 126–27.

11. *Eesti NSV ajalugu*, 3: 509–10; Kareda, *Technique of Economic Sovietisation*, pp. 19–20, 40–41; J. Nõu, "Hoop Eesti põllumajandusele," in *ERRTM*, 3: 88. The figure for the amount of land in the state land reserve is taken from *Eesti NSV ajalugu*; Kareda and Nõu give the slightly higher figure of 758,258 hectares.

12. *Eesti NSV ajalugu*, 3: 510–11; Kareda, *Technique of Economic Sovietisation*, pp. 42–43; Nõu, "Hoop Eesti põllumajandusele," p. 89.

13. *Eesti NSV ajalugu*, 3: 511–12. Kareda lists 113 sovkhozes while Nõu gives a figure of 83. No statistics on the number of sovkhozes in 1940–1941 are provided in *Eesti NSV ajalugu*.

14. Nõu, "Hoop Eesti põllumajandusele," pp. 91–93; *Eesti NSV ajalugu*, 3: 511; Kareda, *Technique of Economic Sovietisation*, pp. 45–49.

15. Nõu, "Hoop Eesti põllumajandusele," pp. 90–91; Kareda, *Technique of Economic Sovietisation*, pp. 49–57.

16. Nõu, "Hoop Eesti põllumajandusele," pp. 95–97.

17. Tõnu Parming, "Population Changes in Estonia, 1935–1970," *Population Studies* 26 (1972): 54–55; M. Kuldkepp, "Inimkaotused punasel aastal," in *ERRTM*, 3: 228–30; Ants Oras, *Baltic Eclipse* (London: Victor Gollancz, 1948), p. 158; Rutt Eliaser, *Passita ja pajata* (Lund: Eesti Kirjanike Kooperatiiv, 1985), pp. 87, 138, 204.

18. Parming, "Population Changes in Estonia," p. 55; Romuald J. Misiunas and Rein Taagepera, *The Baltic States: Years of Dependence, 1940–1980* (Berkeley: University of California Press, 1983), p. 274, suggests a slightly lower estimate (30,000) for evacuees to the USSR.

19. Parming, "Population Changes in Estonia," pp. 54–55; Helmuth Weiss, "Järelümberasumine," in *ERRTM*, 3: 221–22.

20. Hilda Kauri, "Eesti koolist pidi saama kommunistlik taimelava," in *ERRTM*, 3: 199–205.

21. Oras, *Baltic Eclipse*, pp. 93–95, 109–11, 142; *Riigi Teataja*, no. 70 (July 18, 1940): 1028; Hans Kauri, "E. V. Tartu ülikool okupatsioonide ajal," in *ERRTM*, 10: 45–46; M. Jürma, "Laastamine raamatukogudes," in *ERRTM*, 3: 150.

22. H. Salu, "Kirjanduselu punasel aastal," in *ERRTM*, 3: 192–96; E. Reining, "Teatrielu punasel aastal," in *ERRTM*, 3: 171–72.

23. J. Aunver, "Kirik tagakiusamise all," in *ERRTM*, 3: 142–46; Vello Salo, "The Struggle Between the State and the Churches," in Tõnu Parming and Elmar Järvesoo, eds., *A Case Study of a Soviet Republic: The Estonian SSR* (Boulder, Colo.: Westview Press, 1978), pp. 194–97.

CHAPTER 11

1. See, for example, Albert Seaton, *The Russo-German War, 1941–1945* (London: Barker, 1971).

2. "Sündmuste kroonikat 1939–1945," in *ERRTM*, 10: 156–57; Karl Talpak, "Eesti metsavendlus 1941. aastal," in *ERRTM*, 4: 21–22.

3. "Sündmuste kroonikat 1939–1945," pp. 157–58. An official Soviet source puts the size of the destruction battalions at some 5,000 men (*Eesti nõukogude entsüklopeedia*, 8 vols. & supplement [Tallinn: Valgus, 1968–1978], 3: 94), whereas a non-Soviet estimate of the number of active guerrillas in northern Estonia alone is also about 5,000 (Talpak, "Eesti metsavendlus," p. 27).

4. "Sündmuste kroonikat 1939–1945," pp. 157–60; Ants Oras, *Baltic Eclipse* (London: Victor Gollancz, 1948), pp. 202–7.

5. *Eesti NSV ajalugu*, 3 vols. (Tallinn: Eesti Riiklik Kirjastus, 1955–1963; Eesti Raamat, 1971), 3: 529, 537; Arnold Purre, "Olukord punasel frondil ja eesti sõdurite ületulek," in *ERRTM*, 4:167, 169; Alfred Luts, *Heitluste keerises*, 2 vols. (Stockholm: Välis-Eesti & EMP, 1975–1976), 2: 80, 121, 132; Talpak, "Eesti metsavendlus," p. 27; Arnold Purre, "Eesti sõda Nõuk. Liiduga," in *ERRTM*, 7: 25–26.

6. Seppo Myllyniemi, *Die Neuordnung der baltischen Länder, 1941–1944*, Historiallisia Tutkimuksia, no. 90 (Helsinki: Suomen Historiallinen Seura, 1973), p. 229; Luts, *Heitluste keerises*, 2: 183; Purre, "Eesti sõda Nõuk. Liiduga," pp. 33–35; Evald Uustalu, *For Freedom Only: The Story of Estonian Volunteers in the Finnish War of 1940–1944* (Toronto: Northern Publications, 1977), p. 18.

7. Purre, "Eesti sõda Nõuk. Liiduga," pp. 35–36; Uustalu, *For Freedom Only*, pp. 5, 19, 23, 66.

8. "Sündmuste kroonikat 1939–1945," p. 167; Purre, "Eesti sõda Nõuk. Liiduga," pp. 37–38; Myllyniemi, *Neuordnung*, pp. 275–76; Arno Raag, *Saatuslikus kolmnurgas* (Lund: Eesti Kirjanike Kooperatiiv, 1974), p. 194.

9. Purre, "Eesti sõda Nõuk. Liiduga," pp 37–38; Uustalu, *For Freedom Only*, pp.

70–74; "Sündmuste kroonikat 1939–1945," pp. 167–73. For a Soviet view of the last months of the war in Estonia, see *Eesti NSV ajalugu*, 3: 550–60.

10. V. Selge, "Eesti Korpus II maailmasõjas," in *ERRTM*, 7: 157–64; *Eesti rahvas Nõukogude Liidu Suures Isamaasõjas*, 2 vols. (Tallinn: Eesti Raamat, 1971–1977), 1: 280, 286–87, 341; Tõnu Parming, "Population Changes in Estonia, 1935–1970," *Population Studies*, 26 (1972): 54–55n; *Eesti NSV ajalugu*, 3: 560. One estimate for losses among the Estonian Rifle Corps at Velikie Luki gives a figure of 10,000 men dead and wounded; see Meinhard Leetmaa, *Sõjas ja ikestatud Eestis* (Stockholm: Välis-Eesti & EMP, 1979), p. 82.

11. Quotation from Myllyniemi, *Neuordnung*, p. 57; Alexander Dallin, *German Rule in Russia, 1941–1945: A Study in Occupation Policies* (London: Macmillan, 1957), pp. 182–84, 280.

12. Myllyniemi, *Neuordnung*, pp. 87, 89, 159–60; Dallin, *German Rule in Russia*, pp. 276–88.

13. Myllyniemi, *Neuordnung*, pp. 80, 296–97; Dallin, *German Rule in Russia*, pp. 185–86; R. Maasing, "Katseid Eesti sõjaväe uuestiloomiseks," in *ERRTM*, 7: 20.

14. Myllyniemi, *Neuordnung*, pp. 107–10; Oras, *Baltic Eclipse*, pp. 236–37; Oskar Angelus, *Tuhande valitseja maa* (Stockholm: EMP, 1956), pp. 94, 102–3, 139.

15. Johannes Klesment, "Kolm aastat iseseisvuse võitlust võõra okupatsioonide all," in *ERRTM*, 8: 15; Dallin, *German Rule in Russia*, p. 194; Myllyniemi, *Neuordnung*, pp. 204, 213–14, 251.

16. Klesment, "Kolm aastat," pp. 9, 15, 23–24; Edgar Kant, "Jüri Uluotsa memorandum Eesti seisundi kohta 29. juulist 1941," in *ERRTM*, 6: 15–16, 18.

17. Evald Uustalu, "The National Committee of the Estonian Republic," *Journal of Baltic Studies* 7 (1976): 210–17; Helmut Maandi, "Kümne aasta eest," in *ERRTM*, 8: 66–69; Raag, *Saatuslikus kolmnurgas*, pp. 211–12.

18. Klesment, "Kolm aastat," pp. 12–13, 15; David Kirby, "Morality or Expediency: The Baltic Question in British-Soviet Relations, 1941–1942," in V. Stanley Vardys and Romuald J. Misiunas, eds., *The Baltic States in Peace and War, 1917–1945* (University Park: The Pennsylvania State University Press, 1978), pp. 161–72.

19. Harald Nurk, "Eesti majandus saksa okupatsiooni ajal," in *ERRTM*, 7: 72, 104, 111; Oras, *Baltic Eclipse*, pp. 227–32; Endel Kareda, *Technique of Economic Sovietisation*, East and West, no. 3 (London: Boreas, 1947), p. 114.

20. Nurk, "Eesti majandus saksa okupatsiooni ajal," p. 83; Myllyniemi, *Neuordnung*, pp. 219, 225–26, 226n; Kareda, *Technique of Economic Sovietisation*, p. 114.

21. Nurk, "Eesti majandus saksa okupatsiooni ajal," pp. 81–83.

22. Ibid., pp. 83–92, 118; *Eesti NSV ajalugu*, 3: 564, 569; Jaak Survel [Evald Uustalu], *Estonia Today*, East and West, no. 1 (London: Boreas, 1947), p. 11.

23. *Eesti arvudes 1920–1935* (Tallinn: Riigi Statistika Keskbüroo, 1937), p. 12; Emanuel Nodel, "Life and Death of Estonian Jewry," in Arvids Ziedonis, Jr., William L. Winter, and Mardi Valgemäe, eds., *Baltic History* (Columbus, Ohio: Association for the Advancement of Baltic Studies, 1974), pp. 233–34; Parming, "Population

Changes in Estonia," pp. 55, 55n; Tönu Parming, "Population Changes and Processes," in Tönu Parming and Elmar Järvesoo, eds., *A Case Study of a Soviet Republic: The Estonian SSR* (Boulder, Colo.: Westview Press, 1978), p. 24; Oras, *Baltic Eclipse*, pp. 216, 220–21.

24. Parming, "Population Changes and Processes," pp. 24–26; Parming, "Population Changes in Estonia," pp. 55, 55n, 56; *Eesti arvudes*, p. 12; Romuald J. Misiunas and Rein Taagepera, *The Baltic States: Years of Dependence, 1940–1980* (Berkeley: University of California Press, 1983), pp. 275–76. A recent study based mainly on archival materials in Estonia suggests a figure of "more than 20,000" Estonian deaths in German uniform in World War II; see Toe Nõmm, "Eesti üksustest Saksa sõjaväes," *Akadeemia* 2 (1990): 134.

25. Aleksander Kaelas, "Sotsiaalpoliitikast saksa okupatsiooni ajal," in *ERRTM*, 8: 123, 136–37; Oras, *Baltic Eclipse*, pp. 227–32.

26. Hans Kauri, "E. V. Tartu ülikool okupatsioonide ajal," *ERRTM*, 10: 46–55, 59, 65; Survel, *Estonia Today*, pp. 37–38.

27. Oras, *Baltic Eclipse*, pp. 239–40; Endel Nirk, *Estonian Literature* (Tallinn: Eesti Raamat, 1970), pp. 280–84; Ants Oras, *Marie Under* (Lund: Eesti Kirjanike Kooperatiiv, 1963), p. 48; George Kurman, "Estonian Literature," in Parming and Järvesoo, *Case Study of a Soviet Republic*, p. 248.

28. Juhan Kokla, "Eesti ajakirjandus ja saksa okupatsioon," in *ERRTM*, 8: 146–57; Raag, *Saatuslikus kolmnurgas*, pp. 176–83.

29. Vello Salo, *Riik ja kirikud 1940–1974* (Rome: Maarjamaa, 1974), pp. 20–21; Survel, *Estonia Today*, pp. 46–47.

CHAPTER 12

1. Aleksander Kaelas, *Das sowetisch besetzte Estland* (Stockholm: Eesti Rahvusfond, 1958), p. 11; O. Kurs, "On General Tendencies in the Development of the Administrative Division of the Estonian SSR," in *Estonia: Geographical Studies* (Tallinn: Academy of Sciences of the Estonian SSR, 1972), p. 145.

2. Kaelas, *Estland*, pp. 12, 14–15; Kurs, "General Tendencies," p. 146; *Eesti NSV ajalugu*, 3 vols. (Tallinn: Eesti Riiklik Kirjastus, 1955–1963; Eesti Raamat, 1971), 3: 594.

3. *Nõukogude Eesti: Entsüklopeediline teatmeteos*, 2d ed. (Tallinn: Valgus, 1978), pp. 97, 100; Jaan Pennar, "Soviet Nationality Policy and the Estonian Communist Elite," in Tönu Parming and Elmar Järvesoo, eds., *A Case Study of a Soviet Republic: The Estonian SSR* (Boulder, Colo.: Westview Press, 1978), p. 118.

4. *Nõukogude Eesti: Entsüklopeediline teatmeteos*, p. 100; Pennar, "Soviet Nationality Policy," p. 121.

5. Pennar, "Soviet Nationality Policy," pp. 114–15; *Ülevaade Eestimaa Kommunistliku Partei ajaloost*, 3 vols. (Tallinn: Eesti Riiklik Kirjastus, 1961–1963; Eesti Raamat, 1972), 3: 186–87.

6. *Ülevaade Eestimaa Kommunistliku Partei ajaloost*, 3: 187, 192, 316; Romuald J. Misiunas and Rein Taagepera, *The Baltic States: Years of Dependence, 1940–1980* (Berkeley: University of California Press, 1983), p. 74.

7. Arnold Purre, "Teine punane okupatsioon Eestis: Aastad 1944–1950," in *Eesti saatusaastad 1945–1960*, 6 vols. (Stockholm: EMP, 1963–1972), 2: 53–54; *Ülevaade Eestimaa Kommunistliku Partei ajaloost*, 3: 316; Rein Taagepera, "Soviet Collectivization of Estonian Agriculture: The Deportation Phase," *Soviet Studies* 32 (1980): 394–95. Karotamm's opposition to deportations from Estonia has been confirmed in the *glasnost'* era; see Edgar Tõnurist, "Traagiliste sündmuste aasta," in Ene Hion, ed., *Ausalt ja avameelselt EKP VIII pleenumist, Karotammest ja Käbinist, hinge harimatusest* (Tallinn: Perioodika, 1989), pp. 34–36, 44.

8. *Ülevaade Eestimaa Kommunistliku Partei ajaloost*, 3: 316, 319; Purre, "Teine punane okupatsioon: 1944–1950," pp. 59–60; Arnold Purre, "Teine punane okupatsioon Eestis: Aastad 1952–1964," in *Eesti saatusaastad*, 3: 8–9; Misiunas and Taagepera, *Baltic States*, pp. 79–80.

9. *Ülevaade Eestimaa Kommunistliku Partei ajaloost*, 3: 5, 191; Kaelas, *Estland*, p. 22.

10. Purre, "Teine punane okupatsioon: 1944–1950," pp. 10–11; *Eesti NSV ajalugu*, 3: 593–94; Purre, "Teine punane okupatsioon: 1952–1964," pp. 8–9.

11. Purre, "Teine punane okupatsioon: 1944–1950," pp. 9–10; *Eesti nõukogude entsüklopeedia*, 8 vols. & supplement (Tallinn: Valgus, 1968–1978), 4: 234; Endel Kareda, *Estonia in the Soviet Grip: Life and Conditions Under Soviet Occupation, 1947–1949*, East and West, no. 5 (London: Boreas, 1949), p. 87; Paul Winterton, *Report on Russia* (London: Cresset, 1945), pp. 85–86.

12. Kaelas, *Estland*, p. 39; Purre, "Teine punane okupatsioon: 1944–1950," pp. 11–13; Misiunas and Taagepera, *Baltic States*, p. 75.

13. Purre, "Teine punane okupatsioon: 1944–1950," pp. 10–11, 55–56; Purre, "Teine punane okupatsioon: 1952–1964," pp. 8–9.

14. Soviet publications invariably refer to the pro-independence guerrillas as "bandits."

15. Purre, "Teine punane okupatsioon: 1944–1950," pp. 22–24, 31–32; Olaf Tammark, "Mehed kogunevad metsadesse," in *Eesti saatusaastad*, 2: 81.

16. Eerik Heine, "Metsavennad," in *Eesti saatusaastad*, 2: 66–75; Purre, "Teine punane okupatsioon: 1944–1950," pp. 32–33, 35–36, 38–39; Meinhard Leetmaa, *Sõjas ja ikestatud Eestis* (Stockholm: Välis-Eesti & EMP, 1979), pp. 231–33; Tammark, "Mehed kogunevad metsadesse," p. 77.

17. Leetma, *Sõjas ja ikestatud Eestis*, pp. 230–31; Purre, "Teine punane okupatsioon: 1944–1950," pp. 38–39; Rein Taagepera, "Soviet Documentation on the Estonian Pro-Independence Guerrilla Movement, 1945–1952," *Journal of Baltic Studies* 10 (1979): 101–2, 105.

18. *Eesti NSV ajalugu*, 3: 568–69, 596; Elmar Järvesoo, "The Postwar Economic Transformation," in Parming and Järvesoo, *Case Study of a Soviet Republic*, pp. 133–34.

19. Purre, "Teine punane okupatsioon: 1944–1950," pp. 41–43; Arnold Purre, "Tööstus okupeeritud Eestis," in *Eesti saatusaastad*, 3: 114; *Eesti NSV ajalugu*, 3: 570; Järvesoo, "Postwar Economic Transformation," p. 135.

20. Järvesoo, "Postwar Economic Transformation," pp. 135–37; *Nar. khoz. ESSR 1972*, pp. 71–72.

21. *Eesti NSV ajalugu*, 3: 573.

22. Ibid., pp. 576–77. *Nar. khoz. ESSR 1972*, p. 76, gives a slightly higher figure of 86,700 industrial workers in Estonia in 1950.

23. Rein Taagepera, "Soviet Collectivization of Estonian Agriculture: The Taxation Phase," *Journal of Baltic Studies* 10 (1979): 266.

24. Ants Ruusman, "Nõukogude maareformi taastamine pärast Eesti NSV vabastamist saksa fašistlikest okupantidest," in *SPANE*, pp. 47–48, 57, 59–61; Edgar Tõnurist, "Sotsialistliku põllumajanduse arengust Nõukogude Eestis," in *SPANE*, pp. 12–13. Although 80 percent of the expropriated land came from farms over 300 hectares and abandoned farms, the political character of the land reform is seen in the following groups whose lands were also included: "enemies of the people," "collaborators," "bandits," and "those aiding the bandits." Altogether, these groups had held 12.7 percent of the confiscated land. See Ruusmann, "Nõukogude maareformi taastamine," p. 52.

25. *Eesti NSV ajalugu*, 3: 582, 584–86; Purre, "Teine punane okupatsioon: 1944–1950," pp. 45–46. Alfred Kasepalu, "Sotsialistlike põllumajandusettevõtete arvust Nõukogude Eestis aastail 1944–1976," in *SPANE*, p. 126, gives a figure of 96 sovkhozes in 1947.

26. Calculated from data in *Eesti NSV ajalugu*, 3: 586, and J. Nõu, "Hoop Eesti põllumajandusele," in *ERRTM*, 3: 96.

27. Vladimir Kabanov, "NSV Liidu läänerajoonide põllumajanduse kollektiviseerimise historiograafia tähtsamaid probleeme," in *SPANE*, pp. 32–33; Ervin Kivimaa, "Eesti NSV põllumajanduse kollektiviseerimine aastail 1947–1950," in *SPANE*, pp. 74–75.

28. Taagepera, "Taxation Phase," pp. 265, 267, 270, 274–76; Kivimaa, "Eesti NSV põllumajanduse kollektiviseerimine," pp. 72, 76, 83.

29. Kivimaa, "Eesti NSV põllumajanduse kollektiviseerimine," p. 83; Nikolai Karotamm, "Aus ja tubli töö kolhoosis—see on peaasi," in *Eesti NSV kolhoosnikute esimene kongress* (Tallinn: Poliitiline Kirjandus, 1949), pp. 40–41.

30. Taagepera, "Deportation Phase," pp. 381–82.

31. N. Karotamm to J. V. Stalin, January 17, 1949, in Edgar Tõnurist, ed., *Eesti NSV põllumajanduse kollektiviseerimine* (Tallinn: Eesti Raamat, 1978), p. 492.

32. Cf. Taagepera, "Deportation Phase," pp. 394–95.

33. Taagepera, "Taxation Phase," p. 265.

34. *Ülevaade Eestimaa Kommunistliku Partei ajaloost*, 3: 275.

35. Tõnu Parming, "Population Changes and Processes," in Parming and Järvesoo, *Case Study of a Soviet Republic*, pp. 26–27; Järvesoo, "Postwar Economic Transforma-

tion," p. 134; Taagepera, "Deportation Phase," pp. 390–93. As support for his argument, Taagepera cites the recently published description of the deportation of kulaks from Ruusmäe township in Võrumaa (Tõnurist, *Eesti NSV põllumajanduse kollektiviseerimine*, pp. 523–24). Of the thirteen families slated for deportation there, five were able to escape. A recent, unofficial Soviet source — an anonymous letter from fifteen Estonian intellectuals to a Finnish journalist — suggests a figure of 40,000 deportees in 1949; see *Teataja*, October 2, 1982, p. 6.

36. Misiunas and Taagepera, *Baltic States*, pp. 100–1. An eyewitness account by a survivor appears in *Teataja*, June 12, 1982, pp. 3–4.

37. Purre, "Põllumajandus okupeeritud Eestis," in *Eesti saatusaastad*, 3: 20–21; Kasepalu, "Sotsialistlike põllumajandusettevõtete arvust," p. 126; Taagepera, "Taxation Phase," p. 265.

38. *Nõukogude Eesti saavutusi 20 aasta jooksul: Statistiline kogumik* (Tallinn: Eesti Riiklik Kirjastus, 1960), pp. 41, 47, 49; Kasepalu, "Sotsialistlike põllumajandusettevõtete arvust," pp. 121, 125–26.

39. Järvesoo, "Postwar Economic Transformation," pp. 135–36; Elmar Järvesoo, "Progress Despite Collectivization," in Arvids Ziedonis, Jr., Rein Taagepera, and Mardi Valgemäe, eds., *Problems of Mininations: Baltic Perspectives* (San Jose, Calif.: Association for the Advancement of Baltic Studies, 1973), pp. 142, 147; *25 aastat Nõukogude Eestit: Statistiline kogumik* (Tallinn: Eesti Raamat, 1965), pp. 51, 53; *Nar. khoz. ESSR 1972*, p. 155; M. Rubin, "Varumishinnad ja kolhooside rahalised sissetulekud Eesti NSV-s aastail 1950–1960," *ENSVTA Toimetised* 30 (1981): 350.

40. Parming, "Population Changes and Processes," pp. 28, 34; "Sündimus, suremus, abiellumus ja rahvastikuarv 1939. a. (eelkokkuvõte)," *Eesti Statistika*, no. 208 (1939): 162; *Nar. khoz. ESSR 1979*, p. 14.

41. Arnold Purre, "Eesti rahvastik okupeeritud Eestis," in *Eesti saatusaastad*, 5: 22.

42. Raimo Pullat and Karl Siilivask, "Nõukogude Eesti sotsiaalne struktuur," *ENSVTA Toimetised* 26 (1977): 20.

43. Tõnu Parming, "Population Changes in Estonia, 1935–1970," *Population Studies* 26 (1972): 58, 60.

44. Rein Taagepera, "Baltic Population Changes, 1950–1980," *Journal of Baltic Studies* 12 (1981): 47.

45. Parming, "Population Changes in Estonia," p. 56.

46. Rein Taagepera, "The Population Crisis and the Baltics," *Journal of Baltic Studies* 12 (1981): 238–40; Järvesoo, "Postwar Economic Transformation," p. 139; *Nar. khoz. ESSR 1972*, p. 71; Taagepera, "Baltic Population Changes," p. 47.

47. Taagepera, "Baltic Population Changes," p. 40.

48. Estonia showed an increase of 22 percentage points in the urban share of the population in 1939–1959 while the USSR average increase was 16 percentage points; *Narodnoe khoziaistvo SSSR v 1961 godu* (Moscow: Gosstatizdat, 1962), p. 10.

49. Parming, "Population Changes in Estonia," pp. 66–67.

50. *Eesti nõukogude entsüklopeedia*, 8 vols. & supplement (Tallinn: Valgus, 1968–1978), 7: 450.

51. *Tartu: Juht ja teatmik* (Tartu: n.p., 1963), p. 165.

52. *Eesti NSV ajalugu*, 3: 450; *Nõukogude Eesti: Entsüklopeediline teatmeteos*, p. 105.

53. *Nar. khoz. ESSR 1975*, p. 228; Kareda, *Estonia*, pp. 60–66; Jaak Survel, *Estonia Today*, East and West, no. 1 (London: Boreas, 1947), pp. 27–30; Arnold Purre, "Ehitustegevus ja korteriolud," in *Eesti saatusaastad*, 5: 43.

54. Misiunas and Taagepera, *Baltic States*, p. 290.

55. Arnold Purre, "Haridusolud N. Eestis," in *Eesti saatusaastad*, 6: 32, 44; *Eesti NSV ajalugu*, 3: 617–20; Kareda, *Estonia*, p. 48; *Nõukogude Eesti saavutusi*, p. 93.

56. Survel, *Estonia Today*, pp. 38–39; *Eesti NSV ajalugu*, 3: 622–25; Kareda, *Estonia*, pp. 51–54; H. Reinop, *Education in Soviet Estonia* (Tallinn: Eesti Raamat, 1967), p. 34.

57. *Nõukogude Eesti saavutusi*, p. 94.

58. *25 aastat Nõukogude Eesti trükisõna 1940–1965* (Tallinn: Eesti Raamat, 1971), pp. 23, 35–36, 165–67; Richard Antik, *Eesti raamat 1535–1935* (Tartu: n.p., 1936), p. 29; *Narodnoe khoziaistvo SSSR v 1961 godu*, pp. 730, 732.

59. Arvo Mägi, "Kodumaine kirjanduselu," in *Eesti saatusaastad*, 6: 87; Marc Slonim, *Soviet Russian Literature* (Oxford: Oxford University Press, 1967), pp. 278–84.

60. Endel Nirk, *Estonian Literature* (Tallinn: Eesti Raamat, 1970), p. 287; Rein Taagepera, "A Portrait of the 'Historical Gap' in Estonian Literature," *Lituanus* 26, no. 3 (1980): 73–74, 81.

61. Mägi, "Kodumaine kirjanduselu," pp. 88–89; *Eesti kirjanduse biograafiline leksikon* (Tallinn: Eesti Raamat, 1975), pp. 305, 387; George Kurman, "Literary Censorship in General and in Soviet Estonia," *Journal of Baltic Studies* 8 (1977): 8; Misiunas and Taagepera, *Baltic States*, p. 111.

62. George Kurman, "Estonian Literature," in Parming and Järvesoo, *Case Study of a Soviet Republic*, pp. 248–50, 259; Nirk, *Estonian Literature*, pp. 293–94, 355, 362; Mardi Valgemäe, "Drama and the Theatre Arts," in Parming and Järvesoo, *Case Study of a Soviet Republic*, p. 282.

63. Kurman, "Estonian Literature," p. 248; Nirk, *Estonian Literature*, p. 362; *Nõukogude Eesti raamat 1940–1954* (Tallinn: Eesti Riiklik Kirjastus, 1956), pp. 22, 25.

64. *Eesti NSV ajalugu*, 3: 649–55; Kareda, *Estonia*, p. 55; *Nõukogude Eesti: Entsüklopeediline teatmeteos*, pp. 296–98.

65. *Nõukogude Eesti: Entsüklopeediline teatmeteos*, pp. 267–71, 279–81; *Eesti NSV ajalugu*, 3: 655, 657, 659–60; Kareda, *Estonia*, p. 57.

66. *Eesti NSV 1975. a. üldlaulu- ja tantsupeo teatmik* (Tallinn: Eesti Raamat, 1975), p. 34; Aarne Mesikäpp et al., eds., *Laulusajand 1869–1969* (Tallinn: Eesti Raamat, 1969), no pagination; *Nõukogude Eesti: Entsüklopeediline teatmeteos*, p. 280.

67. Mare Põldmäe, "Kaks laulupidu, 1947 ja 1950," *Teater. Muusika. Kino* 9, no. 3 (1990): 32–35.

68. Vello Salo, "The Struggle Between the State and the Churches," in Parming and Järvesoo, *Case Study of a Soviet Republic*, pp. 197–201; Vello Salo, *Riik ja kirikud 1940–1974* (Rome: Maarjamaa, 1974), pp. 31–32.

CHAPTER 13

1. *Rahva Hääl*, September 25, 1956, p. 3; *Nõukogude Eesti: Entsüklopeediline teatmeteos*, 2d ed. (Tallinn: Valgus, 1978), pp. 165–66; Johannes Klesment, "The Forms of Baltic Resistance to the Communists," *The Baltic Review*, no. 8 (1956): 25.

2. Aleksander Kaelas, *Das sowetisch besetzte Estland* (Stockholm: Eesti Rahvus-fond, 1958), pp. 12, 14–15; O. Kurs, "On General Tendencies in the Development of the Administrative Division of the Estonian SSR," in *Estonia: Geographical Studies* (Tallinn: Academy of Sciences of the Estonian SSR, 1972), pp. 146–47; *Nõukogude Eesti: Entsüklopeediline teatmeteos*, pp. 87–88; *Nar. khoz. ESSR 1983*, p. 8.

3. *Nõukogude Eesti: Entsüklopeediline teatmeteos*, p. 100; John L. Scherer, ed., *USSR: Facts and Figures Annual*, vols. 5 & 6 (Gulf Breeze, Fla.: Academic International Press, 1981–1982), 5:40, 6:26; *Kommunisticheskaia partiia Estonii v tsifrakh 1920–1980* (Tallinn: Eesti Raamat, 1983), pp. 108–9, 181–82.

4. Jaan Pennar, "Soviet Nationality Policy and the Estonian Communist Elite," in Tõnu Parming and Elmar Järvesoo, eds., *A Case Study of a Soviet Republic: The Estonian SSR* (Boulder, Colo.: Westview Press, 1978), pp. 117–18; *Rahva Hääl*, January 31, 1976, p. 1; *Eestimaa Kommunistliku Partei XVIII Kongress* (Tallinn: Eesti Raamat, 1981), pp. 135–36; *Kommunisticheskaia partiia Estonii*, pp. 108–9, 181–82.

5. *Kommunisticheskaia partiia Estonii*, pp. 103, 108, 175, 186.

6. An annual list of the ECP's Buro appears in *Ezhegodnik Bol'shoi Sovetskoi Entsiklopedii*, published annually since 1957. The most useful source for biographical information is *Eesti nõukogude entsüklopeedia*, 8 vols. & supplement (Tallinn: Valgus, 1968–1978).

7. *Sovetskaia Estoniia*, April 10, 1983, p. 1; *Rahva Hääl*, March 27, 1985, p. 1.

8. Compiled from *Eesti nõukogude entsüklopeedia*, *Ezhegodnik Bol'shoi Sovetskoi Entsiklopedii*, and *Rahva Hääl*, December 5, 1985, p. 1.

9. *Rahva Hääl*, January 29, 1958, p. 1; *Sirp ja Vasar*, December 17, 1965, p. 1.

10. *Estonian Events*, no. 20 (June 1970): 5; Pennar, "Soviet Nationality Policy," p. 123.

11. *Baltic Events*, nos. 48–49 (February–April 1975): 11; Pennar, "Soviet Nationality Policy," p. 123; *Sovetskaia Estoniia*, January 21, 1956, p. 1; *Rahva Hääl*, May 26, 1970, p. 2.

12. *Sirp ja Vasar*, July 28, 1978, p. 2.

13. See the comments by fifteen anonymous Estonian intellectuals in *Teataja*, October 2, 1982, p. 6.

14. Rein Taagepera, "Nationalism in the Estonian Communist Party," *Bulletin* (Institute for the Study of the USSR) 17, no. 1 (1970): 13.

15. V. Stanley Vardys, "The Role of the Baltic Peoples in Soviet Society," in Roman Szporluk, ed., *The Influence of East Europe and the Soviet West on the USSR* (New York: Praeger, 1976), p. 153.

16. Kaelas, *Estland*, pp. 41–42, 47; "New Chairman of the Estonian KGB," *Radio Liberty Research* RL 266/82 (June 29, 1982): 1–2.

17. *Eesti nõukogude entsüklopeedia*, 2: 43; Kaelas, *Estland*, pp. 41–42.

18. Arnold Purre, "Teine punane okupatsioon Eestis: Aastad 1952–1964," in *Eesti saatusaastad 1945–1960*, 6 vols. (Stockholm: EMP, 1963–1972), 3: 8–9; *Sovetskaia Estoniia*, March 29, 1980, p. 1; E. L. Crowley et al., eds., *Prominent Personalities in the USSR* (Methuen, N.J.: Scarecrow Press, 1968), p. 789; Kaelas, *Estland*, p. 42.

19. *Eesti nõukogude entsüklopeedia*, 4: 21, 5: 294; *Rahva Hääl*, January 19, 1984, p. 1.

20. Kaelas, *Estland*, p. 39; Pennar, "Soviet Nationality Policy," p. 119; *Eesti NSV Ülemnõukogu IX koosseis* (Tallinn: Eesti Raamat, 1976); *Eesti NSV Ülemnõukogu X koosseis* (Tallinn: Eesti Raamat, 1981).

21. Romuald J. Misiunas and Rein Taagepera, *The Baltic States: Years of Dependence, 1940–1980* (Berkeley: University of California Press, 1983), p. 270; *Sovetskaia Estoniia*, April 9, 1983, p. 1.

22. *Eesti Nõukogude Sotsialistliku Vabariigi konstitutsioon (põhiseadus)* (Tallinn: Eesti Raamat, 1978); A. Shtromas, "The Legal Position of Soviet Nationalities and Territorial Units According to the 1977 Constitution of the USSR," *Russian Review* 37 (1978): 265–66, 271; Jaan Pennar, "Reflections on Union Republics in the New Soviet Constitution," *Lituanus* 25, no. 1 (1979): 6.

23. Rein Taagepera, "Nationalism, Collaborationism, and New Leftism," in Parming and Järvesoo, *Case Study of a Soviet Republic*, pp. 78, 83; *Baltic Events*, no. 46 (October 1974): 7.

24. *Teataja*, September 17, 1977, p. 3; V. Stanley Vardys, "Human Rights Issues in Estonia, Latvia, and Lithuania," *Journal of Baltic Studies* 12 (1981): 280–81; Rein Taagepera, *Softening Without Liberalization in the Soviet Union: The Case of Jüri Kukk* (Lanham, Md.: University Press of America, 1984), pp. 115–16, 185–93; *Baltic Forum* 1, no. 1 (1984): 92–93.

25. The nineteen issues of *Lisandusi* have been published in the West in *Lisandusi mõtete ja uudiste vabale levikule Eestis*, 3 vols. (Stockholm: Eesti Vangistatud Vabadusvõitlejate Abistamiskeskus, 1984–1986). See the table of contents for all the issues in volume 1, pp. 221–25.

26. "Student Demonstrations in Tartu, Estonia," *Radio Liberty Special Report* RL 107/77 (May 10, 1977): 1–5; *The Economist*, October 11, 1980, p. 57.

27. Vardys, "Human Rights Issues," pp. 283–84, 292–96; *Teataja*, October 2, 1982, pp. 6–8; *Baltic Forum* 1, no. 1 (1984): 91–92. For a recent analysis of the open letter of 1980, see Sirje Kiin, Rein Ruutsoo, and Andres Tarand, *40 kirja lugu* (Tallinn: Olion, 1990).

28. *Nõukogude Eesti saavutusi 20 aasta jooksul: Statistiline kogumik* (Tallinn: Eesti Riiklik Kirjastus, 1960), pp. 47, 49, 69; *Nar. khoz. ESSR 1975*, pp. 223–24; *Nar. khoz. ESSR 1978*, pp. 187–88; *Nar. khoz. ESSR 1981*, pp. 160–61.

29. *25 aastat Nõukogude Eestit: Statistiline kogumik* (Tallinn: Eesti Raamat, 1965), p. 25; *Nar. khoz. ESSR 1983*, p. 22.

30. Elmar Järvesoo, "The Postwar Economic Transformation," in Parming and Järvesoo, *Case Study of a Soviet Republic*, pp. 174–76; *Nõukogude Eesti: Entsüklopeediline teatmeteos*, pp. 150–51; *Soviet Estonia: Land, People, Culture* (Tallinn: Valgus, 1980), pp. 169–71.

31. *Nõukogude Eesti: Entsüklopeediline teatmeteos*, pp. 115–17; Järvesoo, "Postwar Economic Transformation," pp. 139, 141.

32. *Nõukogude Eesti saavutusi*, p. 21; Järvesoo, "Postwar Economic Transformation," p. 143; *Soviet Estonia: Land, People, Culture*, p. 143; *Nar. khoz. ESSR 1980*, p. 80.

33. V. Tarmisto, "Tootmisharulise ja territoriaalse aspekti ühtsusest rahvamajanduse arendamisel ning juhtimisel," *ENSVTA Toimetised* 19 (1970): 208, 212; Järvesoo, "Postwar Economic Transformation," p. 143.

34. *Nar. khoz. ESSR 1969*, p. 78; *Narodnoe khoziaistvo SSSR v 1969 g.* (Moscow: Statistika, 1970), p. 144.

35. *Nar. khoz. ESSR 1980*, pp. 79–80.

36. Ibid.; *Nar. khoz. ESSR 1972*, p. 71.

37. *Eesti NSV rahvamajandus* (Tallinn: Eesti Riiklik Kirjastus, 1957), p. 36; *Nar. khoz. ESSR 1975*, p. 82.

38. *Eesti NSV rahvamajandus*, pp. 32–33; Järvesoo, "Postwar Economic Transformation," pp. 153, 156, 158, 160, 162.

39. *Eesti NSV rahvamajandus*, pp. 32–33; *Nar. khoz. ESSR 1975*, p. 89; *Nõukogude Eesti: Entsüklopeediline teatmeteos*, pp. 114, 117; *Nar. khoz. ESSR 1980*, p. 92; Henry Ratnieks, "Baltic Oil Shale," *Journal of Baltic Studies* 9 (1978): 159–61.

40. *25 aastat Nõukogude Eestit: Statistiline kogumik*, p. 37; *Nar. khoz. ESSR 1980*, p. 91; Mare Taagepera, "Pollution of the Environment and the Baltics," *Journal of Baltic Studies* 12 (1981): 264; *Nõukogude Eesti: Entsüklopeediline teatmeteos*, p. 118.

41. M. Taagepera, "Pollution," pp. 263–64; *Nõukogude Eesti: Entsüklopeediline teatmeteos*, pp. 118–19; Jaan Pennar, "Greater Demands to Be Made of Estonian Shale Deposits," *Radio Liberty Research* RL 301/81 (July 31, 1981): 1.

42. *Teataja*, September 17, 1977, p. 3; *Nõukogude Eesti: Entsüklopeediline teatmeteos*, p. 118; M. Taagepera, "Pollution," pp. 264–65.

43. Arnold Purre, "Põllumajandus okupeeritut Eestis," in *Eesti saatusaastad*, 3: 35, 66; Edgar Tõnurist, "Sotsialistliku põllumajanduse arengust Nõukogude Eestis," in *SPANE*, pp. 17–21; Meinhard Leetmaa, *Sõjas ja ikestatud Eestis* (Stockholm: Välis-Eesti & EMP, 1979), pp. 247–48; Misiunas and Taagepera, *Baltic States*, p. 134.

44. Tõnurist, "Sotsialistliku põllumajanduse arengust," pp. 23–24; Järvesoo, "Postwar Economic Transformation," pp. 149, 151.

45. *Nõukogude Eesti saavutusi*, pp. 36, 41; *Nar. khoz. ESSR 1975*, p. 121; *Nar. khoz. ESSR 1983*, pp. 73–74.

46. Alfred Kasepalu, "Sotsialistlike põllumajandusettevõtete arvust Nõukogude

Eestis aastail 1944–1976," in *SPANE*, pp. 125–27, 130; *Nõukogude Eesti saavutusi*, p. 41; *Nar. khoz. ESSR 1983*, pp. 73–74.

47. *Nõukogude Eesti saavutusi*, pp. 47, 49; *Nar. khoz. ESSR 1975*, pp. 169, 173, 223; *Nar. khoz. ESSR 1978*, pp. 132, 136, 187; *Nar. khoz. ESSR 1982*, pp. 102, 106.

48. *Nar. khoz. ESSR 1980*, p. 122.

49. Järvesoo, "Postwar Economic Transformation," pp. 144, 146–47, 149; *25 aastat Nõukogude Eestit: Statistiline kogumik*, p. 53; Purre, "Põllumajandus okupeeritud Eestis," p. 48; *Nar. khoz. ESSR 1980*, pp. 129, 134, 140–41, 159.

50. Misiunas and Taagepera, *Baltic States*, pp. 201, 211–12.

51. *Nõukogude Eesti: Entsüklopeediline teatmeteos*, pp. 133–34; *Eestimaa Kommunistliku Partei XVIII Kongress*, p. 21.

52. *Nar. khoz. ESSR 1982*, p. 10; *Nõukogude Eesti: Entsüklopeediline teatmeteos*, p. 41; *Narodnoe khoziaistvo SSSR 1922–1982* (Moscow: Finansy i Statistika, 1982), p. 12; *Rahva Hääl*, January 29, 1985, p. 2.

53. *Nar. khoz. ESSR 1980*, p. 13; *Nar. khoz. ESSR 1981*, pp. 10, 18–19; Rein Taagepera, "Baltic Population Changes, 1950–1980," *Journal of Baltic Studies* 12 (1981): 36, 38.

54. *Nõukogude Eesti: Entsüklopeediline teatmeteos*, p. 42; *Nar. khoz. ESSR 1981*, p. 19; Tõnu Parming, "Population Changes and Processes," in Parming and Järvesoo, *Case Study of a Soviet Republic*, p. 49; Taagepera, "Baltic Population Changes," p. 38; *Narodnoe khoziaistvo SSSR 1922–1982*, pp. 28–29.

55. Tõnu Parming, "Long-term Trends in Family Structure in a Soviet Republic," *Sociology and Social Research* 63 (1979): 456; Egil Levits, "Die demographische Situation in der UdSSR und in den baltischen Staaten unter besonderer Berücksichtigung von nationalen und sprachsoziologischen Aspekten," *Acta Baltica* 21 (1981): 30; Aili Kelam, *Eesti NSV perekond: Sotsioloogiline portree* (Tallinn: Eesti Raamat, 1980), p. 8.

56. *Nar. khoz. ESSR 1972*, p. 35; *Nar. khoz. ESSR 1981*, p. 19; Parming, "Long-term Trends," pp. 457–58.

57. Levits, "Demographische Situation," p. 64; *Nõukogude Eesti: Entsüklopeediline teatmeteos*, p. 42.

58. Taagepera, "Baltic Population Changes," pp. 36, 38, 42, 44; Arnold Purre, "Ethnischer Bestand und Struktur der Bevölkerung Sowjetestlands im Jahr 1970," *Acta Baltica* 11 (1971): 46; Levits, "Demographische Situation," p. 49; *Nar. khoz. ESSR 1983*, pp. 10, 13.

59. Uno Mereste and Maimu Saarepera, *Rahvastiku enesetunnetus* (Tallinn: Eesti Raamat, 1978), p. 188; *Nar. khoz. ESSR 1980*, p. 15.

60. *Vestnik statistiki*, no. 11 (1980): 64; *Nar. khoz. ESSR 1980*, p. 321.

61. *Itogi Vsesoiuznoi perepisi naseleniia 1959 goda: Estonskaia SSR* (Moscow: Gosstatizdat, 1962), p. 94; *Itogi Vsesoiuznoi perepisi naseleniia 1970 goda*, 7 vols. (Moscow: Statistika, 1972–1974), 4: 317; *Vestnik statistiki*, no. 11 (1980): 64.

62. Graham E. Smith, "Die Probleme des Nationalismus in den drei baltischen

Sowjetrepubliken Estland, Lettland und Litauen," *Acta Baltica* 21 (1981): 168; *Vestnik statistiki*, no. 6 (1983): 72–79 and no. 7 (1983): 68–80; *Baltic Events*, no. 43 (April 1974): Appendix.

63. *Nar. khoz. ESSR 1983*, p. 10; *Nõukogude Eesti: Entsüklopeediline teatmeteos*, p. 41.

64. Taagepera, "Baltic Population Changes," p. 40; Zev Katz, ed., *Handbook of Major Soviet Nationalities* (New York: The Free Press, 1975), p. 448; *Naselenie SSSR: Po dannym Vsesoiuznoi perepisi naseleniia 1979 goda* (Moscow: Politizdat, 1980), pp. 4, 8–11.

65. K. Laas, "Rahvastik ja tööjõud," in *Tallinna arengu probleeme* (Tallinn: Eesti Raamat, 1978), p. 98; *Nar. khoz. ESSR 1981*, p. 10; Raimo Pullat and Karl Siilivask, "Nõukogude Eesti sotsiaalne struktuur," *ENSVTA Toimetised* 26 (1977): 21.

66. *Nar. khoz. ESSR 1983*, p. 11.

67. L. Volkov, "Linna generaalplaani põhijooni," in *Tallinna arengu probleeme*, p. 60; *Sirp ja Vasar*, February 10, 1961, p. 4; *Nar. khoz. ESSR 1980*, p. 13.

68. Volkov, "Linna generaalplaani põhijooni," p. 61; *Rahva Hääl*, October 25, 1973, p. 3; *Nar. khoz. ESSR 1983*, pp. 10–11.

69. *Tallinn: Lühientsüklopeedia* (Tallinn: Valgus, 1979), p. 12.

70. Rein Taagepera, "Size and Ethnicity of Estonian Towns and Rural Districts, 1922–1979," *Journal of Baltic Studies* 13 (1982): 122–23. The estimate of 100,000 new workers is given by a group of Estonian dissidents in *Välis-Eesti*, December 14, 1982, p. 6.

71. Taagepera, "Size and Ethnicity," p. 107. The figures for Tallinn in 1979 add up to 100.1 percent due to rounding off.

72. Ibid., pp. 110, 112. The 1934 figures for Kohtla-Järve are given for the small town (*alev*) of Jõhvi, which formed the basis for the new city of Kohtla-Järve, founded in 1946. The Russian percentages for 1934 are taken from *II rahvaloendus Eestis*, 4 vols. (Tallinn: Riigi Statistika Keskbüroo, 1934–1937), 4: 24. The available figures for Pärnu in 1979 are not consistent internally and may involve errors.

73. Taagepera, "Size and Ethnicity," pp. 107, 112, 121.

74. *Nar. khoz. ESSR 1981*, pp. 160–61.

75. Aleksander Kutt, "A Review and the Meaning of Developments in Estonia since 1953," *The Baltic Review*, no. 12 (1957): 22; Leetmaa, *Sõjas ja ikestatud Eestis*, p. 251; *Nar. khoz. ESSR 1981*, p. 164.

76. *Nar. khoz. ESSR 1981*, pp. 164–65.

77. Katz, *Handbook of Major Soviet Nationalities*, pp. 453–54; *Nar. khoz. ESSR 1981*, p. 182; *Narodnoe khoziaistvo SSSR v 1979 g.* (Moscow: Statistika, 1980), pp. 10, 435.

78. Rein Taagepera, "Estonia and the Estonians," in Katz, *Handbook of Major Soviet Nationalities*, p. 83; Järvesoo, "Postwar Economic Transformation," p. 178; *Narodnoe khoziaistvo SSSR v 1980 g.* (Moscow: Finansy i Statistika, 1981), p. 405; *Nar. khoz. ESSR 1980*, p. 234.

79. *Nar. khoz. ESSR 1983*, p. 206; Scherer, *USSR: Facts and Figures Annual*, vol. 6, p. 294; *Teataja*, October 2, 1982, p. 7; Andres Küng, *Estland—en studie i imperialism* (Stockholm: Aldus/Bonniers, 1971), p. 8.

80. Järvesoo, "Postwar Economic Transformation," p. 177; Katz, *Handbook of Major Soviet Nationalities*, p. 458; *Narodnoe khoziaistvo SSSR 1922–1982*, p. 542.

81. Küng, *Estland*, pp. 8–9.

82. *Nõukogude Eesti: Entsüklopeediline teatmeteos*, pp. 105–6, 109–10; *Soviet Estonia: Land, People, Culture*, p. 132; *Nar. khoz. ESSR 1981*, p. 10.

83. *Narodnoe khoziaistvo SSSR v 1961 godu* (Moscow: Gosstatizdat, 1962), p. 574; *Narodnoe khoziaistvo SSSR 1922–1982*, p. 404.

84. Ea Jansen, "Killukesi naisküsimuse ajaloost," *Looming*, no. 3 (1975): 473, 478–79; Mare Taagepera, "Naiste olukord Eestis," in *Metroo 77* (N.p.: n.p., 1977), pp. 76, 82, 84–85; Parming, "Long-term Trends," p. 456.

85. *Nar. khoz. ESSR 1983*, p. 11; *Itogi Vsesoiuznoi perepisi naseleniia 1970 goda*, 4: 383.

86. Vardys, "Human Rights Issues," pp. 293–94; *Teataja*, October 2, 1982, pp. 6–7; *Välis-Eesti*, December 14, 1982, p. 6.

87. M. N. Rutkevich, "Dvuiazychie—vazhnyi faktor razvitiia novoi istoricheskoi obshchnosti," *Istoriia SSSR*, no. 4 (1981): 31; *Naselenie SSSR*, pp. 23–24; *Vestnik statistiki*, no. 8 (1980): 64–69; no. 9 (1980): 61, 65; no. 10 (1980): 67, 70–72; no. 11 (1980), 60–62, 64.

88. Jaan Pennar, Ivan I. Bakalo, and George Z. F. Bereday, *Modernization and Diversity in Soviet Education* (New York: Praeger, 1971), pp. 32, 44–45, 241–42; *Sirp ja Vasar*, March 12, 1965, p. 1.

89. Arnold Purre, "Haridusolud N. Eestis," in *Eesti saatusaastad*, 6: 32n; *Nõukogude Eesti: Entsüklopeediline teatmeteos*, p. 170; *Nar. khoz. ESSR 1981*, pp. 244, 249; *Nar. khoz. ESSR 1983*, p. 229.

90. *Eesti NSV rahvamajandus*, p. 228; Taagepera, "Estonia and the Estonians," p. 83.

91. Hermann Rajamaa, "Schulwesen und pädagogische Zielsetzung im selbständigen Estland und in Sowjet Estland," *Acta Baltica* 1 (1960–1961): 137; *Nõukogude Õpetaja*, May 16, 1981, p. 4; *Teataja*, October 2, 1982, p. 7.

92. Jaan Pennar, "Problems of Teaching Estonian in Tallinn's Russian-language Schools," *Radio Liberty Research* RL 135/82 (March 23, 1982): 1–2; Ann Sheehy, "Estonian-language Olympiad Instituted for Pupils of Russian Schools in Estonia," *Radio Liberty Research* RL 66/82 (February 10, 1982), pp. 1–2.

93. *25 aastat Nõukogude Eestit: Statistiline kogumik*, pp. 110–12; *Nar. khoz. ESSR 1981*, pp. 252–53.

94. *Nõukogude Eesti saavutusi*, p. 95; *Baltic Events*, no. 37 (April 1973), p. 7; Teodor Künnapas and Elmar Järvesoo, "The Structure of Higher Education and Research," in Pärming and Jarvesoo, *Case Study of a Soviet Republic*, p. 366; *Teataja*, October 2, 1982, p. 7.

95. *25 aastat Nõukogude Eestit: Statistiline kogumik*, p. 117; *Nar. khoz. ESSR 1983*, p. 29; *Nõukogude Eesti: Entsüklopeediline teatmeteos*, p. 179.

96. Vardys, "Human Rights Issues," p. 294; *Helsingin Sanomat*, October 26, 1981.

97. *Eesti NSV rahvamajandus*, p. 283: *Nar. khoz. ESSR 1982*, pp. 241–42; *Nar. khoz. ESSR 1985*, pp. 264–65.

98. Katz, *Handbook of Soviet Nationalities*, p. 459; *Pechat' SSSR v 1979 godu* (Moscow: Statistika, 1980), pp. 22–23; *Naselenie SSSR*, pp. 23–24; *Pechat' SSSR v 1980 godu* (Moscow: Statistika, 1981), pp. 24–25.

99. *Eesti NSV rahvamajandus*, p. 283; *Nar. khoz. ESSR 1983*, p. 249; *Nõukogude Eesti: Entsüklopeediline teatmeteos*, p. 197.

100. *25 aastat Nõukogude Eestit: Statistiline kogumik*, p. 125; *Nar. khoz. ESSR 1980*, p. 321; *Nar. khoz. ESSR 1979*, p. 308; *Soviet Estonia: Land, People, Culture*, p. 227.

101. Elsa Grechkina, "Kompleksnyi podkhod k problemam prepodavaniia russkogo iazyka v Estonii," in *Russkii iazyk—iazyk druzhby i sotrudnichestva narodov SSSR* (Moscow: Nauka, 1981), p. 203; *Eesti Päevaleht*, November 15, 1980, pp. 1, 11.

102. *Helsingin Sanomat*, October 10, 1982, p. 8; *Suomen Kuvalehti*, October 22, 1982, p. 46.

103. George Kurman, "Estonian Literature," in Parming and Järvesoo, *Case Study of a Soviet Republic*, pp. 251, 269, 271; *Soviet-occupied Estonia 1963* (Stockholm: Estonian National Council, 1964), pp. 12, 14–15.

104. *Nõukogude Eesti raamat 1940–1954* (Tallinn: Eesti Riiklik Kirjastus, 1956), pp. 22, 25; *Nõukogude Eesti raamat 1955–1965* (Tallinn: Eesti Raamat, 1972), pp. 682–707, 710–47, 752–60, 761–807; *Nõukogude Eesti trükisõna 1966–1975* (Tallinn: Eesti Raamat, 1978), pp. 61–62; *Raamatukroonika*, no. 1 (1981): 127–37; no. 2 (1981): 123–130; no. 3 (1981): 106–12; no. 4 (1981): 112–20.

105. L. Püss, "Ülevaade ilmunud raamatutest," in Voldemar Miller, ed., *Eesti raamat 1575–1975* (Tallinn: Valgus, 1978), p. 290.

106. Endel Nirk, *Estonian Literature* (Tallinn: Eesti Raamat, 1970), p. 292; Mardi Valgemäe, "Drama and the Theatre Arts," in Parming and Järvesoo, *Case Study of a Soviet Republic*, p. 299; Kurman, "Estonian Literature," p. 265. See the bibliographies in *"Loomingu" Raamatukogu*, no. 1 (1974): 75–94, and no. 52 (1978): 79–95.

107. Kurman, "Estonian Literature," pp. 251, 253–55, 257–58; Arvo Mägi, *Estonian Literature* (Stockholm: Baltic Humanitarian Association, 1968), pp. 70–73.

108. Kurman, "Estonian Literature," pp. 259–63; Mägi, *Estonian Literature*, p. 74; Nirk, *Estonian Literature*, pp. 298–300.

109. Valgemäe, "Drama and the Theatre Arts," pp. 283, 287–95, 299–301.

110. Ibid., p. 302; *Nõukogude Eesti: Entsüklopeediline teatmeteos*, pp. 299–309; *Soviet Estonia: Land, People, Culture*, 349–58.

111. *25 aastat Nõukogude Eestit: Statistiline kogumik*, p. 122; *Nar. khoz. ESSR 1980*, p. 315; *Nar. khoz. ESSR 1982*, p. 235.

112. Stephen C. Feinstein, "The Avant-Garde in Soviet Estonia," in Norton Dodge and Alison Holt, eds., *New Art from the Soviet Union* (Washington, D.C.: Acropolis Books, 1977), p. 31.

113. Evi Pihlak, "Hargnevaid suundi eesti 60. aastate maalis," *Kunst*, no. 61/1 (1983): 27–28; *Soviet Estonia: Land, People, Culture*, pp. 323–24; *Nõukogude Eesti: Entsüklopeediline teatmeteos*, p. 274.

114. Monika Topman, *An Outline of Estonian Music* (Tallinn: Perioodika, 1978), pp. 22–23, 26, 33; Harold C. Schonberg, "The World of Music," in Harrison E. Salisbury, ed., *The Soviet Union: The First Fifty Years* (New York: Harcourt, Brace & World, 1967), p. 181; *Nõukogude Eesti: Entsüklopeediline teatmeteos*, pp. 281–82, 288.

115. *1869–1969: Juubelilaulupeo juht* (Tallinn: Eesti Raamat, 1969), pp. 49–55; *Eesti NSV 1975. a. üldlaulu- ja tantsupeo teatmik* (Tallinn: Eesti Raamat, 1975), pp. 25–27; *Nõukogude Eesti: Entsüklopeediline teatmeteos*, p. 286; *Helsingin Sanomat*, July 13, 1980, pp. 13–15; *Sirp ja Vasar*, July 11, 1980, pp. 9–12.

116. Vello Salo, "The Struggle Between the State and the Churches," in Parming and Järvesoo, *Case Study of a Soviet Republic*, pp. 201–4, 208–10; *Nõukogude Eesti: Entsüklopeediline teatmeteos*, pp. 228–29; *Soviet Estonia: Land, People, Culture*, p. 262; *Rahva Hääl*, January 12, 1984, p. 2.

117. Misiunas and Taagepera, *Baltic States*, p. 280.

118. Vardys, "Human Rights Issues," pp. 293–94; *Teataja*, October 2, 1982, p. 6.

CHAPTER 14

1. *Baltic Forum* 4, no. 2 (1987): 86–91; "Lippmaa and Aare on Estonian Ecology," *Baltic Forum* 6, no. 1 (1989): 6–7.

2. *Sirp ja Vasar*, October 30, 1987, p. 14; Mare Taagepera, "The Ecological and Political Problems of Phosphorite Mining in Estonia," *Journal of Baltic Studies* 20 (1989): 174.

3. Rein Taagepera, "Estonia's Road to Independence," *Problems of Communism* 38, no. 6 (1989): 16; "*Glasnost* in the Baltic: Summer Demonstrations," *Baltic Forum* 4, no. 2 (1987): 3.

4. *Homeland*, April 20, 1988, p. 2; *Baltic Forum* 5, no. 1 (1988): 95–97.

5. Endel Pillau, comp., *Eestimaa kuum suvi 1988* (Tallinn: Olion, 1989), pp. 59, 95, 113; Ene Hion, ed., *Kes on kes Eesti poliitikas* (Tallinn: Olion, 1990), pp. 14–15.

6. *Homeland*, August 31, 1988, pp. 1–2.

7. Ibid., September 21, 1988, p. 1; Pillau, *Eestimaa kuum suvi*, p. 149.

8. *Homeland*, May 25, 1988, p. 2; October 5, 1988, pp. 1–2; October 12, 1988, pp. 1–2; *Rahvakongress: Eestimaa Rahvarinde kongress 1.–2. oktoobril 1988* (Tallinn: Perioodika, 1988), pp. 19–21, 23; Rein Taagepera, "Estonia in September 1988: Stalinists, Centrists and Restorationists," *Journal of Baltic Studies* 20 (1989): 175–77.

9. *Homeland*, July 27, 1988, p. 2; March 15, 1989, pp. 1–2.

10. Pillau, *Eestimaa kuum suvi*, p. 136.

11. Ene Hion, ed., *Ausalt ja avameelselt Eesti parteidest*, 2 vols. (Tallinn: Perioodika, 1990), passim.

12. Rein Taagepera, "A Note on the March 1989 Elections in Estonia," *Soviet Studies* 42 (1990): 331–32, 336–37.

13. *Homeland*, December 20, 1989, pp. 1–2; March 21, 1990, p. 1; Rein Taagepera, "The Baltic States," *Electoral Studies* 9 (1990): 303–4, 306–8.

14. *Edasi*, September 26, 1987, p. 3.

15. *Homeland*, November 23, 1988, pp. 1–2; *New York Times*, December 8, 1988, p. A11; Pillau, *Eestimaa kuum suvi*, pp. 205–7.

16. Riina Kionka, "The Estonian Citizens' Committee: An Opposition Movement of a Different Complexion," *Report on the USSR* 2, no. 6 (1990): 30–33; *Homeland*, March 21, 1990, pp. 1, 3.

17. *Homeland*, October 18, 1989, pp. 1–2; *The Estonian Independent*, May 30, 1990, p. 3.

18. *Homeland*, June 7, 1989, p. 1; August 23, 1989, p. 2; December 27, 1989, p. 2; Hion, *Kes on kes*, p. 151.

19. *Baltic Forum* 6, no. 2 (1989): 77–79.

20. *Homeland*, May 17, 1989, p. 1; *The Estonian Independent*, May 16, 1990, p. 1; Dzintra Bungs, "The First Joint Session of the Baltic Parliaments," *Report on the USSR* 2, no. 50 (1990): 16–18.

21. *Homeland*, October 25, 1989, pp. 1–2.

22. Ibid., November 15, 1989, pp. 1–2.

23. Riina Kionka, "Economic Woes and Political Disputes," *Report on the USSR* 3, no. 1 (1991): 45–46; *Homeland*, April 4, 1990, p. 1, March 21, 1990, pp. 1–4.

24. *The Estonian Independent*, November 22, 1990, p. 1.

25. Ibid., May 9, 1990, p. 1; *Päevaleht*, May 9, 1990, p. 1.

26. Rein Taagepera, "The Baltic States," p. 308.

27. *The Estonian Independent*, May 23, 1990, pp. 1–2.

28. Kionka, "Economic Woes," p. 46; *The Estonian Independent*, October 4, 1990, p. 2; *Päevaleht*, January 27, 1991, p. 1.

29. *Homeland*, November 8, 1989, p. 2.

30. Ibid., April 5, 1989, p. 2; *New York Times*, December 18, 1990, p. A11.

31. *Nar. khoz. ESSR 1988*, p. 33; *Statistika Teataja* (1990): 2.

32. *Helsingin Sanomat*, February 1, 1991, p. C5; *Suomen Kuvalehti*, September 14, 1990, pp. 48–52.

33. Toivo Miljan, "The Proposal to Establish Economic Autonomy in Estonia," *Journal of Baltic Studies* 20 (1989): 154–60; *Edasi*, September 26, 1987, p. 3.

34. *New York Times*, December 30, 1990, p. A6.

35. *Nar. khoz. ESSR 1988*, pp. 12, 21; *Eesti arvudes 1989* (Tallinn: Eesti Riiklik Statistikaamet, 1990), pp. 16, 18–19, 133.

36. Egil Levits, "Die demographische Situation in der UdSSR und in den baltischen Staaten unter besonderer Berücksichtigung von nationalen und sprachsoziologischen Aspekten," *Acta Baltica* 21 (1981): 64; *Statistika Teataja* (1990): 1.

37. *Rahva Hääl*, September 19, 1989, p. 2; *Eesti arvudes 1989*, pp. 18, 133.

38. *Vestnik statistiki*, no. 11 (1980): 64; *Rahva Hääl*, September 19, 1989, p. 2; *Narodnoe khoziaistvo SSSR v 1989 g.* (Moscow: Finansy i Statistika, 1990), pp. 35–36.

39. *Vestnik statistiki*, no. 5 (1990): 63.

40. Ibid., no. 11 (1989): 69.

41. *Statistika Teataja* (1990): 1.

42. *The Estonian Independent*, March 7, 1991, p. 3.

43. Riina Kionka, "A Russian in Estonia Speaks Frankly about Non-Estonians," *Report on the USSR* 2, no. 39 (1990): 23.

44. *Statistika Teataja* (1990): 1.

45. For an analysis of Estonian-Russian relations, see Walter C. Clemens, Jr., *Baltic Independence and Russian Empire* (New York: St. Martin's Press, 1991).

46. *Roheline*, April 1990, p. 3.

47. *The Estonian Independent*, August 30, 1990, p. 3.

48. *Homeland*, July 5, 1989; *The Estonian Independent*, October 25, 1990, pp. 1–2. Päts's remains were discovered in the Kalinin (Tver) raion (RSFSR) in June 1990 by experts from Estonia and Lithuania.

49. See, for example, *Ausalt ja avameelselt Eesti suurmeestest* (Tallinn: Perioodika, 1990); Rein Ruutsoo, "Eesti omariiklus ja rahvuslik areng 1918–1940," in Kaarel Haav and Rein Ruutsoo, eds., *Eesti rahvas ja stalinlus* (Tallinn: Olion, 1990), pp. 56, 59; Evald Laasi, "Riigijuhid ajaloo ees," *Looming*, no. 3 (1990): 368, 373.

50. Evald Laasi, "Mõnede lünkade täiteks," *Sirp ja Vasar*, November 27, 1987, pp. 3–4; Evald Laasi, "Sissisõjast Eestis 1945–1953," *Looming*, no. 11 (1989): 1519–27; *1940 god v Estonii: Dokumenty i materialy* (Tallinn: Olion, 1989); *Molotov-Ribbentropi paktist baaside lepinguni: Dokumente ja materjale* (Tallinn: Perioodika, 1989), also published in Russian in 1990.

51. *Homeland*, February 21, 1990, p. 4.

52. *Helsingin Sanomat*, December 2, 1990, p. A18.

53. *Keeleseadusest* (Tallinn: Olion, 1990), pp. 6–12, 17; *Homeland*, January 25, 1989, pp. 1–2; *The Estonian Independent*, January 24, 1991, p. 8.

54. *Eesti ajalugu*, II (Tallinn: Valgus, 1989).

55. *Homeland*, November 29, 1989, p. 2; *Universitatis Tartuensis*, January 11, 1991, p. 3; "Tartu Ülikooli võimalikud arengusuunad 1990. a.–2000. a.," *Ülikool* 1, no. 4 (1989): 55–57.

56. Heino Kiik, "Maria Siberimaal," *Looming*, no. 7 (1987): 873–926, no. 8 (1987): 1011–62, also published as a book (Tallinn: Eesti Raamat, 1988); Raimond Kaugver, *Kirjad laagrist* (Tallinn: Kupar, 1989); Jaan Kross, "Silmade avamise päev," *Looming*, no. 3 (1987): 354–64; Jaan Kross, *Väljakaevamised* (Tallinn: Kupar, 1990). For a description of literary life in Estonia during *glasnost'* by an exile poet and critic, see Ivar Ivask, "At Home in Language and Poetry: Travel Impressions of Estonia, Latvia, Lithuania, and Russia, Autumn 1988," *World Literature Today* 63 (1989): 391–405.

57. *The 21st National Song Festival and the 14th National Dance Festival in Estonia* (Tallinn: Eesti Raamat, 1990), pp. 22, 35–37, 52–54; *The Estonian Independent*, July 4, 1990, p. 1.

58. *Homeland*, February 28, 1990, p. 1, March 21, 1990, p. 3.

59. *The Estonian Independent*, March 7, 1991, pp. 1, 3.

EPILOGUE

1. Czesław Miłosz, "The Lesson of the Baltics," *Baltic Forum* 1, no. 1 (1984): 8–9, 22–23.

2. Hans Kruus, "Väikerahvalik tunnetus eesti ühiskondlikus mõttes," *Ajalooline Ajakiri* 18 (1939): 136–47.

3. *Eesti kirjanduse ajalugu*, 4 vols. (Tallinn: Eesti Raamat, 1965–1984), 1: 401–2 (my translation—TUR).

Bibliography

NEWSPAPERS AND JOURNALS

(Only includes items published either in Estonia or elsewhere in the Estonian language)

Ajalooline Ajakiri (Historical journal). Tartu, 1922–1940.

Eesti Kirjandus (Estonian literature). Tartu, 1906–1940.

Eesti NSV Teaduste Akadeemia Toimetised: Ühiskonnateadused. Izvestiia Akademii Nauk Estonskoi SSR: Obshchestvennye nauki [ENSVTA Toimetised] (Proceedings of the Estonian SSR Academy of Sciences: Social Sciences). Tallinn, 1952–.

Eesti Päevaleht (The Estonian daily newspaper). Stockholm, 1944–.

Eesti Postimees (The Estonian courier). Tartu, 1864–1894; Tallinn, 1894–1905.

Eesti Statistika (Estonian statistics). Tallinn, 1922–1940.

The Estonian Independent. Tallinn, 1990–.

Homeland. Tallinn, 1985–1990.

Keel ja Kirjandus (Language and literature). Tallinn, 1958–.

Looming (Creation). Tallinn, 1923–1941, 1945–.

Nõukogude Kool (Soviet school). Tallinn, 1940–1941, 1945–.

Nõukogude Õpetaja (Soviet teacher). Tallinn, 1940–1941, 1945–.

Päevaleht (The daily newspaper). Tallinn, 1905–1940, 1990–.

Postimees (The courier). Tartu, 1886–1940, 1941–1944, 1991–.

Rahva Hääl (The people's voice). Tallinn, 1940–1941, 1944–.

Riigi Teataja (The state gazette). Tallinn, 1918–1940, 1990–.

Riigi Teataja Lisa (The state gazette supplement). Tallinn, 1921–1940.

Sirp ja Vasar (The hammer and the sickle). Tallinn, 1940–1941, 1944–1989.

Sovetskaia Estoniia (Soviet Estonia). Tallinn, 1940–1941, 1944–.

Teataja (The herald). Tallinn, 1901–1905.

Teataja (The herald). Stockholm, 1944–.

Uudised (The news). Tartu, 1903–1905.

Uus Eesti (New Estonia). Tallinn, 1935–1940.

Vaba Eesti (Free Estonia). Stockholm, 1951–1964.

Välis-Eesti (Estonia abroad). Stockholm, 1944–.

BOOKS AND ARTICLES

1869–1969: Juubelilaulupeo juht (1869–1969: Guide to the anniversary song festival). Tallinn: Eesti Raamat, 1969.

1922. a. üldrahvalugemise andmed (Data from the general population census of 1922). 11 vols. Tallinn: Riigi Statistika Keskbüroo, 1923–1927.

1940 god v Estonii: Dokumenty i materialy (The year 1940 in Estonia: Documents and materials). Tallinn: Olion, 1989.

II rahvaloendus Eestis (The second population census in Estonia). 4 vols. Tallinn: Riigi Statistika Keskbüroo, 1934–1937.

The 21st National Song Festival and the 14th Dance Festival in Estonia. Tallinn: Eesti Raamat, 1990.

25 aastat Nõukogude Eesti trükisõna 1940–1965 (25 years of the Soviet Estonian printed word, 1940–1965). Tallinn: Eesti Raamat, 1971.

25 aastat Nõukogude Eestit: Statistiline kogumik (25 years of Soviet Estonia: Statistical collection). Tallinn: Eesti Raamat, 1965.

Ahven, Eeva. *Eesti kirjakeele arenemine aastail 1900–1917* (The development of written Estonian in the years 1900–1917). Tallinn: Eesti Riiklik Kirjastus, 1958.

Alma mater Tartuensis. Tallinn: Valgus, 1977.

Amburger, Erik. *Geschichte der Behördenorganisation Russlands von Peter dem Grossen bis 1917*. Leiden: E. J. Brill, 1966.

Anderson, Edgar. "The Baltic Entente: Phantom or Reality?" In V. Stanley Vardys and Romuald J. Misiunas, eds., *The Baltic States in Peace and War, 1917–1945*. University Park: The Pennsylvania State University Press, 1978, pp. 126–35.

———. "The Pacts of Mutual Assistance Between the USSR and the Baltic States." In Arvids Ziedonis, Jr., William L. Winter, and Mardi Valgemäe, eds. *Baltic History*. Columbus, Ohio: Association for the Advancement of Baltic Studies, 1974, pp. 239–55.

Andresen, Lembit. *Eesti rahvakoolid 19. sajandil kuni 1880-ndate aastate koolireformini* (Estonian elementary schools in the nineteenth century up to the school reform of the 1880s). Tallinn: Valgus, 1974.

———, ed. *Eesti rahvakoolide seadused 18. ja 19. sajandil* (Estonian elementary school laws in the eighteenth and nineteenth centuries). Tallinn: Eesti NSV Kõrgema ja Kesk-Erihariduse Ministeerium, 1973.

Angelus, Oskar. *Tuhande valitseja maa* (Land of a thousand rulers). Stockholm: EMP, 1956.

Antik, Richard. *Eesti raamat 1535–1935* (The Estonian book, 1535–1935). Tartu: n.p., 1936.

Arens, Olavi. "Bolshevik Policies in Estonia During 1917–18." Paper delivered at the Sixth Conference on Baltic Studies, Toronto, Ontario, Canada, May 11–14, 1978.

———. "The Estonian *Maapäev* During 1917." In V. Stanley Vardys and Romuald J. Misiunas, eds., *The Baltic States in Peace and War, 1917–1945*. University Park: The Pennsylvania State University Press, 1978, pp. 19–30.

———. "Revolutionary Developments in Estonia in 1917–18 and Their Ideological and Political Background." Ph.D. dissertation, Columbia University, 1976.

———. "Soviets in Estonia, 1917/1918." In Andrew Ezergailis and Gert von Pistohlkors, eds., *Die baltischen Provinzen Russlands zwischen den Revolutionen von 1905 und 1917*. Quellen und Studien zur baltischen Geschichte, no. 4. Cologne: Böhlau, 1982, pp. 295–314.

Ariste, Paul. "Über die früheste Entwicklungsstufe der ostseefinnischen Sprachen." *ENSVTA Toimetised* 10 (1961): 260–67.

———. "Uudset liivlaste minevikust" (New findings on the past of the Livonians). *Keel ja Kirjandus* 18 (1975): 442–43.

Ast, Karl. "Demokraatliku Eesti loojakul" (At the sunset of democratic Estonia). *Vaba Eesti*, no. 1 (1955): 1–2, 7.

Aun, Karl. "The Cultural Autonomy of National Minorities in Estonia." *Yearbook of the Estonian Learned Society in America* 1 (1951–1953): 26–41.

Ausalt ja avameelselt Eesti suurmeestest (Honestly and candidly about Estonia's great men). Tallinn: Perioodika, 1990.

"Baltic Yearbook." Appendix to *Baltic Countries* 1, no. 1 (August 1935): 1–11.

Blum, Jerome. "The Rise of Serfdom in Eastern Europe." *American Historical Review* 62 (1957): 807–36.

Blumfeldt, Evald. "Reduktionen på Ösel" (The reduction on Saaremaa). *Svio-Estonica* 14 (1958): 109–71.

Browder, Robert P., and Kerensky, Alexander, eds. *The Russian Provisional Government*, 3 vols. Stanford: Stanford University Press, 1961.

Brundage, James A., ed. and trans. *The Chronicle of Henry of Livonia*. Madison: University of Wisconsin Press, 1961.

Bungs, Dzintra. "The First Joint Session of the Baltic Parliaments." *Report on the USSR* 2, no. 50 (1990): 16–18.

Christiansen, Eric. *The Northern Crusades: The Baltic and Catholic Frontier, 1100–1525*. Minneapolis: University of Minnesota Press, 1980.

Clemens, Walter C., Jr. *Baltic Independence and Russian Empire.* New York: St. Martin's Press, 1991.

Crowe, David M., Jr. "Great Britain and the Baltic States, 1938–1939." In V. Stanley Vardys and Romuald J. Misiunas, eds., *The Baltic States in Peace and War, 1917–1945.* University Park: The Pennsylvania State University Press, 1978, pp. 110–19.

Crowley, E. L., et al., eds., *Prominent Personalities in the USSR.* Methuen, N.J.: Scarecrow Press, 1968.

Dallin, Alexander. "The Baltic States Between Nazi Germany and Soviet Russia." In V. Stanley Vardys and Romuald J. Misiunas, eds., *The Baltic States in Peace and War, 1917–1945.* University Park: The Pennsylvania State University Press, 1978, pp. 97–109.

———. *German Rule in Russia, 1941–1945: A Study in Occupation Policies.* London: Macmillan, 1957.

Dellingshausen, Eduard von. *Im Dienste der Heimat!* Stuttgart: Ausland und Heimat Verlag, 1930.

Eckardt, Julius. *Livland im achtzehnten Jahrhundert.* Vol. 1. Leipzig: F. A. Brockhaus, 1876.

Eesti: 20 aastat iseseisvust sõnas ja pildis (Estonia: Twenty years of independence in words and pictures). Tallinn: Konjunktuurinstituut, 1939.

Eesti ajalugu (History of Estonia). 3 vols. Tartu: Eesti Kirjanduse Selts, 1935–1940.

Eesti arhitektuuri ajalugu (History of Estonian architecture). Tallinn: Eesti Raamat, 1965.

Eesti arvudes 1920–1935 (Estonia in numbers, 1920–1935). Tallinn: Riigi Statistika Keskbüroo, 1937.

Eesti arvudes 1989 (Estonia in numbers, 1989). Tallinn: Eesti Riiklik Statistikaamet, 1990.

Eesti biograafiline leksikon (Estonian biographical dictionary). Tartu: Loodus, 1926–1929.

Eesti biograafilise leksikoni täiendusköide (Estonian biographical dictionary, supplementary volume). Tartu: Loodus, 1940.

Eesti entsüklopeedia (Estonian encyclopedia). 8 vols. & supplement. Tartu: Loodus, 1932–1940.

Eesti karskuse seltside aastaraamat (Yearbook of the Estonian temperance societies). Vol. 8. Tartu: H. Laas, 1905.

Eesti kirjanduse ajalugu (History of Estonian literature). 4 vols. Tallinn: Eesti Raamat, 1965–1984.

Eesti kirjanduse biograafiline leksikon (Biographical dictionary of Estonian literature). Tallinn: Eesti Raamat, 1975.

Eesti kroonika 1932 (Estonian chronicle, 1932). Tartu: Eesti Kirjanduse Selts, 1933.

Eesti kroonika 1936 (Estonian chronicle, 1936). Tartu: Eesti Kirjanduse Selts, 1937.

Eesti kroonika 1938 (Estonian chronicle, 1938). Tartu: Eesti Kirjanduse Selts, 1939.

Eesti kunsti ajalugu (History of Estonian art). 2 vols. Tallinn: Kunst, 1970–1977.

Eestimaa Kommunistliku Partei XVIII Kongress (Eighteenth congress of the Estonian Communist Party). Tallinn: Eesti Raamat, 1981.

Eestimaa Sõja-Revolutsioonikomitee (The Military-Revolutionary Committee of Estonia). Tallinn: Eesti Raamat, 1977.

Eesti majandusajalugu (Economic history of Estonia). Vol. 1. Tartu: Akadeemiline Kooperatiiv, 1937.

Eesti muusika (Estonian music). 2 vols. Tallinn: Eesti Raamat, 1968–1975.

Eesti nõukogude entsüklopeedia, 2d ed. (Estonian Soviet encyclopedia). 10 vols. Tallinn: Valgus, 1985–. Beginning with vol. 5 (1990) title changed to *Eesti entsüklopeedia* (Estonian encyclopedia).

Eesti Nõukogude Sotsialistliku Vabariigi konstitutsioon (põhiseadus) (The constitution of the Estonian Soviet Socialist Republic). Tallinn: Eesti Raamat, 1978.

Eesti NSV 1975. a. üldlaulu- ja tantsupeo teatmik (Handbook of the Estonian SSR national song and dance festival, 1975). Tallinn: Eesti Raamat, 1975.

Eesti NSV ajalugu (History of the Estonian SSR). 3 vols. Tallinn: Eesti Riiklik Kirjastus, 1955–1963; Eesti Raamat, 1971.

Eesti NSV kolhoosnikute esimene kongress (First congress of Estonian SSR kolkhozniks). Tallinn: Poliitiline Kirjandus, 1949.

Eesti NSV rahvamajandus (The national economy of the Estonian SSR). Tallinn: Eesti Riiklik Kirjastus, 1957.

Eesti NSV Ülemnõukogu IX koosseis (Composition of the Ninth Estonian SSR Supreme Soviet). Tallinn: Eesti Raamat, 1976.

Eesti NSV Ülemnõukogu X koosseis (Composition of the Tenth Estonian SSR Supreme Soviet). Tallinn: Eesti Raamat, 1981.

Eesti rahva ajalugu (History of the Estonian people). 3 vols. Tartu: Loodus, 1932–1937.

Eesti rahvas Nõukogude Liidu Suures Isamaasõjas (The Estonian people in the Great Patriotic War of the Soviet Union). 2 vols. Tallinn: Eesti Raamat, 1971–1977.

Eesti riik ja rahvas Teises maailmasõjas (The Estonian state and people in the Second World War). 10 vols. Stockholm: EMP, 1954–1962.

"Eesti saadikute märgukiri Vene keiser Aleksander III-le 19. juunist 1881" (Memorandum from Estonian representatives to the Russian tsar Alexander III on June 19, 1881). *Eesti Kirjandus* 15 (1921): 346–49.

Eesti saatusaastad 1945–1960 (Estonia's fateful years, 1945–1960). 6 vols. Stockholm: EMP, 1963–1972.

Eisen, Matthias J. "Eesti rahva arv" (The size of the Estonian people). *Eesti Kirjandus* 4 (1909): 213–38, 257–66, 289–98, 339–42.

Eliaser, Rutt. *Passita ja pajata* (Without a passport or a pot). Lund: Eesti Kirjanike Kooperatiiv, 1985.

Entsiklopedicheskii slovar' (Encyclopedic dictionary). 41 vols. Leipzig: F. A. Brokgauz; St. Petersburg: I. A. Efron, 1890–1904.

Estonian Official Guide. Baltimore: Baltimore Estonian Society, 1972.

Estonian War of Independence, 1918–1920. New York: Eesti Vabadusvõitlejate Liit, n.d.

Faehlmann, Friedrich R. "Mein Streit mit Nolcken und Liphart." In *Talurahvaliikumine Eestis 1841.–1842. aastal: Dokumentide kogumik.* Tallinn: Eesti Raamat, 1982, pp. 240–47.

Fainshtein, V. "Perekhod ot trekhpol'ia k plodosmenu v Estliandskom pomeshchich'em khoziaistve" (The transition from the three-field system to crop rotation on landed estates in Estland). In *Eesti NSV ajaloo küsimusi,* vol. 7. Tartu Riikliku Ülikooli Toimetised, no. 290. Tartu: Tartu Riiklik Ülikool, 1972, pp. 161–207.

Feinstein, Stephen C. "The Avant-Garde in Soviet Estonia." In Norton Dodge and Alison Holt, eds., *New Art from the Soviet Union.* Washington, D.C.: Acropolis Books, 1977, pp. 31–34.

Garleff, Michael. *Deutschbaltische Politik zwischen den Weltkriegen.* Quellen und Studien zur baltischen Geschichte, no. 2. Bonn-Bad Godesberg: Wissenschaftliches Archiv, 1976.

Gimbutas, Marija. *The Goddesses and Gods of Old Europe, 6500–3500 B.C.: Myths and Cult Images.* Rev. ed. Berkeley: University of California Press, 1982.

Graham, Malbone W. *New Governments of Eastern Europe.* New York: Henry Holt, 1927.

Grechkina, Elsa. "Kompleksnyi podkhod k problemam prepodavaniia russkogo iazyka v Estonii" (A complex approach to the problem of teaching the Russian language in Estonia). In *Russkii iazyk – iazyk druzhby i sotrudnichestva narodov SSSR.* Moscow: Nauka, 1981, pp. 200–5.

Grenzstein, Ado. *Herrenkirche oder Volkskirche?* Tartu: A. Grenzstein, 1899.

Haas, Werner. *Europa will leben: Die nationalen Erneuerungsbewegungen in Wort und Bild.* Berlin: Batschari, 1936.

Haav, Kaarel and Ruutsoo, Rein, eds. *Eesti rahvas ja stalinlus* (The Estonian people and Stalinism). Tallinn: Olion, 1990.

Hajdú, Péter. "Linguistic Background of Genetic Relationships." In Péter Hajdú, ed., *Ancient Cultures of the Uralian Peoples.* Budapest: Corvina Press, 1976, pp. 11–46.

Haltzel, Michael H. "The Baltic Germans." In Edward C. Thaden et al., *Russification in the Baltic Provinces and Finland, 1855–1914.* Princeton, N.J.: Princeton University Press, 1981, pp. 111–204.

Harcave, Sidney. *First Blood: The Russian Revolution of 1905.* New York: Macmillan, 1964.

Hehn, Jürgen von. *Die Umsiedlung der baltischen Deutschen – das letzte Kapitel baltisch-deutscher Geschichte.* Marburger Ostforschungen, no. 40. Marburg/Lahn: J. G. Herder-Institut, 1982.

Helbe, A. "Esseeride tegevusest Eestis Oktoobrirevolutsiooni võidu ja Nõukogude võimu kindlustamise perioodil" (On SR activity in Estonia during the period of the victory of the October Revolution and the consolidation of Soviet power). In *Eesti*

NSV ajaloo küsimusi, vol. 6. Tartu Riikliku Ülikooli Toimetised, no. 258. Tartu: Tartu Riiklik Ülikool, 1970, pp. 355–98.

Helk, Vello. "Die Jesuiten in Dorpat." *Zeitschrift für Ostforschung* 12 (1963): 673–87.

Herranen, Timo, and Myllyntaus, Timo. "Effects of the First World War on the Engineering Industries of Estonia and Finland." *Scandinavian Economic History Review* 32 (1984): 121–42.

Hiden, John and Loit, Aleksander, eds. *The Baltic in International Relations Between the Two World Wars*. Studia Baltica Stockholmiensa, no. 3. Stockholm: Almqvist & Wiksell International, 1988.

Hinkkanen-Lievonen, Merja-Liisa. *British Trade and Enterprise in the Baltic States, 1919–1925*. Studia Historica, no. 14. Helsinki: Suomen Historiallinen Seura, 1984.

Hion, Ene, ed. *Ausalt ja avameelselt Eesti parteidest* (Honestly and candidly about Estonia's political parties). 2 vols. Tallinn: Perioodika, 1990.

———. *Ausalt ja avameelselt EKP Keskkomitee VIII pleenumist, Karotammest ja Käbinist, hinge harimatusest* (Honestly and candidly about the ECP Central Committee's VIII plenum, Karotamm and Käbin, and lack of culture). Tallinn: Perioodika, 1989.

———. *Kes on kes Eesti poliitikas* (Who's who in Estonian politics). Tallinn: Olion, 1990.

Hovi, Kalervo. "Polish-Finnish Cooperation in Border-State Policy, 1919–1922." *Journal of Baltic Studies* 14 (1983): 121–27.

Hurt, Jakob. "Kõne esimesel Eesti üldlaulupeol 1869" (Speech at the first all-Estonian song festival, 1869). In Hans Kruus, ed., *Jakob Hurda kõned ja avalikud kirjad*. Tartu: Eesti Kirjanduse Selts, 1939, pp. 33–48.

———. "Meie koolitatud ja haritud meestest" (On our educated men). In Hans Kruus, ed., *Jakob Hurda kõned ja avalikud kirjad*. Tartu: Eesti Kirjanduse Selts, 1939, pp. 64–79.

———. "Über die pleskauer esten oder die sogenannten setukesen [*sic*]." *Anzeiger der Finnisch-ugrischen Forschungen* 3 (1903): 185–205.

Hyvämäki, Lauri. "Fasistiset ilmiöt Baltian maissa ja Suomessa 1920-luvun lopussa ja 1930-luvulla" (Fascist manifestations in the Baltic countries and Finland at the end of the 1920s and in the 1930s). *Historiallinen Arkisto* 72 (1977): 113–37.

Ibius, Otu. "Balti mõisnike katsed eesti põllumeeseseltside sõltuvuses hoidmiseks XIX sajandi teisel poolel" (The attempts of Baltic estate owners to keep Estonian agricultural societies dependent on them in the second half of the nineteenth century). *ENSVTA Toimetised* 15 (1966): 403–19.

Indreko, Richard. "Soome-ugrilaste päritolust ja asualast" (On the origins and settlement of the Finno-Ugrians). *Virittäjä* 51 (1947): 314–23.

Isakov [Issakov], Sergei G. *Ostzeiskii vopros v russkoi pechati 1860-kh godov* (The Baltic question in the Russian press in the 1860s). Tartu Riikliku Ülikooli Toimetised, no. 107. Tartu: Tartu Riiklik Ülikool, 1961.

Isamaa kalender 1905 aasta jaoks (Fatherland calendar for 1905). Tartu: Schnaken-burg, 1904.

Issakov [Isakov], Sergei G. "Uusi andmeid Eesti Kirjameeste Seltsi sulgemise kohta" (New data on the closing of the Society of Estonian Literati). *Keel ja Kirjandus* 13 (1970): 289–94.

Istoriia Estonskoi SSR (History of the Estonian SSR). 3 vols. Tallinn: Estonskoe Gosudarstvennoe Izdatel'stvo, 1961; Eesti Raamat, 1966–1974.

Itogi Vsesoiuznoi perepisi naseleniia 1959 goda: Estonskaia SSR (Results of the all-Union population census of 1959: The Estonian SSR). Moscow: Gosstatizdat, 1962.

Itogi Vsesoiuznoi perepisi naseleniia 1970 goda (Results of the all-Union population census of 1970). 7 vols. Moscow: Statistika, 1972–1974.

Ivask, Ivar. "At Home in Language and Poetry: Travel Impressions of Estonia, Latvia, Lithuania and Russia, Autumn 1988." *World Literature Today* 63 (1989): 391–405.

Jaanits, Lembit. "Soomeugrilaste hargnemisest arheoloogia andmeil" (The branching apart of the Finno-Ugrians based on archaeological data). *Keel ja Kirjandus* 16 (1973): 711–24.

Jaanits, Lembit; Laul, S.; Lõugas, V.; and Tõnisson, E. *Eesti esiajalugu* (Prehistory of Estonia). Tallinn: Eesti Raamat, 1982.

Jackson, J. Hampden. *Estonia*, 2d ed. London: George Allen & Unwin, 1948.

Jakobson, Carl Robert. *Valitud teosed* (Selected works). 2 vols. Tallinn: Eesti Riiklik Kirjastus, 1959.

Jansen, Ea. *Carl Robert Jakobsoni "Sakala"* (Carl Robert Jakobson's *Sakala*). Tallinn: Eesti Raamat, 1971.

———. "Killukesi naisküsimuse ajaloost" (Aspects of the history of the women's question). *Looming*, no. 3 (1975): 470–80.

———. "'Sakala' kaastööliste sotsiaalsest ja kutselisest jagunemisest" (The social and occupational classification of *Sakala*'s correspondents). *ENSVTA Toimetised* 14 (1965): 435–49.

Janusson, J. "The Economic Structure of Estonia." *Baltic Countries* 1, no. 2 (December 1935): 192–97.

Järvesoo, Elmar. "Early Agricultural Education at Tartu University." *Journal of Baltic Studies* 11 (1980): 341–55.

———. "Estonia's Declaration of Independence in 1918: An Episode of Collision Between National-Revolutionary and Bolshevist Ideologies." In Arvids Ziedonis, Jr., William L. Winter, and Mardi Valgemäe, eds., *Baltic History*. Columbus, Ohio: Association for the Advancement of Baltic Studies, 1974, pp. 161–73.

———. "The Postwar Economic Transformation." In Tõnu Parming and Elmar Jär-vesoo, eds., *A Case Study of a Soviet Republic: The Estonian SSR*. Boulder, Colo.: Westview Press, 1978, pp. 131–90.

———. "Progress Despite Collectivization." In Arvids Ziedonis, Jr., Rein Taagepera, and Mardi Valgemäe, eds., *Problems of Mininations: Baltic Perspectives*. San Jose, Calif.: Association for the Advancement of Baltic Studies, 1973, pp. 137–49.

————. "Die Wirtschaft Estlands und deren strukturelle Veränderungen." *Acta Baltica* 9 (1969): 9–45.

Johansen, Paul. *Siedlung und Agrarwesen der Esten im Mittelalter*. Verhandlungen der Gelehrten Estnischen Gesellschaft, no. 23. Tartu: Gelehrte Estnische Gesellschaft, 1925.

Johansen, Paul, and Mühlen, Heinz von zur. *Deutsch und Undeutsch im mittelalterlichen und frühneuzeitlichen Reval*. Cologne: Böhlau, 1973.

Jordan, Paul. *Die Resultate der ehstländischen Volkszählung vom 29. December 1881 in textlicher Beleuchtung*. Tallinn: Lindfors' Erben, 1886.

————, ed. *Ergebnisse der ehstländischen Volkszählung*. 3 vols. Tallinn: Lindfors' Erben, 1883–1885.

Juhanson, Voldemar. "Esimesed eesti üliõpilased Tartu Ülikoolis ja Eesti Üliõpilaste Selts" (The first Estonian students at Tartu University and the Estonian Student Society). In Juhan Vasar, ed., *Tartu üliõpilaskonna ajalugu seoses eesti üliõpilaskonna ajalooga*. Tartu: Tartu Üliõpilaskond, 1932, pp. 89–122.

Jung-Stilling, Friedrich von, and Anders, W., eds., *Ergebnisse der livländischen Volkszählung*. 3 vols. Riga: Stahl'sche Buchdruckerei, 1883–1885.

Jürgenstein, Anton. "Jaan Tõnissoni elulugu" (Jaan Tõnisson's biography). In *Jaan Tõnisson: Tagasivaateid ja mälestusi tema 60. a. sünnipäevaks*. Tartu: Postimees, 1928, pp. 5–36.

————. "Noor-Eesti: Peatükk uuemast Eesti kulturalisest edenemisloost" (Young-Estonia: A chapter in recent Estonian cultural development). In W. Reiman, ed., *Eesti Kultura*, 4 vols. Tartu: Postimees, 1911–1915, 1: 95–126.

Kaelas, Aleksander. *Das sowetisch besetzte Estland*. Stockholm: Eesti Rahvusfond, 1958.

————. *The Worker in the Soviet Paradise*. East and West, no. 2. London: Boreas, 1947.

Kahk, Juhan. *1858. aasta talurahvarahutused Eestis: Mahtra sõda* (Peasant unrest in Estonia in 1858: The war at Mahtra). Tallinn: Eesti Riiklik Kirjastus, 1958.

————. *Die Krise der feudalen Landwirtschaft in Estland (Das zweite Viertel des 19. Jahrhunderts)*. Tallinn: Eesti Raamat, 1969.

————. *Rahutused ja reformid* (Unrest and reforms). Tallinn: Eesti Riiklik Kirjastus, 1961.

Kahk, Juhan; Ligi, Herbert; and Tarvel, Enn. *Beiträge zur marxistischen Agrargeschichte Estlands der Feudalzeit*. Tallinn: Eesti Raamat, 1974.

Kahu, Meelik. "C. R. Jakobsoni 'Sakala' levikust" (The dissemination of C. R. Jakobson's *Sakala*). *Keel ja Kirjandus* 7 (1964): 138–43, 211–17.

Kareda, Endel. *Estonia in the Soviet Grip: Life and Conditions Under Soviet Occupation, 1947–1949*. East and West, no. 5. London: Boreas, 1949.

————. *Technique of Economic Sovietisation*. East and West, no. 3. London: Boreas, 1947.

Karjahärm, Toomas. "Eesti linnakodanluse poliitilisest formeerumisest 1870-ndate aastate lõpust kuni 1914. aastani (linna- ja duumavalimiste materjalide põhjal)"

(On the political formation of the Estonian urban bourgeoisie from the end of the 1870s to 1914 [based on municipal and duma election materials]). *ENSVTA Toimetised* 23 (1973): 251–65.

————. "Eesti rahvusliku haritlaskonna kujunemisest möödunud sajandi lõpul ja praeguse algul" (On the formation of the Estonian national intelligentsia at the end of the last century and the beginning of the current one). *Keel ja Kirjandus* 16 (1973): 624–30.

Karjahärm, Toomas, and Kivimäe, Sirje. "Maaomavalitsusküsimus Eesti ühiskondlikus liikumises kodanlik-demokraatlike revolutsioonide ajajärgul" (The question of local self-government in the Estonian sociopolitical movement during the period of the bourgeois-democratic revolutions). *ENSVTA Toimetised* 29 (1980): 324–41.

Karjahärm, Toomas, and Pullat, Raimo. *Eesti revolutsiooni tules 1905–1907* (Estonia in the fire of revolution, 1905–1907). Tallinn: Eesti Raamat, 1975.

Karma, Otto. *Tööstuslikult revolutsioonilt sotsialistlikule revolutsioonile Eestis: Tööstuse arenemine 1917. aastani* (From the industrial revolution to the socialist revolution in Estonia: Industrial development to 1917). Tallinn: Eesti NSV Teaduste Akadeemia Ajaloo Institut, 1963.

Karu, Ellen. "Muusikaseltside asutamisest Eestis 19. sajandi teisel poolel" (On the establishment of musical societies in Estonia in the second half of the nineteenth century). In *Eesti talurahva majanduse ja olme arengujooni 19. ja 20. sajandil.* Tallinn: Eesti NSV Teaduste Akadeemia Ajaloo Instituut, 1979, pp. 50–68.

Kasemaa, Olavi. "Orkestrimänguharrastuse ulatus ja levik Eestis aastail 1818–1917" (The extent and spread of amateur orchestras in Estonia in the years 1818–1917). *ENSVTA Toimetised* 32 (1983): 44–66.

Kaslas, Bronius J. *The USSR-German Aggression Against Lithuania.* New York: Robert Speller & Sons, 1973.

Katz, Zev, ed. *Handbook of Major Soviet Nationalities.* New York: The Free Press, 1975.

Keeleseadusest (On the language law). Tallinn: Olion, 1990.

Kelam, Aili. *Eesti NSV perekond: Sotsioloogiline portree* (The Estonian SSR family: A sociological portrait). Tallinn: Eesti Raamat, 1980.

Kiin, Sirje; Ruutsoo, Rein; and Tarand, Andres. *40 kirja lugu* (The story of the letter of the 40). Tallinn: Olion, 1990.

Kionka, Riina. "Economic Woes and Political Disputes." *Report on the USSR* 3, no. 1 (1991): 45–47.

————. "The Estonian Citizens' Committee: An Opposition Movement of a Different Complexion." *Report on the USSR* 2, no. 6 (1990): 30–33.

————. "A Russian Speaks Frankly About Non-Estonians." *Report on the USSR* 2, no. 39 (1990): 22–24.

Kirby, David. "Morality or Expediency: The Baltic Question in British-Soviet Relations, 1941–1942." In V. Stanley Vardys and Romuald J. Misiunas, eds., *The Baltic States in Peace and War, 1917–1945.* University Park: The Pennsylvania State University Press, 1978, pp. 159–72.

Kivimäe, Sirje. "Die Agrarreform Stolypins in den baltischen Gouvernements." In Andrew Ezergailis and Gert von Pistohlkors, eds., *Die baltischen Provinzen Russlands zwischen den Revolutionen von 1905 und 1917*. Quellen und Studien zur baltischen Geschichte, no. 4. Cologne: Böhlau, 1982, pp. 93–114.

Klesment, Johannes. "The Forms of Baltic Resistance to the Communists." *The Baltic Review*, no. 8 (1956): 24–42.

Kommunisticheskaia partiia Estonii v tsifrakh 1920–1980 (The Communist Party of Estonia in numbers, 1920–1980). Tallinn: Eesti Raamat, 1983.

Konks, Jaan. "Maavaldusest Eestimaal aastail 1900–1917 (Landholding in Estland in the years 1900–1917). In *Sotsiaal-majandusliku arengu probleeme XVII–XX sajandil*. Tartu Riikliku Ülikooli Toimetised, no. 454. Tartu: Tartu Riiklik Ülikool, 1979, pp. 73–96.

Köörna, Arno. *Suure Sotsialistliku Oktoobrirevolutsiooni majanduslikud eeldused Eestis*. (Economic preconditions of the Great Socialist October Revolution in Estonia). Tallinn: Eesti Riiklik Kirjastus, 1961.

Köstner, Nikolai. "Rahva arvu kasvamine Eestimaal" (Population growth in Estland). In *Noor-Eesti*, 5 vols. Tartu: Noor-Eesti, 1905–1915, 5: 33–124.

Kreutzwald, Fr. R., comp. *Kalevipoeg: An Ancient Estonian Tale*. Translated by Jüri Kurman. Moorestown, N.J.: Symposia Press, 1982.

Kroeger, Erhard. *Der Auszug aus der alten Heimat*. Tübingen: Verlag der deutschen Hochschullehrer-Zeitung, 1967.

Kruus, Hans. *Eesti Aleksandrikool* (The Estonian Alexander school). Tartu: Noor-Eesti, 1939.

———. *Grundriss der Geschichte des estnischen Volkes*. Tartu: Akadeemiline Kooperatiiv, 1932.

———. "Murdekuudel 1917–1918" (During critical months, 1917–1918). *Looming*, no. 9 (1933): 1026–41.

———. "Opositsioon Tallinna linnaomavalitsuses 1877–1904" (The opposition in the Tallinn city government, 1877–1904). *Ajalooline Ajakiri* 17 (1938): 97–121.

———. *Saksa okkupatsioon Eestis* (The German occupation in Estonia). Tartu: Odamees, 1920.

———. *Talurahva käärimine Lõuna-Eestis XIX sajandi 40-ndail aastail* (Ferment among the peasantry in southern Estonia in the 1840s). Tartu: Eesti Kirjanduse Selts, 1930.

———. "Väikerahvalik tunnetus eesti ühiskondlikus mõttes" (The consciousness of being a small people in Estonian social thought). *Ajalooline Ajakiri* 18 (1939): 136–47.

———, ed. *Eesti ajaloo lugemik* (Estonian history reader). 3 vols. Tartu: Eesti Kirjanduse Selts, 1924–1929.

———, ed. *Punased aastad: Mälestusi ja dokumente 1905. aasta liikumisest Eestis* (Red years: Memoirs and documents from the 1905 movement in Estonia). Tartu: Eesti Kirjanduse Selts, 1932.

Küng, Andres. *A Dream of Freedom: Four Decades of National Survival Versus Russian*

Imperialism in Estonia, Latvia, and Lithuania, 1940–1980. Cardiff, Wales: Boreas, 1980.

————. *Estland—en studie i imperialism* (Estonia—a study in imperialism). Stockholm: Aldus/Bonniers, 1971.

Künnapas, Teodor, and Järvesoo, Elmar. "The Structure of Higher Education and Research." In Tönu Parming and Elmar Järvesoo, eds., *A Case Study of a Soviet Republic: The Estonian SSR.* Boulder, Colo.: Westview Press, 1978, pp. 343–68.

Kurman, George. *The Development of Written Estonian.* Indiana University Publications. Uralic and Altaic Series, no. 90. The Hague: Mouton, 1968.

————. "Estonian Literature." In Tönu Parming and Elmar Järvesoo, eds., *A Case Study of a Soviet Republic: The Estonian SSR.* Boulder, Colo.: Westview Press, 1978, pp. 247–80.

————. "Literary Censorship in General and in Soviet Estonia." *Journal of Baltic Studies* 8 (1977): 3–15.

Kurs, O. "On General Tendencies in the Development of the Administrative Division of the Estonian SSR." In *Estonia: Geographical Studies.* Tallinn: Academy of Sciences of the Estonian SSR, 1972, pp. 144–50.

Kutt, Aleksander. "A Review and the Meaning of Developments in Estonia Since 1953." *The Baltic Review*, no. 12 (1957): 14–40.

Kuuli, Olaf. *Revolutsioon Eestis 1940* (Revolution in Estonia, 1940). Tallinn: Eesti Raamat, 1980.

————. *Vapsidest Isamaaliiduni: Fašismi ja fašismivastase võitluse ajaloost kodanlikus Eestis* (From the League of Veterans to the Fatherland League: On the history of fascism and the antifascist movement in bourgeois Estonia). Tallinn: Eesti Raamat, 1976.

Kuusberg, A., ed. *Materjale Maltsveti-liikumise kohta* (Materials on the Maltsvet movement). Tartu: Loodus, 1931.

Laaman, Eduard. *Eesti iseseisvuse sünd* (The birth of Estonian independence). Stockholm: Vaba Eesti, 1964; first published, 1936.

————. *Eesti ühiskond* (Estonian society). Tartu: Eesti Kirjanduse Selts, 1936.

————. "Põhiseaduse kriisi arenemine 1928–1933" (The development of the constitutional crisis, 1928–1933). In *Põhiseadus ja rahvuskogu.* Tallinn: Rahvuskogu Üldkoosoleku Juhatus, 1937, pp. 29–45.

Laar, Mart, ed. *14. juuni 1941* (June 14, 1941). Stockholm: Välis-Eesti & EMP, 1990.

Laasi, Evald. "Riigijuhid ajaloo ees" (State leaders in the face of history). *Looming*, no. 3 (1990): 368–74.

————. "Sissisõjast Eestis 1945–1953" (On guerrilla war in Estonia, 1945–1953). *Looming*, no. 11 (1989): 1519–27.

Laretei, Heinrich. "Baaside ajastu välispoliitika" (The foreign policy of the era of Soviet bases). In *Minevikust tulevikku.* Stockholm: EÜS Põhjala, 1954, pp. 19–25.

————. *Saatuse mängukanniks* (The plaything of fate). Lund: Eesti Kirjanike Kooperatiiv, 1970.

Nõukogude Eesti: Entsüklopeediline teatmeteos (Soviet Estonia: An encyclopedic reference work). 2d ed. Tallinn: Valgus, 1978.

Nõukogude Eesti raamat 1940–1954 (The Soviet Estonian book, 1940–1954). Tallinn: Eesti Riiklik Kirjastus, 1956.

Nõukogude Eesti raamat 1955–1965 (The Soviet Estonian book, 1955–1965). Tallinn: Eesti Raamat, 1972.

Nõukogude Eesti saavutusi 20 aasta jooksul: Statistiline kogumik (The achievements of Soviet Estonia during twenty years: Statistical collection). Tallinn: Eesti Riiklik Kirjastus, 1960.

Nõukogude Eesti trükisõna 1966–1975 (The printed word in Soviet Estonia, 1966–1975). Tallinn: Eesti Raamat, 1978.

Obzor Estliandskoi gubernii za 1913 god (Survey of the province of Estland for 1913). Tallinn: Estliandskaia Gubernskaia Tipografiia, 1914. Prilozhenie no. 23.

Õisman, J. "Maareformi teostamine Eestis" (The implementation of land reform in Estonia). *Eesti Statistika*, nos. 6–8 (1922): 49–68.

Öpik, Elina. *Talurahva mõisavastane võitlus Eestis Põhjasõja esimesel poolel 1700–1710* (The anti-estate struggle by the peasantry in Estonia in the first half of the Great Northern War, 1700–1710). Tallinn: Eesti NSV Teaduste Akadeemia Ajaloo Instituut, 1964.

Oras, Ants. *Baltic Eclipse*. London: Victor Gollancz, 1948.

―――. *Marie Under*. Lund: Eesti Kirjanike Kooperatiiv, 1963.

Ots, August. *Mehed sündmuste kurvidel* (Men at turning points). Stockholm: Andromeda, 1976.

"Pact of Mutual Assistance Between the USSR and Estonia." *Lituanus* 14, no. 2 (1968): 94–96.

Page, Stanley. *The Formation of the Baltic States*. New York: Howard Fertig, 1970; first published, 1959.

Palgi, Daniel, ed. *Raamatu osa Eesti arengus* (The role of the book in the development of Estonia). Tartu: Eesti Kirjanduse Selts, 1935.

Palli, Heldur. "19. sajandi maarahvastiku loomuliku liikumise uurimisest: Probleeme ja allikaid" (Research on population in rural Estonia in the nineteenth century: Problems and sources). *ENSV TA Toimetised* 32 (1983): 127–38.

―――. *Estestvennoe dvizhenie sel'skogo naseleniia Estonii 1650–1799* (Population movement in rural Estonia, 1650–1799). 3 vols. Tallinn: Eesti Raamat, 1980.

―――. "Historical Demography of Estonia in the 17th and 18th Centuries and Computers." In *Studia historica in honorem Hans Kruus*. Tallinn: Eesti NSV Teaduste Akadeemia Ajaloo Instituut, 1971, pp. 205–22.

―――. "O razvitii narodonaseleniia Estonii v sravnitel'no-istoricheskom plane (XIII–XVIII vv.)" (On the development of the population of Estonia in comparative-historical perspective [thirteenth to the eighteenth centuries]). *ENSV TA Toimetised* 23 (1974): 356–75.

Palm, August. *Eesti Kirjanduse Selts 1907–1932* (The Estonian Literary Society, 1907–1932). Tartu: Eesti Kirjanduse Selts, 1932.

Parming, Tönu. *The Collapse of Liberal Democracy and the Rise of Authoritarianism in Estonia*. London: Sage, 1975.

———. "The Electoral Achievements of the Communist Party in Estonia, 1920–1940." *Slavic Review* 42 (1983): 426–47.

———. "From the Republic of Estonia to the Estonian Soviet Socialist Republic: The Transfer of Rule and Sovereignty, 1939–1940." Unpublished manuscript.

———. "Long-term Trends in Family Structure in a Soviet Republic." *Sociology and Social Research* 63 (1979): 443–66.

———. "The Pattern of Participation of the Estonian Communist Party in National Politics, 1918–1940." *Slavonic and East European Review* 59 (1981): 397–412.

———. "Population Changes and Processes." In Tönu Parming and Elmar Järvesoo, eds., *A Case Study of a Soviet Republic: The Estonian SSR*. Boulder, Colo.: Westview Press, 1978, pp. 21–74.

———. "Population Changes in Estonia, 1935–1970." *Population Studies* 26 (1972): 53–78.

Parming, Tönu, and Järvesoo, Elmar, eds. *A Case Study of a Soviet Republic: The Estonian SSR*. Boulder, Colo.: Westview Press, 1978.

Paulson, Ivar. *The Old Estonian Folk Religion*. Translated by Juta Kõvamees Kitching and H. Kõvamees. Indiana University Publications. Uralic and Altaic Series, no. 108. The Hague: Mouton, 1971.

Pechat' SSSR v 1979 godu (The printed word in the USSR in 1979). Moscow: Statistika, 1980.

Pechat' SSSR v 1980 godu (The printed word in the USSR in 1980). Moscow: Statistika, 1981.

Pennar, Jaan. "Greater Demands to Be Made of Estonian Shale Deposits." *Radio Liberty Research* RL 301/81 (July 31, 1981).

———. "Problems of Teaching Estonian in Tallinn's Russian-language Schools." *Radio Liberty Research* RL 135/82 (March 23, 1982).

———. "Reflections on Union Republics in the New Soviet Constitution." *Lituanus* 25, no. 1 (1979): 5–16.

———. "Soviet Nationality Policy and the Estonian Communist Elite." In Tönu Parming and Elmar Järvesoo, eds., *A Case Study of a Soviet Republic: The Estonian SSR*. Boulder, Colo.: Westview Press, 1978, pp. 105–27.

Pennar, Jaan; Bakalo, Ivan I.; and Bereday, George Z. F. *Modernization and Diversity in Soviet Education*. New York: Praeger, 1971.

Peterson, Aleksei. "Taluelamu käsitlus eestikeelses perioodikas aastail 1850–1917" (The treatment of the farmhouse in Estonian-language periodicals in the years 1850–1917). *Etnograafiamuuseumi aastaraamat* 23 (1968): 29–52.

Petri, Johan Christoph. *Ehstland und die Ehsten oder historisch-geographisch-statistisches Gemälde von Ehsteland*. 3 vols. Gotha: n.p., 1802.

Pihlak, Evi. "Hargnevaid suundi eesti 60. aastate maalis" (Diverse trends in Estonian painting in the 1960s). *Kunst*, no. 61/1 (1983): 26–32.

Piip, Ants. *Tormine aasta* (Stormy year). Stockholm: Vaba Eesti, 1966; first published, 1934.

Piirimäe, Helmut, comp. *Tartu ülikooli ajalugu* (The history of Tartu University). Vol. 1, *1632–1798*. Tallinn: Eesti Raamat, 1982.

Pillau, Endel, comp. *Eestimaa kuum suvi 1988* (Estonia's hot summer of 1988). Tallinn: Olion, 1989.

Pistohlkors, Gert von. "Juhan Kahk's Interpretation of Feudal Agrarian Economy in Estonia and Northern Livonia, 1825–1850: A Review Article." *Journal of Baltic Studies* 9 (1978): 367–75.

———. *Ritterschaftliche Reformpolitik zwischen Russifizierung und Revolution.* Göttinger Bausteine zur Geschichtswissenschaft, no. 48. Göttingen: Musterschmidt, 1978.

Põld, Peeter. *Eesti kooli ajalugu* (History of the Estonian school). Tartu: Akadeemiline Kooperatiiv, 1933.

———. "Tartu Ülikool" (Tartu University). In *Eesti: Maa, rahvas, kultuur.* Tartu: Haridusministeeriumi Kirjastus, 1926, pp. 983–1005.

Põldmäe, Mare. "Kaks laulupidu, 1947 ja 1950" (Two song festivals, 1947 and 1950). *Teater. Muusika. Kino* 9, no. 3 (1990): 32–35.

Põldmäe, Rudolf. "Eesti ainestik Vennaste-uniteedi arhiivis Herrnhutis Saksamaal" (Estonian materials in the archives of the Moravian Brethren in Herrnhut, Germany). *Ajalooline Ajakiri* 19 (1940): 73–84.

———. *Esimene Eesti üldlaulupidu 1869* (The first all-Estonian song festival, 1869). Tallinn: Eesti Raamat, 1969.

———. *Kaks laulupidu: 1879–1880* (Two song festivals: 1879–1880). Tallinn: Eesti Raamat, 1976.

"Polozhenie estov v 1860-kh godakh" (The condition of the Estonians in the 1860s). *Russkaia starina* 100 (1899): 655–65.

Poska-Grünthal, Vera. *Naine ja naisliikumine: Peajooni naisliikumise ajaloost ja probleemistikust* (Woman and the women's movement: The main lines of the history and problems of the women's movement). Tartu: Eesti Kirjanduse Selts, 1936.

———. *See oli Eestis 1919–1944* (It took place in Estonia, 1919–1944). Stockholm: Välis-Eesti & EMP, 1975.

Pravoslavie i liuteranstvo v Pribaltiiskom krae po noveishim dannym russkoi pechati (Orthodoxy and Lutheranism in the Baltic region according to the latest data of the Russian press). St. Petersburg: Gosudarstvennaia Tipografiia, 1911.

Puksov, Friedrich. *Eesti raamatu arengulugu seoses kirja ja raamatu üldise arenemisega* (The development of the Estonian book in connection with the general development of writing and the book). Tallinn: Eesti Raamatukoguhoidjate Ühing, 1933.

Pullat, Raimo. "Eesti kodanluse kujunemisest Tallinnas aastail 1871–1912" (On the formation of the Estonian bourgeoisie in Tallinn in the years 1871–1912). *ENSV TA Toimetised* (1964): 49–55.

———. *Eesti linnad ja linlased XVIII sajandi lõpust 1917. aastani* (Estonian cities and townspeople from the end of the eighteenth century to 1917). Tallinn: Eesti Raamat, 1972.

———. *Linnad kodanlikus Eestis: Ajaloolis-demograafiline käsitlus* (Cities in bourgeois Estonia: Historical-demographic treatment). Tallinn: Eesti Raamat, 1978.

———. *Peterburi eestlased: Ajaloolis-demograafiline käsitlus XVIII sajandi algusest kuni 1917. aastani* (The St. Petersburg Estonians: Historical-demographic treatment from the start of the eighteenth century to 1917). Tallinn: Eesti Raamat, 1981.

———, ed. *Tartu ajalugu* (History of Tartu). Tallinn: Eesti Raamat, 1980.

Pullat, Raimo, and Siilivask, Karl. "Nõukogude Eesti sotsiaalne struktuur" (The social structure of Soviet Estonia). *ENSVTA Toimetised* 26 (1977): 13–21, 142–56.

Purre, Arnold. "Estlands Industrie unter sowjetischer Herrschaft." *Acta Baltica* 9 (1969): 47–69.

———. "Ethnischer Bestand und Struktur der Bevölkerung Sowjetestlands im Jahr 1970." *Acta Baltica* 11 (1971): 41–60.

Püss, L. "Ülevaade ilmunud raamatutest" (Overview of published books). In Voldemar Miller, ed., *Eesti raamat 1575–1975*. Tallinn: Valgus, 1978, pp. 261–309.

Raag, Arno. *Saatuslikus kolmnurgas* (In a fateful triangle). Lund: Eesti Kirjanike Kooperatiiv, 1974.

Raamot, Ilmar. *Mälestused* (Memoirs). Vol. 1. Turku: Vaba Eesti, 1975.

Rahvakongress: Eestimaa Rahvarinde kongress 1.–2. oktoobril 1988 (People's congress: The congress of the Estonian Popular Front, October 1–2, 1988). Tallinn: Perioodika, 1988.

Rajamaa, Hermann. "Schulwesen und pädagogische Zielsetzung im selbständigen Estland und in Sowjet Estland." *Acta Baltica* 1 (1960–1961): 131–47.

Ränk, Gustav. *Die Bauernhausformen im baltischen Raum*. Würzburg: Holzer, 1962.

———. "The Estonian Dwelling-House." In *Apophoreta Tartuensia*. Stockholm: Eesti Teaduslik Selts Rootsis, 1949, pp. 95–107.

Rashin, A. G. *Naselenie Rossii za sto let, 1811–1913 gg.* (The population of Russia during 100 years, 1811–1913). Moscow: Gosstatizdat, 1956.

Ratnieks, Henry. "Baltic Oil Shale." *Journal of Baltic Studies* 9 (1978): 155–63.

Rauch, Georg von. *The Baltic States: The Years of Independence, 1917–1940*. Berkeley: University of California Press, 1974.

Raud, Märt. *Sulg ja raamat* (The pen and the book). Lund: Eesti Kirjanike Kooperatiiv, 1962.

Raud, Villem. *Developments in Estonia, 1939–1941*. Tallinn: Perioodika, 1979.

Raun, Alo. "Nõukogude Liidu relvastatud jõudude liikumised Eestis seoses niinimetatud vastastikuse abistamise paktiga" (The movement of Soviet armed forces in Estonia in connection with the so-called mutual assistance pact). Unpublished manuscript.

Raun, Toivo U. "1905 as a Turning Point in Estonian History." *East European Quarterly* 14 (1980): 327–33.

——. "The Development of Estonian Literacy in the 18th and 19th Centuries." *Journal of Baltic Studies* 10 (1979): 115–26.

——. "The Estonians." In Edward C. Thaden et al., *Russification in the Baltic Provinces and Finland, 1855–1914*. Princeton, N.J.: Princeton University Press, 1981, pp. 287–354.

——. "Estonian Social and Political Thought, 1905–February 1917." In Andrew Ezergailis and Gert von Pistohlkors, eds., *Die baltischen Provinzen Russlands zwischen den Revolutionen von 1905 und 1917*. Quellen und Studien zur baltischen Geschichte, no. 4. Cologne: Böhlau, 1982, pp. 59–72.

——. "Language Development and Policy in Estonia." In Isabelle T. Kreindler, ed., *Sociolinguistic Perspectives on Soviet National Languages: Their Past, Present and Future*. Contributions to the Sociology of Language, 40. Berlin: Mouton de Gruyter, 1985, pp. 13–35.

——. "The Revolution of 1905 and the Movement for Estonian National Autonomy, 1896–1907." Ph.D. dissertation, Princeton University, 1969.

——. "The Revolution of 1905 in the Baltic Provinces and Finland." *Slavic Review* 43 (1984): 453–67.

——. "The Role of Journalism in the Estonian National Awakening." In Aleksander Loit, ed., *National Movements in the Baltic Countries During the 19th Century*. Studia Baltica Stockholmiensia, no. 2. Stockholm: Almqvist & Wiksell International, 1985, pp. 389–401.

Rebane, P. Peter. "The *Jüriöö Mäss* (St. George's Night Rebellion) of 1343." In Arvids Ziedonis, Jr., William L. Winter, and Mardi Valgemäe, eds., *Baltic History*. Columbus, Ohio: Association for the Advancement of Baltic Studies, 1974, pp. 35–48.

Rei, August. *The Drama of the Baltic Peoples*, 2d ed. Stockholm: Vaba Eesti, 1970.

——. *Mälestusi tormiselt teelt* (Memoirs of a stormy road). Stockholm: Vaba Eesti, 1961.

——, ed. *Nazi-Soviet Conspiracy and the Baltic States: Diplomatic Documents and Other Evidence*. London: Boreas, 1948.

Reiman, Hugo. "II rahvaloenduse tulemusi" (Results of the second population census). *Eesti Statistika*, no. 156 (1934): 557–68.

——. "Demographic Survey of Estonia." *Baltic Countries* 1, no. 1 (August 1935): 52–61.

——. "Rahvused Eestis" (Nationalities in Estonia). *Eesti Statistika*, nos. 164–65 (1935): 353–61.

Reinhop, H. *Education in Soviet Estonia*. Tallinn: Eesti Raamat, 1967.

Revoliutsiia 1905–1907 gg. v Estonii: Sbornik dokumentov i materialov (The revolution of 1905–1907 in Estonia: Collection of documents and materials). Tallinn: Estonskoe Gosudarstvennoe Izdatel'stvo, 1955.

Revolutsioon, kodusõda ja välisriikide interventsioon Eestis (1917–1920) (Revolution, civil war, and foreign intervention in Estonia, 1917–1920). 2 vols. Tallinn: Eesti Raamat, 1977–1982.

Ridala, Esmo. "Peajooni Eesti välispoliitikast 1934–1940" (The main lines of Estonian foreign policy, 1934–1940). *Eesti Teadusliku Seltsi Rootsis Aastaraamat* 8 (1977–1979): 37–60.

Rigberg, Benjamin. "The Efficacy of Tsarist Censorship Operations, 1894–1917." *Jahrbücher für Geschichte Osteuropas* NF 14 (1966): 327–46.

[Rigby, Elisabeth]. *Letters from the Shores of the Baltic.* London: John Murray, 1849.

Rogger, Hans. *Russia in the Age of Modernisation and Revolution, 1881–1917.* London: Longman, 1983.

Rothschild, Joseph. *East Central Europe Between the Two World Wars.* A History of East Central Europe, vol. 9. Seattle: University of Washington Press, 1974.

Royal Institute of International Affairs. *The Baltic States.* Westport, Conn.: Greenwood Press, 1970; first published, 1938.

Rubin, M. "Varumishinnad ja kolhooside rahalised sissetulekud Eesti NSV-s aastail 1950–1960" (Procurement prices and the money income of kolkhozes in the Estonian SSR in the years 1950–1960). *ENSVTA Toimetised* 30 (1981): 349–61.

Rutkevich, M. N. "Dvuiazychie—vazhnyi faktor razvitiia novoi istoricheskoi obshchnosti" (Bilingualism—an important factor in the development of a new historical community). *Istoriia SSSR*, no. 4 (1981): 22–32.

Ruubel, Peeter. *Poliitilised ja ühiskondlikud voolud Eestis* (Political and social currents in Estonia). Tallinn: Varrak, 1920.

Saar, A. "Saksa vangilaagrites" (In German prison camps). In *K. Päts: Tema elu ja töö.* Tallinn: n.p., 1934, pp. 222–35.

Saar, J. *Enamlaste riigipöörde katse Tallinnas 1. detsember 1924* (The attempted Bolshevik coup in Tallinn on December 1, 1924). Tallinn: Valvur, 1925.

Saat, Joosep [Ioosep]. *Nõukogude võim Eestis: Oktoober 1917-märts 1918* (Soviet power in Estonia: October 1917–March 1918). Tallinn: Eesti Raamat, 1975.

Saat, Ioosep [Joosep], and Siilivask, Karl. *Velikaia Oktriabr'skaia Sotsialisticheskaia Revoliutsiia v Estonii* (The Great October Socialist Revolution in Estonia). Tallinn: Eesti Raamat, 1977.

Salo, Vello. *Riik ja kirikud 1940–1974* (The state and the churches, 1940–1974). Rome: Maarjamaa, 1974.

———. "The Struggle Between the State and the Churches." In Tönu Parming and Elmar Järvesoo, eds., *A Case Study of a Soviet Republic: The Estonian SSR.* Boulder, Colo.: Westview Press, 1978, pp. 191–222.

———, comp. *Population Losses in Estonia, June 1940–August 1941,* I. Scarborough, Ont.: Maarjamaa, 1989.

Salu, Herbert. *Eesti vanem kirjandus* (Older Estonian literature). Vadstena, Sweden: Tõrvik, 1953.

Scherer, John L., ed. *USSR: Facts and Figures Annual.* Vols. 5 & 6. Gulf Breeze, Fla.: Academic International Press, 1981–1982.

Schonberg, Harold C. "The World of Music." In Harrison E. Salisbury, ed., *The Soviet Union: The First Fifty Years.* New York: Harcourt, Brace & World, 1967, pp. 175–98.

Seaton, Albert. *The Russo-German War, 1941–1945*. London: Barker, 1971.

Sepp, Hendrik. "Põhja-Eesti majanduslik olustik XIX sajandi teisel poolel" (Economic conditions in northern Estonia in the second half of the nineteenth century). *Ajalooline Ajakiri* 17 (1938): 4–20.

Seraphim, Ernst. "Die baltischen Provinzen in der zweiten Hälfte des 19. Jahrhunderts." *Deutsche Monatsschrift für Russland* 1 (1912): 577–95.

Shakhovskoi, Sergei V. *Iz arkhiva kniazia S. V. Shakhovskogo: Materialy dlia istorii nedavnego proshlogo Pribaltiiskoi okrainy* (From the archive of Prince S. V. Shakhovskoi: Materials for the history of the recent past of the Baltic borderland). 3 vols. St. Petersburg: V. Eriks, 1909–1910.

Sheehy, Ann. "Estonian-language Olympiad Instituted for Pupils of Russian Schools in Estonia." *Radio Liberty Research* RL 66/82 (February 10, 1982).

Shtromas, A. "The Legal Position of Soviet Nationalities and Territorial Units According to the 1977 Constitution of the USSR." *Russian Review* 37 (1978): 265–72.

Siilivask, Karl. *Veebruarist oktoobrini 1917* (From February to October 1917). Tallinn: Eesti Raamat, 1972.

Siiras, Jaan. *Viro neuvostokurimuksessa: Piirteitä Viron tapahtumista ja kehityksestä bolševikkivallan aikana vv. 1939–1941* (Estonia in the Soviet maelstrom: Sketches of Estonian events and development during the period of Bolshevik rule, 1939–1941). Porvoo: Werner Söderström, 1942.

Slonim, Marc. *Soviet Russian Literature*. Oxford: Oxford University Press, 1967.

Smith, Graham E. "Die Probleme des Nationalismus in den drei baltischen Sowjetrepubliken Estland, Lettland und Litauen." *Acta Baltica* 21 (1981): 143–77.

Sontag, Raymond J., and Beddie, James S., eds. *Nazi-Soviet Relations, 1939–1941: Documents from the Archives of the German Foreign Office*. Washington, D.C.: Department of State, 1948.

Soom, Arnold. *Der Herrenhof in Estland im 17. Jahrhundert*. Lund: Eesti Teaduslik Selts Rootsis, 1954.

Sõrmus, R. "Streigid tööstuses" (Strikes in industry). *Eesti Statistika*, no. 98 (1930): 37–39.

———. "Töötülid 1939. a." (Labor disputes in 1939). *Eesti Statistika* (1940): 205–7.

Soviet Estonia: Land, People, Culture. Tallinn: Valgus, 1980.

Soviet-occupied Estonia 1963. Stockholm: Estonian National Council, 1964.

"Student Demonstrations in Tartu, Estonia." *Radio Liberty Special Report* RL 107/77 (May 10, 1977).

Suits, Gustav. *Sihid ja vaated* (Goals and views). Helsinki: Yrjö Weilin, 1906.

"Sündimus, suremus, abiellumus ja rahvastikuarv 1938. a. (eelkokkuvõte)" (The birth rate, death rate, frequency of marriage, and size of the population in 1938 [preliminary summary]). *Eesti Statistika*, no. 208 (1939): 161–62.

"Sündimus, suremus, abiellumus ja rahvastikuarv 1939. a. (eelkokkuvõte)" (The birth rate, death rate, frequency of marriage, and size of the population in 1939 [preliminary summary]). *Eesti Statistika* (1940): 147.

"Sündivus, surevus, abielluvus ja rahvastikuarv 1932. a. (eelkokkuvõte)" (The birth rate, death rate, frequency of marriage, and size of the population in 1932 [preliminary summary]). *Eesti Statistika*, no. 136 (1933): 164.

Survel, Jaak [Evald Uustalu]. *Estonia Today*. East and West, no. 1. London: Boreas, 1947.

Suur Sotsialistlik Oktoobrirevolutsioon Eestis (The Great Socialist October Revolution in Estonia). Tallinn: Eesti Riiklik Kirjastus, 1957.

Taagepera, Mare. "The Ecological and Political Problems of Phosphorite Mining in Estonia." *Journal of Baltic Studies* 20 (1989): 165–74.

———. "Naiste olukord Eestis" (The status of women in Estonia). In *Metroo 77*. N.p: n.p., 1977, pp. 76–86.

———. "Pollution of the Environment and the Baltics." *Journal of Baltic Studies* 12 (1981): 260–74.

Taagepera, Rein. "Baltic Population Changes, 1950–1980." *Journal of Baltic Studies* 12 (1981): 35–57.

———. "The Baltic States." *Electoral Studies* 9 (1990): 303–11.

———. "Civic Culture and Authoritarianism in the Baltic States, 1930–1940." *East European Quarterly* 7 (1973): 407–12.

———. "De-Choicing of Elections: July 1940 in Estonia." *Journal of Baltic Studies* 14 (1983): 215–46.

———. "Estonia and the Estonians." In Zev Katz, ed., *Handbook of Major Soviet Nationalities*. New York: The Free Press, 1975, pp. 75–95.

———. "Estonia in September 1988: Stalinists, Centrists and Restorationists." *Journal of Baltic Studies* 20 (1989): 175–90.

———. "Estonia's Road to Independence." *Problems of Communism* 38, no. 6 (1989): 11–26.

———. "Inequality Indices for Baltic Farm Size Distribution, 1929–1940." *Journal of Baltic Studies* 3 (1972): 26–34.

———. "Nationalism, Collaborationism, and New Leftism." In Tönu Parming and Elmar Järvesoo, eds., *A Case Study of a Soviet Republic: The Estonian SSR*. Boulder, Colo.: Westview Press, 1978, pp. 75–103.

———. "Nationalism in the Estonian Communist Party." *Bulletin* (Institute for the Study of the USSR) 17, no. 1 (1970): 3–15.

———. "A Note on the March 1989 Elections in Estonia." *Soviet Studies* 42 (1990): 329–39.

———. "The Population Crisis and the Baltics." *Journal of Baltic Studies* 12 (1981): 234–44.

———. "A Portrait of the 'Historical Gap' in Estonian Literature." *Lituanus* 26, no. 3 (1980): 73–86.

———. "Size and Ethnicity of Estonian Towns and Rural Districts, 1922–1979." *Journal of Baltic Studies* 13 (1982): 105–27.

———. *Softening Without Liberalization in the Soviet Union: The Case of Jüri Kukk.* Lanham, Md.: University Press of America, 1984.

———. "Soviet Collectivization of Estonian Agriculture: The Deportation Phase." *Soviet Studies* 32 (1980): 379–97.

———. "Soviet Collectivization of Estonian Agriculture: The Taxation Phase." *Journal of Baltic Studies* 10 (1979): 263–82.

———. "Soviet Documentation on the Estonian Pro-Independence Guerrilla Movement, 1945–1952." *Journal of Baltic Studies* 10 (1979): 91–106.

Takkin, Arnold. *Eesti Esimese maailmasõja aastail* (Estonia during the years of the First World War). Tallinn: Eesti Riiklik Kirjastus, 1961.

Tallinn: Lühientsüklopeedia (Tallinn: Short encyclopedia). Tallinn: Valgus, 1979.

Tallinna arengu probleeme (Problems of Tallinn's development). Tallinn: Eesti Raamat, 1978.

Tambek, Elmar. *Tõus ja mõõn* (Ebb and flow). 2 vols. Toronto: Orto, 1964.

Tamman, A. *Eesti üldised laulupeod XIX aastasajal* (All-Estonian song festivals of the nineteenth century). Tallinn: Albert Org, 1923.

Tampere, Herbert. "Eesti regivärsilise rahvalaulu meloodika stiilitüübid" (Types of melodic styles in the Estonian regivärss folk song). *Etnograafiamuuseumi aastaraamat* 11 (1965): 50–66.

Tarmisto, V. "Tootmisharulise ja territoriaalse aspekti ühtsusest rahvamajanduse arendamisel ning juhtimisel" (The unity of branches of production and territorial aspects in the development and direction of the national economy). *ENSVTA Toimetised* 19 (1970): 208–19.

Tartu: Juht ja teatmik (Tartu: Guide and handbook). Tartu: n.p., 1963.

Tarvel, Enn. *Adramaa* (Ploughland). Tallinn: Eesti Raamat, 1972.

Tarvel, Peeter. "J. Tõnissoni rahvuspoliitilisi vaateid" (J. Tõnisson's views in the area of national policy). In *Jaan Tõnisson töös ja võitluses.* Tartu: Koguteose "Jaan Tõnissoni" komitee, 1938, pp. 415–68.

Taube, Arved Freiherr von. "Von Brest-Litovsk bis Libau: Die baltisch-deutsche Führungsschicht und die Mächte in den Jahren 1918/1919." In Jürgen von Hehn, Hans von Rimscha, and Hellmuth Weiss, eds., *Von den baltischen Provinzen zu den baltischen Staaten: Beiträge zur Entstehungsgeschichte der Republiken Estland und Lettland 1918–1920.* Marburg/Lahn: J. G. Herder-Institut, 1977, pp. 70–236.

"Testimony of Estonia's Foreign Minister Karl Selter." *Lituanus* 14, no. 2 (1968): 50–61.

Thaden, Edward C. "Estland, Livland, and the Ukraine: Reflections on Eighteenth-Century Autonomy." *Journal of Baltic Studies* 12 (1981): 312–17.

——— et al. *Russification in the Baltic Provinces and Finland, 1855–1914.* Princeton, N.J.: Princeton University Press, 1981.

Tobien, Alexander von. *Die Agrargesetzgebung Livlands im 19. Jahrhundert.* 2 vols. Berlin: Puttkammer & Mühlbrecht, 1899; Riga: G. Löffler, 1911.

——. *Die livländische Ritterschaft in ihrem Verhältnis zum Zarismus und russischen Nationalismus.* 2 vols. Riga: G. Löffler, 1925; Berlin: Water de Gruyter, 1930.

Toivonen, Y. H. "Suomalais-ugrilaisten alkukodista" (The original homeland of the Finno-Ugrians). *Virittäjä* 57 (1953): 5–35.

Tomberg, A. "Abiellumus, sündimus, suremus ja rahvastiku iive 1938. a." (Frequency of marriage, the birth rate, the death rate, and population increase in 1938). *Eesti Statistika,* no. 218 (1940): 8–44.

Tomingas, William. *Vaikiv ajastu Eestis* (The era of silence in Estonia). New York: Eesti Ajaloo Instituut, 1961.

Tomson, Edgar. "The Annexation of the Baltic States." In Thomas T. Hammond, ed., *The Anatomy of Communist Takeovers.* New Haven, Conn.: Yale University Press, 1975, pp. 214–28.

Tõnurist, Edgar, ed. *Eesti NSV põllumajanduse kollektiviseerimine* (Collectivization of agriculture in the Estonian SSR). Tallinn: Eesti Raamat, 1978.

——, ed. *Sotsialistliku põllumajanduse areng Nõukogude Eestis* (The development of socialist agriculture in Soviet Estonia). Tallinn: Valgus, 1976.

"Tööliste arv Eesti tööstuses 1923–1924. a." (The number of workers in Estonian industry, 1923–1924). *Eesti Statistika,* no. 39 (1925): Appendix I, 1–14.

Tooms, Anatol. "Opteermisliikumine ja Eesti jõudnud optandid" (The repatriation movement and the repatriates who arrived in Estonia). *Eesti Statistika,* no. 5 (1922): 5–22.

——. "Rahvahääletused põhiseaduse muutmiseks" (Referendums to change the constitution). *Eesti Statistika,* no. 145 (1933): 605–17.

Toomus, Friido. *Konstantin Päts ja riigireformi aastad* (Konstantin Päts and the years of state reform). Tartu: Loodus, 1938.

Topman, Monika. *An Outline of Estonian Music.* Tallinn: Perioodika, 1978.

Tormis, Lea. *Eesti balletist* (On the Estonian ballet). Tallinn: Eesti Raamat, 1967.

——. *Eesti teater 1920–1940: Sõnalavastus* (The Estonian theater, 1920–1940: Nonmusical productions). Tallinn: Eesti Raamat, 1978.

Traat, August. "Vallareform Eestis 1866. aastal" (The rural township reform in Estonia in 1866). *ENSV TA Toimetised* 27 (1968): 11–23.

Tuglas, Friedebert. *Ado Grenzsteini lahkumine* (Ado Grenzstein's departure). Tartu: Noor-Eesti, 1926.

——. *Eesti Kirjameeste Selts* (The Society of Estonian Literati). Tallinn: Eesti Riiklik Kirjastus, 1958; first published, 1932.

Uibopuu, Henn-Jüri. "The Constitutional Development of the Estonian Republic." *Journal of Baltic Studies* 4 (1973): 11–35.

Ülevaade Eestimaa Kommunistliku Partei ajaloost (Overview of the history of the Estonian Communist Party). 3 vols. Tallinn: Eesti Riiklik Kirjastus, 1961–1963; Eesti Raamat, 1972.

Uluots, Jüri. *Grundzüge der Agrargeschichte Estlands.* Tartu: Akadeemiline Kooperatiiv, 1935.

Urban, William. *The Baltic Crusade*. Dekalb: Northern Illinois University Press, 1975.

——. *The Livonian Crusade*. Washington, D.C.: University Press of America, 1981.

Uustalu, Evald. *Eesti Vabariik 1918–1940* (The Republic of Estonia, 1918–1940). Lund: Eesti Kirjanike Kooperatiiv, 1968.

——. *For Freedom Only: The Story of Estonian Volunteers in the Finnish War of 1940–1944*. Toronto: Northern Publications, 1977.

——. *The History of Estonian People*. London: Boreas, 1952.

——. "The National Committee of the Estonian Republic." *Journal of Baltic Studies* 7 (1976): 209–19.

——. "Die Staatsgründung Estlands." In Jürgen von Hehn, Hans von Rimscha, and Hellmuth Weiss, eds., *Von den baltischen Provinzen zu den baltischen Staaten: Beiträge zur Entstehungsgeschichte der Republiken Estland und Lettland, 1917–1918*. Marburg/Lahn: J. G. Herder-Institut, 1971, pp. 275–92.

——. *Tagurpidi sõudes: Mälestusi ajavahemikult 1914–1943* (Rowing Backward: Memoirs from the period 1914–1943). Stockholm: Teataja, 1982.

Vahtre, Sulev. *Eestimaa talurahvas hingeloenduste andmeil (1782–1858)* (The Estonian peasantry on the basis of soul revisions, 1782–1858). Tallinn: Eesti Raamat, 1973.

Valgemäe, Mardi. "Drama and the Theatre Arts." In Tõnu Parming and Elmar Järvesoo, eds., *A Case Study of a Soviet Republic: The Estonian SSR*. Boulder, Colo.: Westview Press, 1978, pp. 281–317.

Vardys, V. Stanley. "The Baltic Peoples." *Problems of Communism* 16, no. 5 (1967): 55–64.

——. "Human Rights Issues in Estonia, Latvia, and Lithuania." *Journal of Baltic Studies* 12 (1981): 275–98.

——. "Modernization and Baltic Nationalism." *Problems of Communism* 24, no. 5 (1975): 32–48.

——. "The Rise of Authoritarianism in the Baltic States." In V. Stanley Vardys and Romuald J. Misiunas, eds., *The Baltic States in Peace and War, 1917–1945*. University Park: The Pennsylvania State University Press, 1978, pp. 65–80.

——. "The Role of the Baltic Peoples in Soviet Society." In Roman Szporluk, ed., *The Influence of East Europe and the Soviet West on the USSR*. New York: Praeger, 1976, pp. 147–79.

Vassar, Artur. "Eesti talurahva vaated maavaldusele XIX sajandi teisel poolel" (The Estonian peasantry's views on landholding in the second half of the nineteenth century). In *Eesti talurahva sotsiaalseid vaateid XIX sajandil*. Tallinn: Eesti NSV Teaduste Akadeemia Ajaloo Instituut, 1977, pp. 124–86.

Vilms, J. "Maaomavalitsuse uuenduskatsed Eestis" (Attempts at local government reform in Estonia). *Vaba Sõna*, no. 12 (1915): 319–23.

Vuorela, Toivo. *The Finno-Ugric Peoples*. Translated by John Atkinson. Indiana University Publications. Uralic and Altaic series, no. 39. The Hague: Mouton, 1964.

Waite, Robert G. L. *Vanguard of Nazism: The Free Corps Movement in Post-War Germany, 1918–1933*. Cambridge, Mass.: Harvard University Press, 1952.

Warma, August. *Diplomaadi kroonika* (A diplomat's chronicle). Lund: Eesti Kirjanike Kooperatiiv, 1971.

Webermann, Otto A. "Probleme des baltischen Raumes als Forschungsaufgabe." *Ural-Altaische Jahrbücher* 35 (1964): 284–300.

Weske, Mihkel. "Über den Culturfortschritt im Leben der Esten." *Sitzungsberichte der gelehrten estnischen Gesellschaft zu Dorpat* (1876): 37–50.

Wheeler-Bennett, John. *Brest-Litovsk: The Forgotten Peace, March 1918.* London: Macmillan, 1956; first published, 1938.

Winterton, Paul. *Report on Russia.* London: Cresset, 1945.

Wittram, Reinhard. *Baltische Geschichte: Die Ostseelande Livland, Estland, Kurland 1180–1918.* Munich: R. Oldenbourg, 1954.

———. *Geschichte der baltischen Deutschen: Grundzüge und Durchblicke.* Stuttgart: W. Kohlhammer, 1939.

Zetterberg, Seppo. *Suomi ja Viro 1917–1919* (Finland and Estonia, 1917–1919). Historiallisia Tutkimuksia, no. 102. Helsinki: Suomen Historiallinen Seura, 1977.

Index

Aav, Evald, 137
Aavik, Johannes, 92, 136
Aavik, Juhan, 238
Academia Gustaviana. *See* Tartu
    University
Adramaa (ploughland), 19, 21, 30;
    peasants, 21, 31
Agrarian laws: (1802), 47; (1804), 43,
    47; (1816), 47; (1819), 47; (1849),
    49; (1860), 49
Agrarian League, 100, 109. *See also*
    Farmers' Party; United Agrarian Party
Agricultural societies, Estonian, 70, 89
Agriculture: major crops, 8, 19, 30, 41,
    69–70, 129, 202; in prehistoric
    times, 8–10; three-field system, 9,
    19, 40–41, 69; in medieval Livonia,
    19; under Swedish and Polish rule,
    30; dairy and cattle farming, 40, 69,
    129, 203; in early tsarist era, 40–43;
    innovation in, 41, 69–70, 89,
    200–201; in 1940–1941, 152–53;
    under German occupation, 164–65;
    collectivization, 176–81; in post-
    Stalin era, 200–203; Estonia as ex-

perimental laboratory, 201; privatiza-
    tion, 233. *See also* Land reform
Aleshin, Georgii, 191
Alexander I, 46, 74
Alexander II, 49, 57, 61
Alexander III, 65–66
All-Estonian Congress (1905), 84–85,
    93, 246n.6
Alliksaar, Artur, 216
Altaic theory, 6
Altmark, Peace of, 28
Alver, Betti, 136, 186, 215
Andresen, Nigol, 172, 174, 186
Anvelt, Jaan, 102, 107, 115
Arbujad, 136
Art: professional art schools, 137, 185,
    212; Union of Artists, 187; bourgeois
    nationalism in, 187; graphics, 217;
    international contacts, 217
Ast, Karl, 123
Atlantic Charter, 163

Baltic Assembly, 229
Baltic Constitutional Party, 84, 86
Baltic Council, 229

Baltic entente, 124–25
Baltic Germans: origins, 15–17; in cit-
    ies, 18, 23, 38, 52–53, 60, 73,
    131–32; as *Kulturträger*, 23; promote
    education, 54; and administrative
    Russification, 60–61; views of Esto-
    nians, 63; emigration, 72, 130, 143,
    154; dominance of Lutheran Church,
    80, 94; reaction to 1905, 86; re-
    strictions in World War I, 94–95; and
    German occupation (1918), 106; in
    Estonian War of Independence, 108;
    in *Landeswehr* War, 109–10. *See also*
    Clergy; Diets; Nobility
Balto-Finns, 5–7
Báthory, Stefan, 27, 29
Bible, first Estonian translation of, 53
Bloody Sunday, 83
Boat-ax culture, 8, 13
Bolsheviks, 87, 100–102; in power
    (1917–1918), 102–4; in Estonian
    War of Independence, 107–11. *See
    also* Estonian Communist Party
Bornhöhe, Eduard, 78
Bourgeoisie, Estonian, 60, 73, 88, 91,
    132
Bourgeois nationalism, 171, 186–87
Brest-Litovsk, Treaty of, 104
Brömsebro, Treaty of, 28
Buxhoevden, Albert von, 15–16

Castrén, M. A., 6
Catherine II, 39, 46, 54
Catholic Church, 18, 22–24, 32
Censorship: in late tsarist era, 78;
    liberalization of, 87, 93; in 1917–
    1918, 103; in 1930s, 120; under
    German occupation, 167–68; Sta-
    linism and, 186
Chamber of Deputies (1938–1940),
    121–22, 145–46, 149
Charles XI, 30–31, 38
Charles XII, 33
Christian Nationalist Party, 109, 113.
    See also National Center

Clergy, 219; in medieval Livonia, 22;
    Germans as, 22, 32, 51, 80, 94, 136;
    status, 22, 51, 72; use of vernacular,
    32; Estonians as, 32, 80, 94, 136;
    selection, 80; persecution and depor-
    tation, 156, 188; flight to West, 168.
    See also Lutheran Church; Orthodox
    Church
Collectivization of agriculture, 176–81
Comb-ceramic culture, 7–8
Comintern, 115
Commerce. *See* Trade
Commissars for peasant affairs, 61
Committee for State Security (KGB),
    193
Conference on Security and Coopera-
    tion in Europe (CSCE), 230
Congress of Estonia, 227–28, 230–31
Congress of People's Deputies
    (Moscow), 227–29
Constitutional Democrats, 86
Constitutions: (1920), 112–13,
    115–16, 133, 135, 252n.13; (1933),
    117–18; (1937), 121–22, 162,
    253n.17; (1940), 149–50; (1977),
    195
Continental Blockade, 47
Cooperative movement, 89
Cottagers (*vabadikud*), 21–22, 49–51
Council of Ministers, 172–73, 194
Council of People's Commissars,
    149–50, 172. *See also* Council of
    Ministers
Counter-Reformation, 29, 32
Cultural autonomy law (1925), 133

Defense League, 119, 144–45
Democrats (Democratic Bloc), 100,
    103–4. *See also* National Center;
    National Party
Denmark, 16–18, 25, 27–29
Deportations: political leaders of inde-
    pendent Estonia, 150–51; in
    1940–1941, 153–54; return of some
    deportees, 154, 189, 204, 219; dur-

ing Stalinist era, 173, 181; and collectivization, 178–79, 236, 283n.35
Depression, 115–16, 125–27, 129
Destruction battalions, 157–58, 279n.3
Diets (*Landtage*), 29, 40, 47, 60; origins of, 18; temporary abolition of, 39; proposed reforms in, 88; abolition (1917), 100
Dissent and dissidents, in Soviet Estonia, 195–97, 223, 225–26
Duke Magnus, 25, 27
Duma, 87–88

Education: in medieval Livonia, 24; first secondary schools, 32–33; first elementary schools, 33; Catherine II and, 54; more advanced in Livland, 54; in memorandum to Alexander III, 65; Russification and, 66–67, 79–80, 85; Estonian Alexander School, 67, 74–76; and Society of Estonian Literati, 75, 79; in late tsarist era, 93–94; in independent Estonia, 134–35; Sovietization, 155; under German occupation, 167; in Stalinist era, 184–85; in post-Stalin era, 211–13; in *glasnost'* era, 237. *See also* Tartu University
Eenpalu (Einbund), Kaarel, 119, 122
Eesti Postimes, 63–64, 76, 260–61n.12
Eichfeld, Johan, 185, 194
Eisen, Johann Georg, 46, 54
Emigration, 45, 90; restrictions on, 48; within Russian empire, 72, 90; of Baltic Germans, 72, 130, 143, 154; flight to West in World War II, 166
Environmental issues, 196, 200, 223, 228, 235–36
Erik XIV, 25
Ernesaks, Gustav, 187–88, 218, 238
ESSR State Art Institute, 185, 212
Estland, definition of, 28, 256n.3
Estonian Academy of Sciences, 155, 237–38

Estonian Agricultural Academy, 185, 212
Estonian Alexander School, 59, 67, 74–76
Estonian Christian Union, 226, 228
Estonian Citizens' Committees, 228
Estonian Communist Party (ECP): attempted coup in Estonia (1924), 115; in 1940, 145–46; membership, 150, 170, 190–91; Buro of Central Committee, 150, 170–72, 191–93; ethnic composition, 170, 190; social composition, 170, 191; purge in, 171–73; nationalism in, 192–93; 1988 plenum, 225; decline in membership, 231
Estonian Constituent Assembly: elections in 1918, 102, 104–5, 250n.19; elections in 1919, 109
Estonian Democratic Movement, 195–96
Estonian Heritage Society, 224, 228, 235–36
Estonian intelligentsia, 38, 72; origins of, 56; cultural emphasis, 63; loyalty to tsar, 66; Russification and, 67, 76–77; German influence on, 77; radicalization of, 82–83; in post-Stalin era, 213, 224
Estonian Learned Society, 56
Estonian Legion, 158–59
Estonian Literary Society, 92
Estonian Military Revolutionary Committee, 102
Estonian National Front, 195–96
Estonian National Independence Party, 226, 228
Estonian national military units, 95, 101–2, 105
Estonian national movement, 59, 63–66, 74, 240–41; origins of, 57–58; memorandum to Alexander III, 65–66; pessimism in, 74–76; demand for autonomy in 1905, 85
Estonian National Museum, 92

Estonian Popular Front, 224–27, 229–31, 235

Estonian Progressive People's Party (EPPP), 84, 86–88, 100

Estonian provisional government (1918–1919), 105, 107–8, 111

Estonian Rifle Corps, 160, 170–71, 280n.10

Estonian Social Democratic Workers' Party (1905–1906), 83, 87

Estonian Social Democrats: in elections, 100–101, 103, 109, 113; support independence, 104; in cabinets, 114. See also Socialist Workers' Party

Estonian Socialist Revolutionaries, 100, 101, 103–5, 109, 113. See also Socialist Workers' Party

Estonian-Soviet mutual assistance pact (1939), 140–41, 143–44

Estonian SSR Academy of Sciences, 185, 213

Estonian War of Independence: early Soviet successes, 107–8; Finnish loans and volunteers, 108; strength of opposing forces, 108; Landeswehr War, 109–10; role of Russian Whites, 108, 110; peace negotiations, 110; interpretations of, 110–11

Estonian Working People's League, 145–46

Estonian Workers' Commune, 107, 110

Estonia Society, 76, 92–93

Estonia Theater, 137, 175, 187, 218

Everyone (Iggaüks) Declaration, 47

Faehlmann, Friedrich Robert, 56

Farmers' Party, 113–14, 119, 163. See also Agrarian League; United Agrarian Party

Fatherland League, 119, 145

Finland, 76, 104, 132, 139–40, 143, 159, 197; aid to Estonia in 1918–1919, 108; opposes border-state alliance, 124; Estonian flight to, 166;

contacts with in post-Stalin era, 189, 214, 217–18, 232, 238

Finno-Ugrians, 5–7, 242

Fölkersahm, Hamilkar von, 49

Folklore, Estonian, 56, 77

Forest brethren, 174–75. See also Guerrilla movements

Forselius, Bengt Gottfried, 32–33

France, 106–7, 124, 139

Gelehrte Estnische Gesellschaft, 56

Generalplan Ost, 161

Germanization, 23, 62, 72, 106, 161, 166

Germany, 62–63, 139, 142, 146, 166; occupation of Estonia (1918), 105–7; relations with Estonia, 123–25; non-aggression pact with Estonia, 125; trade with Estonia, 127; conquest of Estonia, 157–58; occupation of Estonia (1941–1944), 158–68

Golovin, Evgenii A., 39

Goltz, Rüdiger von der, 109–10

Gorbachev, Mikhail, 222, 227, 230, 236

Great Britain, 106–8, 110, 124, 127, 139, 142, 163–64

Great Hunger, 31

Great Northern War, 30–31, 33–34, 37–38, 50, 54

Grenzstein, Ado, 67, 80, 82

Guerrilla movements, under Soviet rule, 157–58, 174–75, 279n.3

Guilds, 23, 32, 52–53

Gustavus Adolphus, 29, 33

Hanseatic League, 23

Head tax, 43

Henry of Livonia, 9–11, 16, 24

Herder, Johann Gottfried, 56

Himmler, Heinrich, 161–62

Hint, Aadu, 186–87

Hitler, Adolph, 139, 142, 160–62

Homesteaders' Party, 113, 163. See also United Agrarian Party

Horse and Machinery Lending Stations, 152–53, 177
Hurt, Jakob, 63–67 passim, 74, 75, 82, 242

IME (Self-management plan), 227, 233
Independent Socialists. *See* Estonian Socialist Revolutionaries
Industrial workers, 70, 73–74, 89–90, 126, 165, 176, 199
Industry: in late tsarist era, 70–71, 89; in World War I, 95; impact of Depression, 125–26; nationalization, 151; under German occupation, 164–65; in Stalinist era, 175–76; Estonia as experimental laboratory, 198; decline of growth rates, 198–99; in *glasnost'* era, 232. *See also* Oil-shale industry
Institute of Theology, 168, 188
Intermovement, 225–26, 231, 235
Ird, Kaarel, 187, 216
Iudenich, Nikolai, 110
Ivan the Terrible, 25, 27

Jakobson, August, 172–73, 187, 194–95
Jakobson, Carl Robert, 64–70 passim, 74, 75, 78, 100
Jannau, Heinrich von, 46, 54
Jannsen, Johann Voldemar, 55–56, 63–64, 66, 70, 75–76, 82, 216
Järvi, Neeme, 217, 237
Jesuits, 32
Jews, fate of in World War II, 165; 226
Jõeäär, Aleksander, 172, 174
Journalism. *See* Press
Jüriöö Mäss (St. George's Night Rebellion), 20–21

Käbin, Ivan (Johannes), 171–72, 191–93, 195, 220
Kalevala, 56
Kalevipoeg, 56, 77
Kallas, Siima, 233
Kalmar Union, 24

Kangro, Bernard, 136
Kapp, Eugen, 187
Karindi, Alfred, 188
Karotamm, Nikolai, 150, 171, 178–79, 224, 282n.7
Kaugver, Raimond, 238
Kelam, Tunne, 226
Kerensky, Alexander, 101–2
Kes, Hans, 32–33
KGB, 193
Khrushchev, Nikita S., 169, 189, 193–94, 200–201
Kiik, Heino, 238
Kingissepp, Viktor, 102, 110, 115, 170
Kitzberg, August, 78, 92
Klauson, Valter, 194
Koell, Johann, 24
Kohtla-Järve, 170, 175, 183, 198, 206–8, 235, 290n.72
Koidula, Lydia, 77–79, 188
Köler, Johann, 64–65, 67, 75, 216
Kolkhozes, 152, 178–81, 200–202
Kolõvan. *See* Tallinn
Konik, Konstantin, 105
Kornilov, Lavr, 102
Kosov, Vasilii, 172
Kreenholm factory (Narva), 52, 70, 74
Kreutzwald, Friedrich Reinhold, 55–56, 75, 77
Kross, Jaan, 215–16, 238
Kruus, Hans, 87, 144, 155, 172, 185, 242
Kudriavtsev, Aleksandr, 191
Kuhlbars, Friedrich, 78
Kukk, Jüri, 196
Kumm, Boris, 150, 171, 173–74
Kunda culture, 7
Kuressaare, name restored, 231
Kurland, 29, 39, 54, 59, 66, 86, 88, 95

Laasi, Evald, 236
Labor Party: in elections (1917–1932), 100, 103–4, 109, 113; in cabinets, 114. *See also* National Center
Laidoner, Johan, 107, 118–19, 144–45

Landesrat (1918), 106
Landeswehr War, 109–10
Landmarschall, 40
Landratskollegium, 40
Land reform: in independent Estonia, 114, 128–29, 132; in Soviet era, 152, 177, 283n.24
Language, Estonian: linguistic classification, 5; orthographic reforms by Forselius, 32; lectureship at Tartu University, 56; as language of administration, 62, 85; modernization and standardization, 77, 92, 136; in education, 85, 93, 212–13; borrowing from Finnish, 136; proportion of printing in, 185–87, 213–14; status in *glasnost'* era, 235, 237. *See also* Printing, in Estonian
Language law (1989), 237
Lapua movement, 116
Larka, Andres, 118
Latvia, 109, 123, 139–41, 144–46, 163–64, 183, 208, 222, 229–31, 241; partition of Valga with Estonia, 112; entente with Estonia and Lithuania, 124–25; lack of trade with Estonia, 127
Latvians, 3, 8–9, 17, 19, 62–63, 80, 108, 226, 242, 255n.3; electoral alliance with Estonians, 88; in Estonian War of Independence, 108
Lauristin, Johannes, 149–50, 158, 225
Lauristin, Marju, 225
League of Estonian Women, 132
League of Nations, 124–25, 241
League of Veterans of the Estonian War of Independence, 116–20, 122–23, 165
Lebedev, Konstantin, 191–92
Leberecht, Hans, 187
Leinberg, Juhan, 45
Leis, Malle, 217
Lembitu, 16
Lenin, Vladimir I., 105, 172
Lentsman, Leonid, 191–92

Lettgallians, 15–16, 237n.3
Liiv, Juhan, 78
Lindanise. *See* Tallinn
Linda Shipping Society, 71
Literacy, 54–55, 79, 133–34
Literature, Estonian: first example of, 32–33; national epic (*Kalevipoeg*), 56, 77; during national awakening, 77–78; critical realism, 78; Young-Estonia, 91–92; *Siuru* and *arbujad*, 136; A. H. Tammsaare, 136; in 1940–1941, 155–56; under German occupation, 167; Stalinism and, 186–87; role of Estonian writers in West, 187; in post-Stalin era, 214–16; in *glasnost'* era, 238
Lithuania, 123–32 passim, 139, 141, 144–46, 163–64, 183, 222, 229–31, 241
Lithuanians, 8–9, 17, 242
Litzmann, Karl, 161–62
Livland, definition of, 29, 238n.4
Livland Public Benefit and Economic Society, 41, 70
Livonian Order. *See* Teutonic Knights
Livonians, 6, 12, 15–17, 19, 237n.2
Livonian Wars, 25, 27–29, 31–32
Lohse, Hinrich, 161
Lutheran Church: origins, 24; and Counter-Reformation, 32; and Orthodox Church, 45, 48–49, 53–54, 80, 94, 135; and Moravian Brethren, 53; administration, 80, 94, 135–36; Soviet regime and, 156, 188, 218–19; Nazi regime and, 168; in *glasnost'* era, 238. *See also* Clergy; Orthodox Church

Maapäev (provincial assembly), 100–108 passim, 249n.15
Machine Tractor Stations, 152–53, 177, 200
Made, Tiit, 233
Mäe, Hjalmar, 159, 161–63
Mahtra, peasant unrest at, 44–45

Maltsvet the Prophet, 45
Manasein, Nikolai A., 66
Manorialism, 42–43
Marahwa Näddala-Leht, 55
Masing, Otto Wilhelm, 55–56
Mensheviks, 87, 100–101. *See also*
    Estonian Social Democrats
Meri, Lennart, 237
Merilaas, Kersti, 186, 215
Merkel, Garlieb, 42, 46
MGB, 173, 193
Mobilization, in World War II, 154,
    158–59
Molotov-Ribbentrop Pact, 130, 139,
    143–44, 196, 223–24, 226, 229,
    236
Molotov, Viacheslav M., 139–41
Moravian Brethren, 53–54
Municipal government, 18, 60, 88,
    101–2, 106, 122
Music: choral and orchestral societies,
    76, 137; opera, 137, 187, 218;
    conservatories, 137, 185, 212; Union
    of Composers, 187; bourgeois na-
    tionalism in, 187; modernism in,
    217; international contacts, 218. *See
    also* Song festivals
Müürisepp, Aleksei, 173, 194–95

Narva, 18, 22, 112, 115, 137, 158–59,
    170; in Great Northern War, 33; as
    industrial center, 52, 70, 89–91, 198;
    population, 52, 73, 90, 131, 206,
    235; in 1905, 83; in 1917–1918,
    101, 104, 107; destruction in World
    War II, 175. *See also* Population,
    ethnic composition
National Center, 113–14, 116, 163. *See
    also* Labor Party; National Party
National Committee of the Estonian
    Republic, 163
National Front for the Implementation
    of the Constitution, 121–22
Nationalism. *See* Estonian national
    movement

Nationalization, 151
National Party, 109, 113–14. *See also*
    Democrats; National Center; Radical
    Democrats
Nazi-Soviet Pact. *See* Molotov-
    Ribbentrop Pact
Nevskii, Aleksandr, 17
Nicholas I, 54
Nicholas II, 83–84, 94
Niklus, Mart, 196
NKVD, 173
Nobility, 29–31, 51, 60, 68, 72, 86,
    104, 257nn.2, 3; origins, 18; in
    medieval Livonia, 22, 24–25; and
    Livonian wars, 28; growing power in
    eighteenth century, 38–39; expansion
    of estates, 40–41; views on serf
    emancipation, 46, 48–49; expropria-
    tion of estates, 128
North Estonian dialect, 53, 77
Northwestern (White Russian) Army,
    108, 110

October Manifesto, 84
Oil-shale industry, 126, 165, 175–76,
    198–200
Olbrei, Rahel, 137
Order of the Knights of Christ, 15. *See
    also* Sword Brethren
Orthodox Church, 94, 135, 156, 168,
    218; conversion movement in 1840s,
    45, 48, 53; conversions in 1880s, 80
Ostarbeiter, 166

Päevaleht, 135, 168
Päll, Eduard, 173–74
Parek, Lagle, 226
Pärn, Jakob, 78
Pärnu, 18, 22, 63, 70–71, 137,
    158–59, 170; Tartu University at, 33;
    as commercial center, 51–52; popula-
    tion, 52, 90–91, 131, 206–7, 235
Pärt, Arvo, 217
Partisans. *See* Guerrilla movements

Päts, Konstantin, 88, 162; as editor of *Teataja*, 82; in 1905, 85–86; head of Estonian provisional government, 105, 107–8; arrested by Germans, 106; head of state, 114, 119–22; carries out coup d'état, 118–19; as President, 122–23; foreign policy, 125; in crisis of 1939–1940, 140, 142–46; deported to USSR, 145; reburied in Estonia, 236

Päts, Riho, 188

Paul I, 39, 43

Peasant legislation. *See* Agrarian laws

Peasantry: obligations, 20, 30, 43–44, 47, 68; resistance, 20–21, 28, 34, 44–45; social differentiation, 21, 50, 72; petitions, 31, 61, 68; emancipation, 40, 47–48; attitudes toward tsar, 45; self-government, 61–62; landownership, 68–89, 89

People's Commissariat of Internal Affairs (NKVD), 173. *See also* KGB

Perno Postimees, 56, 63

Peter I, 29, 33, 38, 43

Peterson, Kristjan Jaak, 56, 216, 242

Peterson-Särgava, Ernst, 78

Petri, Johan Christoph, 42, 46

Petrograd. *See* St. Petersburg

Petserimaa, 112, 169

Pietism, 53

Piip, Ants, 105–6, 120, 140, 142

Plague, 34, 49–50

Pobedonostsev, Konstantin, 80

Poland, 24–25, 27–30, 39, 124, 129, 132

Poland-Lithuania. *See* Poland

Political parties (1917–1940): in *Maapäev*, 100; municipal elections, 101; in soviets, 101; Russian Constituent Assembly elections, 103; Estonian Constituent Assembly elections (1918), 104; Estonian Constituent Assembly elections (1919), 109; State Assembly elections (1920–1932), 113; Communist fronts, 113–15; in cabinets, 114; constitutional crisis and, 116–19; abolition of, 119; Fatherland League, 119; National Front for Implementation of the Constitution, 121–22; in *glasnost'* era, 225–26. *See also* individual parties

Population: medieval Livonia, 19; losses in 1561–1700, 31; losses in Great Northern War, 34; growth in tsarist era, 49–50, 71–73, 90–91; ethnic composition, 52, 71–73, 91, 130–32, 182, 184, 204–5, 207–8, 290n.72; independent Estonia, 129–32; losses in 1940–1941, 154; losses under German occupation, 165–66, 281n.24; Stalinist era, 181–82; post-Stalin era, 203–5; ethnic composition, 233–35; in *glasnost'* era, 233–35; demographic tables, 246–49. *See also* Narva; Tallinn; Tartu

Poska, Jaan, 100–103, 109

Postimees, 78–79, 82, 168

Press: *Marahwa Näddala-Leht*, 55; and J. V. Jannsen, 55–56, 63, 70, 75–76; role in national movement, 56, 75–76; and C. R. Jakobson, 65, 78; and Abo Grenzstein, 67, 82; first daily newspaper, 78–79; and Jaan Tõnisson, 82; and Konstantin Päts, 82; in 1905, 83, 85; *Vaba Sõna*, 87–88; in late tsarist era, 93; in independent Estonia, 135; major dailies, 135, 168, 186, 214; under German occupation, 167–68; in Stalinist era, 185–86; Estonian-language share of, 213; in *glasnost'* era, 236–37. *See also* Printing, in Estonian

Printing, in Estonian: medieval Livonia, 24; seventeenth century, 32; tsarist era, 55, 78, 93; independent Estonia, 135; Stalinist era, 185–86; post-Stalin era, 213–14. *See also* Press

Provisional Government (Russian), 99–102

Public opinion polls, in *glasnost'* era, 228–29
Pulli, 7
Pusta, Kaarel R., 105–6

Radical Democrats, 100, 103. *See also* National Center
Rahva Hääl, 145, 186, 214
Railroads, 71
Raudsepp, Hugo, 136, 155–56, 186
Referendum, on independence (1991), 239
Reformation, 24–25
Regional economic council, 193–94, 198
Regivärss folk song, 12, 55, 77, 217–18
Rehielamu (barn-dwelling), 10, 132
Rei, August, 109, 114, 118, 140–41, 144, 276–77n.23
Reinvald, Ado, 78
Religion in prehistoric times, 12–13. *See also* Catholic Church; Lutheran Church; Orthodox Church
Revolution of 1905: as turning point, 81, 83, 86; causes, 83; strikes and unrest, 83–86; October Manifesto, 84; All-Estonian Congress, 84–85; punitive expeditions, 85–86; impact on worker activism, 91
Riga, 16, 18, 71–72, 100, 106
Riga Polytechnic Institute, 70, 80
Ristikivi, Karl, 156, 167
Ritsing, Richard, 238
Ritterschaften, see Diets; Nobility
Ritterschaftshauptmann, 29, 40
Rosenberg, Alfred, 161–62
Rosen Declaration, 42
Rosenplänter, Johann Heinrich, 56
Rummo, Paul-Eerik, 215–16
Russia, 12, 25, 27–28, 32, 105; relations with Baltic German nobility, 38–40; tsarist view of Baltic provinces, 62–63; and Estonian War of Independence, 107–8, 110. *See also* Soviet Union

Russian Constituent Assembly elections, 103–4, 109, 111
Russian-Estonians: definition of, 170; immigration to Estonia, 182, 204–5, 234; role in Estonian Communist Party, 170–71, 190–93; role in Estonian Rifle Corps, 171; role in ESSR government, 173, 194–95
Russian Orthodoxy. *See* Orthodox Church
Russian Social Democratic Workers' Party, 83, 85–87. *See also* Bolsheviks; Mensheviks
Russification: in late tsarist era, 59–63, 66–67, 73, 75–76, 79–80, 85; under Stalin, 182–83, 186–87; in post-Stalin era, 196–97, 205, 210–11, 219–220; in *glasnost'* era, 234
Rüütel, Arnold, 195

Saare-Lääne, bishopric of, 17–18, 25
Saaremaa (Ösel), 9, 11; resistance to German conquest, 16–17; in *Jüriöö Mäss*, 20; under Denmark and Sweden, 28–29; nobility corporation, 39, 60, 88; diet, 40; sale of peasant land, 69; revolt on (1919), 111; Soviet bases, 141; in World War II, 159
St. Petersburg (Petrograd), 40, 71, 90, 99, 102, 107
Sakala, 65, 78, 242–43n.12
Samarin, Iurii, 63
Samizdat, 196
Sang, August, 186, 215
Säre, Karl, 150, 158, 171
Saul, Bruno, 191, 194, 228
Savisaar, Edgar, 224, 230–31, 233
Sazonov, Sergei, 171–72
Scandinavia, 9, 13, 104, 124, 127, 129, 217, 230, 242. *See also* Denmark, Sweden
Schirren, Carl, 63
Second Congress of Estonian Soldiers, 105
Selter, Karl, 140–41

Semigallians, 17, 237n.3
Serfdom, 37–38; origins, 19–20; growing burdens of, 30; Rosen Declaration and, 42; critics of, 42, 46; dismantling of, 45–48
Setus, 112
Shakhovskoi, Sergei V., 66–67, 80
Sigismund III, 28
Sink, Kuldar, 217
Sirge, Rudolf, 216
Sirk, Artur, 116, 120, 271n.19
Siuru, 136
Slaves, 11, 22
Socialist realism, 155, 186, 214
Socialist Revolutionaries, 101, 103. *See also* Estonian Socialist Revolutionaries
Socialist Workers' Party: in elections, 113; in cabinets, 114; origins, 114; oppose constitutional reform, 117; support Päts, 118–19, 123; and League of Veterans, 118; World War II resistance, 163. *See also* Estonian Social Democrats; Estonian Socialist Revolutionaries
Society of Estonian Literati, 59, 67, 75–76, 79, 92
Song festivals, 59; J. V. Jannsen and, 75–76; impact on musical culture, 75–76, 137, 188; number of participants and audience, 75–76, 92–93, 137, 188, 218, 238; Stalinism and, 187–88; unofficial national anthem at, 188, 218
Soul tax, 43
Soviets, in 1917–1918, 101–2, 107
Soviet Union: and attempted coup (1924), 115; relations with Estonia, 123–25; nonaggression pact with Estonia, 125; pressure on Estonia (1939), 139–40; mutual assistance pact (1939), 140–43; bases in Estonia (1939–1940), 141–44; ultimatum to Estonia (1940), 144; annexation of Estonia, 145–46. *See also* Russia
Sovkhozes, 152, 177, 180, 201–2, 260n.13
Sovnarkhoz, 193–94, 198
Speek, Peeter, 82
Stalin, Iosif V., 141, 157, 172, 176
Standard of living, 132, 151–52, 164, 184, 208–9, 219–20, 241–42
State Assembly (*Riigikogu*), 113–14, 116–19, 133
State Council (1938–1940), 121, 145
Statthalterschaft, 39
Stensby, Treaty of, 17–18
Stolypin, P. A., 89
Strandmann, Otto, 109
Strikes, 74, 83–84, 91, 126–27
Supreme Council, in *glasnost'* era, 230–32
Supreme Soviet of ESSR, 142, 173, 194–95, 227–29, 231–32
Suits, Gustav, 87, 92
Sweden, 16–17, 25, 27–32, 166, 217–18
Sword Brethren, 16–17. *See also* Teutonic Knights

Tallinn, 25, 115, 140–41, 158–59, 170, 255n.5; origins, 10, 16; city government, 18, 60, 88, 118; population, 22, 32, 34, 52, 73, 90–91, 131, 183–84, 206–7; in medieval Livonia, 22–23; in Livonian Wars, 27; under Swedish rule, 32–33; as commercial center, 51–52; as industrial center, 70–71; 89–91, 198; in 1905, 83–85; in 1917–1919, 101–3, 105, 108; destruction in World War II, 175; in post-Stalin era, 206–7; in *glasnost'* era, 234. *See also* Population, ethnic composition
Tallinn Bloodbath, 84
Tallinn Conservatory, 137
Tallinn Pedagogical Institute, 185, 212
Tallinn Polytechnical Institute, 185, 212

Tallinn State Conservatory, 185, 212. *See also* Tallinn Conservatory

Tallinn Technical University (Institute), 135

Talvik, Heiti, 136, 186

Tammsaare, A. H., 136–37, 241

Tartu, 5, 32–33, 70–71, 88–89, 118, 158–59, 170; bishopric of, 17–18; in medieval Livonia, 18, 22; population, 22, 32, 52, 73, 90, 131, 184, 206; as cultural center, 74–75; in 1905, 83–85; in 1917–1918, 101, 103–4; Peace of (1920), 110, 124; destruction in World War II, 175. *See also* Population, ethnic composition

Tartu University, 185; in seventeenth century, 33; agricultural science at, 41; lectureship in Estonian language, 56; and Russification, 80; in 1905, 85; growing Estonian role at, 94; in independent Estonia, 134–35; Sovietization, 155; under German occupation, 167; protests at, 196; in post-Stalin era, 212–13; in *glasnost'* era, 223, 237

Täyssinä, Peace of, 27

Teataja, 82, 86

Teemant, Jaan, 84–85, 114, 120

Television, in Soviet Estonia, 205, 214, 236–37

Temperance societies, 76

Teutonic Knights, 17–18, 22, 24–25, 28

Theater, Estonia, 78, 92, 136–37, 156, 187, 216–17

Tief, Otto, 163

Titma, Mikk, 233

Toi, Roman, 238

Tolli, Vive, 217

Tõnisson, Jaan, 100, 118, 122, 242; ideology, 82, 87; in 1905, 84, 86; in First Duma, 88; in Estonian foreign delegation, 105; head of state, 114; removed as editor of *Postimees*, 120

Toome, Indrek, 228

Tormis, Veljo, 217–18

Trade, 9, 51–52, 71, 127, 197

Trotsky, Leon, 105

Tubin, Eduard, 218

Tuglas, Friedebert, 92, 186

Üksjalad, 21, 31

Uluots, Juri, 140, 142, 159, 162–63, 167

Under, Marie, 136, 167, 241

United Agrarian Party, 113–14, 116. *See also* Agrarian League; Farmers' Party; Homesteaders' Party

United Nations, 241

United States, 107, 124, 127, 163–64

Unt, Mati, 216

Uralic theory, 6

Urbanization, 22, 32, 52, 284n.48; late tsarist era, 73, 90; independent Estonia, 131–32; Stalinist era, 183–84; post-Stalin era, 205–8; in *glasnost'* era, 234–35. *See also* Narva; Tallinn; Tartu

Uudised, 82–83, 85

Uusikaupunki, Peace of, 38

Vaba Sõna, 87–88

Vader, Artur, 191–92, 195

Vaino, Karl, 191–93, 203, 210, 220, 224

Valdemar II, 16

Valdemārs, Krišjānis, 64

Väljas, Vaino, 192, 224–25, 228, 233

Vanemuine Society, 75–76, 92–93

Vanemuine Theater, 137, 187, 216

Varangians, 9, 11–12

Vares, Johannes, 144–46, 149–50, 171, 173

Vassals, 18, 21–22, 31

Veimer, Arnold, 149, 171–74, 194

Veske, Mihkel, 78

Veski, Johannes Voldemar, 136

Vetemaa, Enn, 215–16

Vettik, Tuudur, 188

Viipuri Manifesto, 88

Vikings, 9, 11–12
Vilde, Eduard, 78, 92
Vilms, Jüri, 87, 105–6
Vilna question, 123–24
Vint, Tõnis, 217
Virulane, 78
Vyborg. *See* Viipuri Manifesto

Wanradt, Simon, 24
Western Allies, 108, 110, 174–75. *See also* France; Great Britain; United States
William II, 106
Wilson, Woodrow, 107
Winter War, 143
Women: in prehistoric times, 10–11; in higher education, 94, 135; receive right to vote, 132; in politics, 133, 209–10; in labor force, 133, 209; Party membership, 170, 191
World War I, 94–95, 99

Yaroslav the Wise, 12
Young Communist League, 184, 209
Young-Estonia, 87, 92, 173

Zemstvos, 60, 65, 82, 100
Zhdanov, Andrei A., 144–46
Zhdanovshchina, 186
Zinov'ev, Grigorii, 115
Zinov'ev, Mikhail A., 66–67
Zinzendorf, Nikolaus von, 53